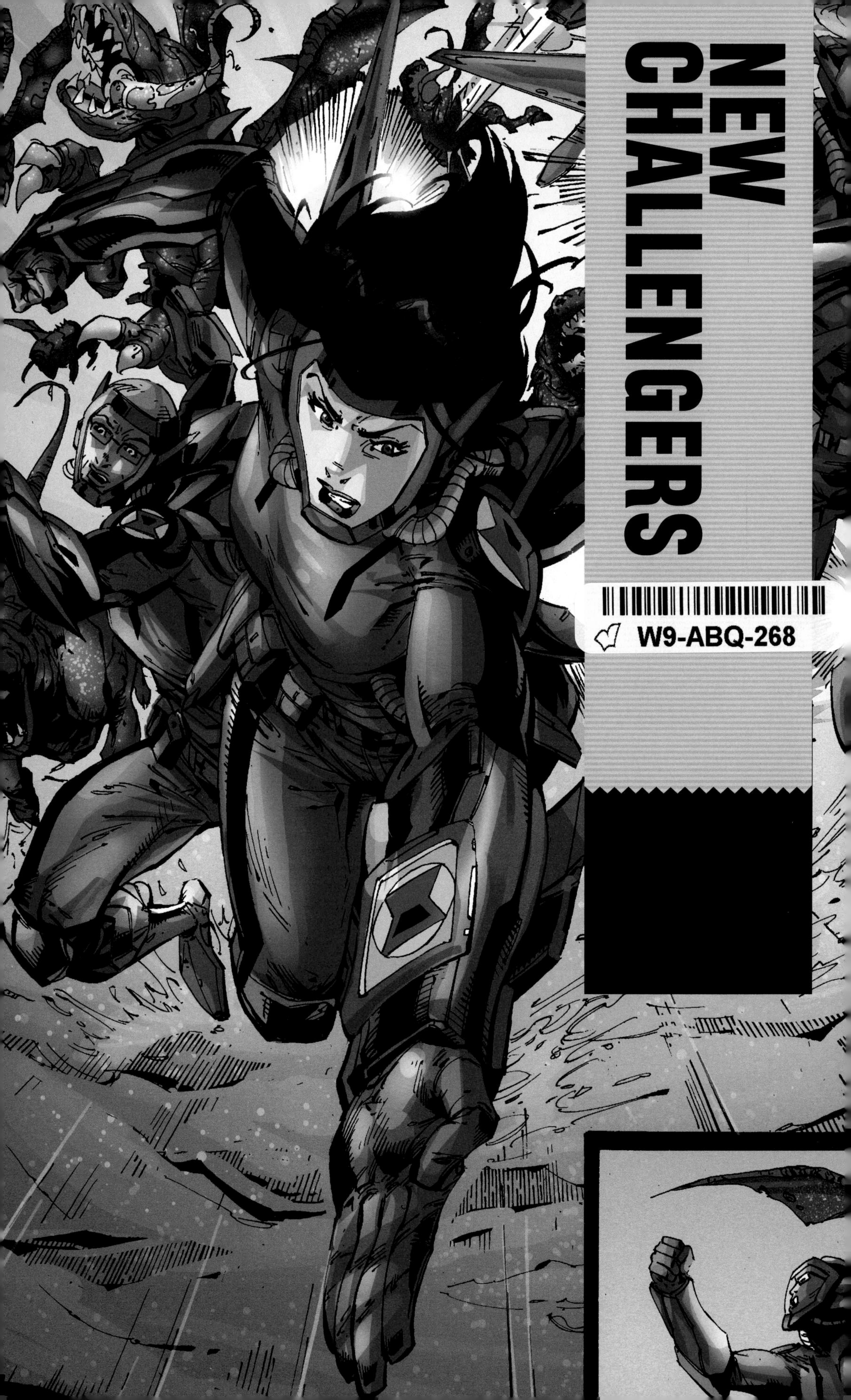
NEW
CHALLENGERS

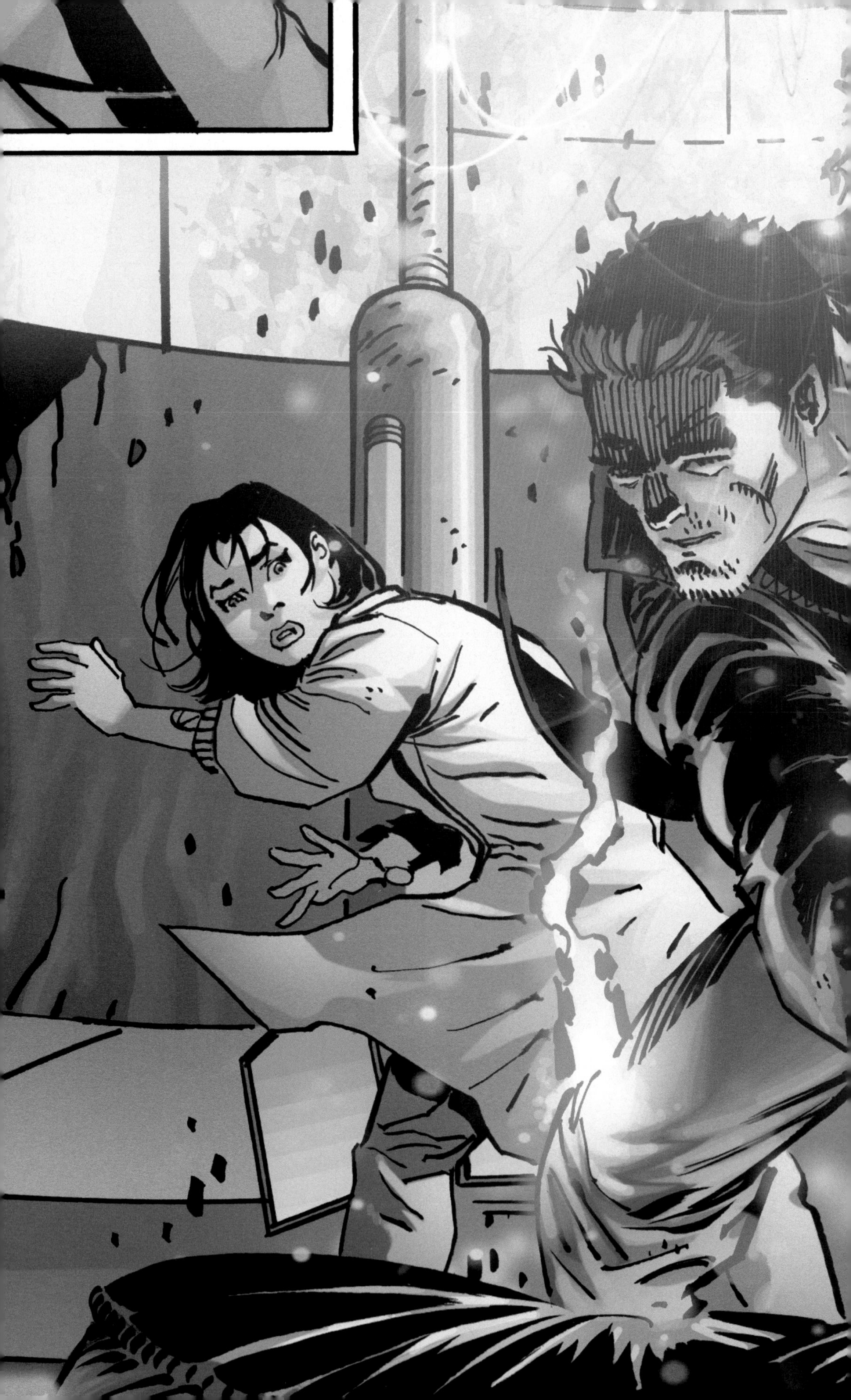

NEW CHALLENGERS

pencillers

ANDY KUBERT
V KEN MARION

writers

SCOTT SNYDER
AARON GILLESPIE

inkers

KLAUS JANSON
SANDU FLOREA

colorists

BRAD ANDERSON
DINEI RIBEIRO

letterer

DERON BENNETT

collection cover artists

ANDY KUBERT with **BRAD ANDERSON**

SUPERMAN created by **JERRY SIEGEL** and **JOE SHUSTER**
by special arrangements with the Jerry Siegel Family

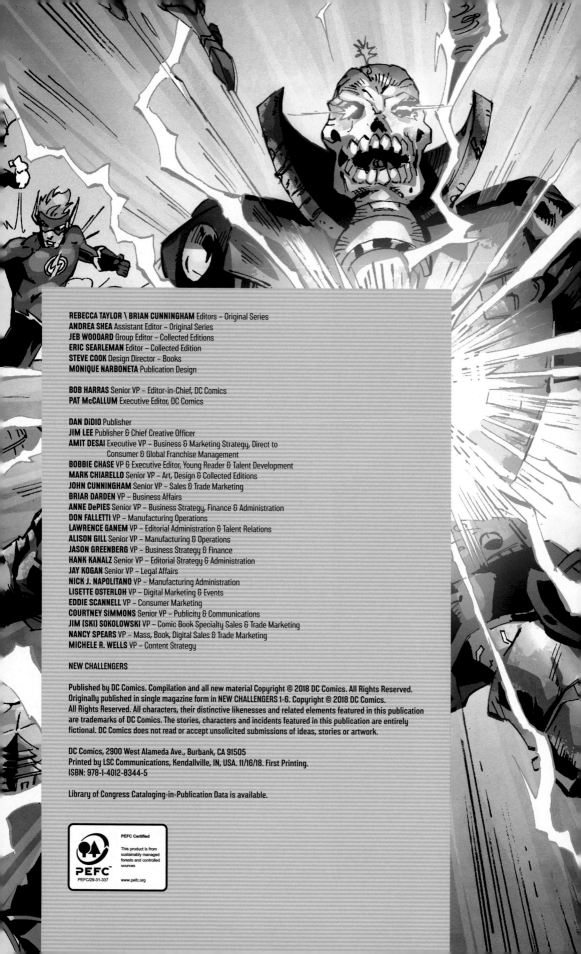

REBECCA TAYLOR \ BRIAN CUNNINGHAM Editors – Original Series
ANDREA SHEA Assistant Editor – Original Series
JEB WOODARD Group Editor – Collected Editions
ERIC SEARLEMAN Editor – Collected Edition
STEVE COOK Design Director – Books
MONIQUE NARBONETA Publication Design

BOB HARRAS Senior VP – Editor-in-Chief, DC Comics
PAT McCALLUM Executive Editor, DC Comics

DAN DiDIO Publisher
JIM LEE Publisher & Chief Creative Officer
AMIT DESAI Executive VP – Business & Marketing Strategy, Direct to Consumer & Global Franchise Management
BOBBIE CHASE VP & Executive Editor, Young Reader & Talent Development
MARK CHIARELLO Senior VP – Art, Design & Collected Editions
JOHN CUNNINGHAM Senior VP – Sales & Trade Marketing
BRIAR DARDEN VP – Business Affairs
ANNE DePIES Senior VP – Business Strategy, Finance & Administration
DON FALLETTI VP – Manufacturing Operations
LAWRENCE GANEM VP – Editorial Administration & Talent Relations
ALISON GILL Senior VP – Manufacturing & Operations
JASON GREENBERG VP – Business Strategy & Finance
HANK KANALZ Senior VP – Editorial Strategy & Administration
JAY KOGAN Senior VP – Legal Affairs
NICK J. NAPOLITANO VP – Manufacturing Administration
LISETTE OSTERLOH VP – Digital Marketing & Events
EDDIE SCANNELL VP – Consumer Marketing
COURTNEY SIMMONS Senior VP – Publicity & Communications
JIM (SKI) SOKOLOWSKI VP – Comic Book Specialty Sales & Trade Marketing
NANCY SPEARS VP – Mass, Book, Digital Sales & Trade Marketing
MICHELE R. WELLS VP – Content Strategy

NEW CHALLENGERS

DC Comics, 2900 West Alameda Ave., Burbank, CA 91505
Printed by LSC Communications, Kendallville, IN, USA. 11/16/18. First Printing.
ISBN: 978-1-4012-8344-5

Library of Congress Cataloging-in-Publication Data is available.

PEFC
PEFC/29-31-337
PEFC Certified
This product is from sustainably managed forests and controlled sources
www.pefc.org

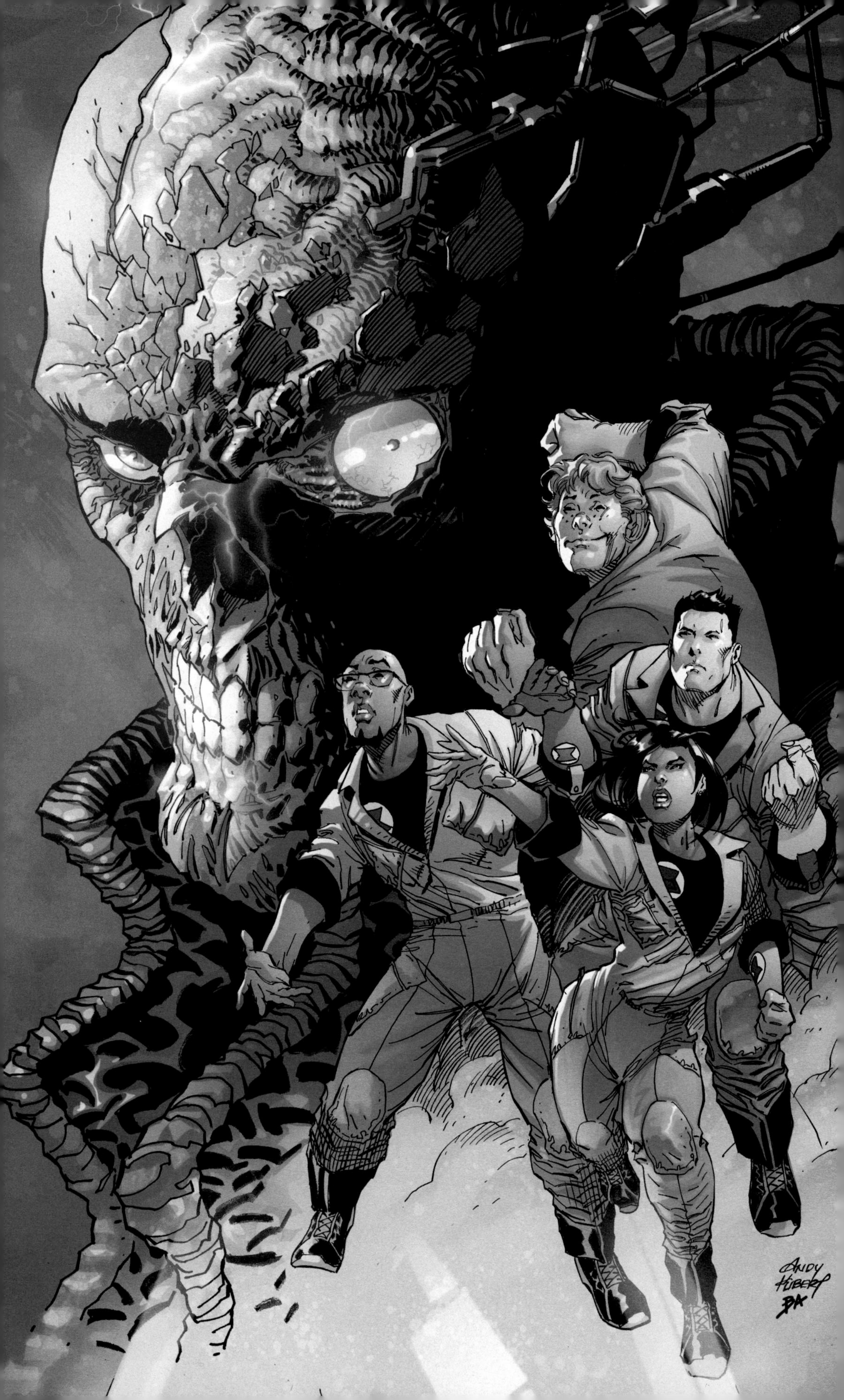
ANDY KUBERT
BA

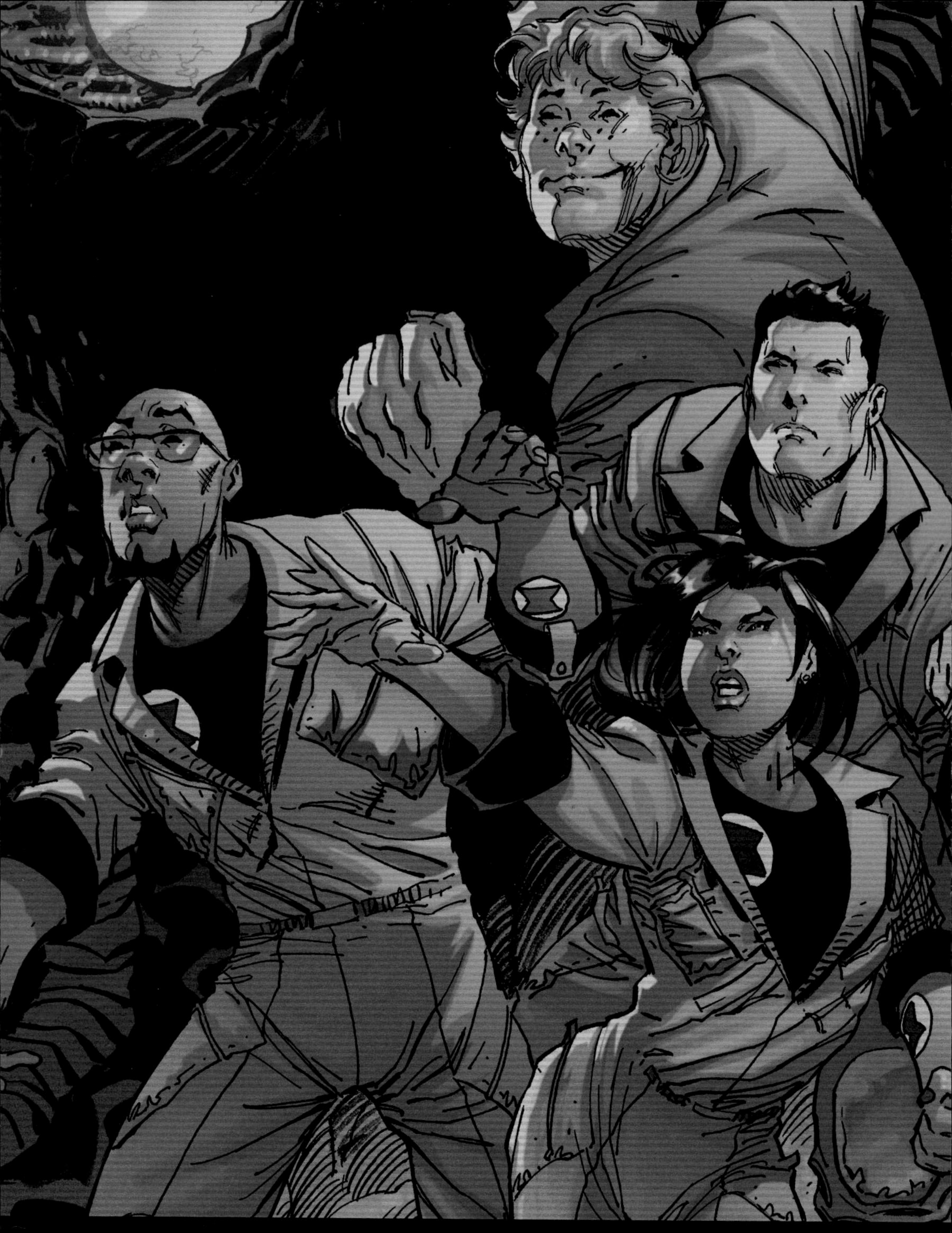

NEW CHALLENGERS
#1

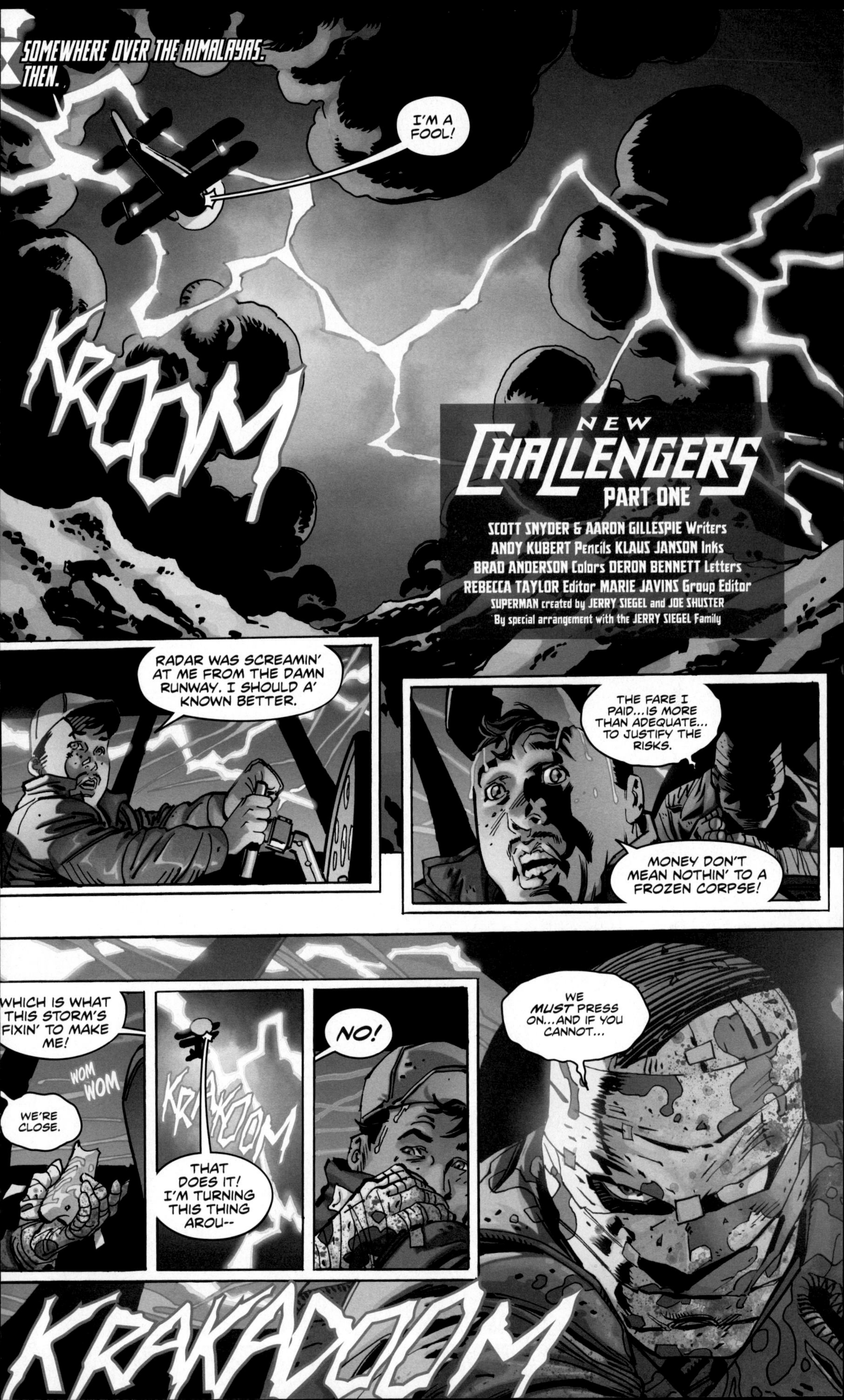

SOMEWHERE OVER THE HIMALAYAS. THEN.
I'M A FOOL!
KROOM
NEW CHALLENGERS
PART ONE
SCOTT SNYDER & AARON GILLESPIE Writers
ANDY KUBERT Pencils KLAUS JANSON Inks
BRAD ANDERSON Colors DERON BENNETT Letters
REBECCA TAYLOR Editor MARIE JAVINS Group Editor
SUPERMAN created by JERRY SIEGEL and JOE SHUSTER
By special arrangement with the JERRY SIEGEL Family
RADAR WAS SCREAMIN' AT ME FROM THE DAMN RUNWAY. I SHOULD A' KNOWN BETTER.
THE FARE I PAID...IS MORE THAN ADEQUATE...TO JUSTIFY THE RISKS.
MONEY DON'T MEAN NOTHIN' TO A FROZEN CORPSE!
WHICH IS WHAT THIS STORM'S FIXIN' TO MAKE ME!
WOM WOM
WE'RE CLOSE.
KRAKOOM
THAT DOES IT! I'M TURNING THIS THING AROU--
NO!
WE *MUST* PRESS ON...AND IF YOU CANNOT...
KRAKADOOM

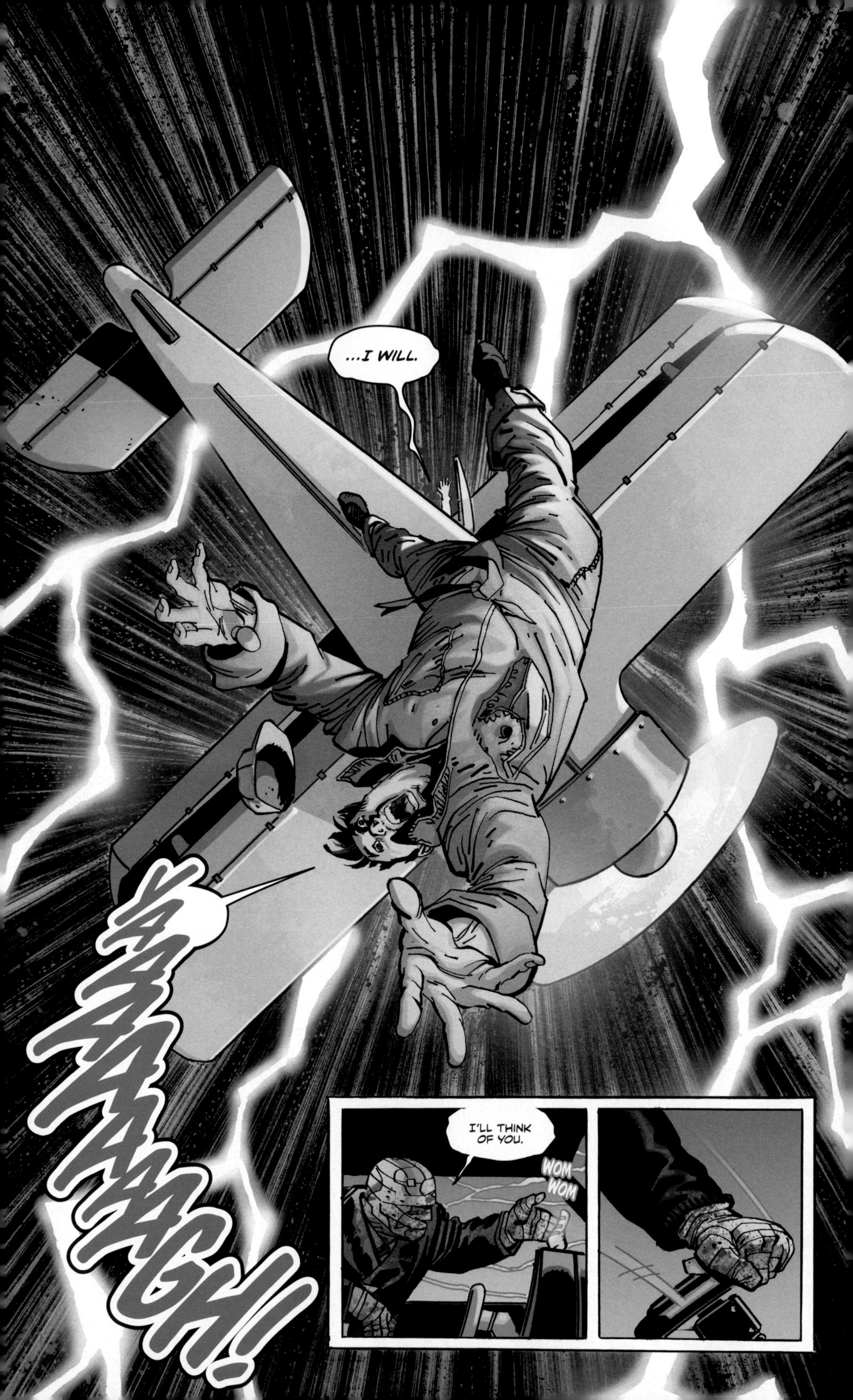
...I WILL.
YAAAAAAGH!
I'LL THINK OF YOU.
WOM WOM

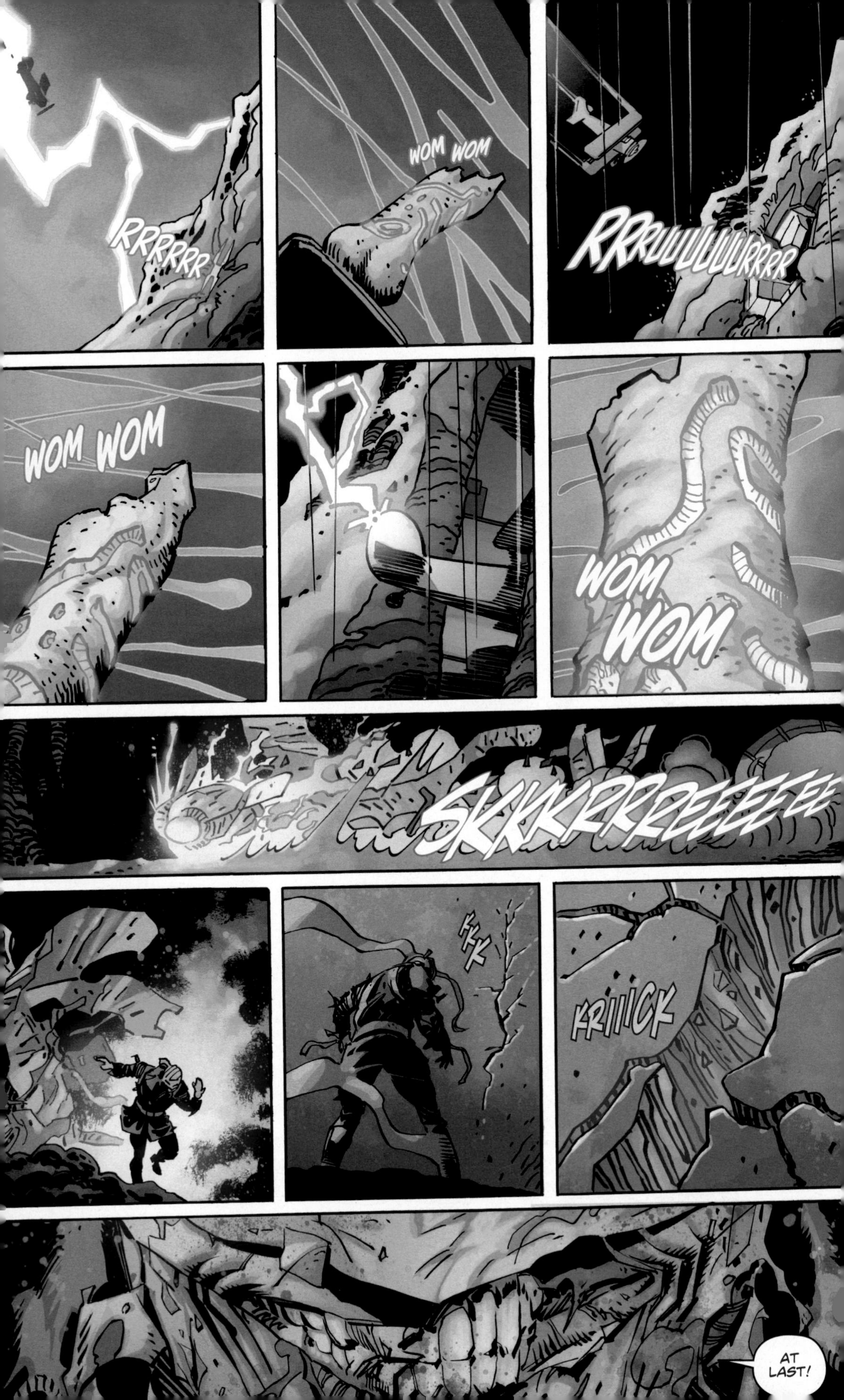
RRRRRR
WOM WOM
RRRUUUUUURRRR
WOM WOM
WOM WOM
SKKRRRREEEEEE
KKK
KRIIICK
AT LAST!

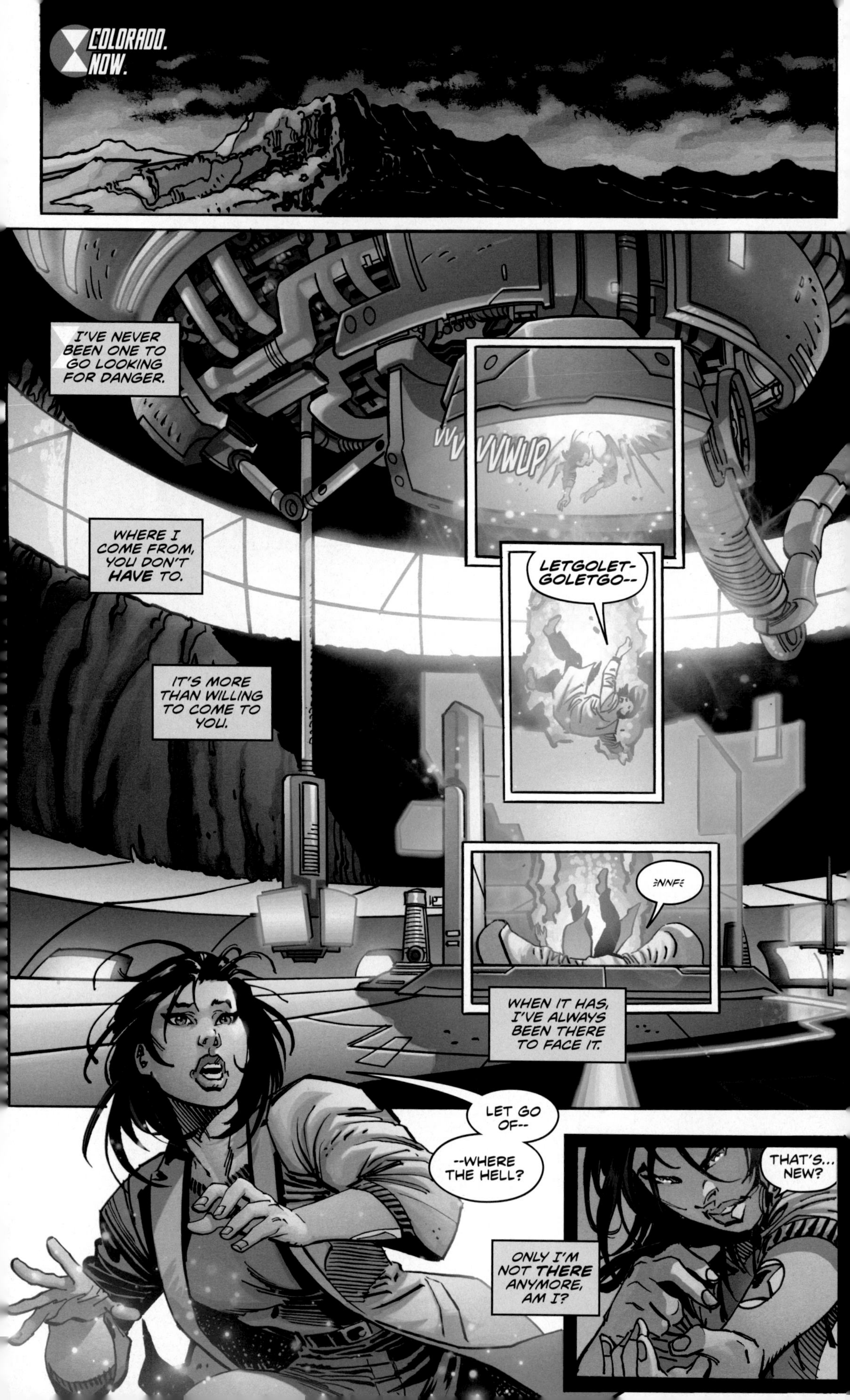
COLORADO.
NOW.
I'VE NEVER BEEN ONE TO GO LOOKING FOR DANGER.
VVVVVWUP
WHERE I COME FROM, YOU DON'T HAVE TO.
IT'S MORE THAN WILLING TO COME TO YOU.
LETGOLET-GOLETGO--
NNF
WHEN IT HAS, I'VE ALWAYS BEEN THERE TO FACE IT.
LET GO OF--
--WHERE THE HELL?
THAT'S... NEW?
ONLY I'M NOT THERE ANYMORE, AM I?

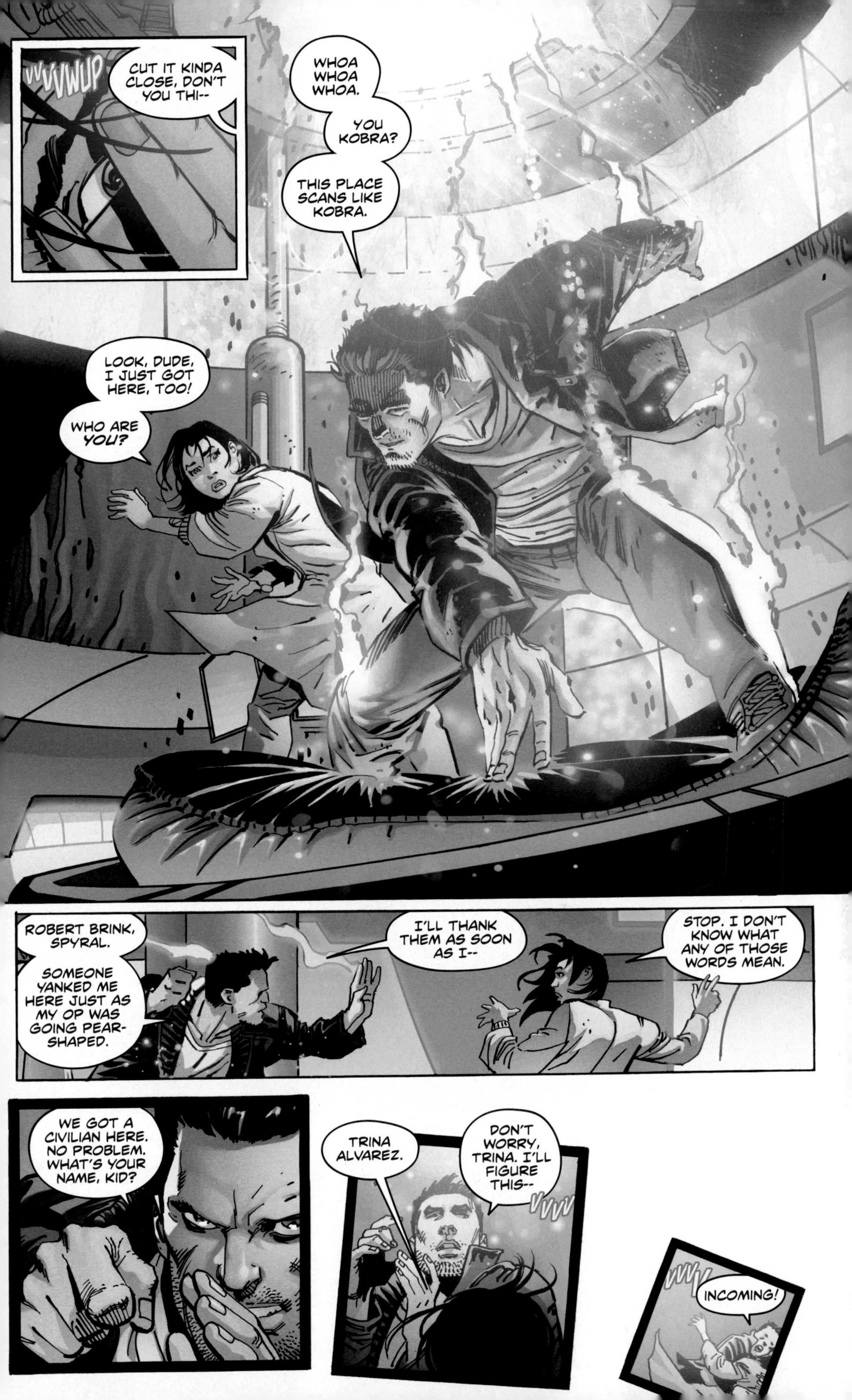
VVVVWUP
CUT IT KINDA CLOSE, DON'T YOU THI--
WHOA WHOA WHOA.
YOU KOBRA?
THIS PLACE SCANS LIKE KOBRA.
LOOK, DUDE, I JUST GOT HERE, TOO!
WHO ARE YOU?
ROBERT BRINK, SPYRAL.
SOMEONE YANKED ME HERE JUST AS MY OP WAS GOING PEAR-SHAPED.
I'LL THANK THEM AS SOON AS I--
STOP. I DON'T KNOW WHAT ANY OF THOSE WORDS MEAN.
WE GOT A CIVILIAN HERE. NO PROBLEM. WHAT'S YOUR NAME, KID?
TRINA ALVAREZ.
DON'T WORRY, TRINA. I'LL FIGURE THIS--
VVVV
VVVV
INCOMING!

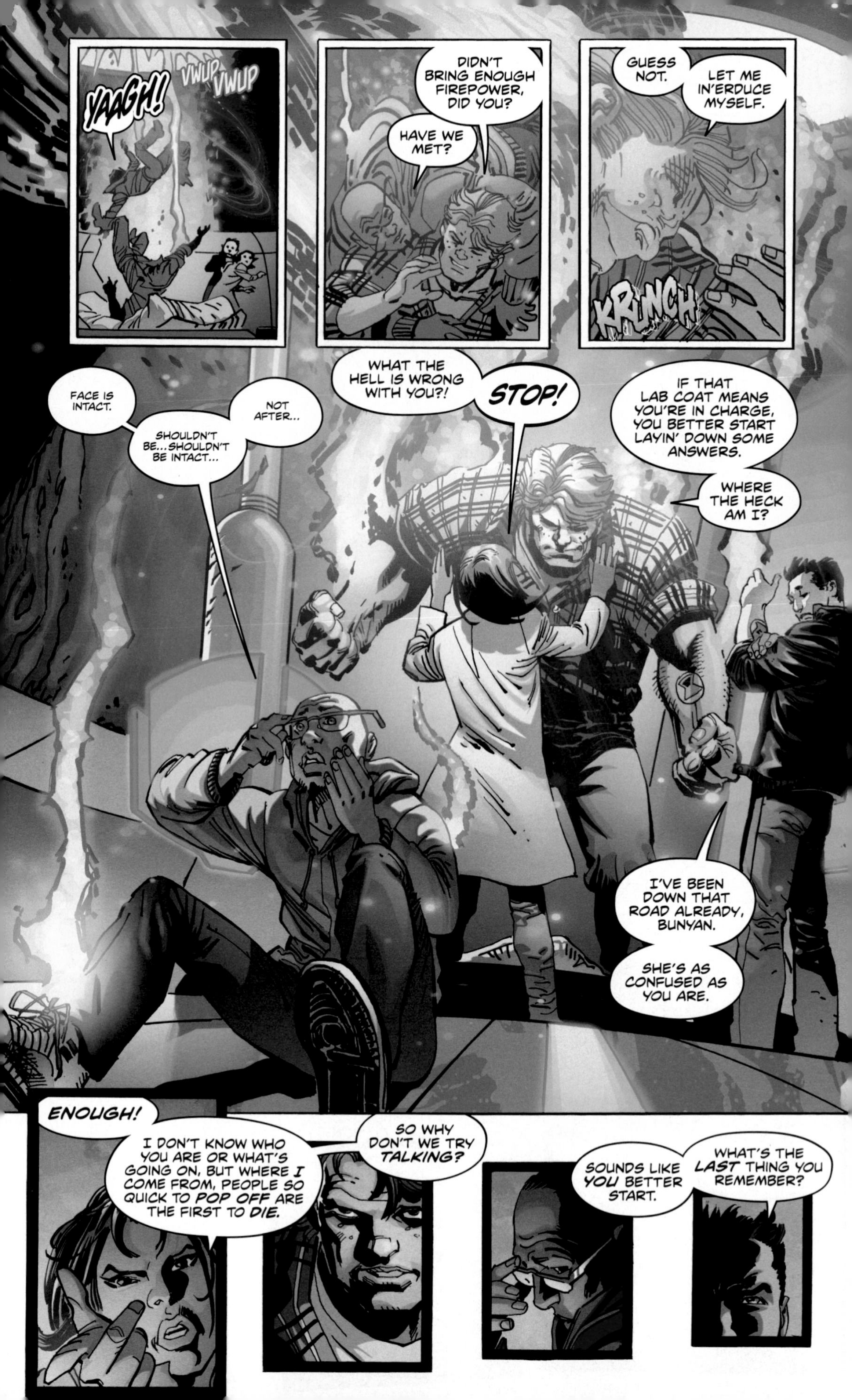
YAAGH!
VWUP VWUP
DIDN'T BRING ENOUGH FIREPOWER, DID YOU?
HAVE WE MET?
GUESS NOT.
LET ME IN'ERDUCE MYSELF.
KRUNCH
FACE IS INTACT.
SHOULDN'T BE...SHOULDN'T BE INTACT...
NOT AFTER...
WHAT THE HELL IS WRONG WITH YOU?!
STOP!
IF THAT LAB COAT MEANS YOU'RE IN CHARGE, YOU BETTER START LAYIN' DOWN SOME ANSWERS.
WHERE THE HECK AM I?
I'VE BEEN DOWN THAT ROAD ALREADY, BUNYAN.
SHE'S AS CONFUSED AS YOU ARE.
ENOUGH!
I DON'T KNOW WHO YOU ARE OR WHAT'S GOING ON, BUT WHERE I COME FROM, PEOPLE SO QUICK TO POP OFF ARE THE FIRST TO DIE.
SO WHY DON'T WE TRY TALKING?
SOUNDS LIKE YOU BETTER START.
WHAT'S THE LAST THING YOU REMEMBER?

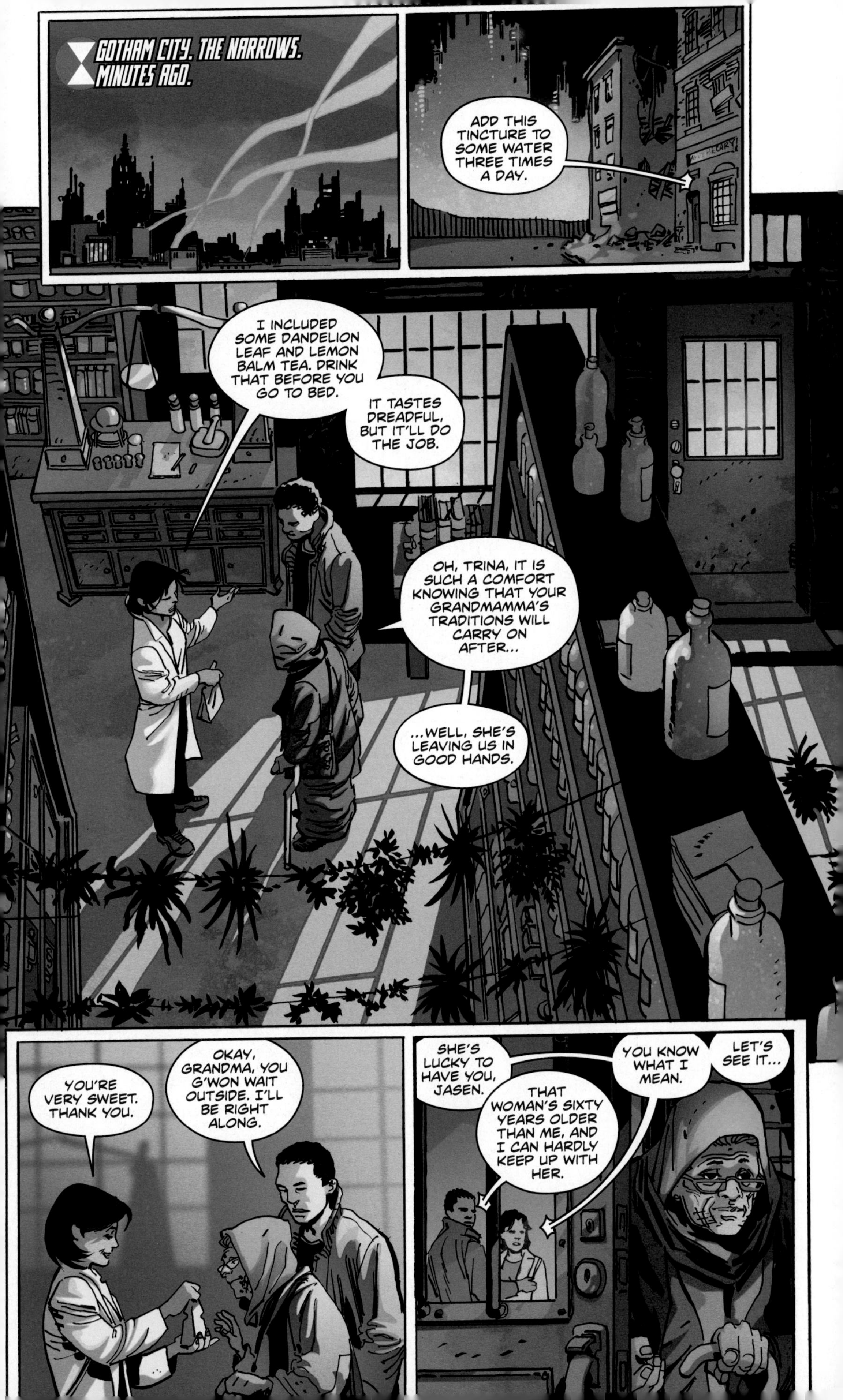
GOTHAM CITY. THE NARROWS. MINUTES AGO.
ADD THIS TINCTURE TO SOME WATER THREE TIMES A DAY.
I INCLUDED SOME DANDELION LEAF AND LEMON BALM TEA. DRINK THAT BEFORE YOU GO TO BED.
IT TASTES DREADFUL, BUT IT'LL DO THE JOB.
OH, TRINA, IT IS SUCH A COMFORT KNOWING THAT YOUR GRANDMAMMA'S TRADITIONS WILL CARRY ON AFTER...
...WELL, SHE'S LEAVING US IN GOOD HANDS.
YOU'RE VERY SWEET. THANK YOU.
OKAY, GRANDMA, YOU G'WON WAIT OUTSIDE. I'LL BE RIGHT ALONG.
SHE'S LUCKY TO HAVE YOU, JASEN.
THAT WOMAN'S SIXTY YEARS OLDER THAN ME, AND I CAN HARDLY KEEP UP WITH HER.
YOU KNOW WHAT I MEAN.
LET'S SEE IT...

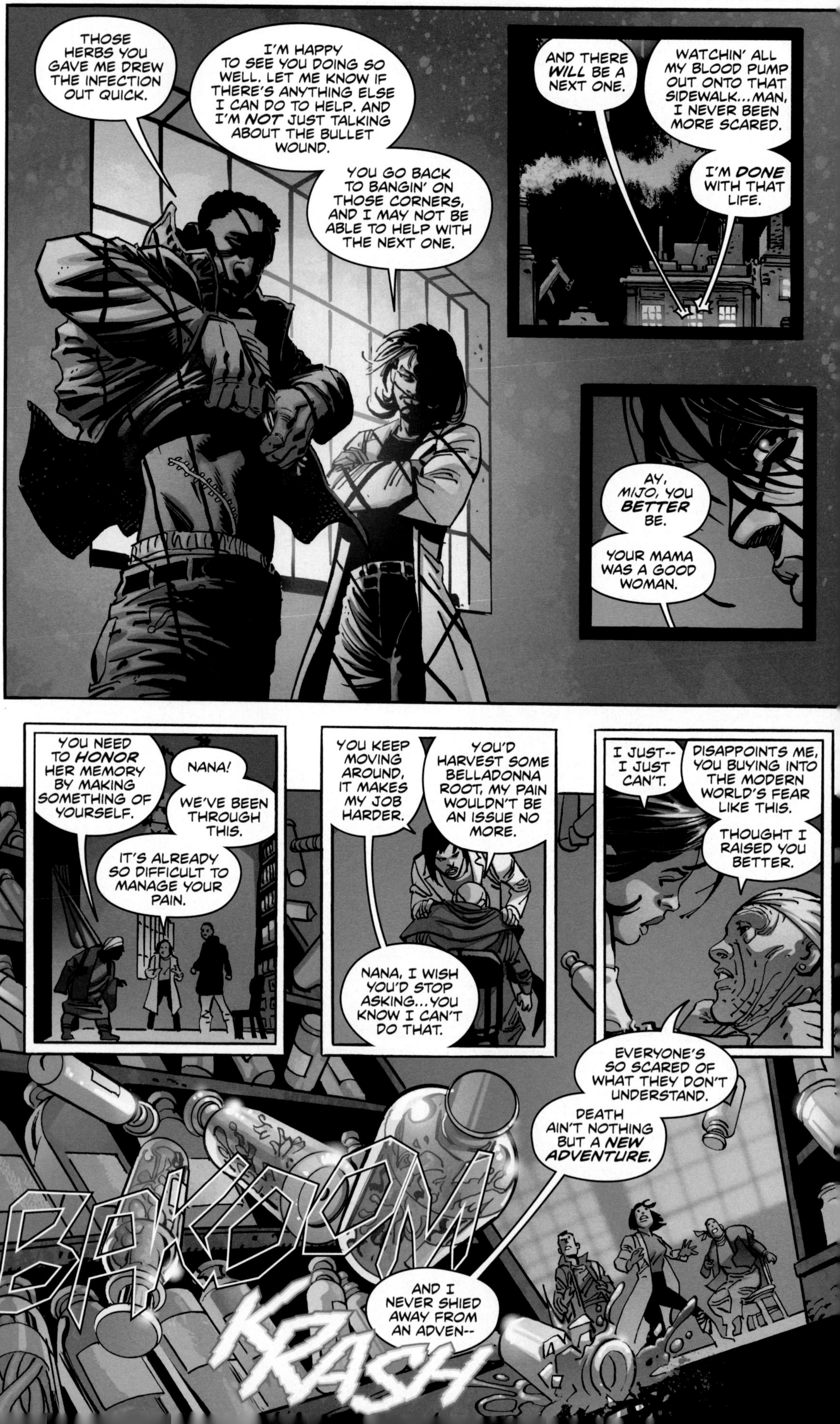
THOSE HERBS YOU GAVE ME DREW THE INFECTION OUT QUICK.
I'M HAPPY TO SEE YOU DOING SO WELL. LET ME KNOW IF THERE'S ANYTHING ELSE I CAN DO TO HELP. AND I'M *NOT* JUST TALKING ABOUT THE BULLET WOUND.
YOU GO BACK TO BANGIN' ON THOSE CORNERS, AND I MAY NOT BE ABLE TO HELP WITH THE NEXT ONE.
AND THERE *WILL* BE A NEXT ONE.
WATCHIN' ALL MY BLOOD PUMP OUT ONTO THAT SIDEWALK...MAN, I NEVER BEEN MORE SCARED.
I'M *DONE* WITH THAT LIFE.
AY, MIJO, YOU *BETTER* BE.
YOUR MAMA WAS A GOOD WOMAN.
YOU NEED TO *HONOR* HER MEMORY BY MAKING SOMETHING OF YOURSELF.
NANA!
WE'VE BEEN THROUGH THIS.
IT'S ALREADY SO DIFFICULT TO MANAGE YOUR PAIN.
YOU KEEP MOVING AROUND, IT MAKES MY JOB HARDER.
YOU'D HARVEST SOME BELLADONNA ROOT, MY PAIN WOULDN'T BE AN ISSUE NO MORE.
NANA, I WISH YOU'D STOP ASKING...YOU KNOW I CAN'T DO THAT.
I JUST-- I JUST CAN'T.
DISAPPOINTS ME, YOU BUYING INTO THE MODERN WORLD'S FEAR LIKE THIS.
THOUGHT I RAISED YOU BETTER.
EVERYONE'S SO SCARED OF WHAT THEY DON'T UNDERSTAND.
DEATH AIN'T NOTHING BUT A *NEW ADVENTURE*.
AND I NEVER SHIED AWAY FROM AN ADVEN--
BRAKOOM
KRASH

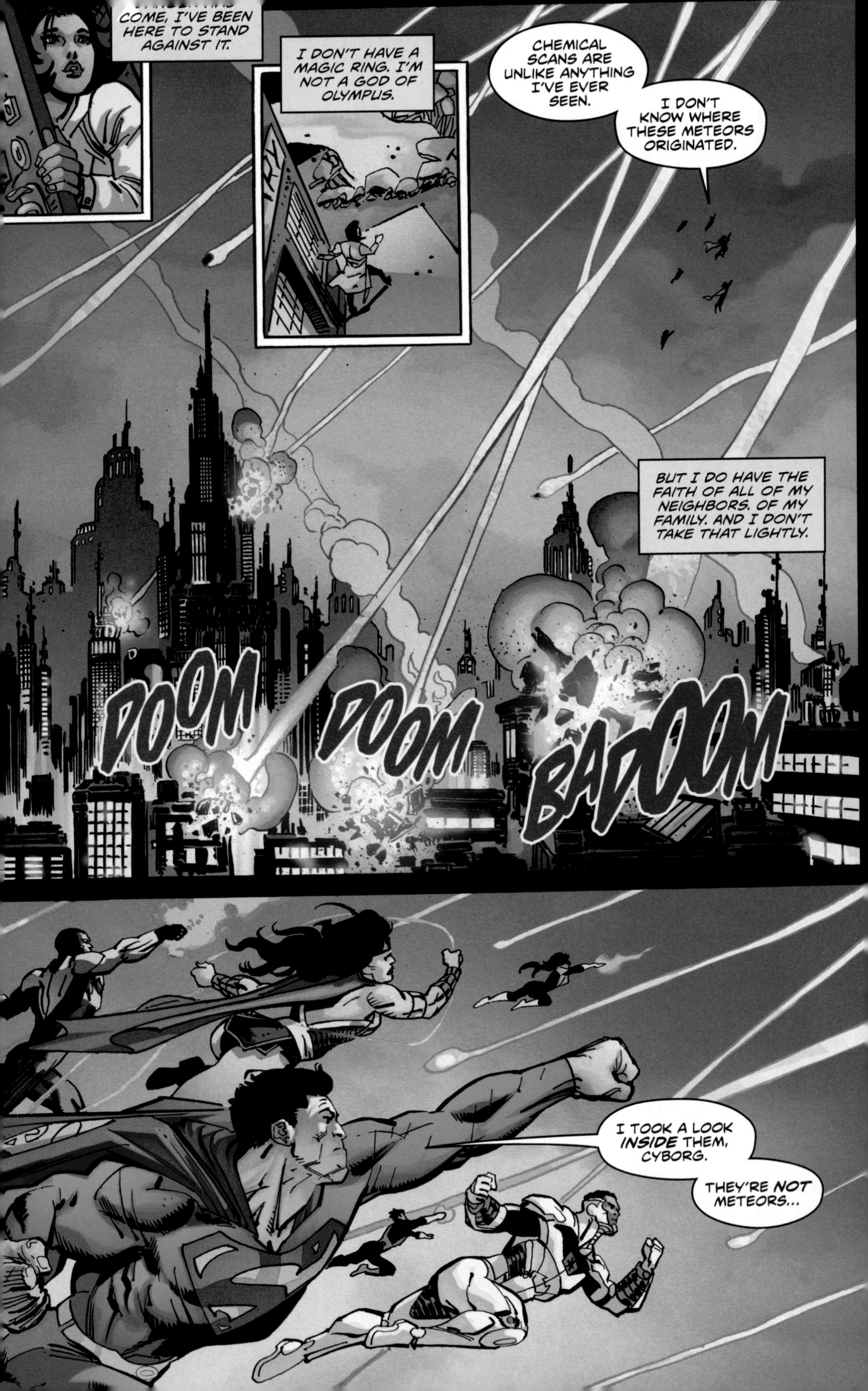
COME, I'VE BEEN HERE TO STAND AGAINST IT.
I DON'T HAVE A MAGIC RING. I'M NOT A GOD OF OLYMPUS.
CHEMICAL SCANS ARE UNLIKE ANYTHING I'VE EVER SEEN.
I DON'T KNOW WHERE THESE METEORS ORIGINATED.
BUT I DO HAVE THE FAITH OF ALL OF MY NEIGHBORS. OF MY FAMILY. AND I DON'T TAKE THAT LIGHTLY.
DOOM
DOOM
BADOOM
I TOOK A LOOK INSIDE THEM, CYBORG.
THEY'RE NOT METEORS...

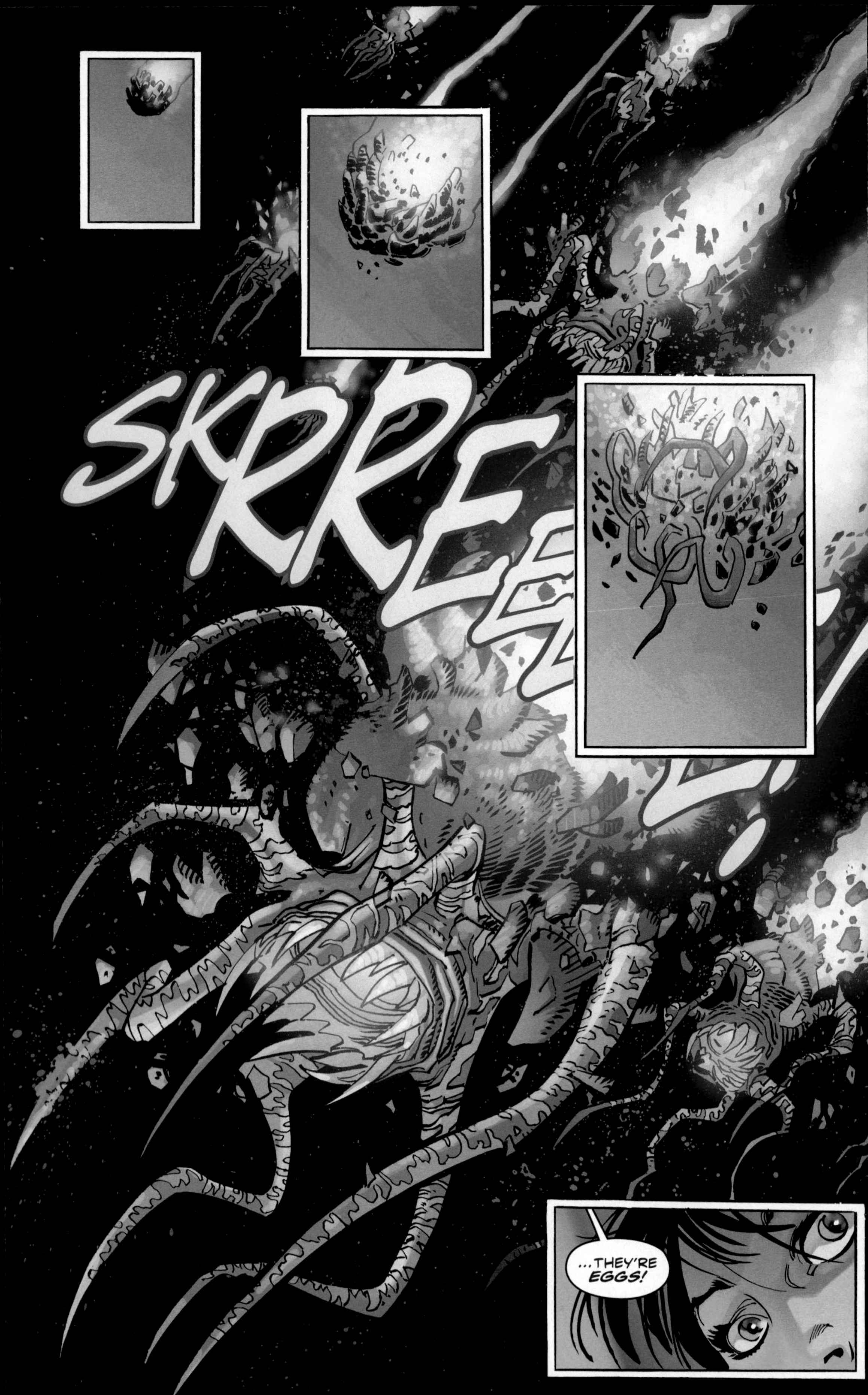
SKREEEEE!
...THEY'RE EGGS!

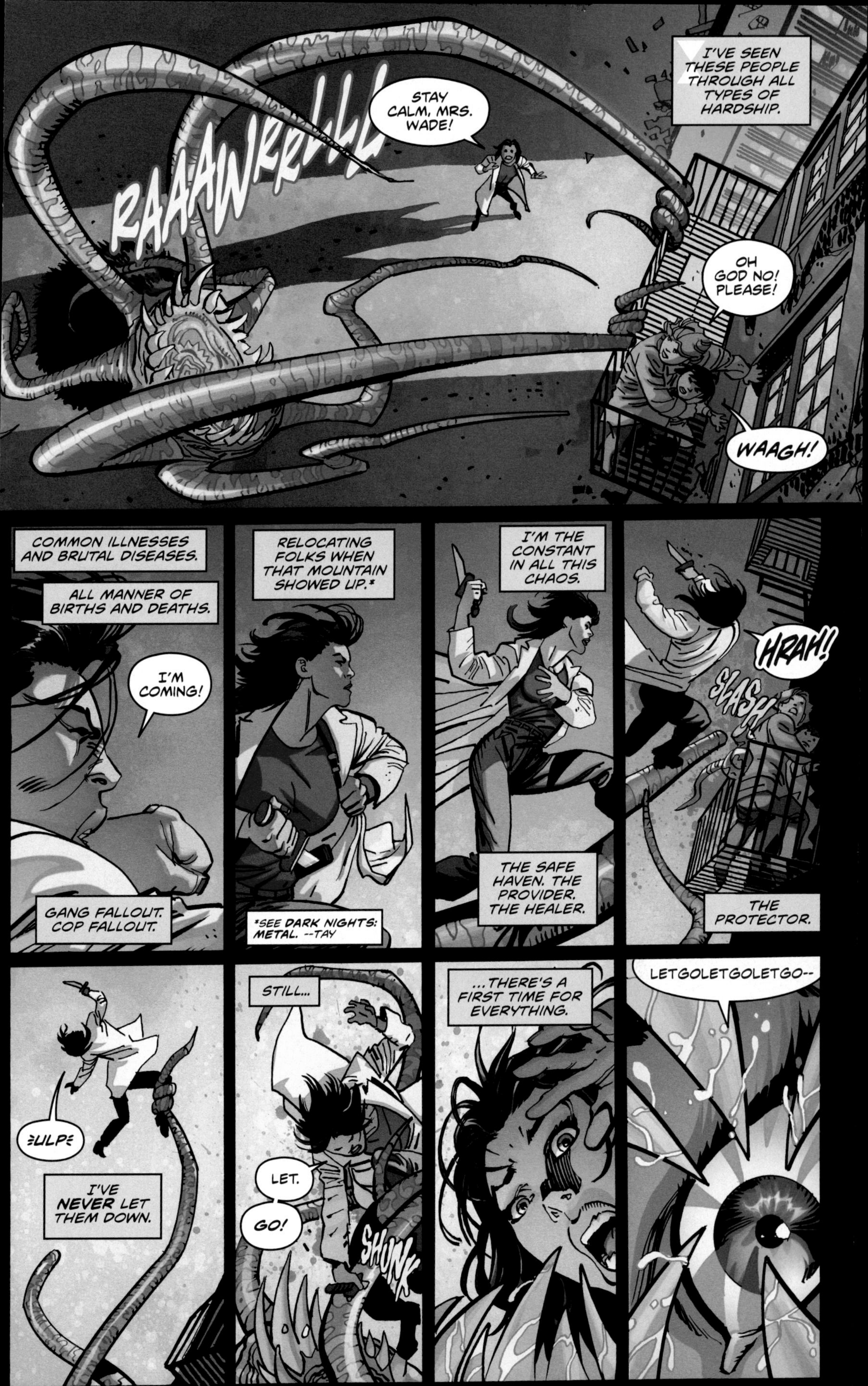
RAAAWRRLLL
STAY CALM, MRS. WADE!
I'VE SEEN THESE PEOPLE THROUGH ALL TYPES OF HARDSHIP.
OH GOD NO! PLEASE!
WAAGH!
COMMON ILLNESSES AND BRUTAL DISEASES.
ALL MANNER OF BIRTHS AND DEATHS.
I'M COMING!
GANG FALLOUT. COP FALLOUT.
RELOCATING FOLKS WHEN THAT MOUNTAIN SHOWED UP.*
*SEE DARK NIGHTS: METAL. --TAY
I'M THE CONSTANT IN ALL THIS CHAOS.
THE SAFE HAVEN. THE PROVIDER. THE HEALER.
HRAH!
SLASH
THE PROTECTOR.
ULP
I'VE NEVER LET THEM DOWN.
STILL...
LET.
GO!
SHUNK
...THERE'S A FIRST TIME FOR EVERYTHING.
LETGOLETGOLETGO--

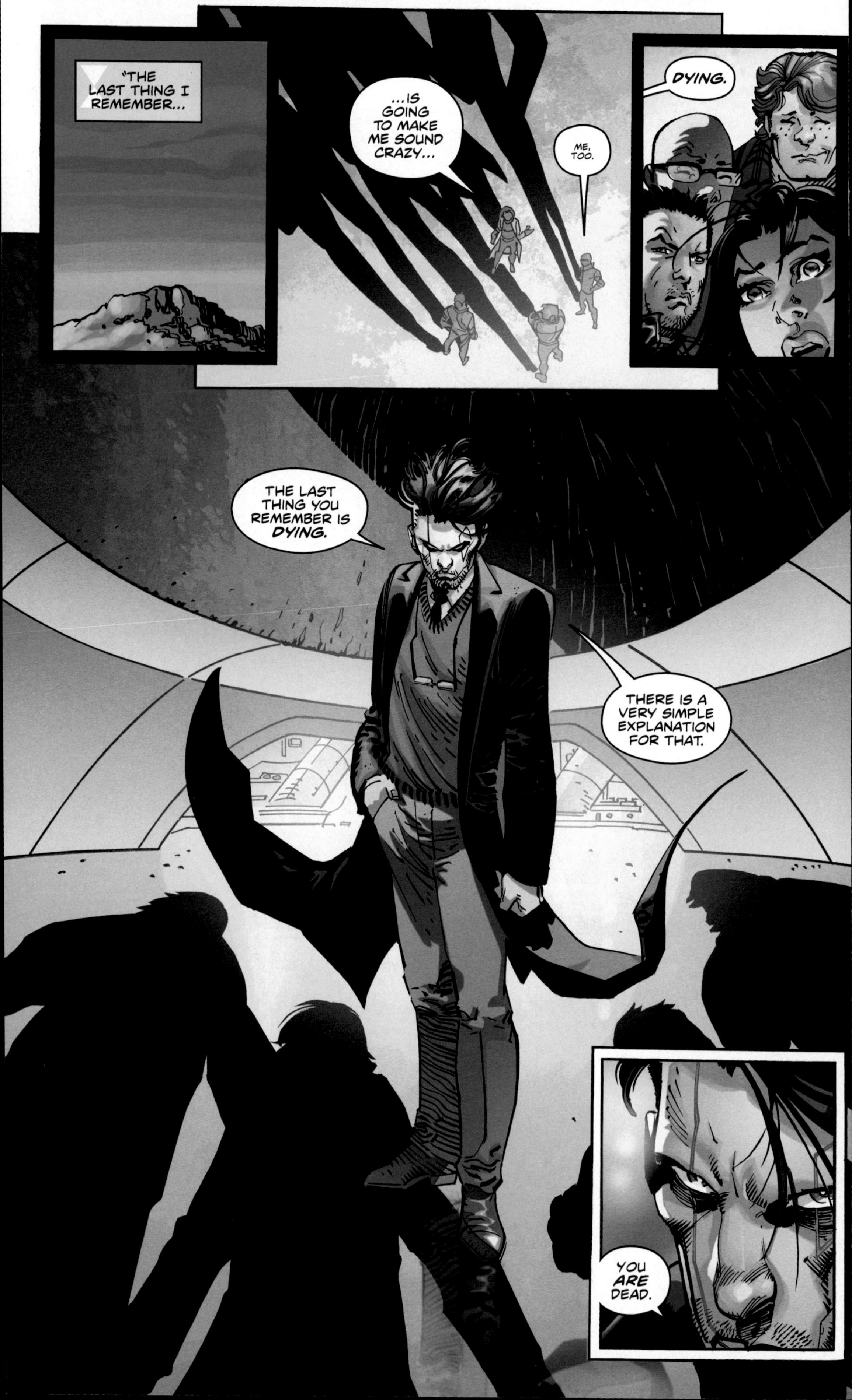
"THE LAST THING I REMEMBER...
...IS GOING TO MAKE ME SOUND CRAZY...
ME, TOO.
DYING.
THE LAST THING YOU REMEMBER IS DYING.
THERE IS A VERY SIMPLE EXPLANATION FOR THAT.
YOU ARE DEAD.

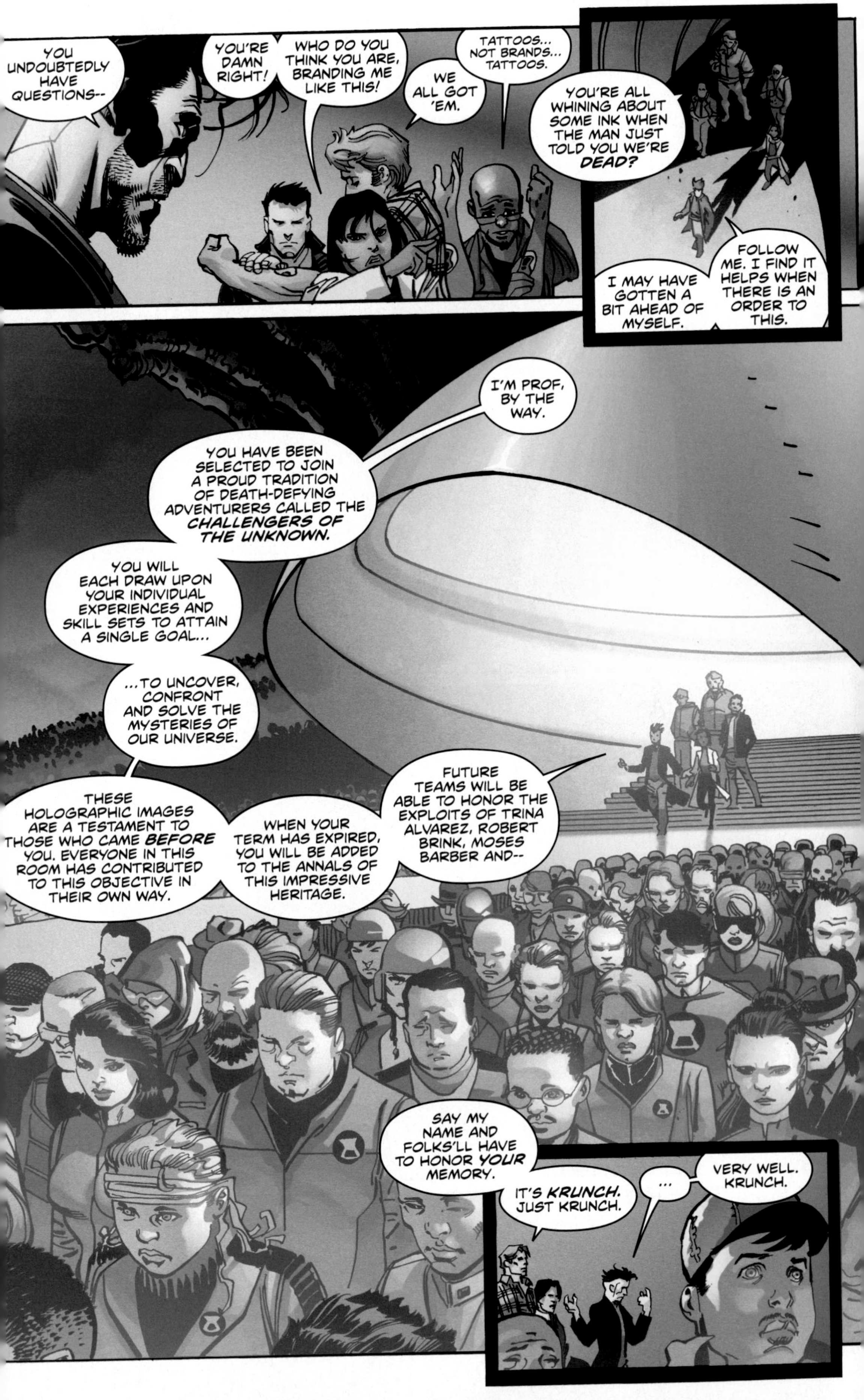
YOU UNDOUBTEDLY HAVE QUESTIONS--
YOU'RE DAMN RIGHT!
WHO DO YOU THINK YOU ARE, BRANDING ME LIKE THIS!
WE ALL GOT 'EM.
TATTOOS... NOT BRANDS... TATTOOS.
YOU'RE ALL WHINING ABOUT SOME INK WHEN THE MAN JUST TOLD YOU WE'RE ***DEAD?***
I MAY HAVE GOTTEN A BIT AHEAD OF MYSELF.
FOLLOW ME. I FIND IT HELPS WHEN THERE IS AN ORDER TO THIS.
I'M PROF, BY THE WAY.
YOU HAVE BEEN SELECTED TO JOIN A PROUD TRADITION OF DEATH-DEFYING ADVENTURERS CALLED THE ***CHALLENGERS OF THE UNKNOWN.***
YOU WILL EACH DRAW UPON YOUR INDIVIDUAL EXPERIENCES AND SKILL SETS TO ATTAIN A SINGLE GOAL...
...TO UNCOVER, CONFRONT AND SOLVE THE MYSTERIES OF OUR UNIVERSE.
THESE HOLOGRAPHIC IMAGES ARE A TESTAMENT TO THOSE WHO CAME ***BEFORE*** YOU. EVERYONE IN THIS ROOM HAS CONTRIBUTED TO THIS OBJECTIVE IN THEIR OWN WAY.
WHEN YOUR TERM HAS EXPIRED, YOU WILL BE ADDED TO THE ANNALS OF THIS IMPRESSIVE HERITAGE.
FUTURE TEAMS WILL BE ABLE TO HONOR THE EXPLOITS OF TRINA ALVAREZ, ROBERT BRINK, MOSES BARBER AND--
SAY MY NAME AND FOLKS'LL HAVE TO HONOR ***YOUR*** MEMORY.
IT'S ***KRUNCH.*** JUST KRUNCH.
...
VERY WELL. KRUNCH.

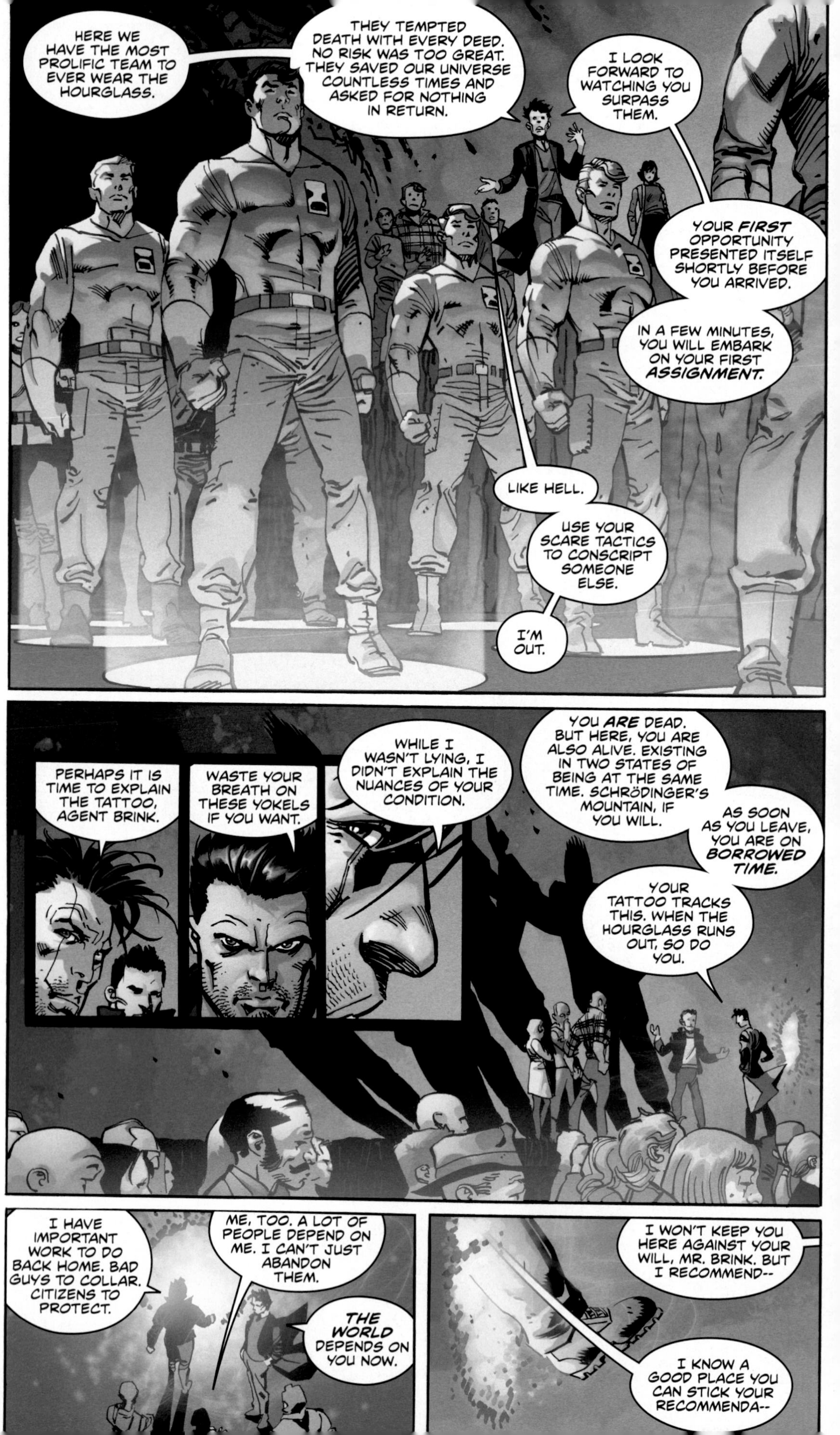
HERE WE HAVE THE MOST PROLIFIC TEAM TO EVER WEAR THE HOURGLASS.
THEY TEMPTED DEATH WITH EVERY DEED. NO RISK WAS TOO GREAT. THEY SAVED OUR UNIVERSE COUNTLESS TIMES AND ASKED FOR NOTHING IN RETURN.
I LOOK FORWARD TO WATCHING YOU SURPASS THEM.
YOUR *FIRST* OPPORTUNITY PRESENTED ITSELF SHORTLY BEFORE YOU ARRIVED.
IN A FEW MINUTES, YOU WILL EMBARK ON YOUR FIRST *ASSIGNMENT.*
LIKE HELL.
USE YOUR SCARE TACTICS TO CONSCRIPT SOMEONE ELSE.
I'M OUT.
PERHAPS IT IS TIME TO EXPLAIN THE TATTOO, AGENT BRINK.
WASTE YOUR BREATH ON THESE YOKELS IF YOU WANT.
WHILE I WASN'T LYING, I DIDN'T EXPLAIN THE NUANCES OF YOUR CONDITION.
YOU *ARE* DEAD. BUT HERE, YOU ARE ALSO ALIVE. EXISTING IN TWO STATES OF BEING AT THE SAME TIME. SCHRÖDINGER'S MOUNTAIN, IF YOU WILL.
AS SOON AS YOU LEAVE, YOU ARE ON *BORROWED TIME.*
YOUR TATTOO TRACKS THIS. WHEN THE HOURGLASS RUNS OUT, SO DO YOU.
I HAVE IMPORTANT WORK TO DO BACK HOME. BAD GUYS TO COLLAR. CITIZENS TO PROTECT.
ME, TOO. A LOT OF PEOPLE DEPEND ON ME. I CAN'T JUST ABANDON THEM.
THE WORLD DEPENDS ON YOU NOW.
I WON'T KEEP YOU HERE AGAINST YOUR WILL, MR. BRINK. BUT I RECOMMEND--
I KNOW A GOOD PLACE YOU CAN STICK YOUR RECOMMENDA--

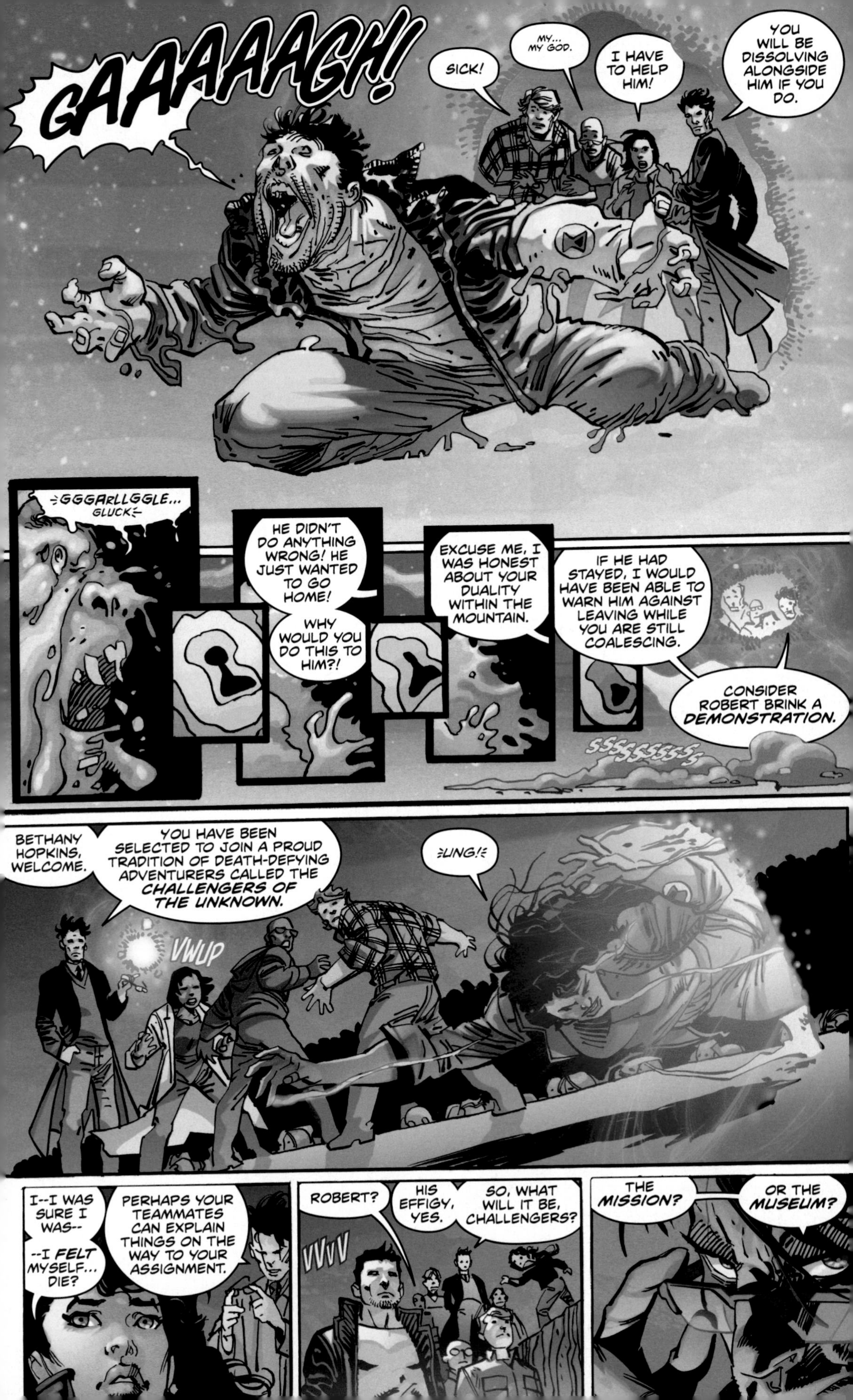
GAAAAAGH!
SICK!
MY... MY GOD.
I HAVE TO HELP HIM!
YOU WILL BE DISSOLVING ALONGSIDE HIM IF YOU DO.
GGGARLLGGLE... GLUCK
HE DIDN'T DO ANYTHING WRONG! HE JUST WANTED TO GO HOME!
WHY WOULD YOU DO THIS TO HIM?!
EXCUSE ME, I WAS HONEST ABOUT YOUR DUALITY WITHIN THE MOUNTAIN.
IF HE HAD STAYED, I WOULD HAVE BEEN ABLE TO WARN HIM AGAINST LEAVING WHILE YOU ARE STILL COALESCING.
CONSIDER ROBERT BRINK A *DEMONSTRATION.*
SSSSSSSSSS
BETHANY HOPKINS, WELCOME.
YOU HAVE BEEN SELECTED TO JOIN A PROUD TRADITION OF DEATH-DEFYING ADVENTURERS CALLED THE *CHALLENGERS OF THE UNKNOWN.*
UNG!
VWUP
I--I WAS SURE I WAS--
--I *FELT* MYSELF... DIE?
PERHAPS YOUR TEAMMATES CAN EXPLAIN THINGS ON THE WAY TO YOUR ASSIGNMENT.
ROBERT?
HIS EFFIGY, YES.
SO, WHAT WILL IT BE, CHALLENGERS?
VVVV
THE *MISSION?*
OR THE *MUSEUM?*

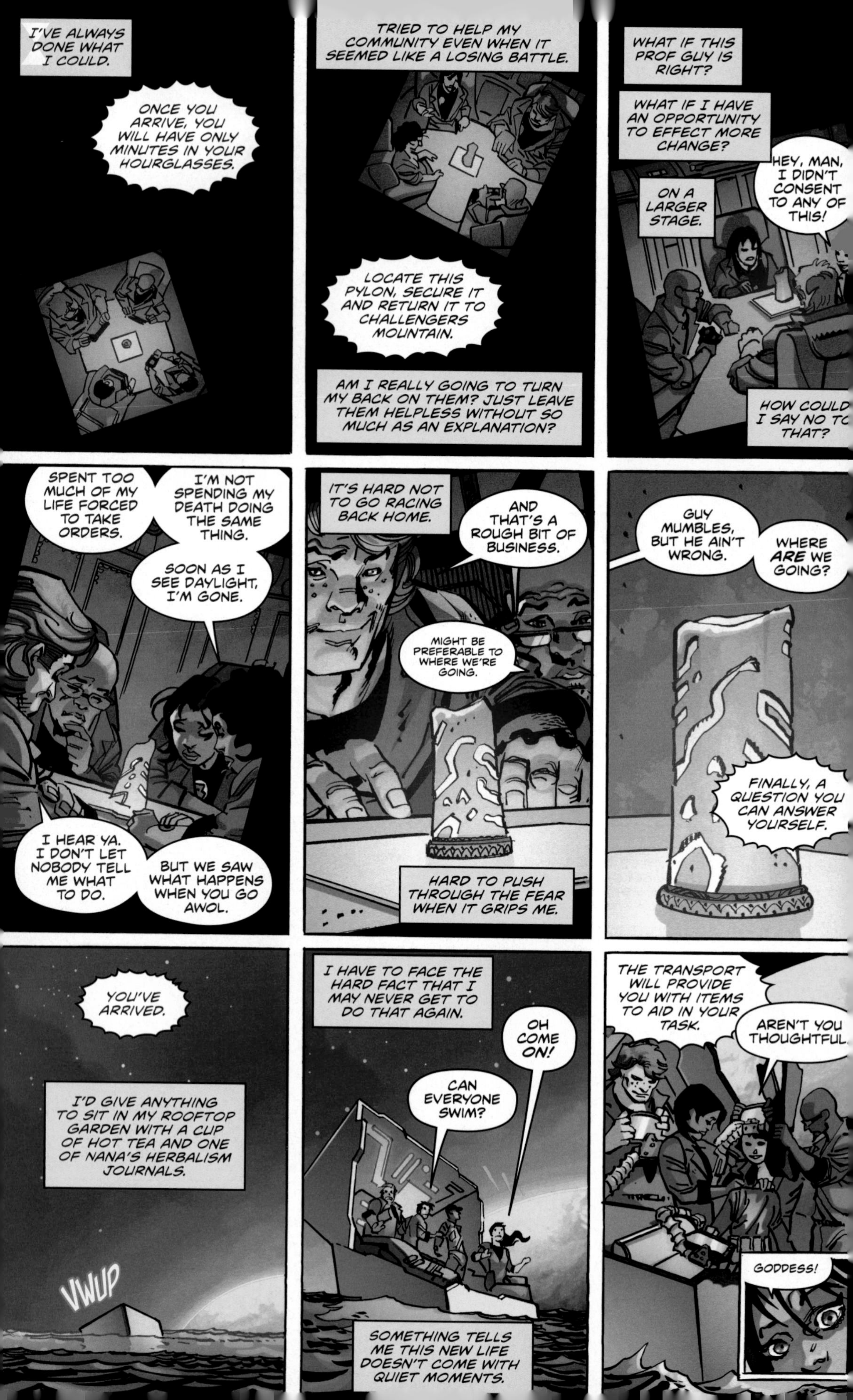

I'VE ALWAYS DONE WHAT I COULD.
ONCE YOU ARRIVE, YOU WILL HAVE ONLY MINUTES IN YOUR HOURGLASSES.
TRIED TO HELP MY COMMUNITY EVEN WHEN IT SEEMED LIKE A LOSING BATTLE.
LOCATE THIS PYLON, SECURE IT AND RETURN IT TO CHALLENGERS MOUNTAIN.
AM I REALLY GOING TO TURN MY BACK ON THEM? JUST LEAVE THEM HELPLESS WITHOUT SO MUCH AS AN EXPLANATION?
WHAT IF THIS PROF GUY IS RIGHT?
WHAT IF I HAVE AN OPPORTUNITY TO EFFECT MORE CHANGE?
ON A LARGER STAGE.
HEY, MAN, I DIDN'T CONSENT TO ANY OF THIS!
HOW COULD I SAY NO TO THAT?
SPENT TOO MUCH OF MY LIFE FORCED TO TAKE ORDERS.
I'M NOT SPENDING MY DEATH DOING THE SAME THING.
SOON AS I SEE DAYLIGHT, I'M GONE.
I HEAR YA. I DON'T LET NOBODY TELL ME WHAT TO DO.
BUT WE SAW WHAT HAPPENS WHEN YOU GO AWOL.
IT'S HARD NOT TO GO RACING BACK HOME.
AND THAT'S A ROUGH BIT OF BUSINESS.
MIGHT BE PREFERABLE TO WHERE WE'RE GOING.
HARD TO PUSH THROUGH THE FEAR WHEN IT GRIPS ME.
GUY MUMBLES, BUT HE AIN'T WRONG.
WHERE ARE WE GOING?
FINALLY, A QUESTION YOU CAN ANSWER YOURSELF.
YOU'VE ARRIVED.
I'D GIVE ANYTHING TO SIT IN MY ROOFTOP GARDEN WITH A CUP OF HOT TEA AND ONE OF NANA'S HERBALISM JOURNALS.
VWUP
I HAVE TO FACE THE HARD FACT THAT I MAY NEVER GET TO DO THAT AGAIN.
OH COME ON!
CAN EVERYONE SWIM?
SOMETHING TELLS ME THIS NEW LIFE DOESN'T COME WITH QUIET MOMENTS.
THE TRANSPORT WILL PROVIDE YOU WITH ITEMS TO AID IN YOUR TASK.
AREN'T YOU THOUGHTFUL.
GODDESS!

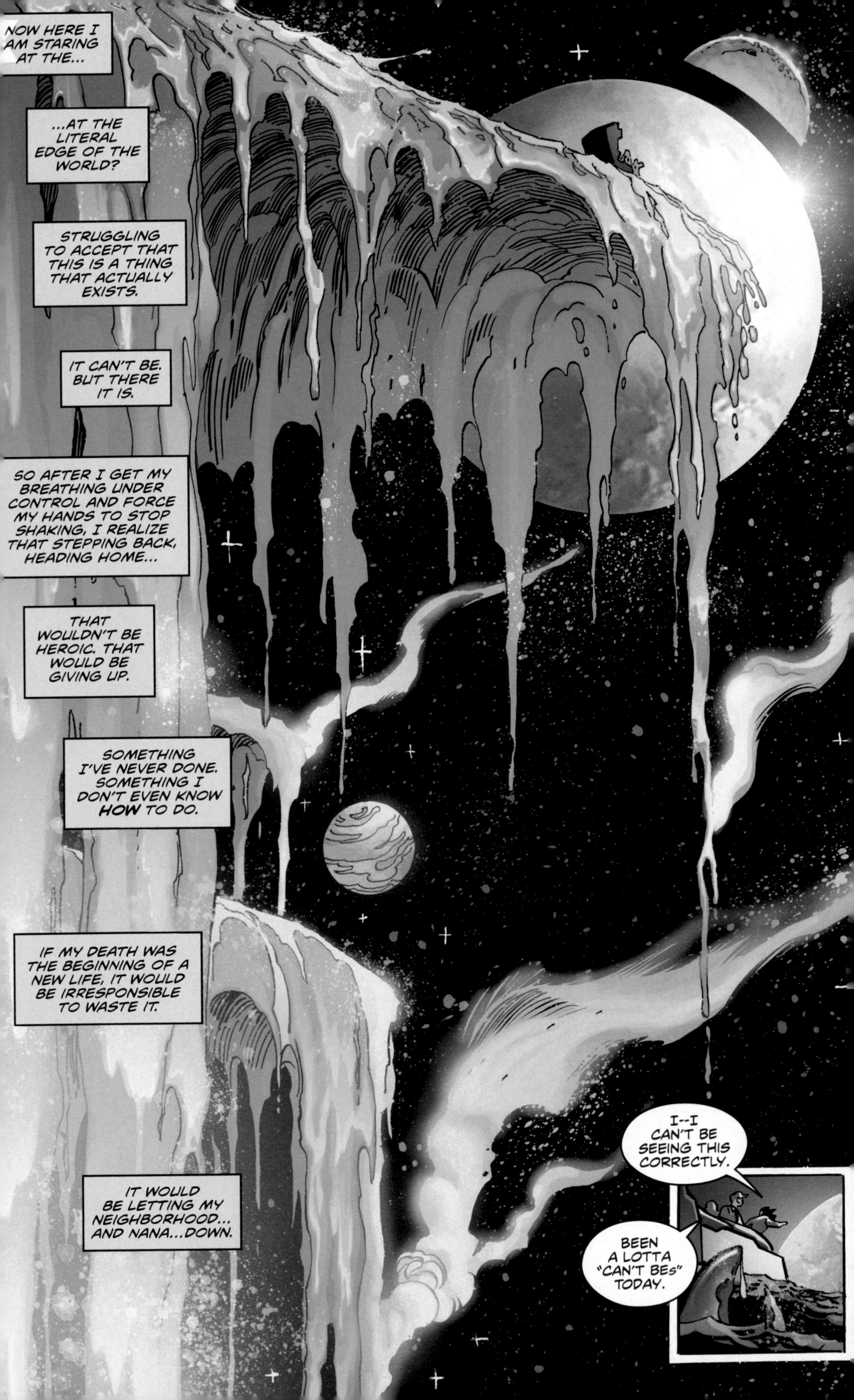
NOW HERE I AM STARING AT THE...
...AT THE LITERAL EDGE OF THE WORLD?
STRUGGLING TO ACCEPT THAT THIS IS A THING THAT ACTUALLY EXISTS.
IT CAN'T BE. BUT THERE IT IS.
SO AFTER I GET MY BREATHING UNDER CONTROL AND FORCE MY HANDS TO STOP SHAKING, I REALIZE THAT STEPPING BACK, HEADING HOME...
THAT WOULDN'T BE HEROIC. THAT WOULD BE GIVING UP.
SOMETHING I'VE NEVER DONE. SOMETHING I DON'T EVEN KNOW HOW TO DO.
IF MY DEATH WAS THE BEGINNING OF A NEW LIFE, IT WOULD BE IRRESPONSIBLE TO WASTE IT.
IT WOULD BE LETTING MY NEIGHBORHOOD... AND NANA...DOWN.
I--I CAN'T BE SEEING THIS CORRECTLY.
BEEN A LOTTA "CAN'T BEs" TODAY.

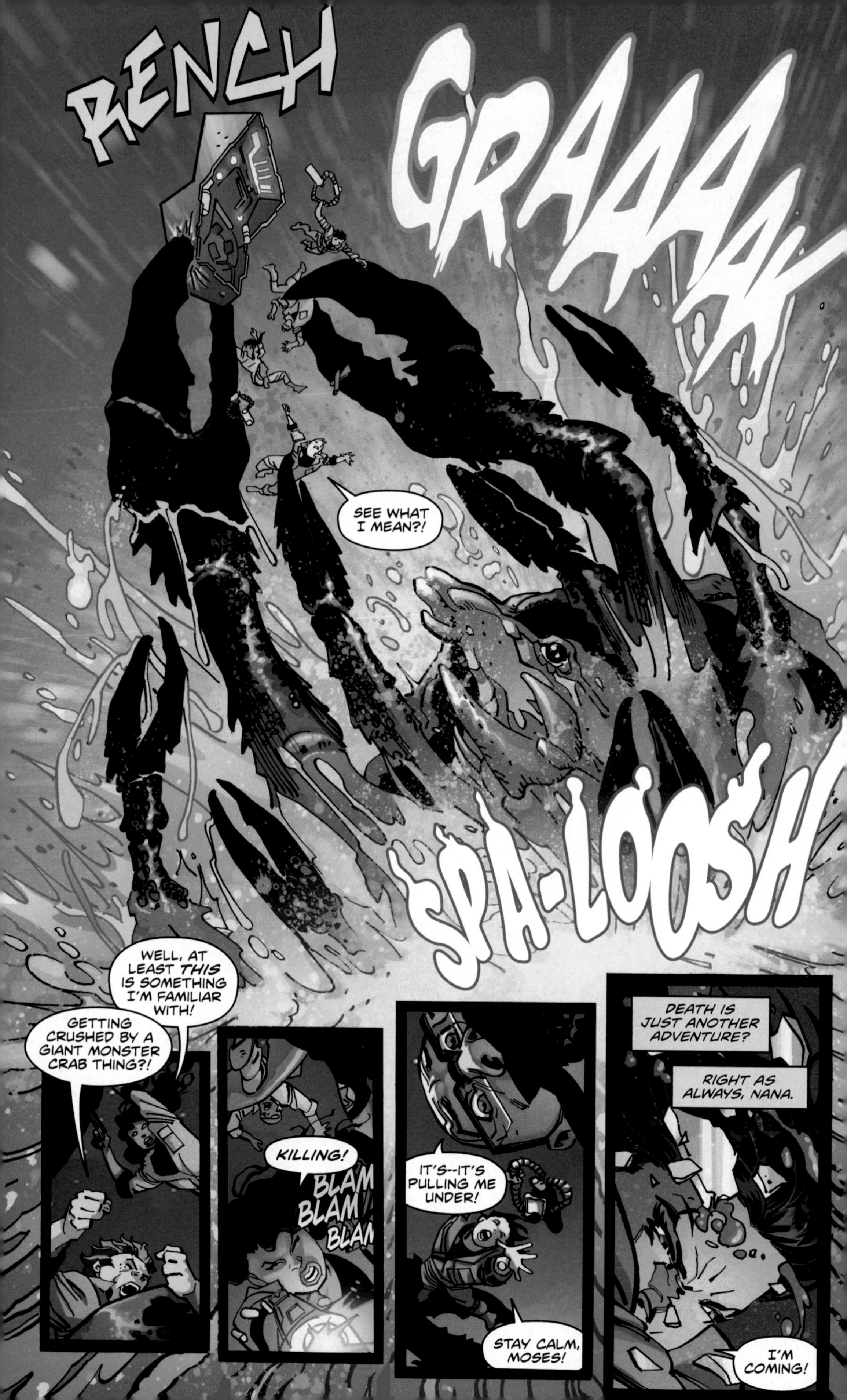
RENCH
GRAAAAK
SEE WHAT I MEAN?!
SPA-LOOSH
GETTING CRUSHED BY A GIANT MONSTER CRAB THING?!
WELL, AT LEAST *THIS* IS SOMETHING I'M FAMILIAR WITH!
KILLING!
BLAM BLAM BLAM
IT'S--IT'S PULLING ME UNDER!
STAY CALM, MOSES!
DEATH IS JUST ANOTHER ADVENTURE?
RIGHT AS ALWAYS, NANA.
I'M COMING!

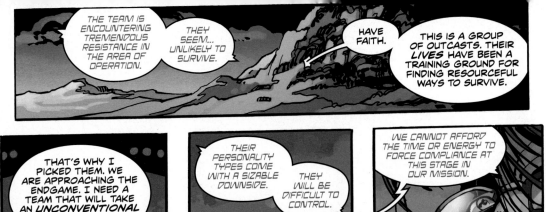

THE TEAM IS ENCOUNTERING TREMENDOUS RESISTANCE IN THE AREA OF OPERATION.

THEY SEEM... UNLIKELY TO SURVIVE.

HAVE FAITH.

THIS IS A GROUP OF OUTCASTS. THEIR *LIVES* HAVE BEEN A TRAINING GROUND FOR FINDING RESOURCEFUL WAYS TO SURVIVE.

THAT'S WHY I PICKED THEM. WE ARE APPROACHING THE ENDGAME. I NEED A TEAM THAT WILL TAKE AN *UNCONVENTIONAL* APPROACH TO THE OPPOSITION.

THEIR PERSONALITY TYPES COME WITH A SIZABLE DOWNSIDE.

THEY WILL BE DIFFICULT TO CONTROL.

WE CANNOT AFFORD THE TIME OR ENERGY TO FORCE COMPLIANCE AT THIS STAGE IN OUR MISSION.

LOOK, I KNOW IT IS LITERALLY YOUR JOB TO QUESTION ME.

BUT COULD YOU GIVE IT A REST?

I FIND IT DIFFICULT TO PLAN THE NEXT STEPS WITH YOUR RELENTLESS BUZZING OVER MY SHOULDER.

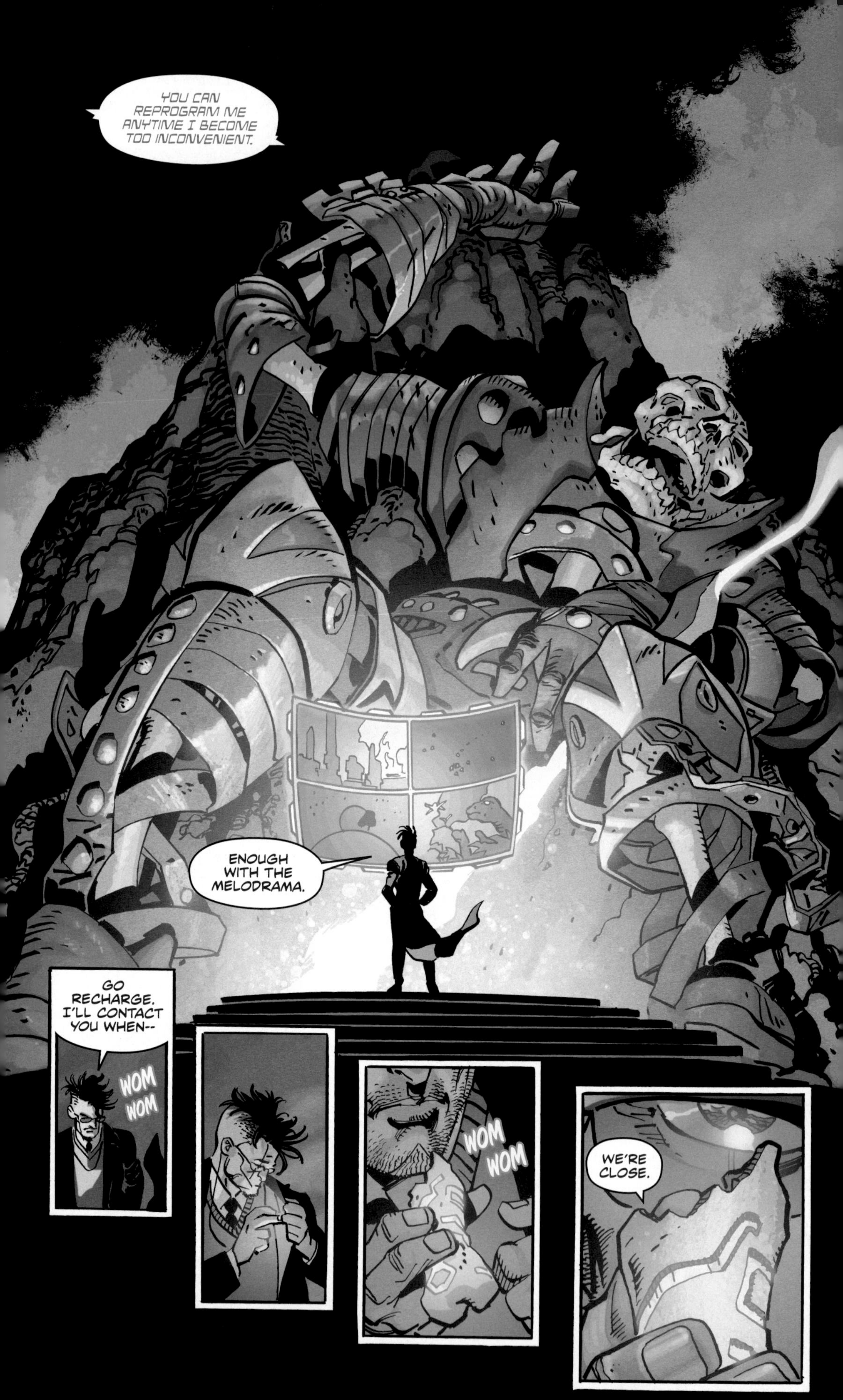
YOU CAN REPROGRAM ME ANYTIME I BECOME TOO INCONVENIENT.
ENOUGH WITH THE MELODRAMA.
GO RECHARGE. I'LL CONTACT YOU WHEN--
WOM WOM
WOM WOM
WE'RE CLOSE.

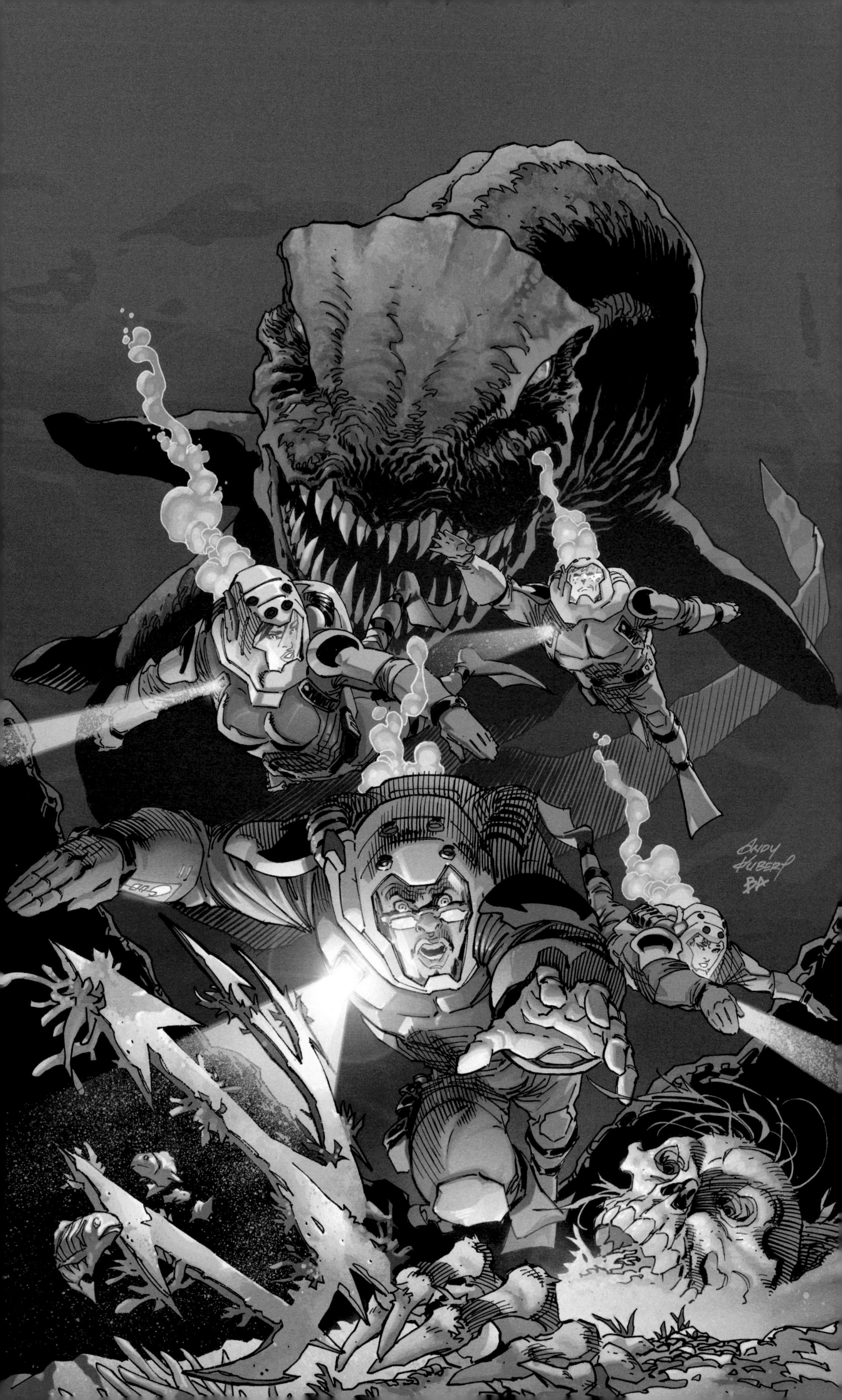
ANDY
KUBERT
BA

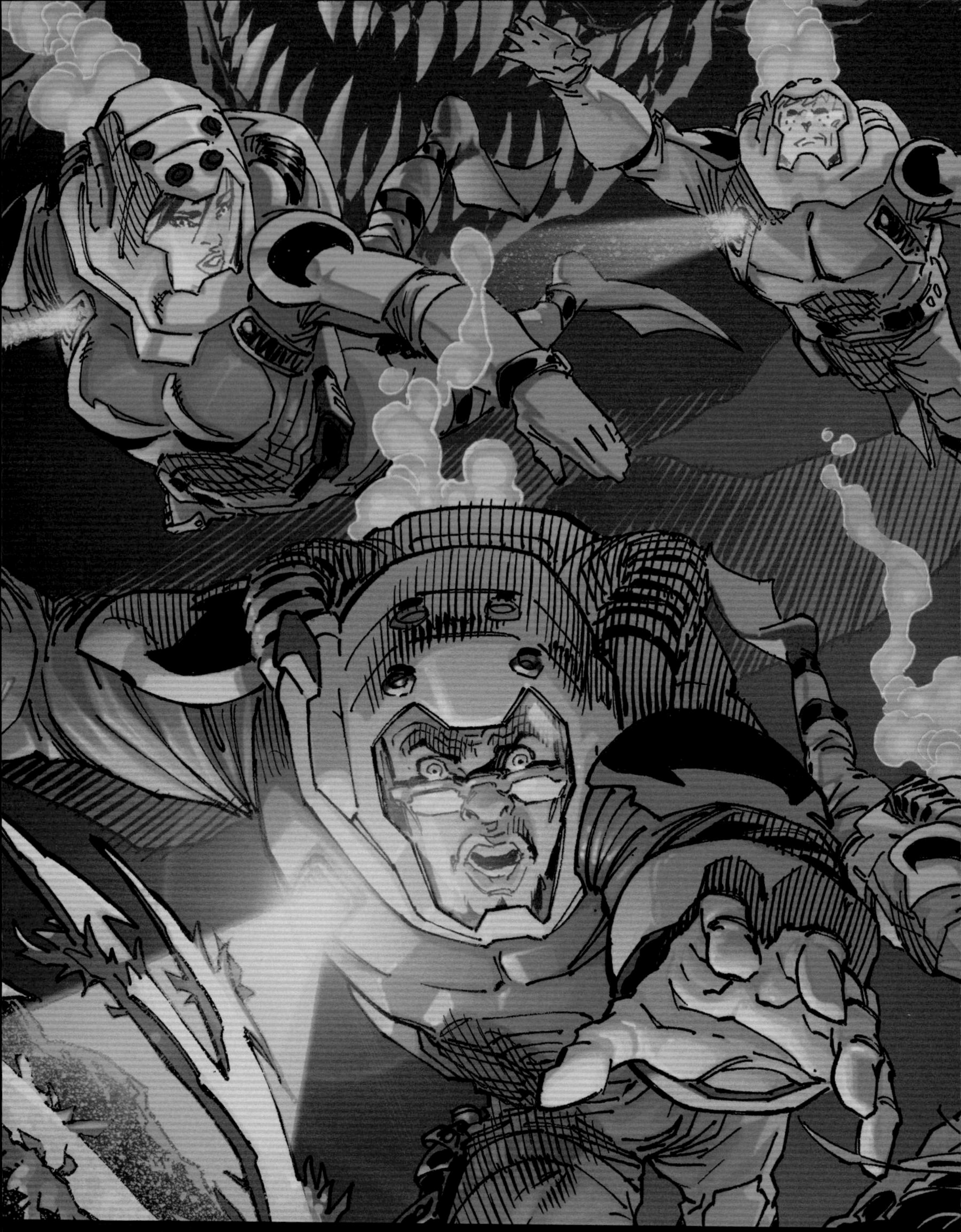

NEW CHALLENGERS
#2

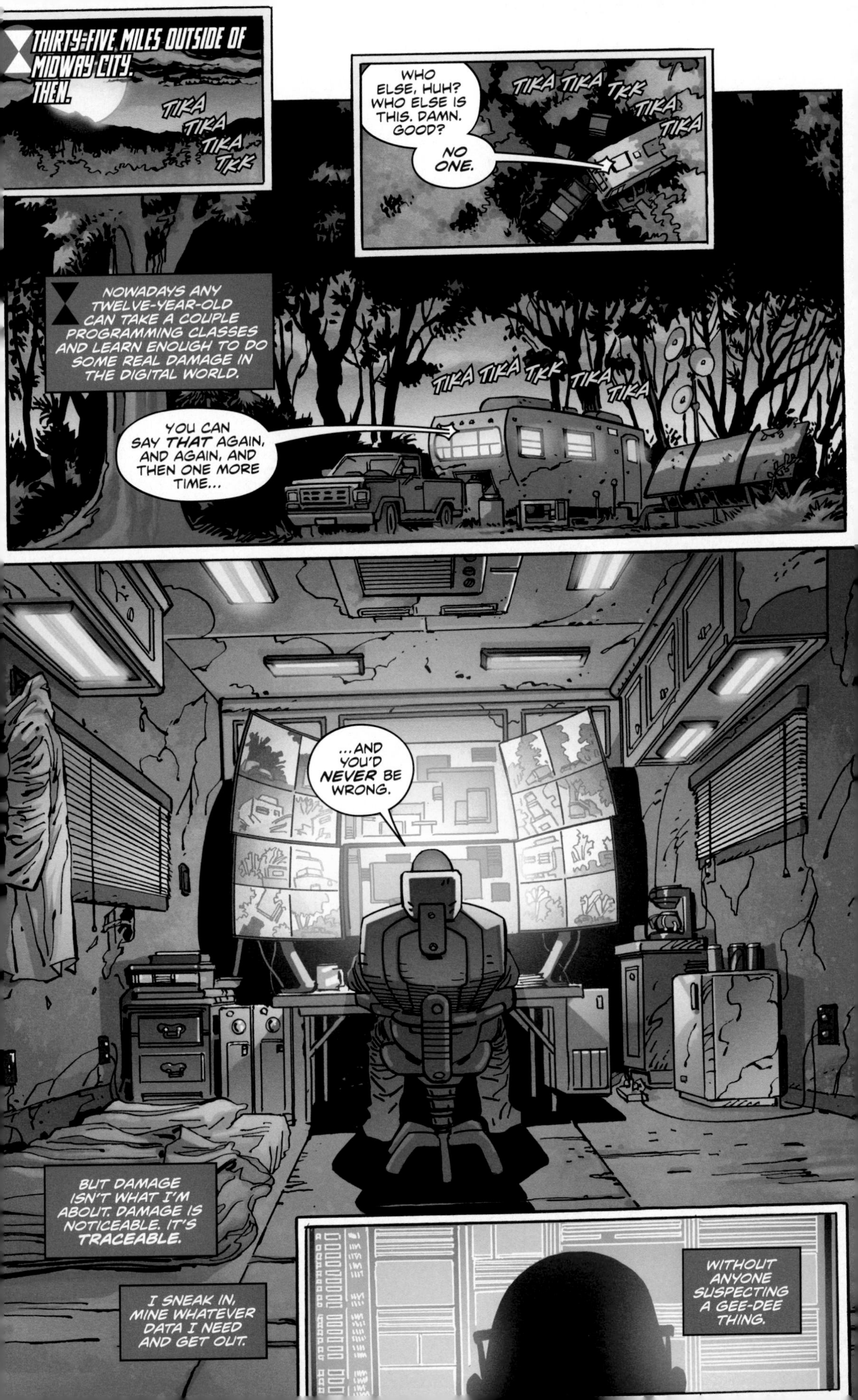
THIRTY-FIVE MILES OUTSIDE OF MIDWAY CITY. THEN.
TIKA TIKA TIKA TKK
WHO ELSE, HUH? WHO ELSE IS THIS. DAMN. GOOD?
NO ONE.
TIKA TIKA TKK TIKA TIKA
NOWADAYS ANY TWELVE-YEAR-OLD CAN TAKE A COUPLE PROGRAMMING CLASSES AND LEARN ENOUGH TO DO SOME REAL DAMAGE IN THE DIGITAL WORLD.
TIKA TIKA TKK TIKA TIKA
YOU CAN SAY THAT AGAIN, AND AGAIN, AND THEN ONE MORE TIME...
...AND YOU'D NEVER BE WRONG.
BUT DAMAGE ISN'T WHAT I'M ABOUT. DAMAGE IS NOTICEABLE. IT'S TRACEABLE.
I SNEAK IN, MINE WHATEVER DATA I NEED AND GET OUT.
WITHOUT ANYONE SUSPECTING A GEE-DEE THING.

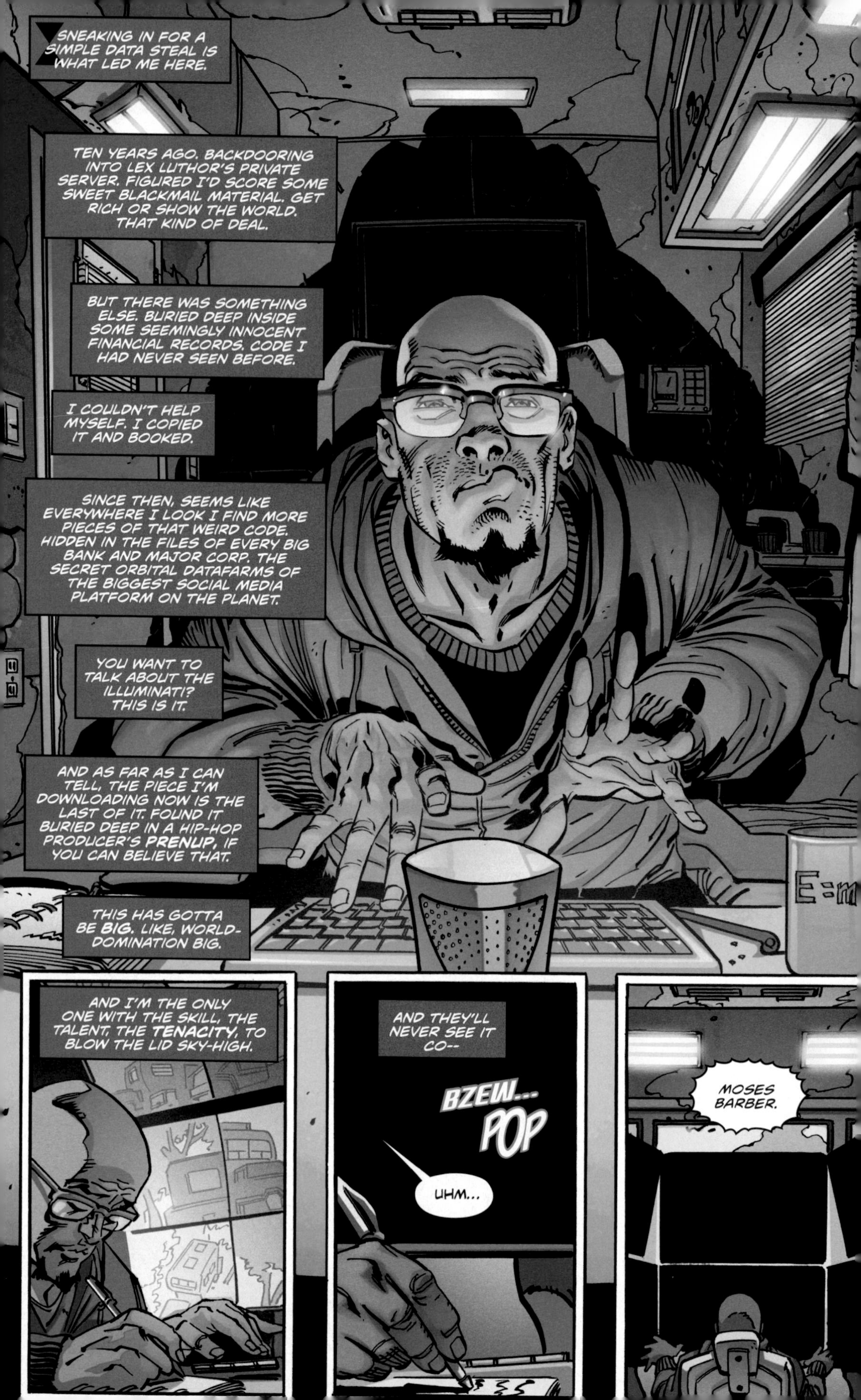
SNEAKING IN FOR A SIMPLE DATA STEAL IS WHAT LED ME HERE.
TEN YEARS AGO. BACKDOORING INTO LEX LUTHOR'S PRIVATE SERVER. FIGURED I'D SCORE SOME SWEET BLACKMAIL MATERIAL. GET RICH OR SHOW THE WORLD. THAT KIND OF DEAL.
BUT THERE WAS SOMETHING ELSE. BURIED DEEP INSIDE SOME SEEMINGLY INNOCENT FINANCIAL RECORDS. CODE I HAD NEVER SEEN BEFORE.
I COULDN'T HELP MYSELF. I COPIED IT AND BOOKED.
SINCE THEN, SEEMS LIKE EVERYWHERE I LOOK I FIND MORE PIECES OF THAT WEIRD CODE. HIDDEN IN THE FILES OF EVERY BIG BANK AND MAJOR CORP. THE SECRET ORBITAL DATAFARMS OF THE BIGGEST SOCIAL MEDIA PLATFORM ON THE PLANET.
YOU WANT TO TALK ABOUT THE ILLUMINATI? THIS IS IT.
AND AS FAR AS I CAN TELL, THE PIECE I'M DOWNLOADING NOW IS THE LAST OF IT. FOUND IT BURIED DEEP IN A HIP-HOP PRODUCER'S **PRENUP**, IF YOU CAN BELIEVE THAT.
THIS HAS GOTTA BE **BIG**. LIKE, WORLD-DOMINATION BIG.
E=m
AND I'M THE ONLY ONE WITH THE SKILL, THE TALENT, THE **TENACITY**, TO BLOW THE LID SKY-HIGH.
AND THEY'LL NEVER SEE IT CO--
BZEW... POP
UHM...
MOSES BARBER.

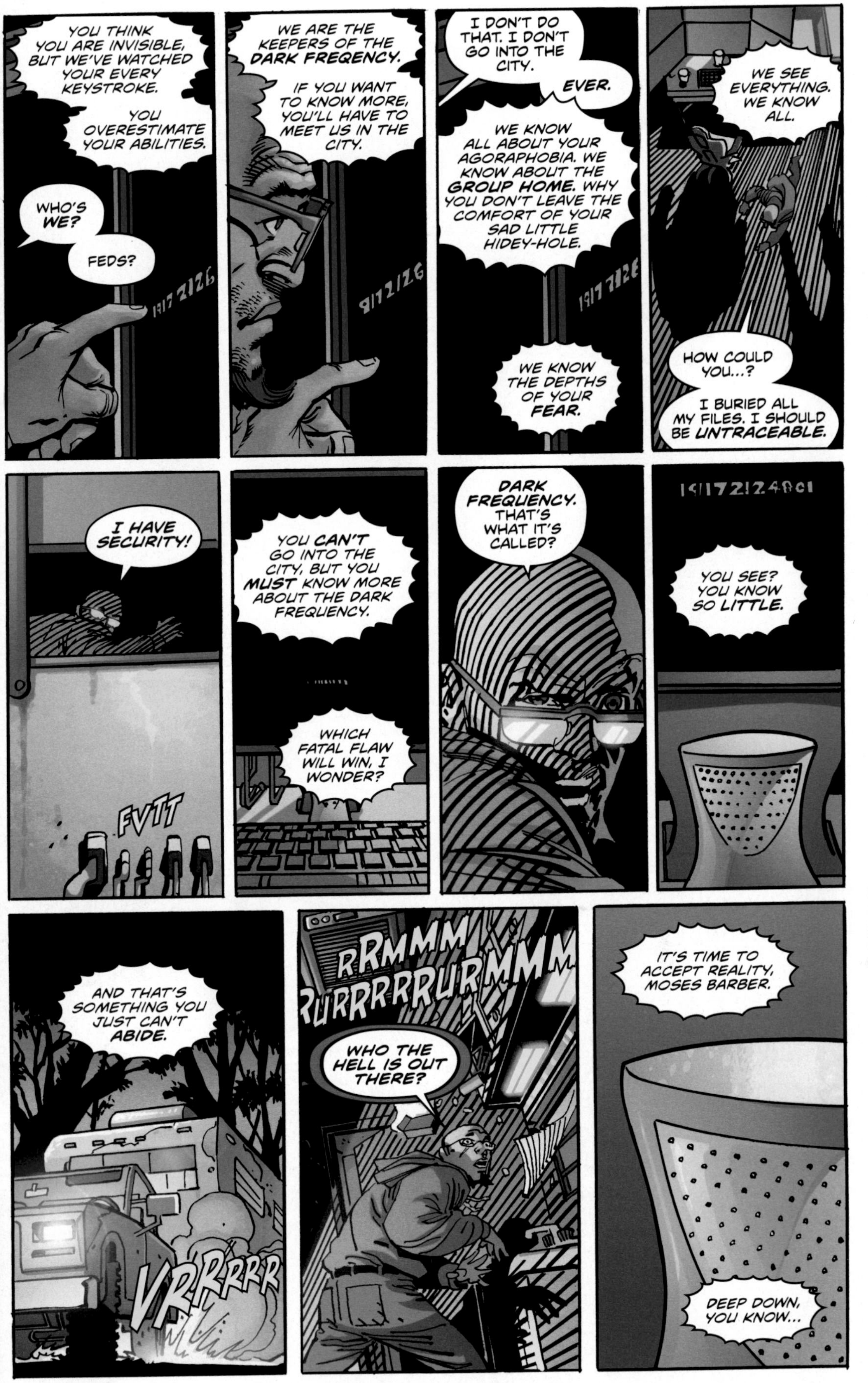
YOU THINK YOU ARE INVISIBLE, BUT WE'VE WATCHED YOUR EVERY KEYSTROKE.
YOU OVERESTIMATE YOUR ABILITIES.
WHO'S WE?
FEDS?
WE ARE THE KEEPERS OF THE DARK FREQENCY.
IF YOU WANT TO KNOW MORE, YOU'LL HAVE TO MEET US IN THE CITY.
I DON'T DO THAT. I DON'T GO INTO THE CITY.
EVER.
WE KNOW ALL ABOUT YOUR AGORAPHOBIA. WE KNOW ABOUT THE GROUP HOME. WHY YOU DON'T LEAVE THE COMFORT OF YOUR SAD LITTLE HIDEY-HOLE.
WE KNOW THE DEPTHS OF YOUR FEAR.
WE SEE EVERYTHING. WE KNOW ALL.
HOW COULD YOU...?
I BURIED ALL MY FILES. I SHOULD BE UNTRACEABLE.
I HAVE SECURITY!
FVTT
YOU CAN'T GO INTO THE CITY, BUT YOU MUST KNOW MORE ABOUT THE DARK FREQUENCY.
WHICH FATAL FLAW WILL WIN, I WONDER?
DARK FREQUENCY. THAT'S WHAT IT'S CALLED?
YOU SEE? YOU KNOW SO LITTLE.
AND THAT'S SOMETHING YOU JUST CAN'T ABIDE.
VRRRRR
RRMMM
RURRRRRURMMM
WHO THE HELL IS OUT THERE?
IT'S TIME TO ACCEPT REALITY, MOSES BARBER.
DEEP DOWN, YOU KNOW...

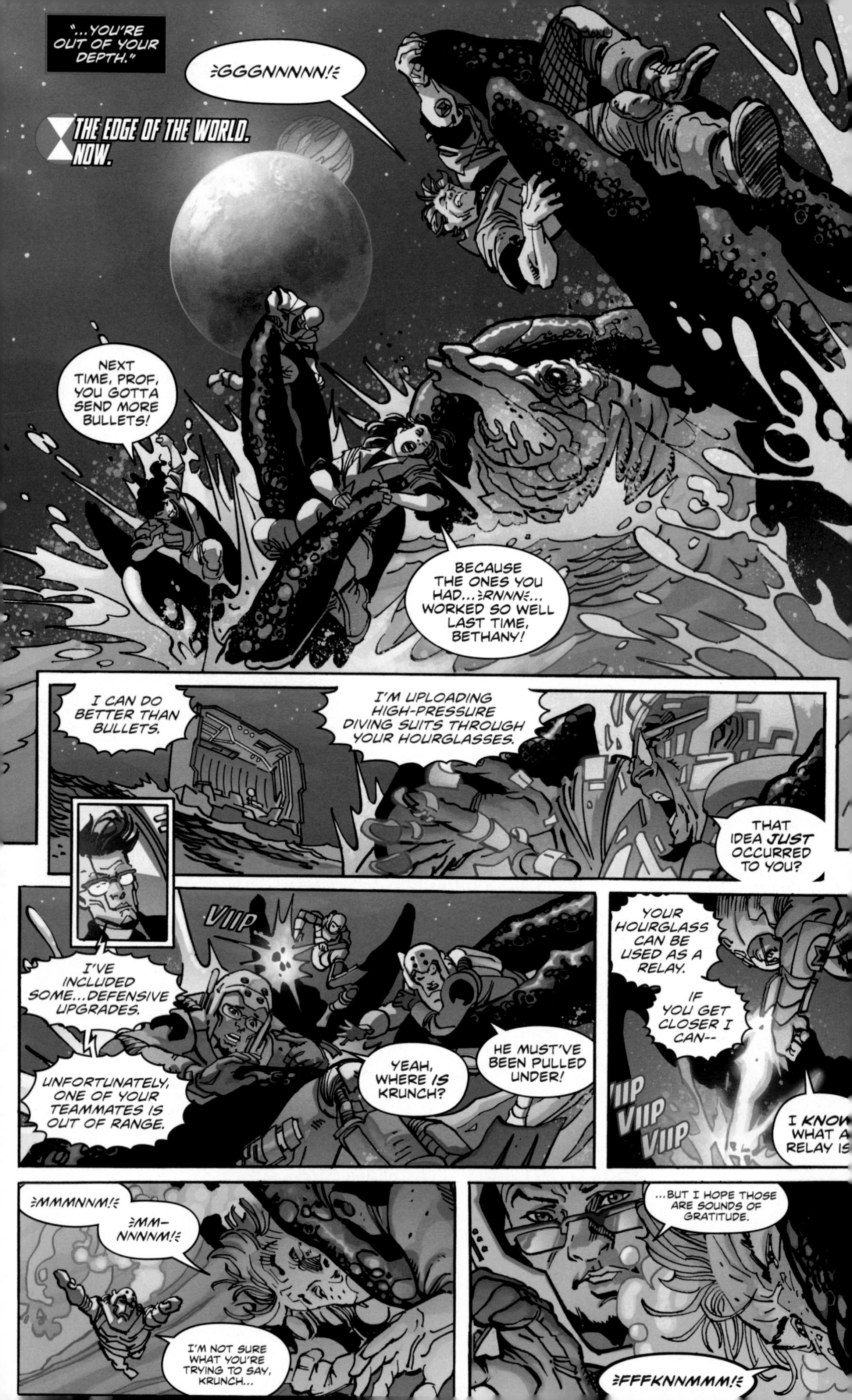

"...YOU'RE OUT OF YOUR DEPTH."
GGGNNNNN!
THE EDGE OF THE WORLD. NOW.
NEXT TIME, PROF, YOU GOTTA SEND MORE BULLETS!
BECAUSE THE ONES YOU HAD... RNNN... WORKED SO WELL LAST TIME, BETHANY!
I CAN DO BETTER THAN BULLETS.
I'M UPLOADING HIGH-PRESSURE DIVING SUITS THROUGH YOUR HOURGLASSES.
THAT IDEA JUST OCCURRED TO YOU?
VIIP
I'VE INCLUDED SOME...DEFENSIVE UPGRADES.
UNFORTUNATELY, ONE OF YOUR TEAMMATES IS OUT OF RANGE.
YEAH, WHERE IS KRUNCH?
HE MUST'VE BEEN PULLED UNDER!
YOUR HOURGLASS CAN BE USED AS A RELAY.
IF YOU GET CLOSER I CAN--
VIIP VIIP VIIP
I KNOW WHAT A RELAY IS
MMMNNM!
MM-NNNNM!
I'M NOT SURE WHAT YOU'RE TRYING TO SAY, KRUNCH...
...BUT I HOPE THOSE ARE SOUNDS OF GRATITUDE.
FFFKNNMMM!

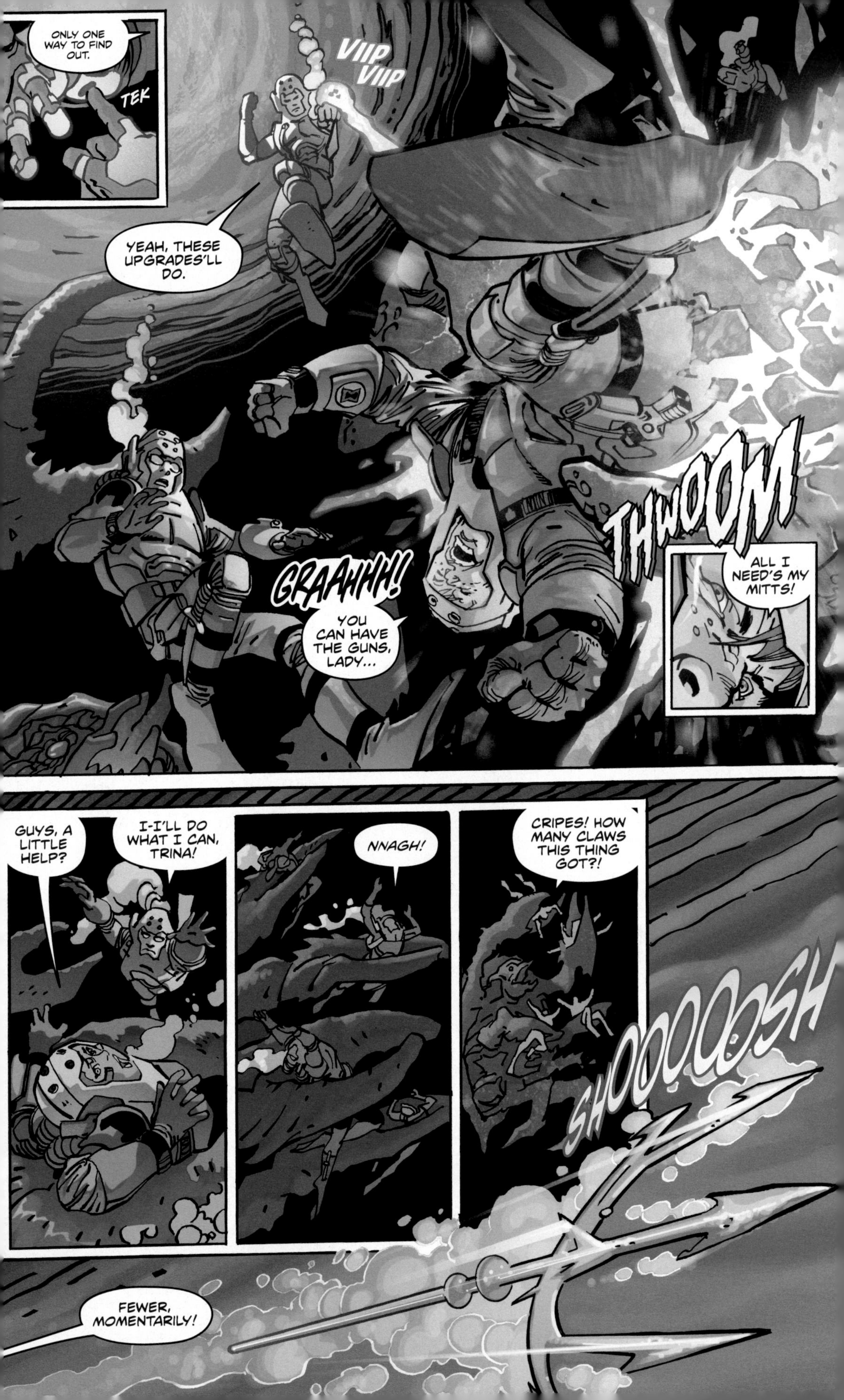
ONLY ONE WAY TO FIND OUT.
TEK
VIIP VIIP
YEAH, THESE UPGRADES'LL DO.
THWOOM
GRAAHHH!
YOU CAN HAVE THE GUNS, LADY...
ALL I NEED'S MY MITTS!
GUYS, A LITTLE HELP?
I-I'LL DO WHAT I CAN, TRINA!
NNAGH!
CRIPES! HOW MANY CLAWS THIS THING GOT?!
SHOOOOOSH
FEWER, MOMENTARILY!

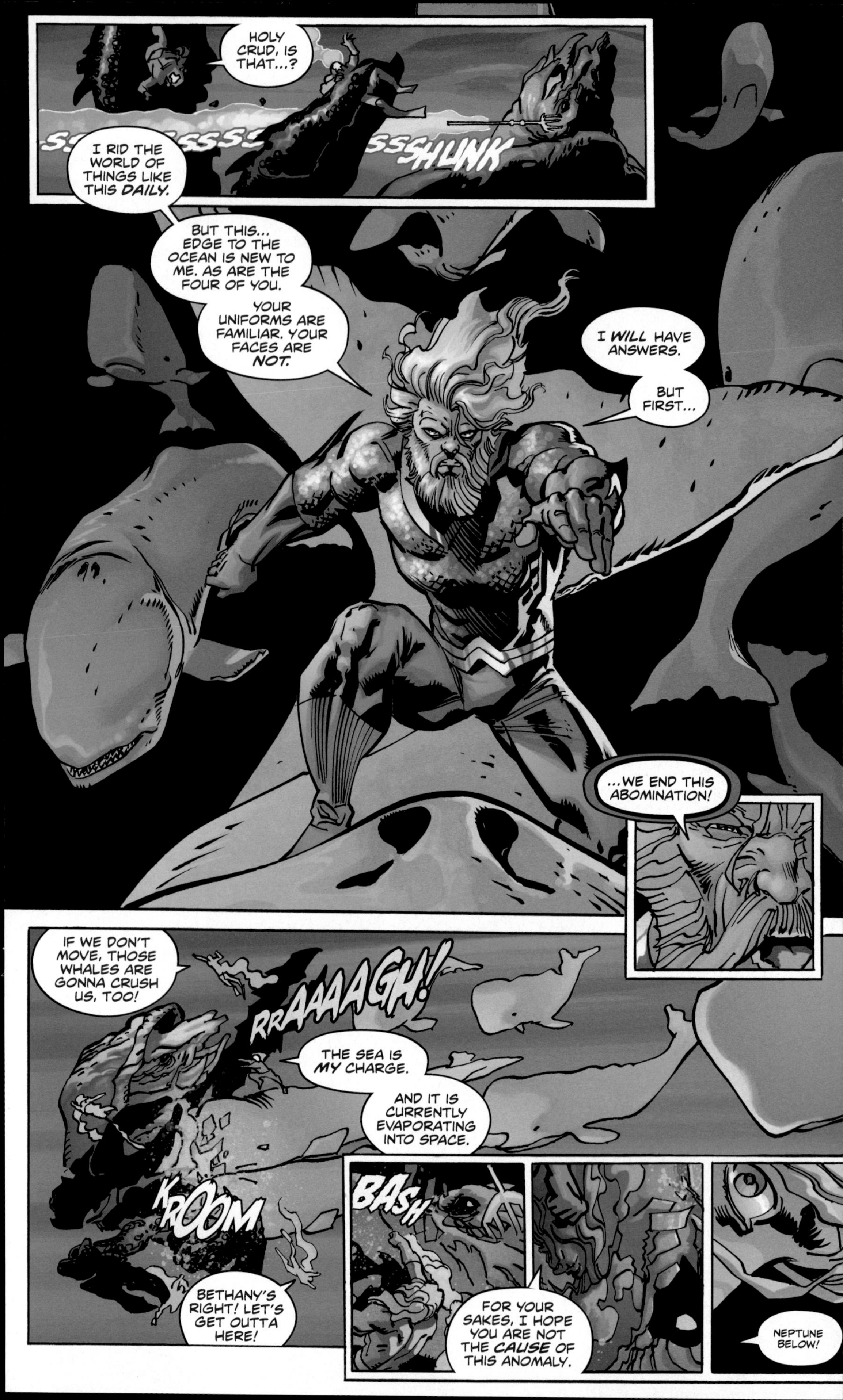
HOLY CRUD, IS THAT...?
SSSSSSSSSSSSHUNK
I RID THE WORLD OF THINGS LIKE THIS DAILY.
BUT THIS... EDGE TO THE OCEAN IS NEW TO ME. AS ARE THE FOUR OF YOU.
YOUR UNIFORMS ARE FAMILIAR. YOUR FACES ARE NOT.
I WILL HAVE ANSWERS.
BUT FIRST...
...WE END THIS ABOMINATION!
IF WE DON'T MOVE, THOSE WHALES ARE GONNA CRUSH US, TOO!
RRAAAAGH!
THE SEA IS MY CHARGE.
AND IT IS CURRENTLY EVAPORATING INTO SPACE.
KROOM
BETHANY'S RIGHT! LET'S GET OUTTA HERE!
BASH
FOR YOUR SAKES, I HOPE YOU ARE NOT THE CAUSE OF THIS ANOMALY.
NEPTUNE BELOW!

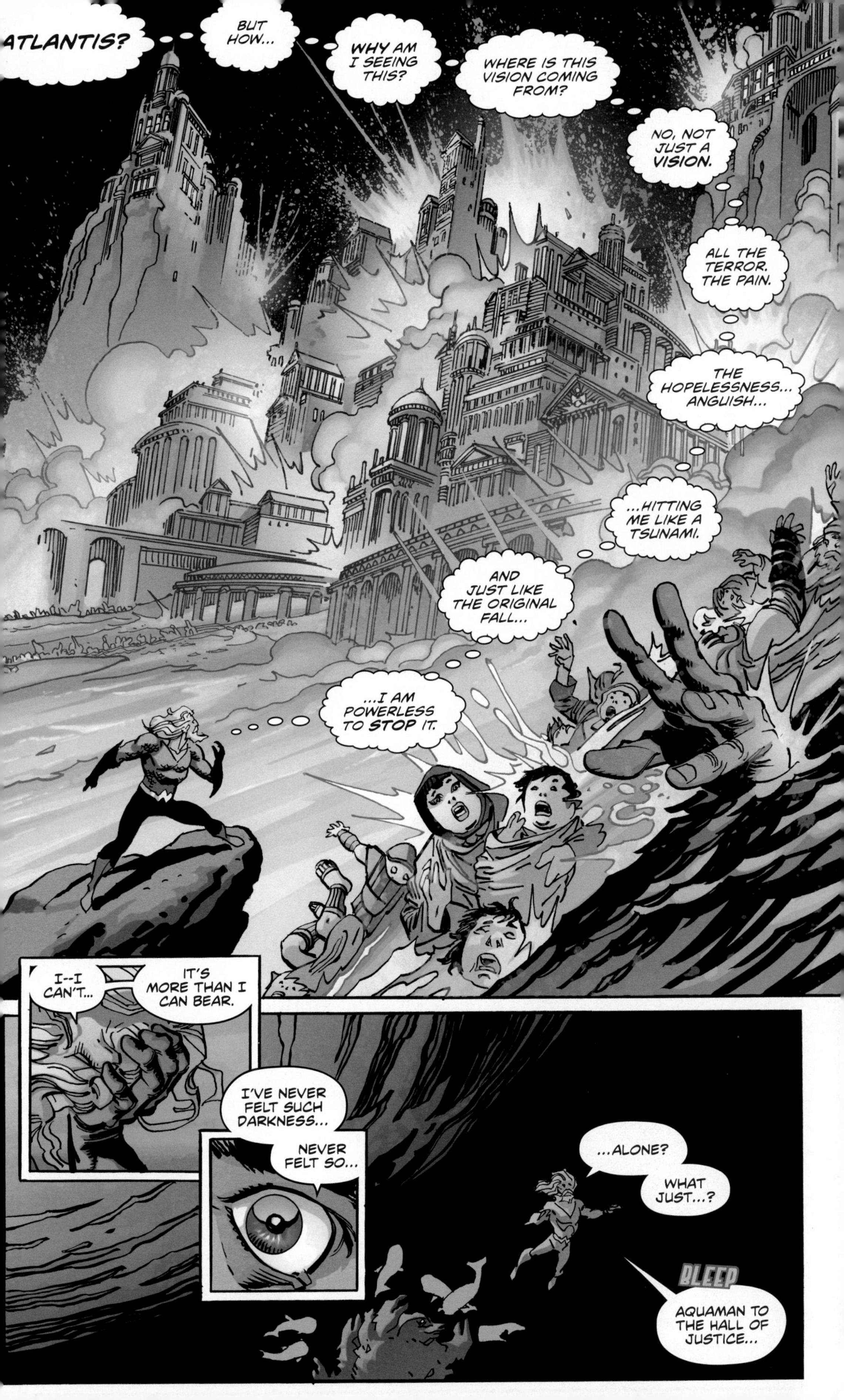
ATLANTIS?
BUT HOW...
WHY AM I SEEING THIS?
WHERE IS THIS VISION COMING FROM?
NO, NOT JUST A VISION.
ALL THE TERROR. THE PAIN.
THE HOPELESSNESS... ANGUISH...
...HITTING ME LIKE A TSUNAMI.
AND JUST LIKE THE ORIGINAL FALL...
...I AM POWERLESS TO STOP IT.
I--I CAN'T...
IT'S MORE THAN I CAN BEAR.
I'VE NEVER FELT SUCH DARKNESS...
NEVER FELT SO...
...ALONE?
WHAT JUST...?
BLEEP
AQUAMAN TO THE HALL OF JUSTICE...

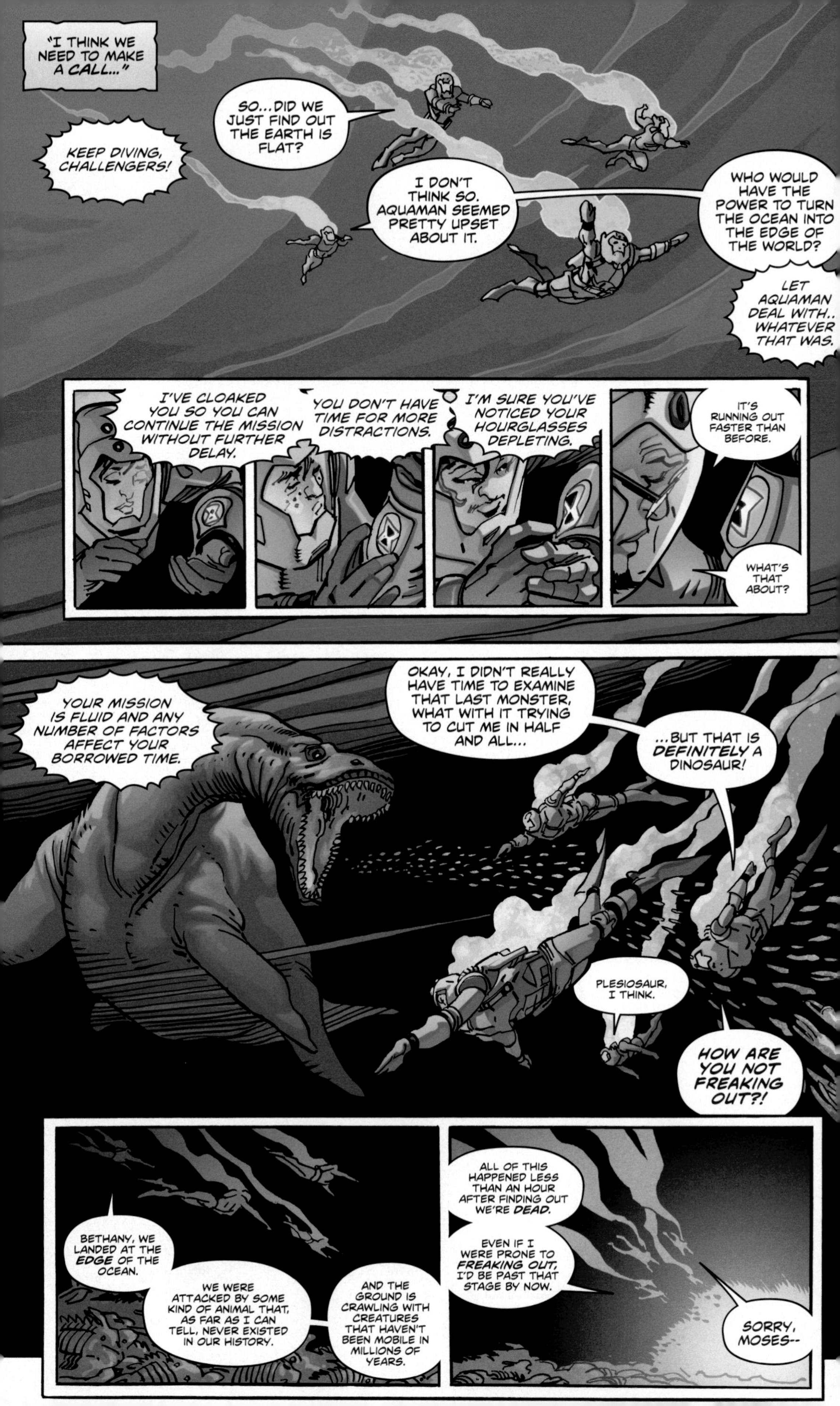
"I THINK WE NEED TO MAKE A *CALL*..."
KEEP DIVING, CHALLENGERS!
SO...DID WE JUST FIND OUT THE EARTH IS *FLAT*?
I DON'T THINK SO. AQUAMAN SEEMED PRETTY UPSET ABOUT IT.
WHO WOULD HAVE THE POWER TO TURN THE OCEAN INTO THE EDGE OF THE WORLD?
LET AQUAMAN DEAL WITH.. WHATEVER THAT WAS.
I'VE CLOAKED YOU SO YOU CAN CONTINUE THE MISSION WITHOUT FURTHER DELAY.
YOU DON'T HAVE TIME FOR MORE DISTRACTIONS.
I'M SURE YOU'VE NOTICED YOUR HOURGLASSES DEPLETING.
IT'S RUNNING OUT FASTER THAN BEFORE.
WHAT'S THAT ABOUT?
YOUR MISSION IS FLUID AND ANY NUMBER OF FACTORS AFFECT YOUR BORROWED TIME.
OKAY, I DIDN'T REALLY HAVE TIME TO EXAMINE THAT LAST MONSTER, WHAT WITH IT TRYING TO CUT ME IN HALF AND ALL...
...BUT THAT IS *DEFINITELY* A DINOSAUR!
PLESIOSAUR, I THINK.
HOW ARE YOU NOT FREAKING OUT?!
BETHANY, WE LANDED AT THE *EDGE* OF THE OCEAN.
WE WERE ATTACKED BY SOME KIND OF ANIMAL THAT, AS FAR AS I CAN TELL, NEVER EXISTED IN OUR HISTORY.
AND THE GROUND IS CRAWLING WITH CREATURES THAT HAVEN'T BEEN MOBILE IN MILLIONS OF YEARS.
ALL OF THIS HAPPENED LESS THAN AN HOUR AFTER FINDING OUT WE'RE *DEAD*.
EVEN IF I WERE PRONE TO *FREAKING OUT*, I'D BE PAST THAT STAGE BY NOW.
SORRY, MOSES--

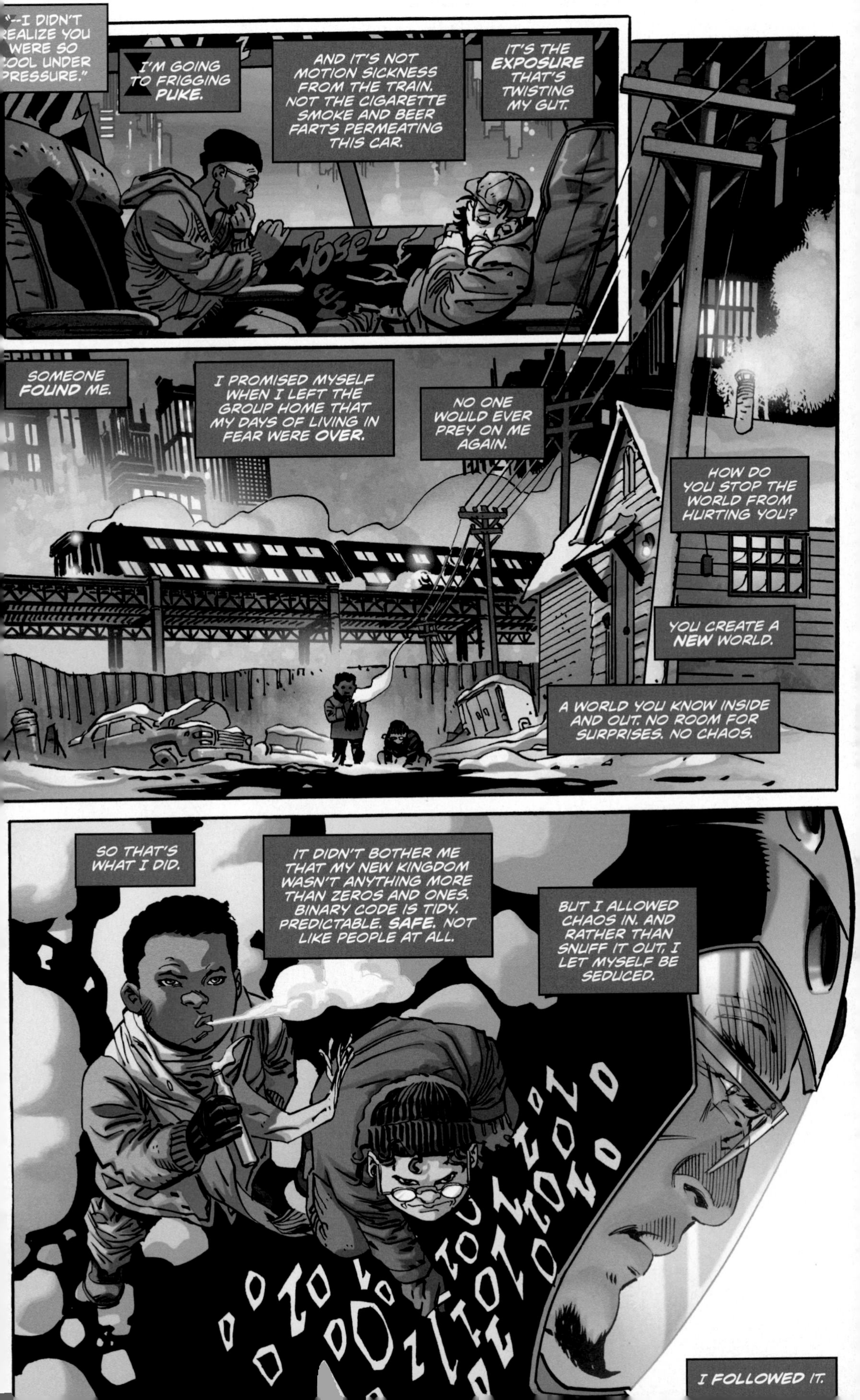
"--I DIDN'T REALIZE YOU WERE SO COOL UNDER PRESSURE."
I'M GOING TO FRIGGING PUKE.
AND IT'S NOT MOTION SICKNESS FROM THE TRAIN. NOT THE CIGARETTE SMOKE AND BEER FARTS PERMEATING THIS CAR.
IT'S THE EXPOSURE THAT'S TWISTING MY GUT.
JOSE
SOMEONE FOUND ME.
I PROMISED MYSELF WHEN I LEFT THE GROUP HOME THAT MY DAYS OF LIVING IN FEAR WERE OVER.
NO ONE WOULD EVER PREY ON ME AGAIN.
HOW DO YOU STOP THE WORLD FROM HURTING YOU?
YOU CREATE A NEW WORLD.
A WORLD YOU KNOW INSIDE AND OUT. NO ROOM FOR SURPRISES. NO CHAOS.
SO THAT'S WHAT I DID.
IT DIDN'T BOTHER ME THAT MY NEW KINGDOM WASN'T ANYTHING MORE THAN ZEROS AND ONES. BINARY CODE IS TIDY. PREDICTABLE. SAFE. NOT LIKE PEOPLE AT ALL.
BUT I ALLOWED CHAOS IN. AND RATHER THAN SNUFF IT OUT, I LET MYSELF BE SEDUCED.
I FOLLOWED IT.

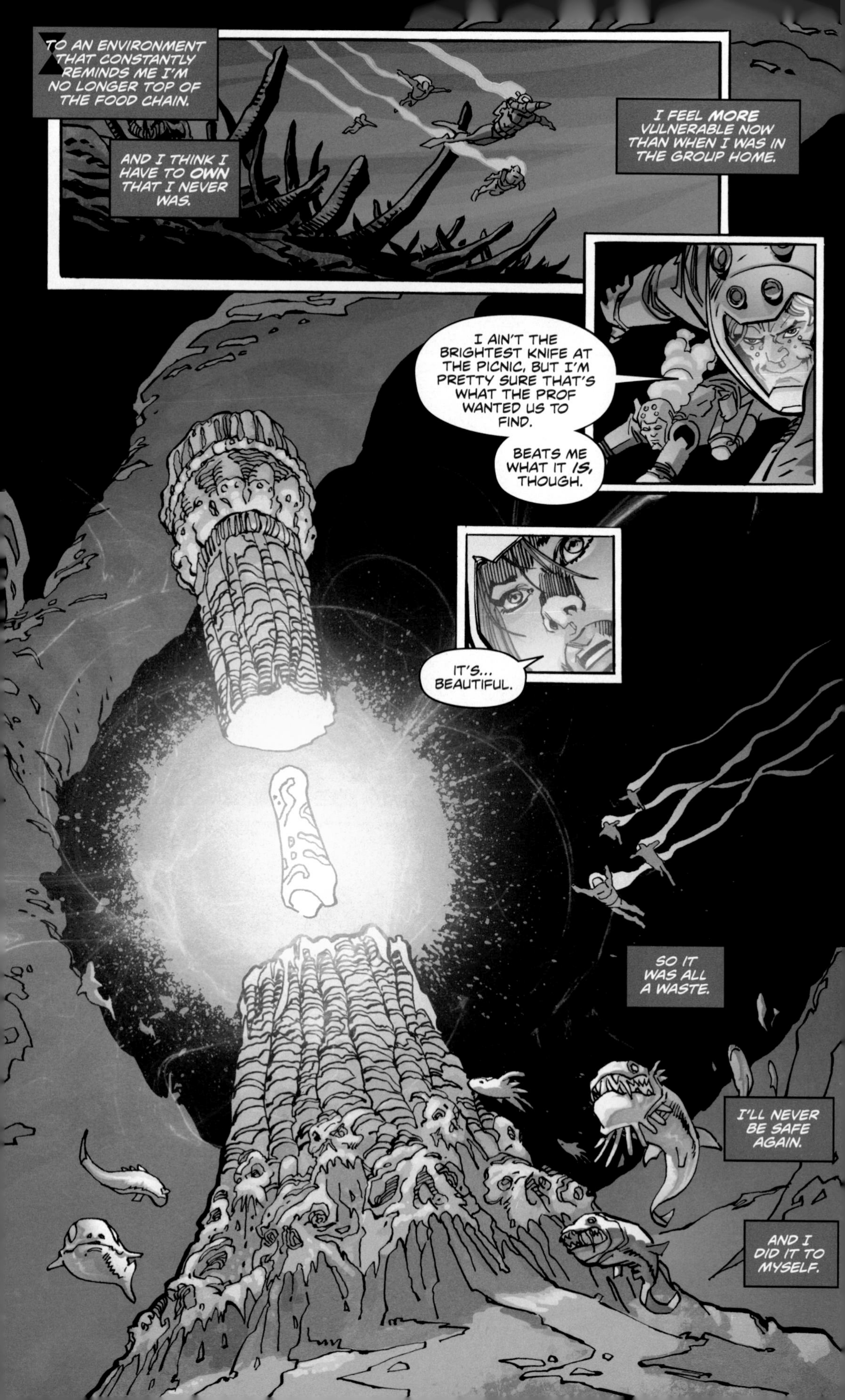
TO AN ENVIRONMENT THAT CONSTANTLY REMINDS ME I'M NO LONGER TOP OF THE FOOD CHAIN.
AND I THINK I HAVE TO OWN THAT I NEVER WAS.
I FEEL MORE VULNERABLE NOW THAN WHEN I WAS IN THE GROUP HOME.
I AIN'T THE BRIGHTEST KNIFE AT THE PICNIC, BUT I'M PRETTY SURE THAT'S WHAT THE PROF WANTED US TO FIND.
BEATS ME WHAT IT IS, THOUGH.
IT'S... BEAUTIFUL.
SO IT WAS ALL A WASTE.
I'LL NEVER BE SAFE AGAIN.
AND I DID IT TO MYSELF.

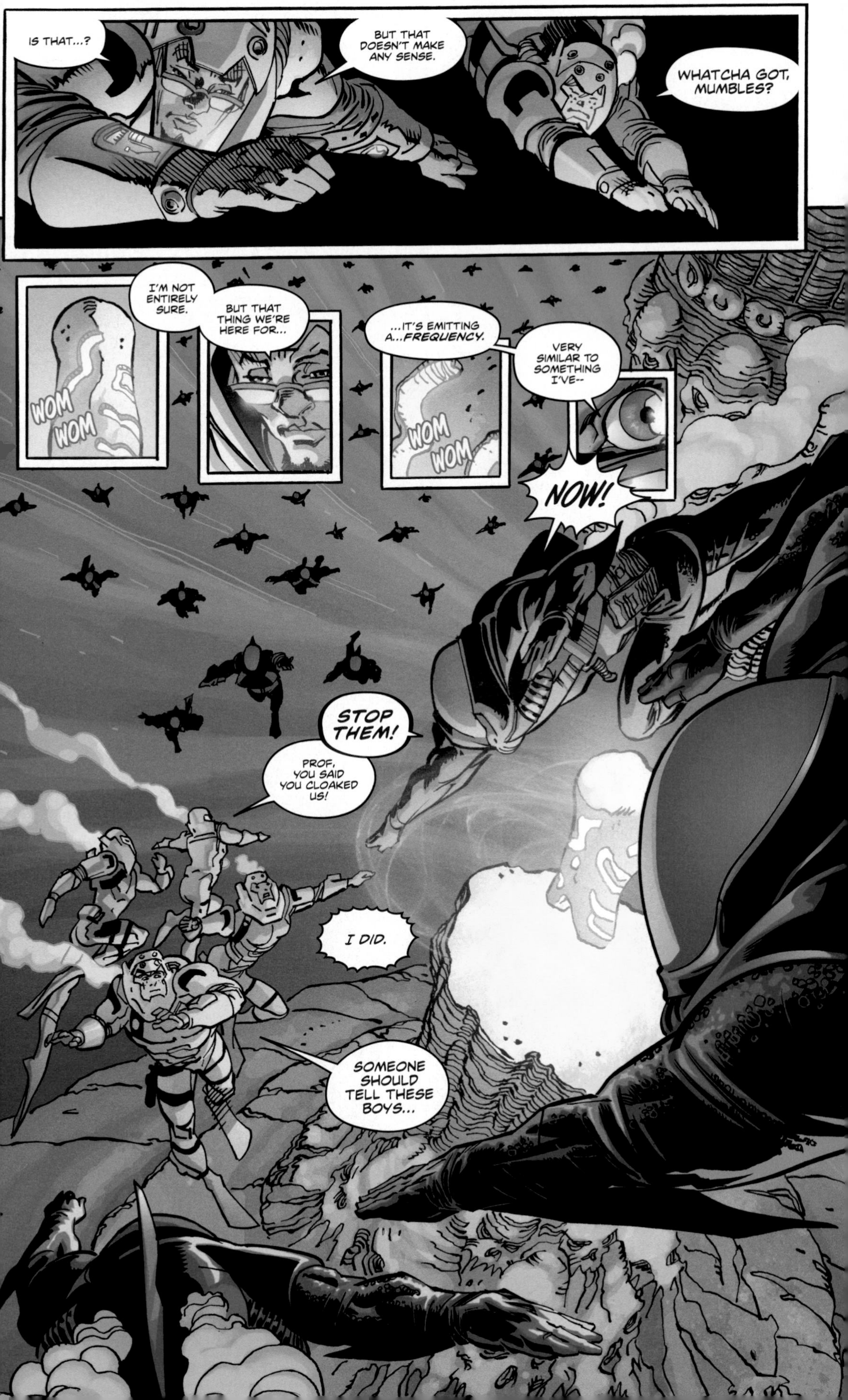
IS THAT...?
BUT THAT DOESN'T MAKE ANY SENSE.
WHATCHA GOT, MUMBLES?
I'M NOT ENTIRELY SURE.
WOM WOM
BUT THAT THING WE'RE HERE FOR...
...IT'S EMITTING A...FREQUENCY.
WOM WOM
VERY SIMILAR TO SOMETHING I'VE--
NOW!
STOP THEM!
PROF, YOU SAID YOU CLOAKED US!
I DID.
SOMEONE SHOULD TELL THESE BOYS...

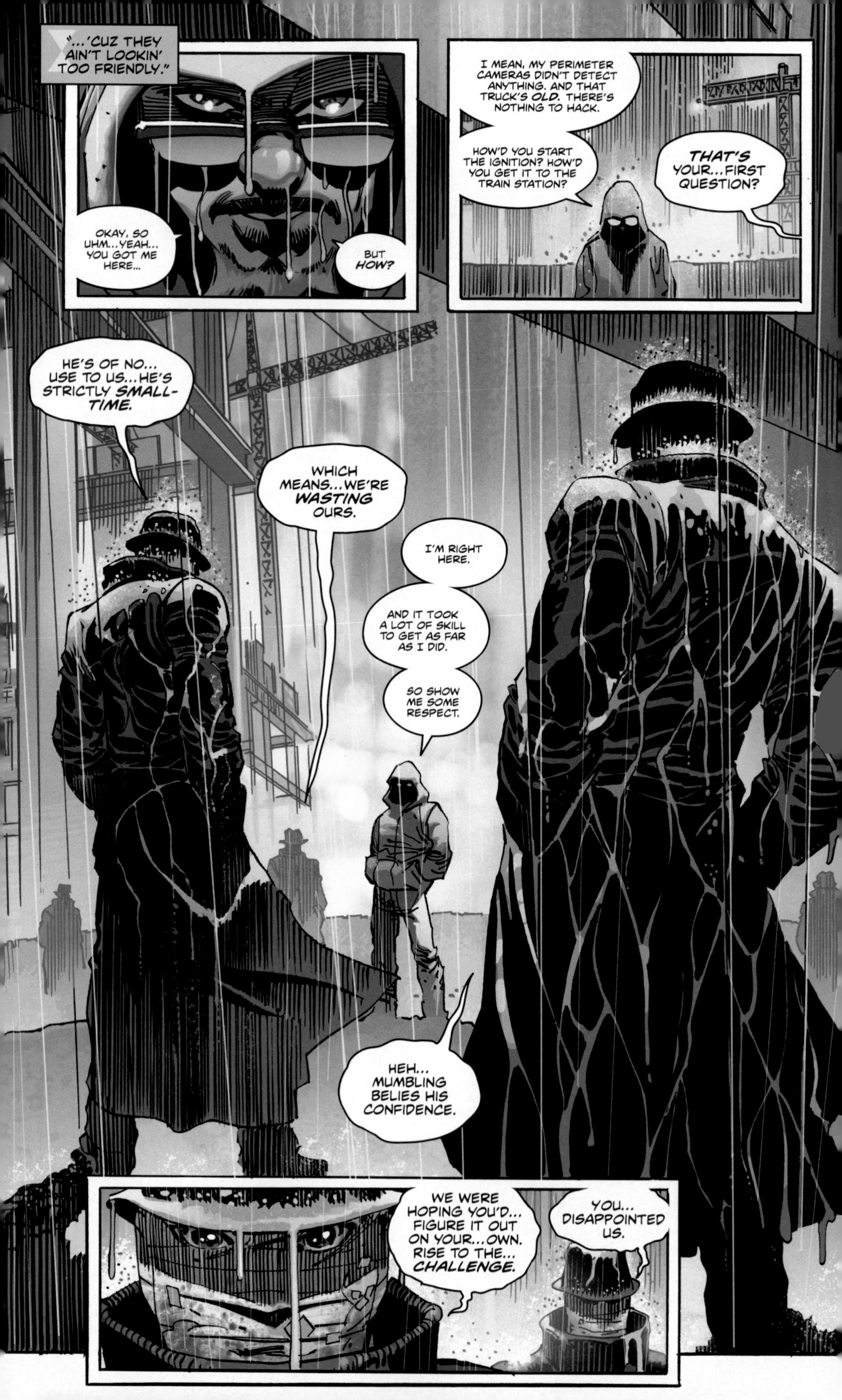
"...'CUZ THEY AIN'T LOOKIN' TOO FRIENDLY."
OKAY, SO UHM...YEAH... YOU GOT ME HERE...
BUT HOW?
I MEAN, MY PERIMETER CAMERAS DIDN'T DETECT ANYTHING. AND THAT TRUCK'S OLD. THERE'S NOTHING TO HACK.
HOW'D YOU START THE IGNITION? HOW'D YOU GET IT TO THE TRAIN STATION?
THAT'S YOUR...FIRST QUESTION?
HE'S OF NO... USE TO US...HE'S STRICTLY SMALL-TIME.
WHICH MEANS...WE'RE WASTING OURS.
I'M RIGHT HERE.
AND IT TOOK A LOT OF SKILL TO GET AS FAR AS I DID.
SO SHOW ME SOME RESPECT.
HEH... MUMBLING BELIES HIS CONFIDENCE.
WE WERE HOPING YOU'D... FIGURE IT OUT ON YOUR...OWN. RISE TO THE... CHALLENGE.
YOU... DISAPPOINTED US.

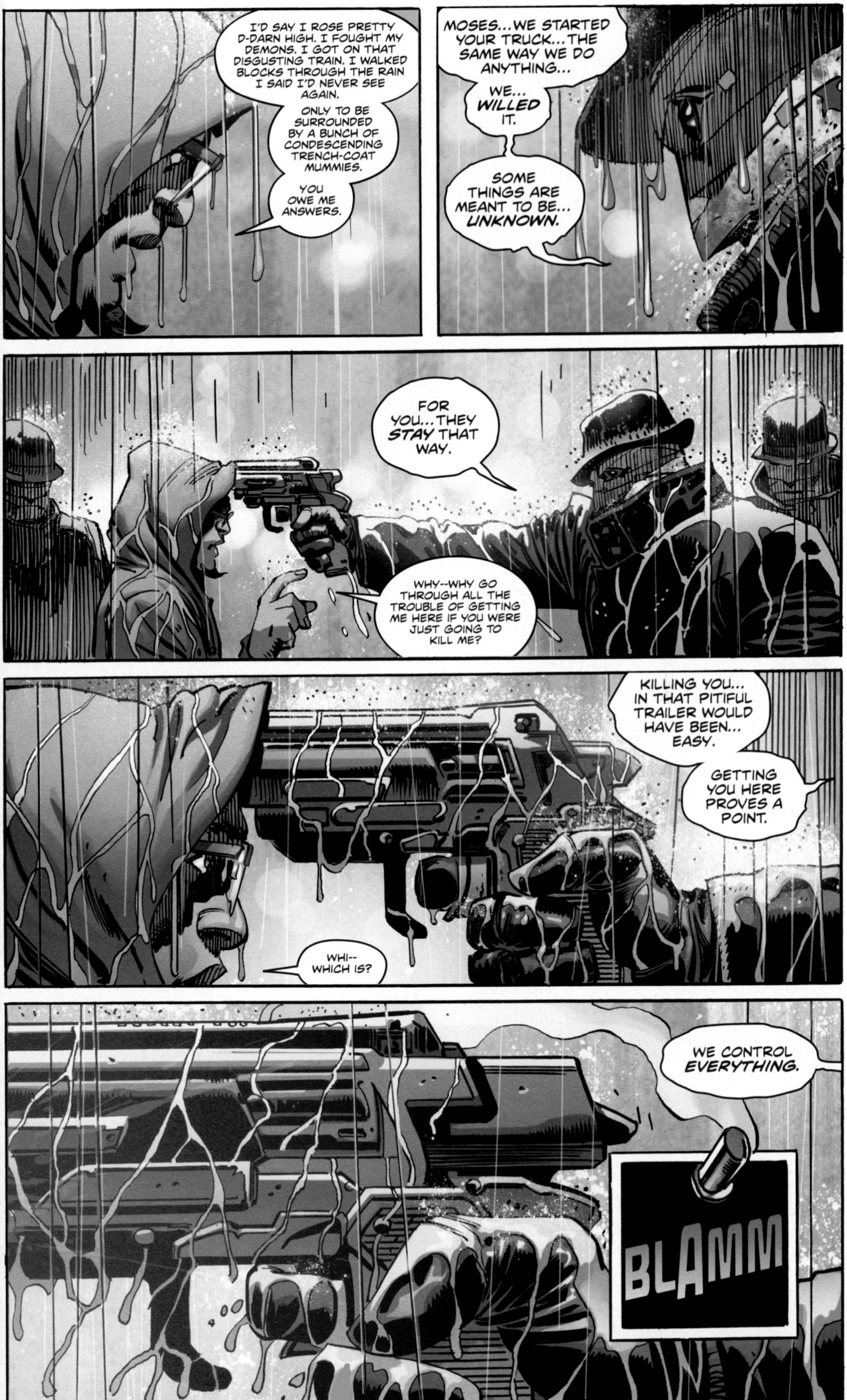
I'D SAY I ROSE PRETTY D-DARN HIGH. I FOUGHT MY DEMONS. I GOT ON THAT DISGUSTING TRAIN. I WALKED BLOCKS THROUGH THE RAIN I SAID I'D NEVER SEE AGAIN.
ONLY TO BE SURROUNDED BY A BUNCH OF CONDESCENDING TRENCH-COAT MUMMIES.
YOU OWE ME ANSWERS.
MOSES...WE STARTED YOUR TRUCK...THE SAME WAY WE DO ANYTHING...
WE... WILLED IT.
SOME THINGS ARE MEANT TO BE... UNKNOWN.
FOR YOU...THEY STAY THAT WAY.
WHY--WHY GO THROUGH ALL THE TROUBLE OF GETTING ME HERE IF YOU WERE JUST GOING TO KILL ME?
KILLING YOU... IN THAT PITIFUL TRAILER WOULD HAVE BEEN... EASY.
GETTING YOU HERE PROVES A POINT.
WHI-- WHICH IS?
WE CONTROL EVERYTHING.
BLAMM

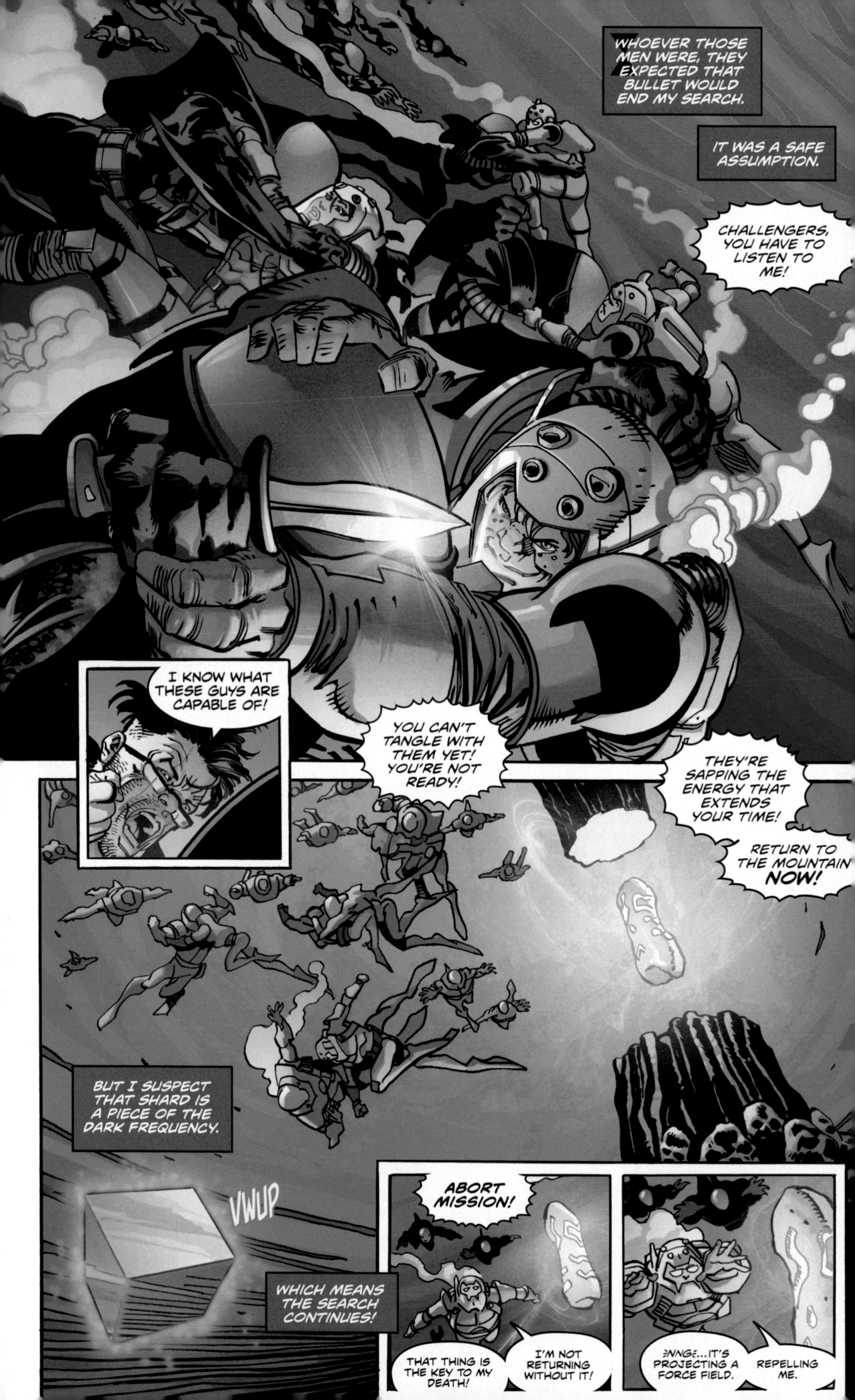

WHOEVER THOSE MEN WERE, THEY EXPECTED THAT BULLET WOULD END MY SEARCH.
IT WAS A SAFE ASSUMPTION.
CHALLENGERS, YOU HAVE TO LISTEN TO ME!
I KNOW WHAT THESE GUYS ARE CAPABLE OF!
YOU CAN'T TANGLE WITH THEM YET! YOU'RE NOT READY!
THEY'RE SAPPING THE ENERGY THAT EXTENDS YOUR TIME!
RETURN TO THE MOUNTAIN NOW!
BUT I SUSPECT THAT SHARD IS A PIECE OF THE DARK FREQUENCY.
VWUP
WHICH MEANS THE SEARCH CONTINUES!
ABORT MISSION!
THAT THING IS THE KEY TO MY DEATH!
I'M NOT RETURNING WITHOUT IT!
NNG≡...IT'S PROJECTING A FORCE FIELD.
REPELLING ME.

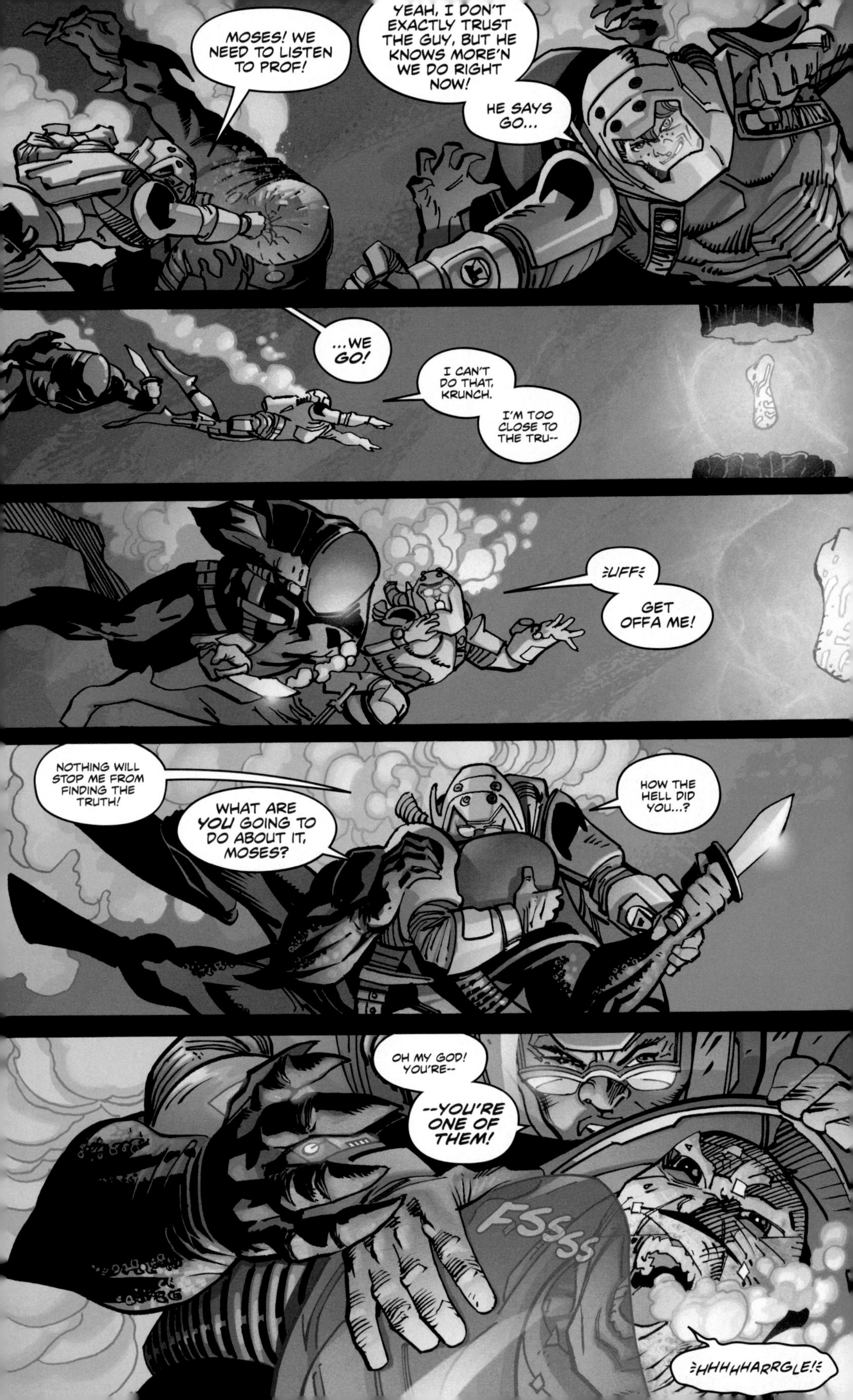
MOSES! WE NEED TO LISTEN TO PROF!
YEAH, I DON'T EXACTLY TRUST THE GUY, BUT HE KNOWS MORE'N WE DO RIGHT NOW!
HE SAYS GO...
...WE GO!
I CAN'T DO THAT, KRUNCH.
I'M TOO CLOSE TO THE TRU--
UFF
GET OFFA ME!
NOTHING WILL STOP ME FROM FINDING THE TRUTH!
WHAT ARE YOU GOING TO DO ABOUT IT, MOSES?
HOW THE HELL DID YOU...?
OH MY GOD! YOU'RE--
--YOU'RE ONE OF THEM!
FSSSS
HHHHHARRGLE!

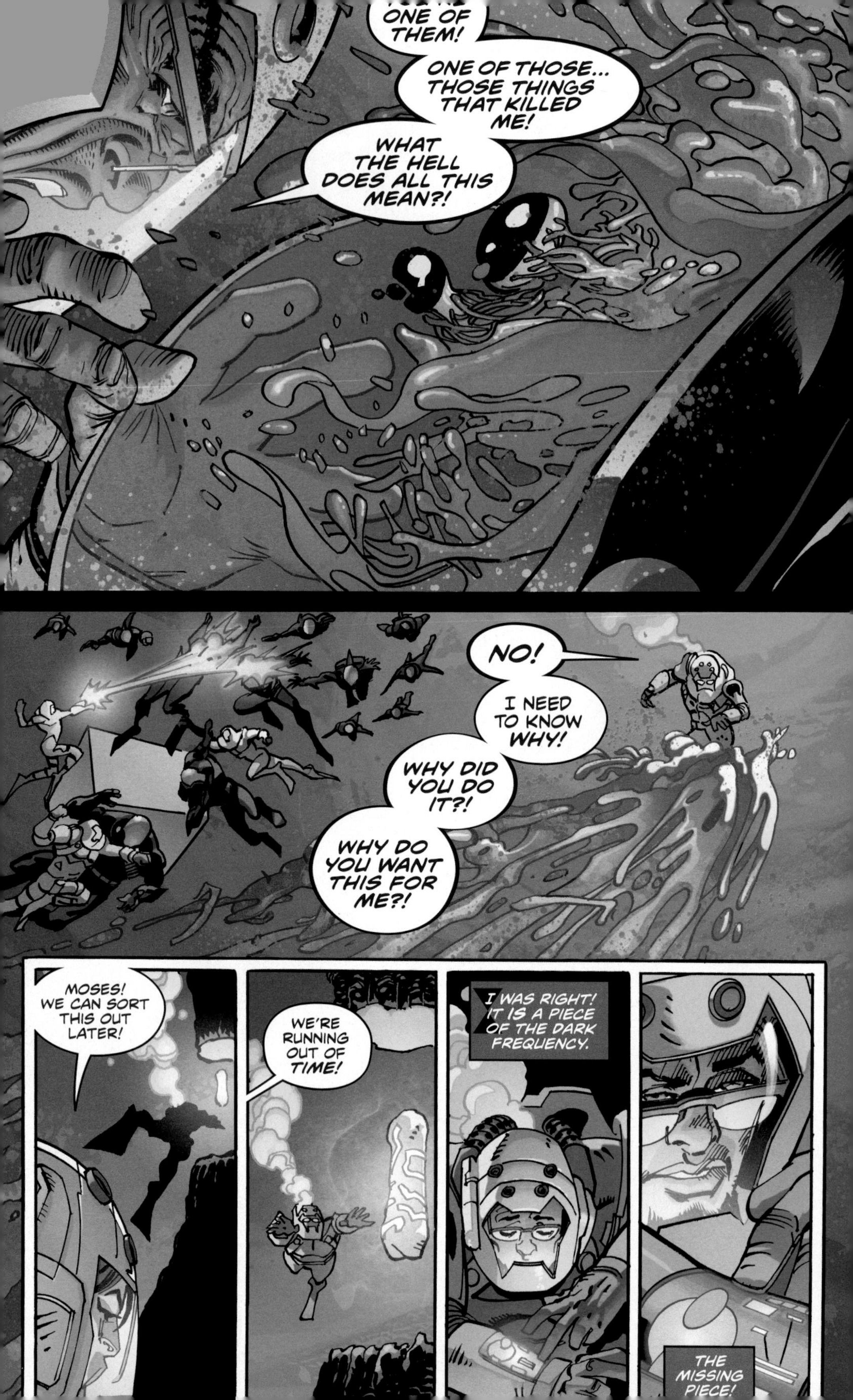
ONE OF THEM!
ONE OF THOSE... THOSE THINGS THAT KILLED ME!
WHAT THE HELL DOES ALL THIS MEAN?!
NO!
I NEED TO KNOW WHY!
WHY DID YOU DO IT?!
WHY DO YOU WANT THIS FOR ME?!
MOSES! WE CAN SORT THIS OUT LATER!
WE'RE RUNNING OUT OF TIME!
I WAS RIGHT! IT IS A PIECE OF THE DARK FREQUENCY.
THE MISSING PIECE!

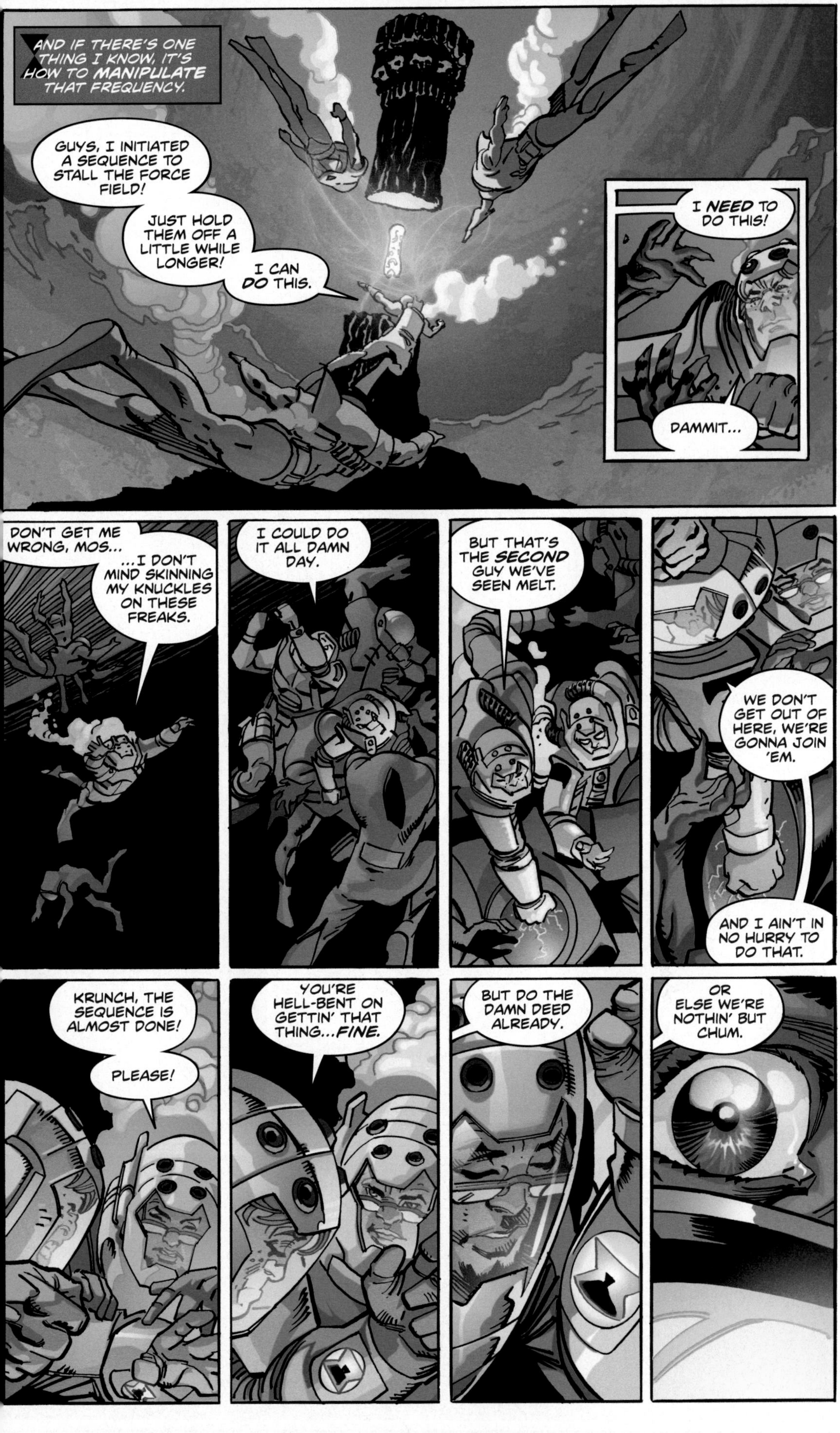

AND IF THERE'S ONE THING I KNOW, IT'S HOW TO MANIPULATE THAT FREQUENCY.
GUYS, I INITIATED A SEQUENCE TO STALL THE FORCE FIELD!
JUST HOLD THEM OFF A LITTLE WHILE LONGER!
I CAN DO THIS.
I NEED TO DO THIS!
DAMMIT...
DON'T GET ME WRONG, MOS...
...I DON'T MIND SKINNING MY KNUCKLES ON THESE FREAKS.
I COULD DO IT ALL DAMN DAY.
BUT THAT'S THE SECOND GUY WE'VE SEEN MELT.
WE DON'T GET OUT OF HERE, WE'RE GONNA JOIN 'EM.
AND I AIN'T IN NO HURRY TO DO THAT.
KRUNCH, THE SEQUENCE IS ALMOST DONE!
PLEASE!
YOU'RE HELL-BENT ON GETTIN' THAT THING...FINE.
BUT DO THE DAMN DEED ALREADY.
OR ELSE WE'RE NOTHIN' BUT CHUM.

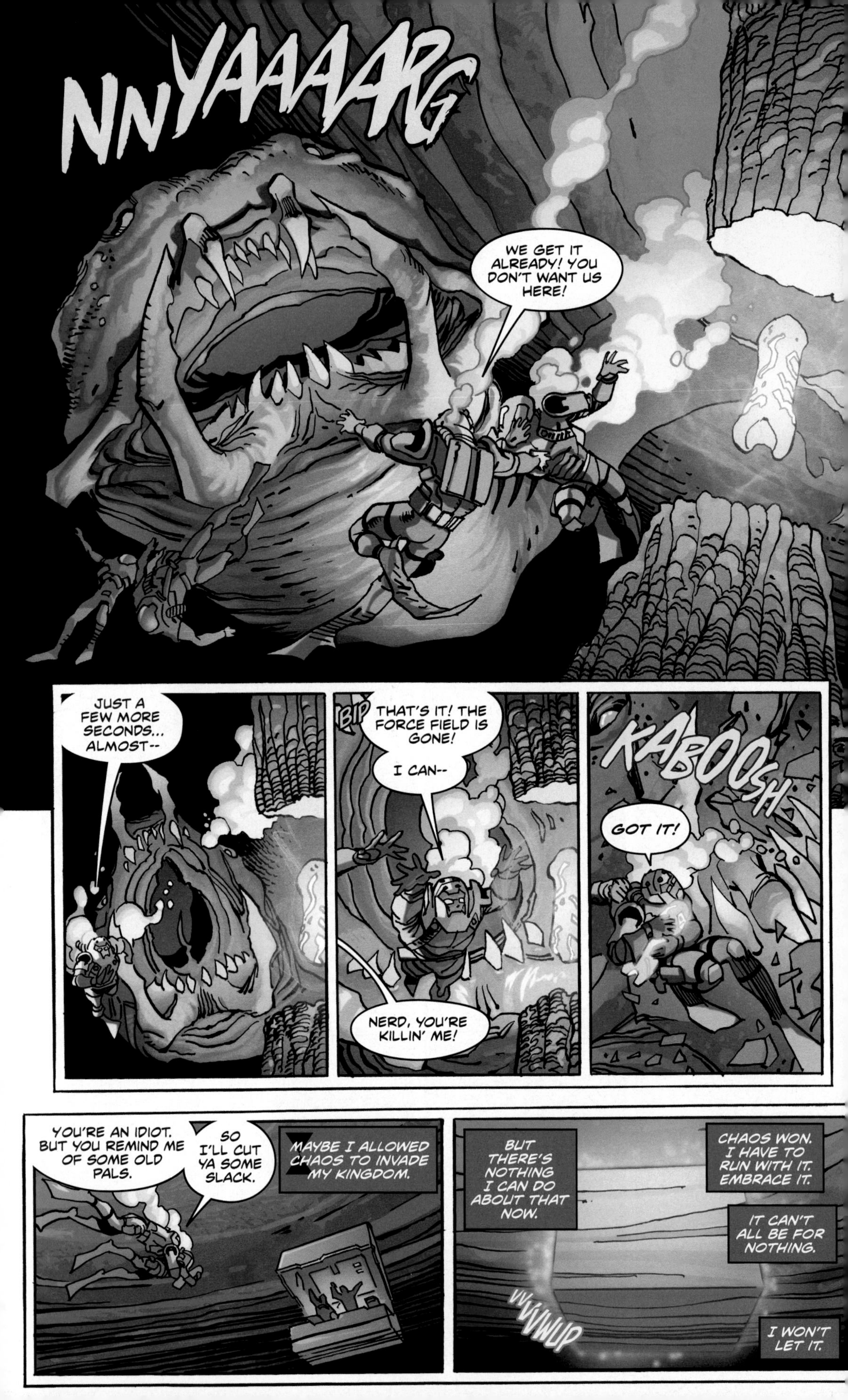
NNYAAAARG
WE GET IT ALREADY! YOU DON'T WANT US HERE!
JUST A FEW MORE SECONDS... ALMOST--
BIP
THAT'S IT! THE FORCE FIELD IS GONE!
I CAN--
NERD, YOU'RE KILLIN' ME!
KABOOSH
GOT IT!
YOU'RE AN IDIOT. BUT YOU REMIND ME OF SOME OLD PALS.
SO I'LL CUT YA SOME SLACK.
MAYBE I ALLOWED CHAOS TO INVADE MY KINGDOM.
BUT THERE'S NOTHING I CAN DO ABOUT THAT NOW.
CHAOS WON. I HAVE TO RUN WITH IT. EMBRACE IT.
IT CAN'T ALL BE FOR NOTHING.
VVVWUP
I WON'T LET IT.

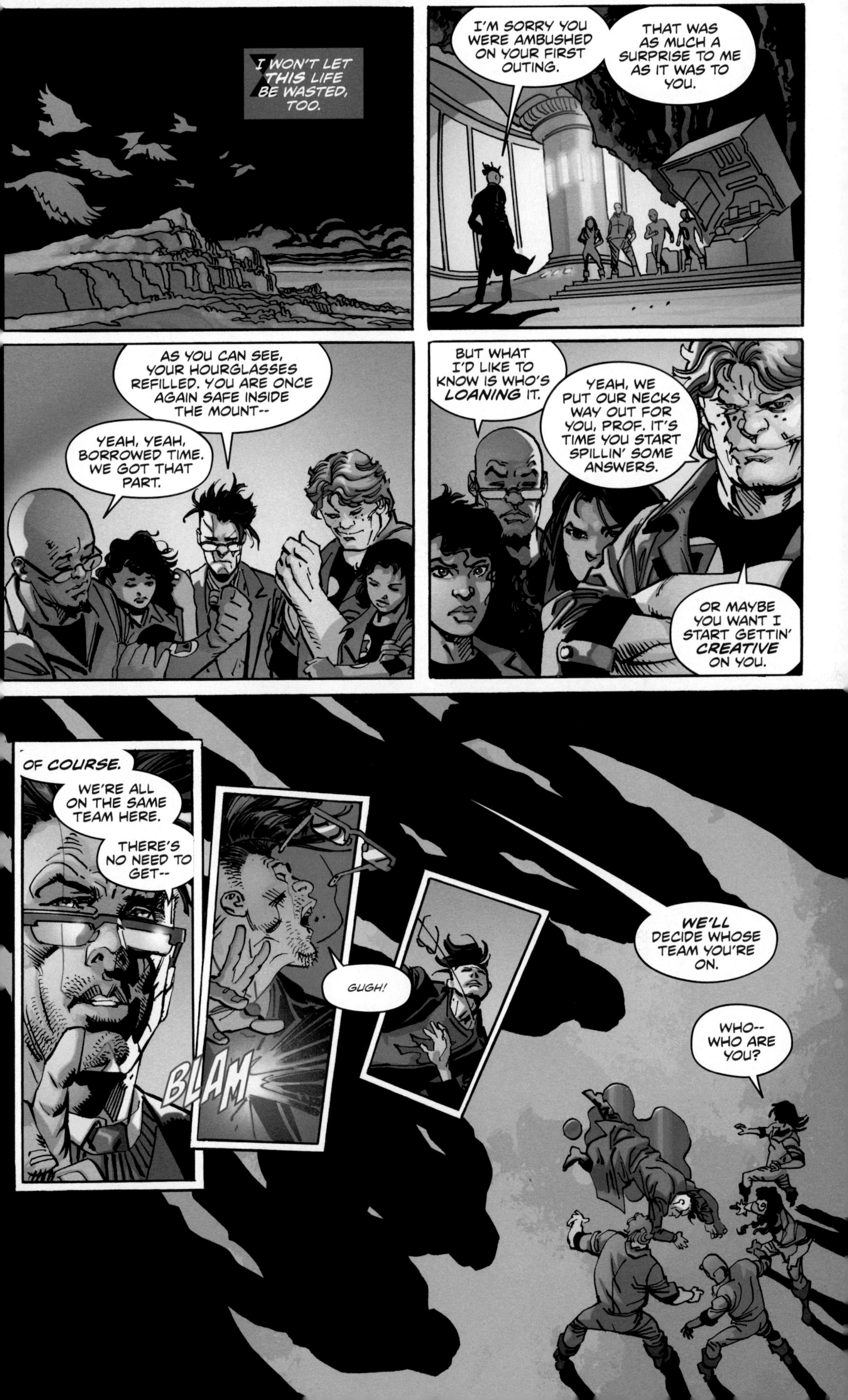
I WON'T LET THIS LIFE BE WASTED, TOO.
I'M SORRY YOU WERE AMBUSHED ON YOUR FIRST OUTING.
THAT WAS AS MUCH A SURPRISE TO ME AS IT WAS TO YOU.
AS YOU CAN SEE, YOUR HOURGLASSES REFILLED. YOU ARE ONCE AGAIN SAFE INSIDE THE MOUNT--
YEAH, YEAH, BORROWED TIME. WE GOT THAT PART.
BUT WHAT I'D LIKE TO KNOW IS WHO'S LOANING IT.
YEAH, WE PUT OUR NECKS WAY OUT FOR YOU, PROF. IT'S TIME YOU START SPILLIN' SOME ANSWERS.
OR MAYBE YOU WANT I START GETTIN' CREATIVE ON YOU.
OF COURSE.
WE'RE ALL ON THE SAME TEAM HERE.
THERE'S NO NEED TO GET--
BLAM
GUGH!
WE'LL DECIDE WHOSE TEAM YOU'RE ON.
WHO-- WHO ARE YOU?

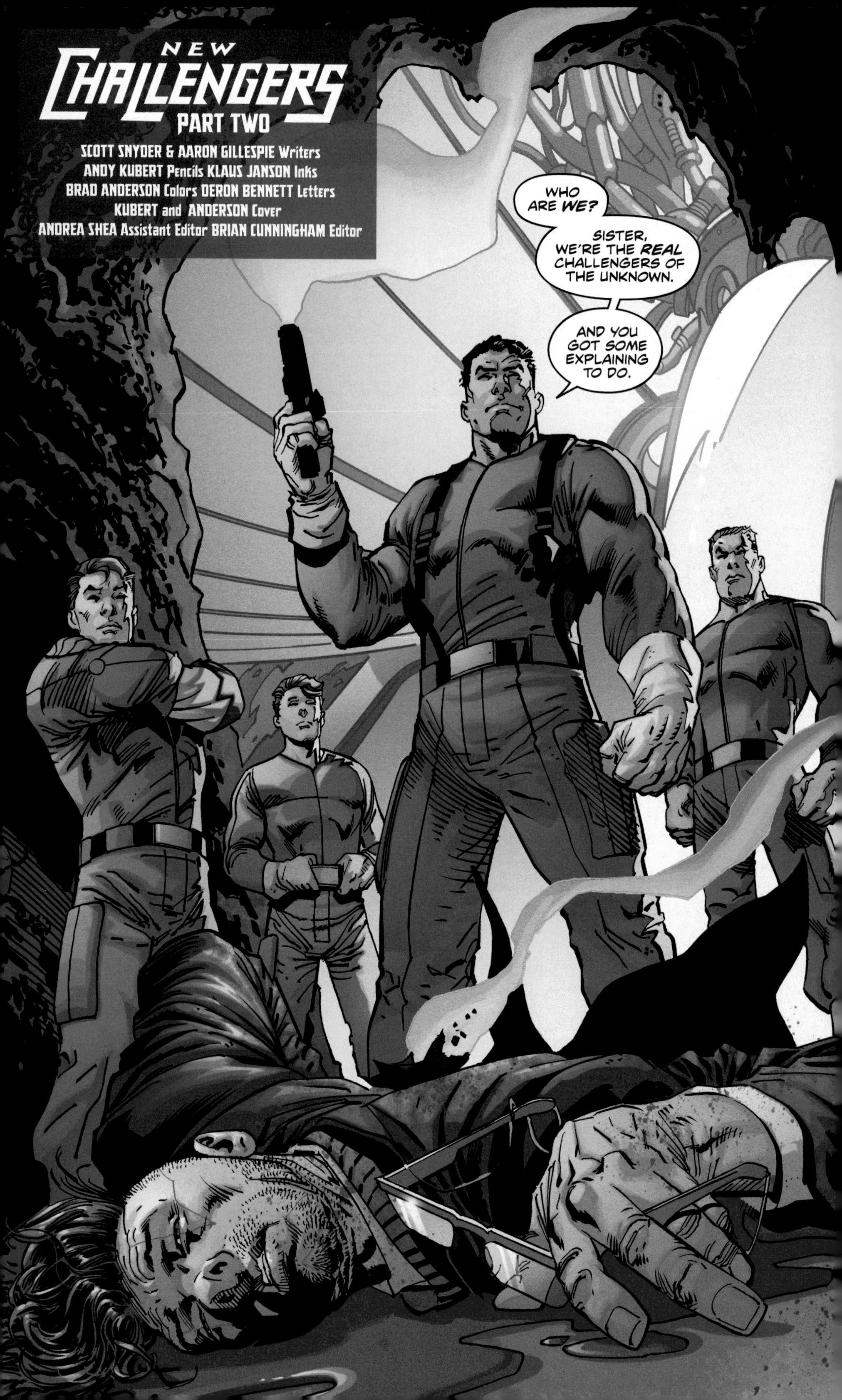
NEW
CHALLENGERS
PART TWO
SCOTT SNYDER & AARON GILLESPIE Writers
ANDY KUBERT Pencils KLAUS JANSON Inks
BRAD ANDERSON Colors DERON BENNETT Letters
KUBERT and ANDERSON Cover
ANDREA SHEA Assistant Editor BRIAN CUNNINGHAM Editor
WHO ARE WE?
SISTER, WE'RE THE REAL CHALLENGERS OF THE UNKNOWN.
AND YOU GOT SOME EXPLAINING TO DO.

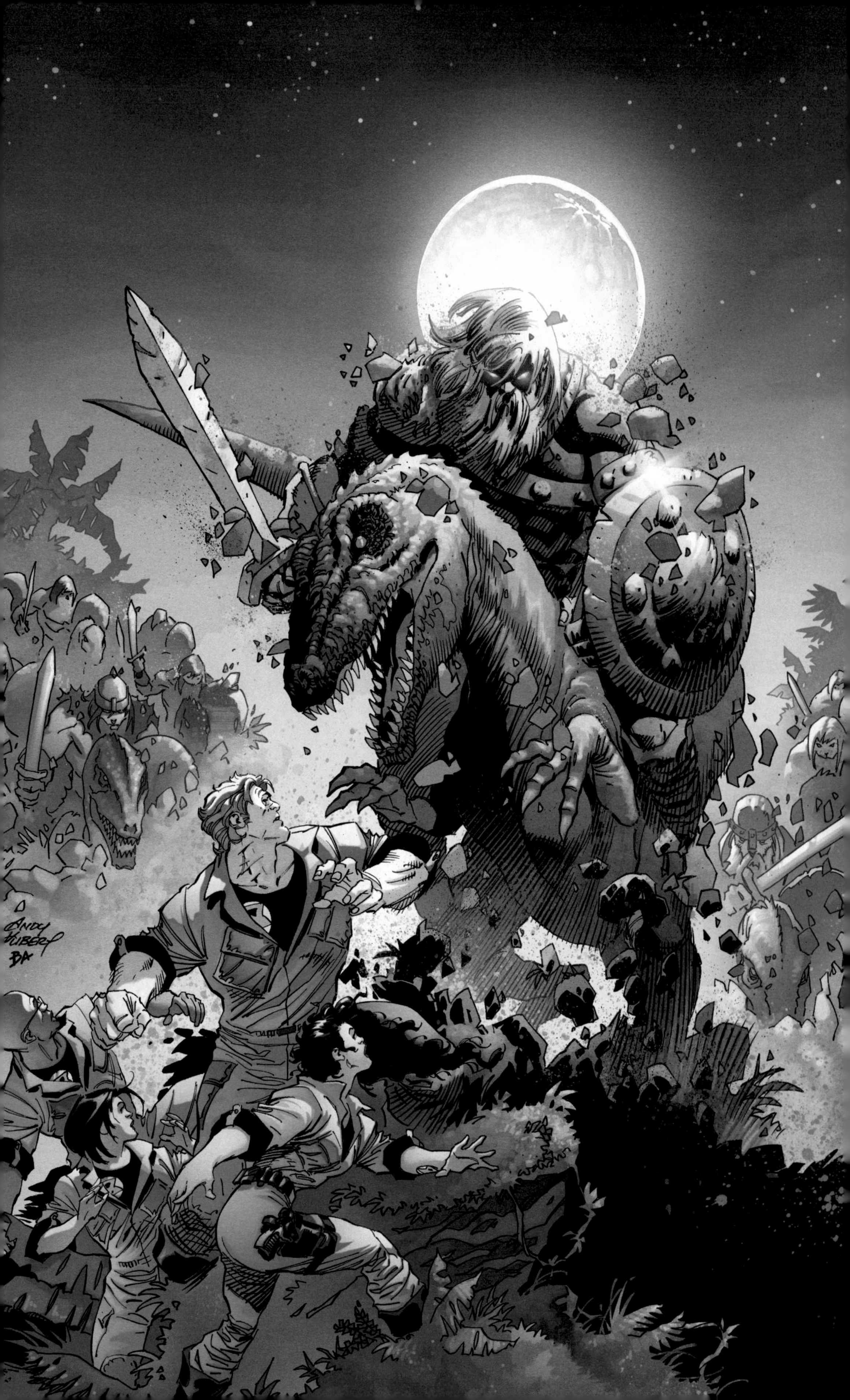
ANDY KUBERT
BA

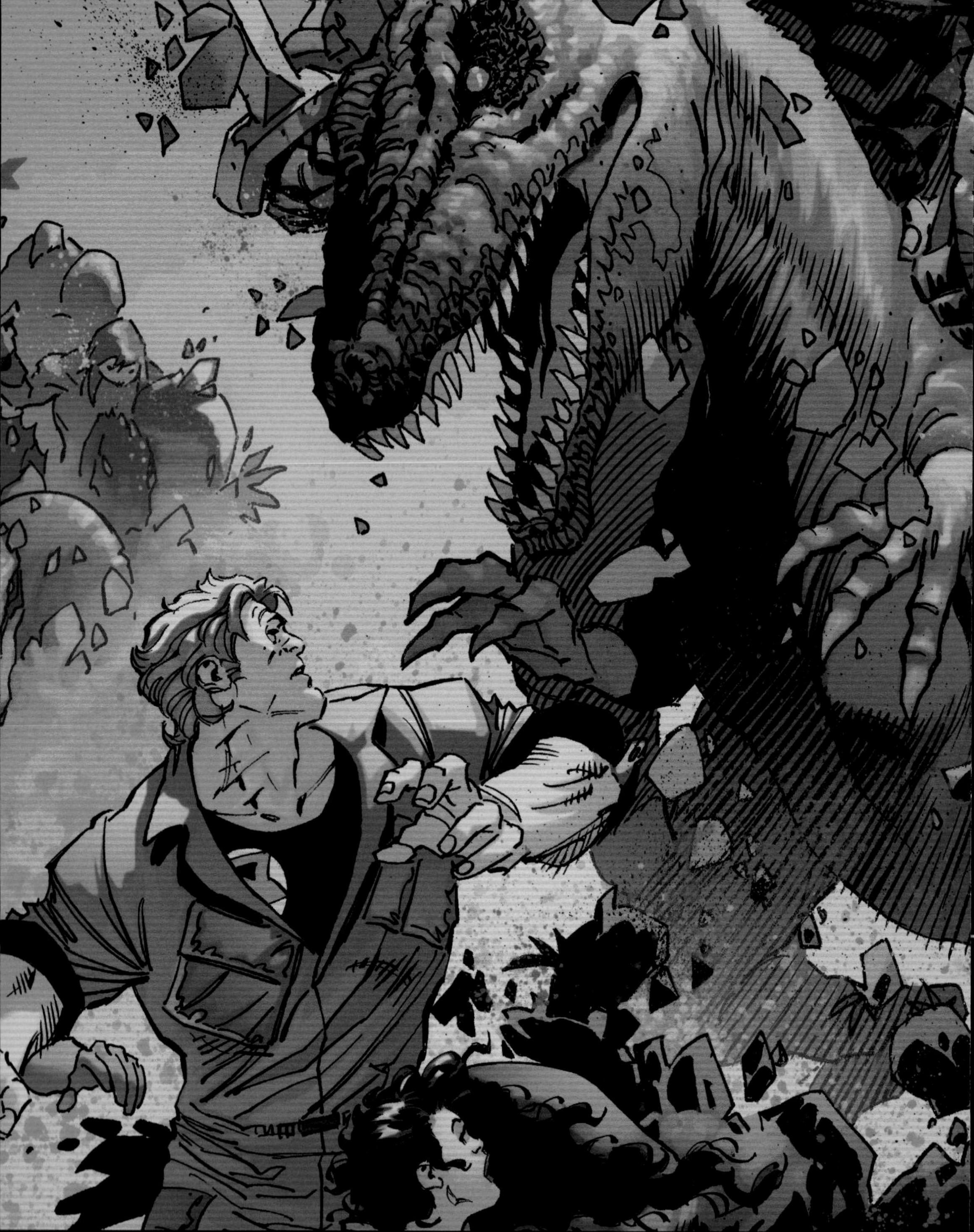

NEW CHALLENGERS
#3

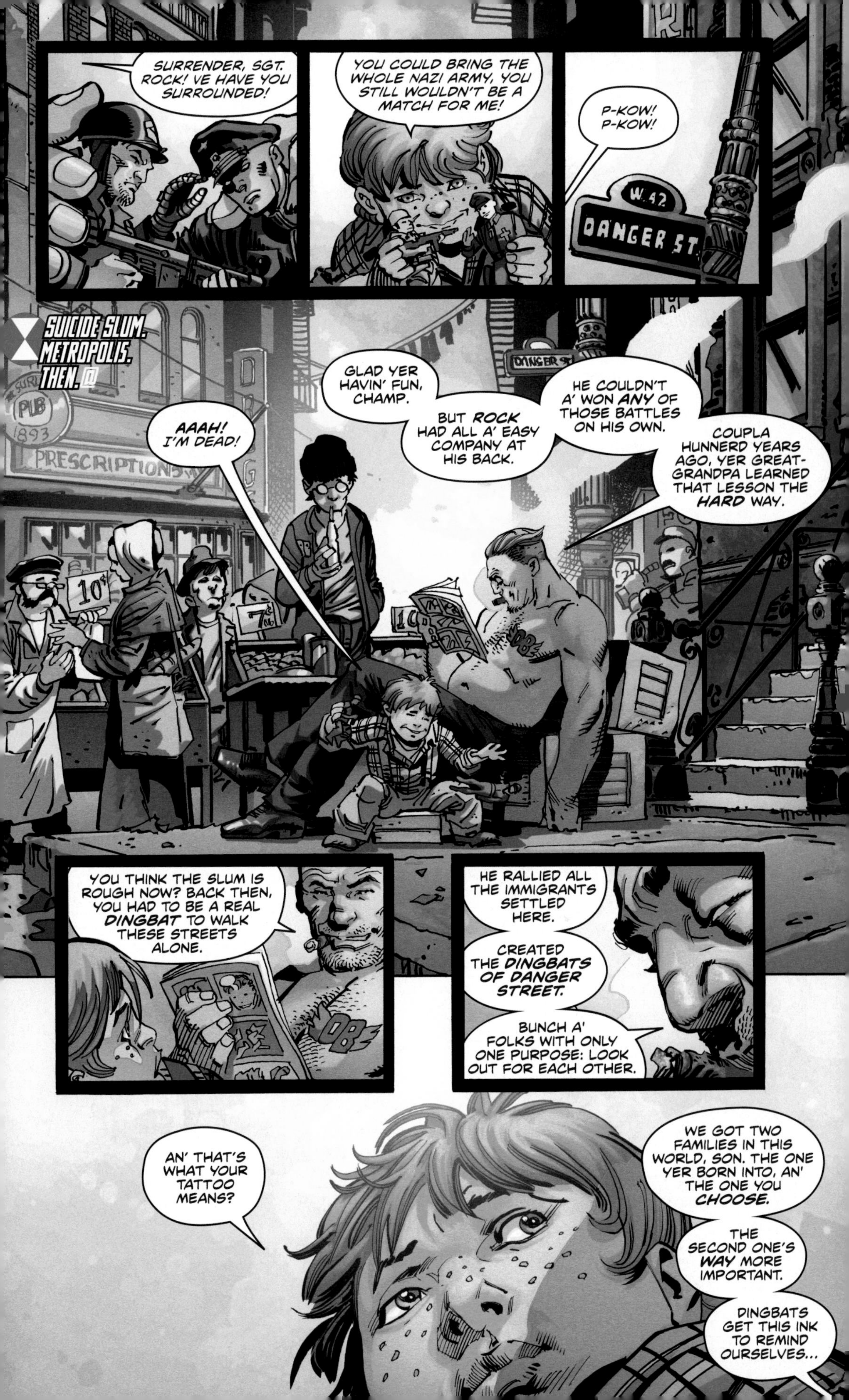
SURRENDER, SGT. ROCK! VE HAVE YOU SURROUNDED!
YOU COULD BRING THE WHOLE NAZI ARMY, YOU STILL WOULDN'T BE A MATCH FOR ME!
P-KOW! P-KOW!
W. 42
DANGER ST.
SUICIDE SLUM. METROPOLIS. THEN.
GLAD YER HAVIN' FUN, CHAMP.
BUT ROCK HAD ALL A' EASY COMPANY AT HIS BACK.
HE COULDN'T A' WON ANY OF THOSE BATTLES ON HIS OWN.
COUPLA HUNNERD YEARS AGO, YER GREAT-GRANDPA LEARNED THAT LESSON THE HARD WAY.
AAAH! I'M DEAD!
PRESCRIPTIONS
PUB
1893
YOU THINK THE SLUM IS ROUGH NOW? BACK THEN, YOU HAD TO BE A REAL DINGBAT TO WALK THESE STREETS ALONE.
HE RALLIED ALL THE IMMIGRANTS SETTLED HERE.
CREATED THE DINGBATS OF DANGER STREET.
BUNCH A' FOLKS WITH ONLY ONE PURPOSE: LOOK OUT FOR EACH OTHER.
AN' THAT'S WHAT YOUR TATTOO MEANS?
WE GOT TWO FAMILIES IN THIS WORLD, SON. THE ONE YER BORN INTO, AN' THE ONE YOU CHOOSE.
THE SECOND ONE'S WAY MORE IMPORTANT.
DINGBATS GET THIS INK TO REMIND OURSELVES...

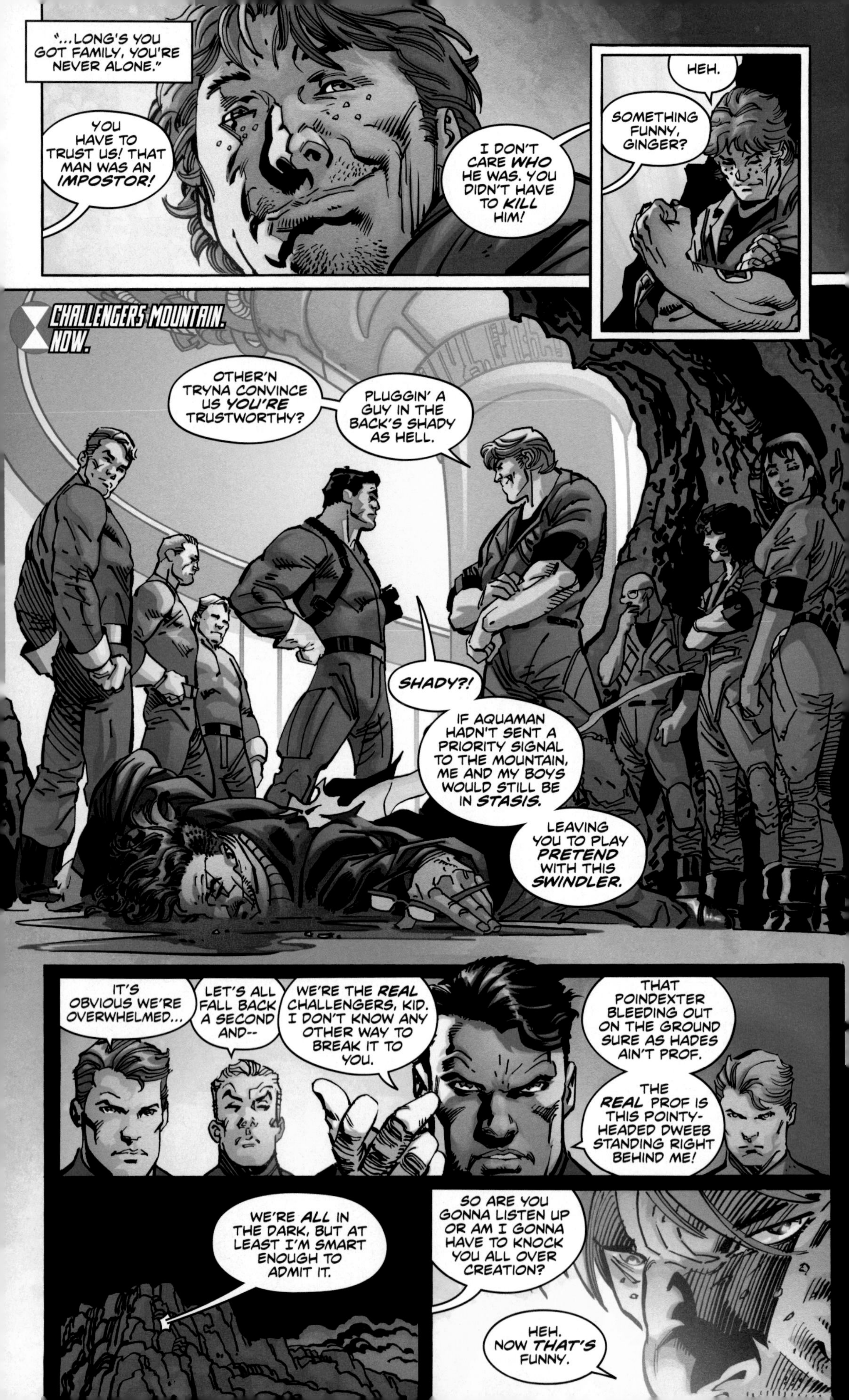
"...LONG'S YOU GOT FAMILY, YOU'RE NEVER ALONE."
YOU HAVE TO TRUST US! THAT MAN WAS AN IMPOSTOR!
I DON'T CARE WHO HE WAS. YOU DIDN'T HAVE TO KILL HIM!
HEH.
SOMETHING FUNNY, GINGER?
CHALLENGERS MOUNTAIN. NOW.
OTHER'N TRYNA CONVINCE US YOU'RE TRUSTWORTHY?
PLUGGIN' A GUY IN THE BACK'S SHADY AS HELL.
SHADY?!
IF AQUAMAN HADN'T SENT A PRIORITY SIGNAL TO THE MOUNTAIN, ME AND MY BOYS WOULD STILL BE IN STASIS.
LEAVING YOU TO PLAY PRETEND WITH THIS SWINDLER.
IT'S OBVIOUS WE'RE OVERWHELMED...
LET'S ALL FALL BACK A SECOND AND--
WE'RE THE REAL CHALLENGERS, KID. I DON'T KNOW ANY OTHER WAY TO BREAK IT TO YOU.
THAT POINDEXTER BLEEDING OUT ON THE GROUND SURE AS HADES AIN'T PROF.
THE REAL PROF IS THIS POINTY-HEADED DWEEB STANDING RIGHT BEHIND ME!
WE'RE ALL IN THE DARK, BUT AT LEAST I'M SMART ENOUGH TO ADMIT IT.
SO ARE YOU GONNA LISTEN UP OR AM I GONNA HAVE TO KNOCK YOU ALL OVER CREATION?
HEH. NOW THAT'S FUNNY.

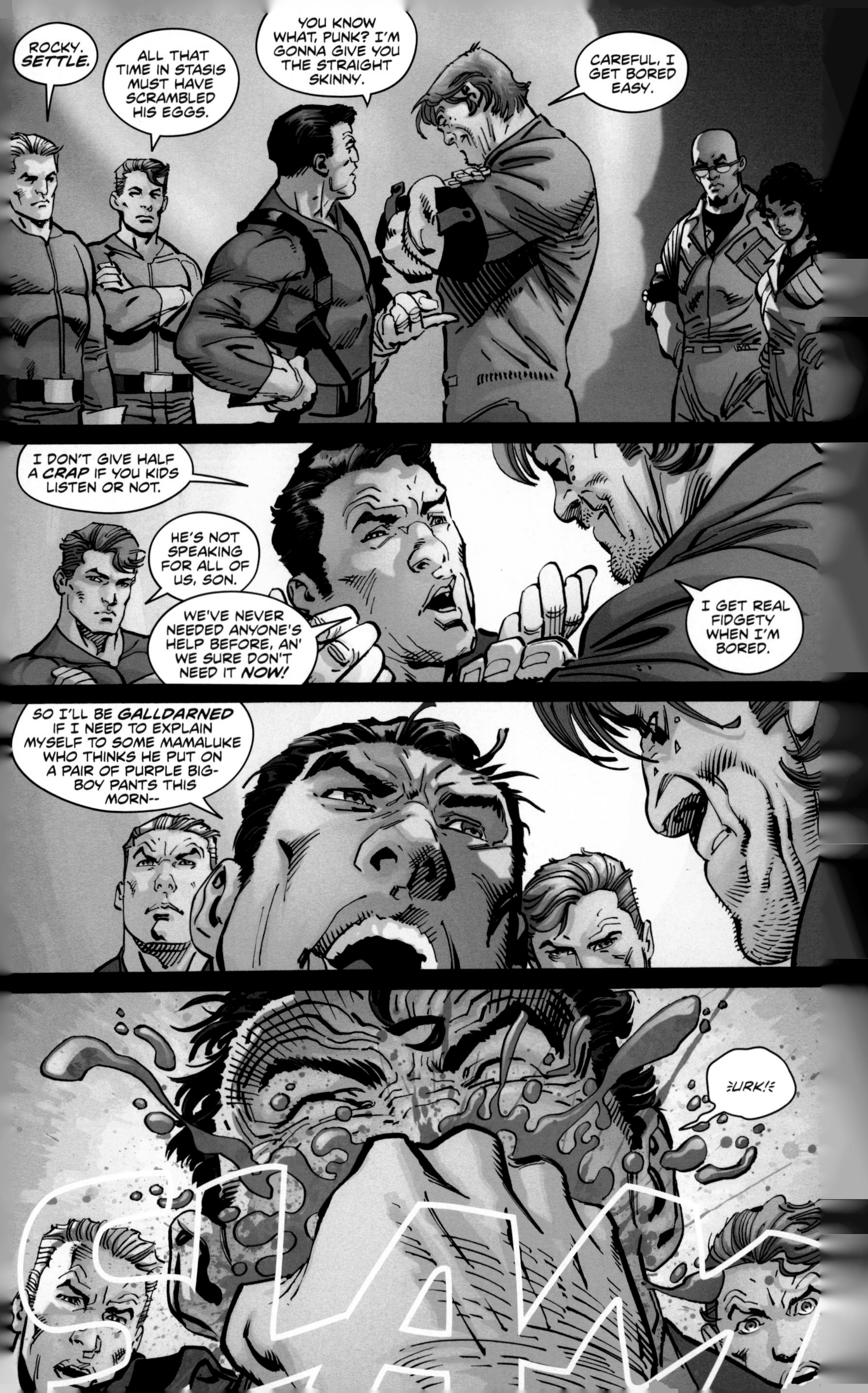
ROCKY. SETTLE.
ALL THAT TIME IN STASIS MUST HAVE SCRAMBLED HIS EGGS.
YOU KNOW WHAT, PUNK? I'M GONNA GIVE YOU THE STRAIGHT SKINNY.
CAREFUL, I GET BORED EASY.
I DON'T GIVE HALF A CRAP IF YOU KIDS LISTEN OR NOT.
HE'S NOT SPEAKING FOR ALL OF US, SON.
WE'VE NEVER NEEDED ANYONE'S HELP BEFORE, AN' WE SURE DON'T NEED IT NOW!
I GET REAL FIDGETY WHEN I'M BORED.
SO I'LL BE GALLDARNED IF I NEED TO EXPLAIN MYSELF TO SOME MAMALUKE WHO THINKS HE PUT ON A PAIR OF PURPLE BIG-BOY PANTS THIS MORN--
URK!

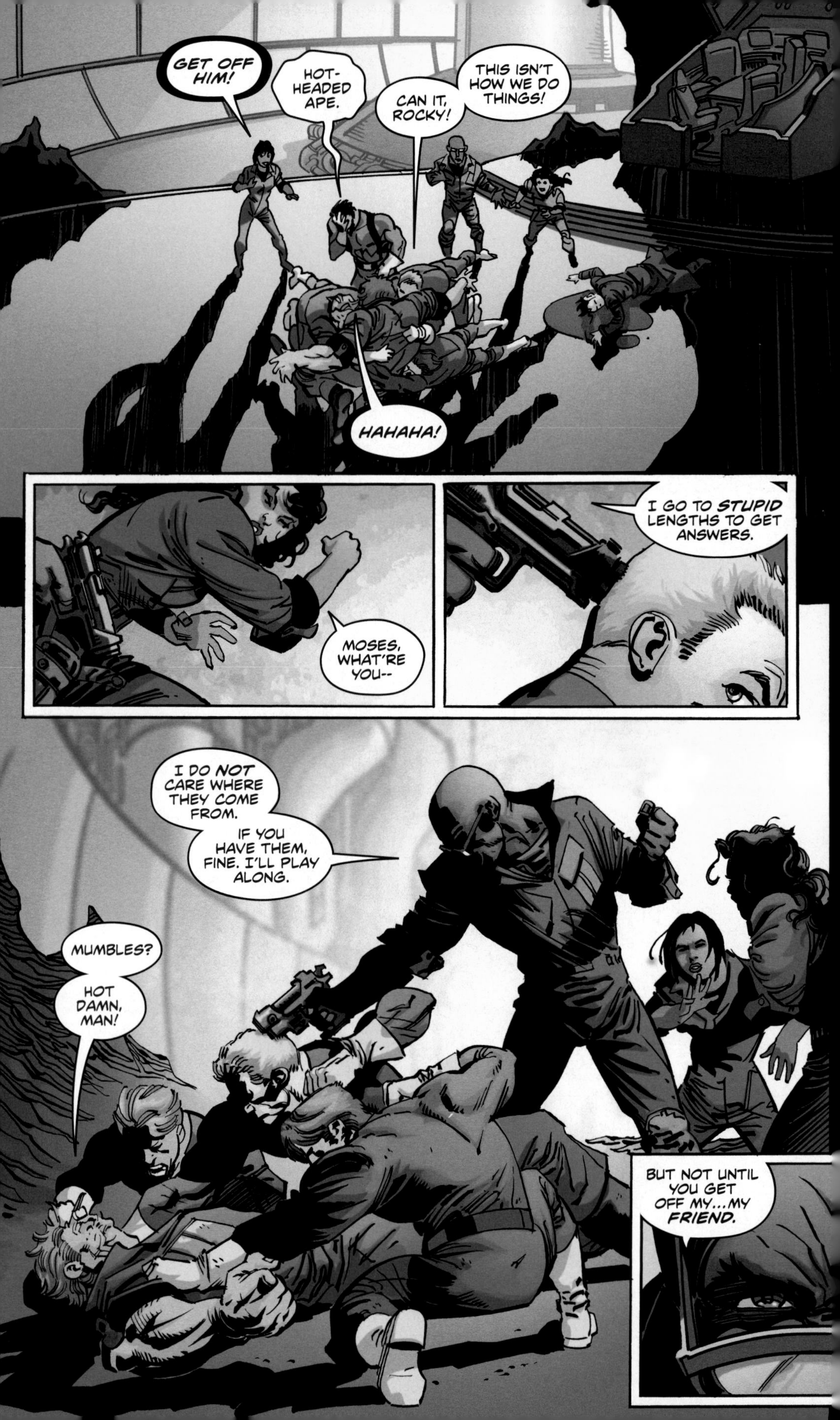
GET OFF HIM!
HOT-HEADED APE.
CAN IT, ROCKY!
THIS ISN'T HOW WE DO THINGS!
HAHAHA!
MOSES, WHAT'RE YOU--
I GO TO STUPID LENGTHS TO GET ANSWERS.
I DO NOT CARE WHERE THEY COME FROM.
IF YOU HAVE THEM, FINE. I'LL PLAY ALONG.
MUMBLES?
HOT DAMN, MAN!
BUT NOT UNTIL YOU GET OFF MY...MY FRIEND.

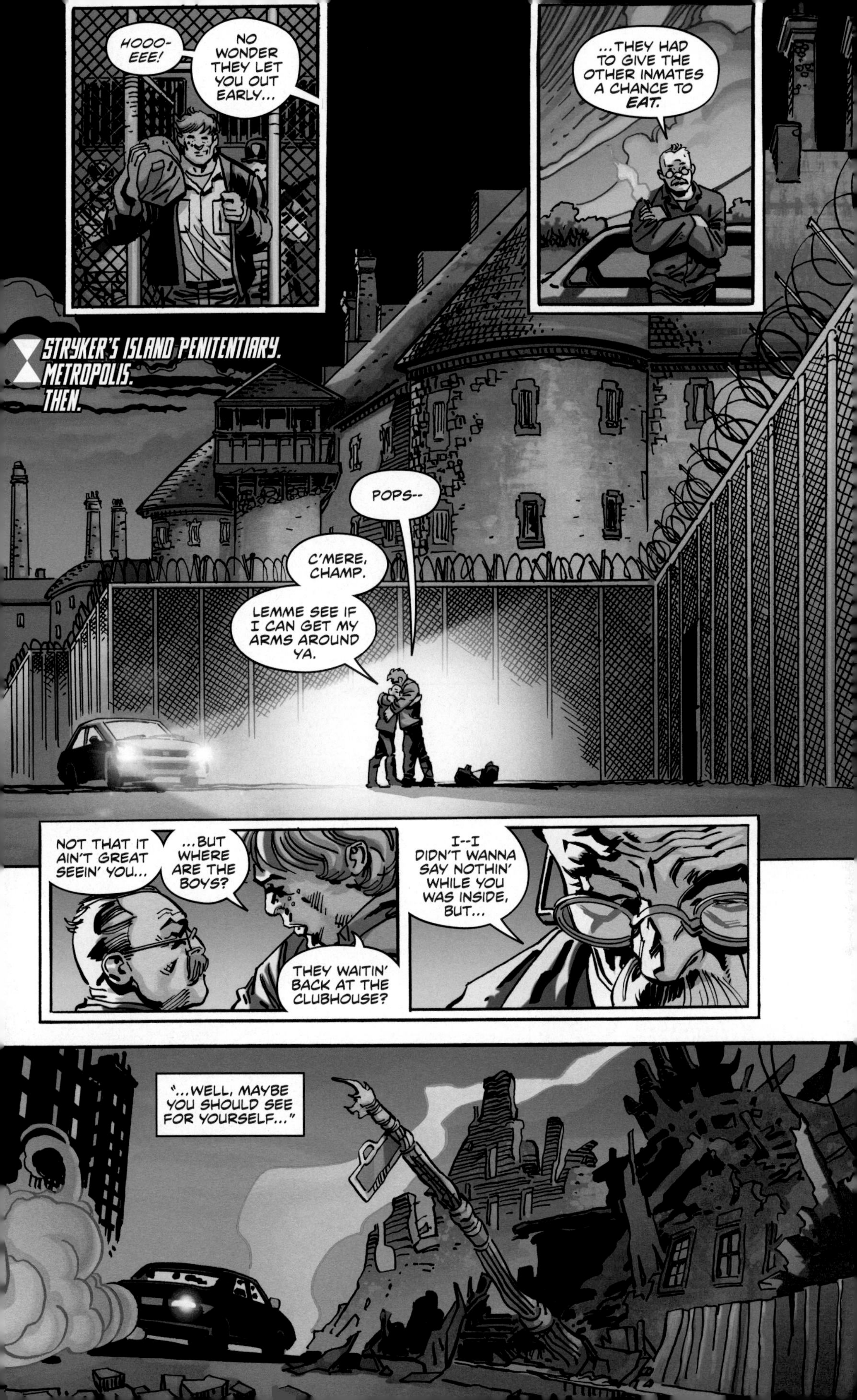
HOOO-EEE!
NO WONDER THEY LET YOU OUT EARLY...
...THEY HAD TO GIVE THE OTHER INMATES A CHANCE TO EAT.
STRYKER'S ISLAND PENITENTIARY.
METROPOLIS.
THEN.
POPS--
C'MERE, CHAMP.
LEMME SEE IF I CAN GET MY ARMS AROUND YA.
NOT THAT IT AIN'T GREAT SEEIN' YOU...
...BUT WHERE ARE THE BOYS?
THEY WAITIN' BACK AT THE CLUBHOUSE?
I--I DIDN'T WANNA SAY NOTHIN' WHILE YOU WAS INSIDE, BUT...
"...WELL, MAYBE YOU SHOULD SEE FOR YOURSELF..."

WHAT THE HOLY HELL HAPPENED HERE?

INTERGANG.

THEY FOUND OUT IT WAS *YOU* STOLE THEIR NEW APOKOLIPS CANNON.

HEARD YOU STASHED IT BEFORE YOU GOT PINCHED USIN' IT ON THAT ARMORED CAR.

"THEY ROUNDED UP THE REST OF THE DINGBATS. WHEN THEY DIDN'T GET THE ANSWERS THEY WAS LOOKING FOR...THEY ASKED *HARDER.*"

THEY...THEY DIDN'T KNOW...I NEVER HAD A CHANCE TO TELL THEM WHERE I HID IT.

"SON, I DON'T THINK IT WOULD HAVE MATTERED IF THEY *DID.*"

"THOSE INTERGANG BOYS WERE LOOKING TO SEND A *MESSAGE.*"

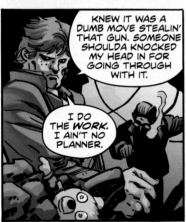

KNEW IT WAS A DUMB MOVE STEALIN' THAT GUN. SOMEONE SHOULDA KNOCKED MY HEAD IN FOR GOING THROUGH WITH IT.

I DO THE *WORK.* I AIN'T NO PLANNER.

"GOOD LOOKS... NON-FAT... BANANAS...

"...THEY ALL DIED MESSY 'CUZ OF ME."

SON, THIS ISN'T *A LITTLE LEAGUE TEAM.* THEY KNEW THE SCORE WHEN THEY JOINED--

DON'T MATTER. I WAS SUPPOSED TO *SHIELD* THEM.

I SHOULDA BEEN HERE!

KROOM

DON'T TALK STUPID.

YOU HAD BEEN HERE, YOU'D BE ON A COLD SLAB RIGHT NEXT TO THEM. NO MAYBES ABOUT IT.

FACE IT, SON, WE'RE THE *LAST* OF THE DINGBATS.

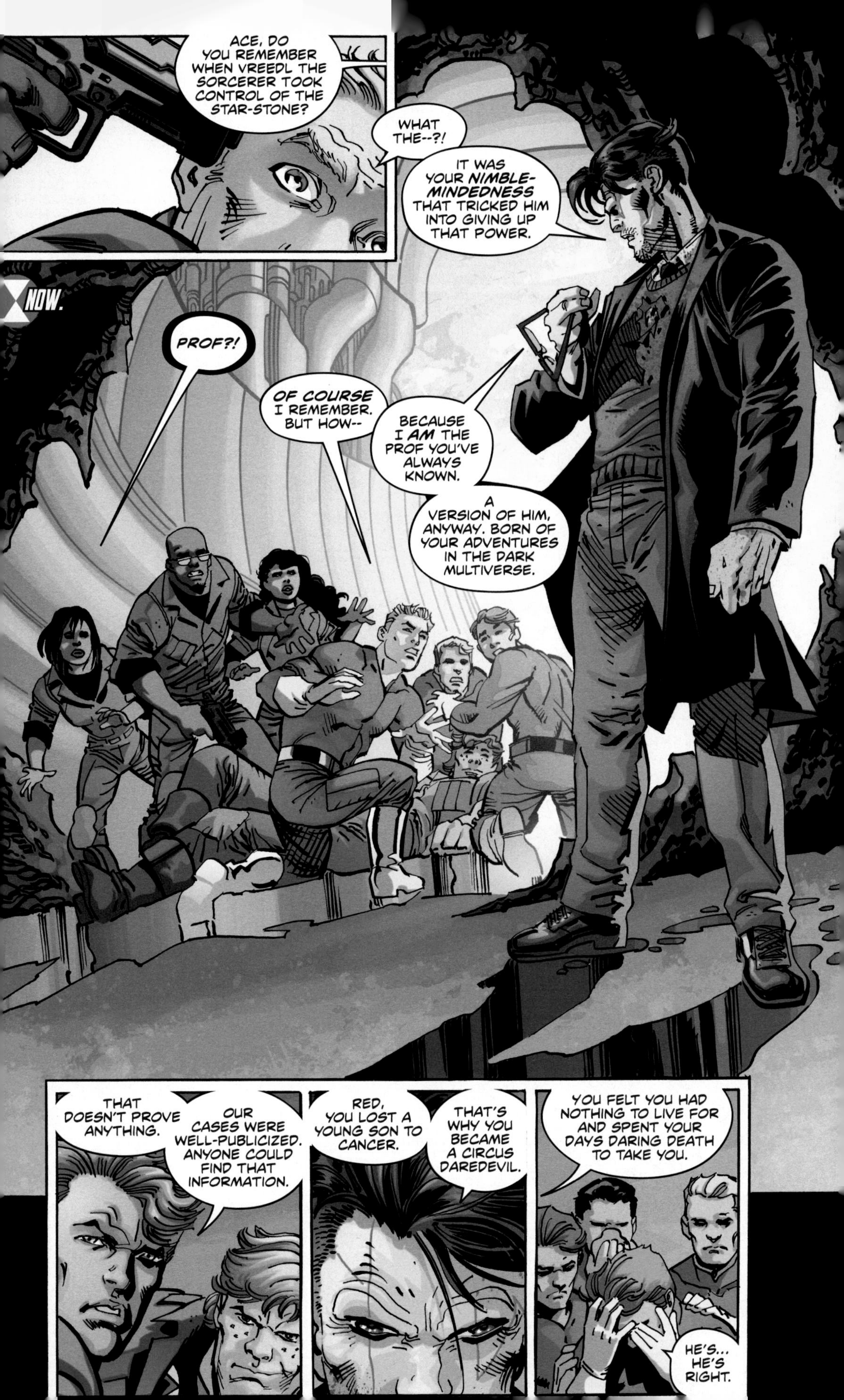
ACE, DO YOU REMEMBER WHEN VREEDL THE SORCERER TOOK CONTROL OF THE STAR-STONE?
WHAT THE--?!
IT WAS YOUR NIMBLE-MINDEDNESS THAT TRICKED HIM INTO GIVING UP THAT POWER.
NOW.
PROF?!
OF COURSE I REMEMBER. BUT HOW--
BECAUSE I AM THE PROF YOU'VE ALWAYS KNOWN.
A VERSION OF HIM, ANYWAY. BORN OF YOUR ADVENTURES IN THE DARK MULTIVERSE.
THAT DOESN'T PROVE ANYTHING.
OUR CASES WERE WELL-PUBLICIZED. ANYONE COULD FIND THAT INFORMATION.
RED, YOU LOST A YOUNG SON TO CANCER.
THAT'S WHY YOU BECAME A CIRCUS DAREDEVIL.
YOU FELT YOU HAD NOTHING TO LIVE FOR AND SPENT YOUR DAYS DARING DEATH TO TAKE YOU.
HE'S... HE'S RIGHT.

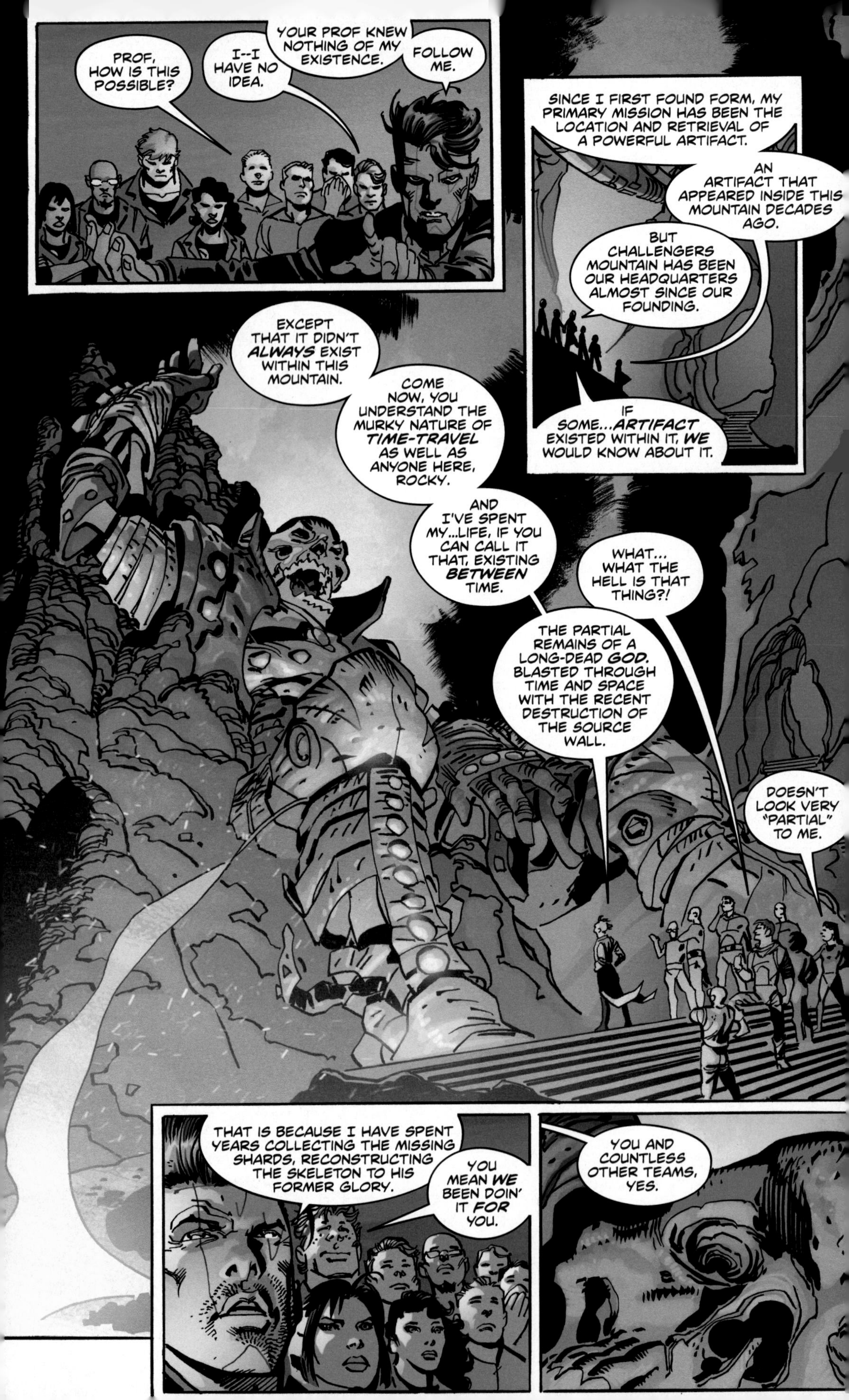
PROF, HOW IS THIS POSSIBLE?
I--I HAVE NO IDEA.
YOUR PROF KNEW NOTHING OF MY EXISTENCE.
FOLLOW ME.
SINCE I FIRST FOUND FORM, MY PRIMARY MISSION HAS BEEN THE LOCATION AND RETRIEVAL OF A POWERFUL ARTIFACT.
AN ARTIFACT THAT APPEARED INSIDE THIS MOUNTAIN DECADES AGO.
BUT CHALLENGERS MOUNTAIN HAS BEEN OUR HEADQUARTERS ALMOST SINCE OUR FOUNDING.
IF SOME...ARTIFACT EXISTED WITHIN IT, WE WOULD KNOW ABOUT IT.
EXCEPT THAT IT DIDN'T ALWAYS EXIST WITHIN THIS MOUNTAIN.
COME NOW, YOU UNDERSTAND THE MURKY NATURE OF TIME-TRAVEL AS WELL AS ANYONE HERE, ROCKY.
AND I'VE SPENT MY...LIFE, IF YOU CAN CALL IT THAT, EXISTING BETWEEN TIME.
WHAT... WHAT THE HELL IS THAT THING?!
THE PARTIAL REMAINS OF A LONG-DEAD GOD. BLASTED THROUGH TIME AND SPACE WITH THE RECENT DESTRUCTION OF THE SOURCE WALL.
DOESN'T LOOK VERY "PARTIAL" TO ME.
THAT IS BECAUSE I HAVE SPENT YEARS COLLECTING THE MISSING SHARDS, RECONSTRUCTING THE SKELETON TO HIS FORMER GLORY.
YOU MEAN WE BEEN DOIN' IT FOR YOU.
YOU AND COUNTLESS OTHER TEAMS, YES.

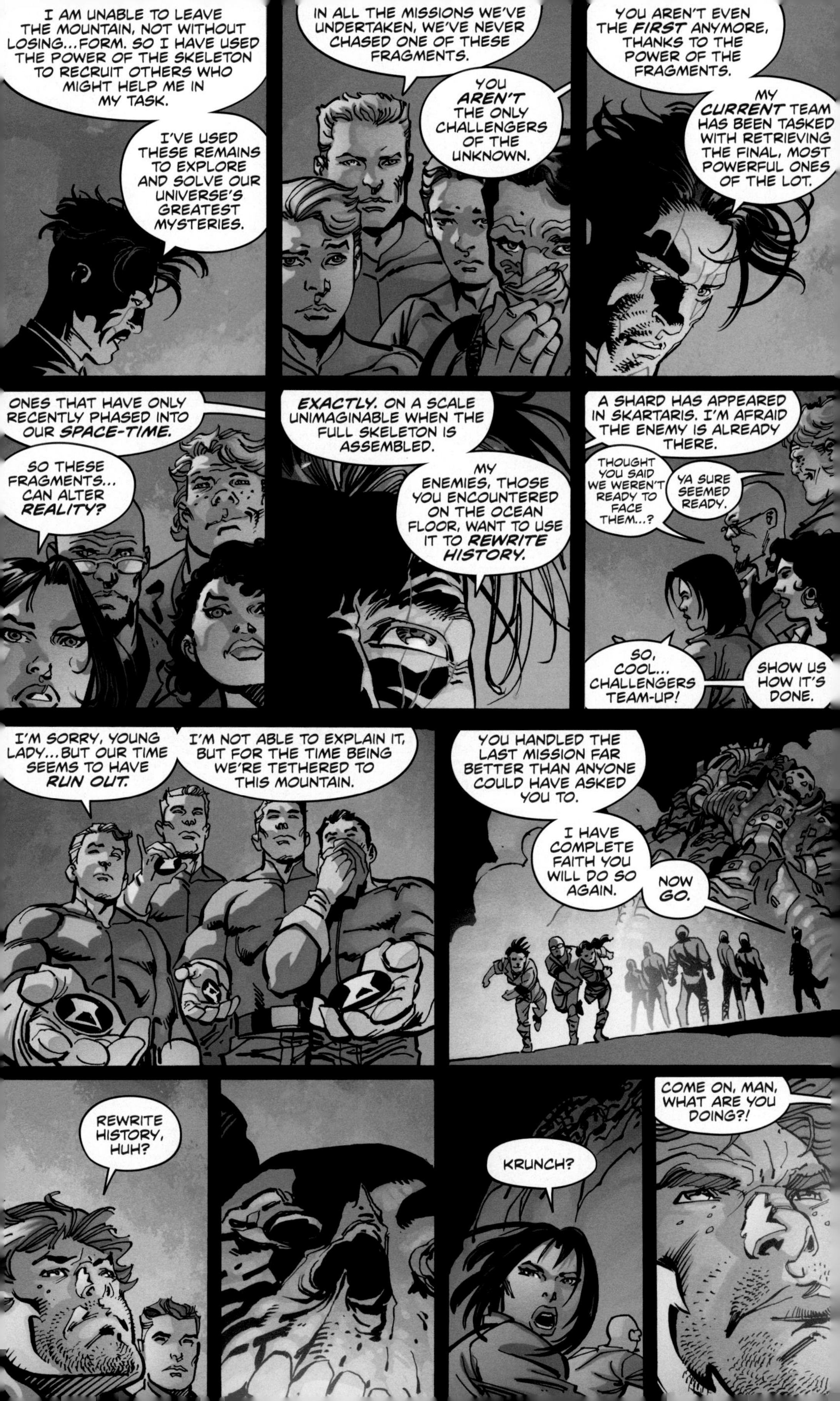
I AM UNABLE TO LEAVE THE MOUNTAIN, NOT WITHOUT LOSING...FORM. SO I HAVE USED THE POWER OF THE SKELETON TO RECRUIT OTHERS WHO MIGHT HELP ME IN MY TASK.
I'VE USED THESE REMAINS TO EXPLORE AND SOLVE OUR UNIVERSE'S GREATEST MYSTERIES.
IN ALL THE MISSIONS WE'VE UNDERTAKEN, WE'VE NEVER CHASED ONE OF THESE FRAGMENTS.
YOU AREN'T THE ONLY CHALLENGERS OF THE UNKNOWN.
YOU AREN'T EVEN THE FIRST ANYMORE, THANKS TO THE POWER OF THE FRAGMENTS.
MY CURRENT TEAM HAS BEEN TASKED WITH RETRIEVING THE FINAL, MOST POWERFUL ONES OF THE LOT.
ONES THAT HAVE ONLY RECENTLY PHASED INTO OUR SPACE-TIME.
SO THESE FRAGMENTS... CAN ALTER REALITY?
EXACTLY. ON A SCALE UNIMAGINABLE WHEN THE FULL SKELETON IS ASSEMBLED.
MY ENEMIES, THOSE YOU ENCOUNTERED ON THE OCEAN FLOOR, WANT TO USE IT TO REWRITE HISTORY.
A SHARD HAS APPEARED IN SKARTARIS. I'M AFRAID THE ENEMY IS ALREADY THERE.
THOUGHT YOU SAID WE WEREN'T READY TO FACE THEM...?
YA SURE SEEMED READY.
SO, COOL... CHALLENGERS TEAM-UP!
SHOW US HOW IT'S DONE.
I'M SORRY, YOUNG LADY...BUT OUR TIME SEEMS TO HAVE RUN OUT.
I'M NOT ABLE TO EXPLAIN IT, BUT FOR THE TIME BEING WE'RE TETHERED TO THIS MOUNTAIN.
YOU HANDLED THE LAST MISSION FAR BETTER THAN ANYONE COULD HAVE ASKED YOU TO.
I HAVE COMPLETE FAITH YOU WILL DO SO AGAIN.
NOW GO.
REWRITE HISTORY, HUH?
KRUNCH?
COME ON, MAN, WHAT ARE YOU DOING?!

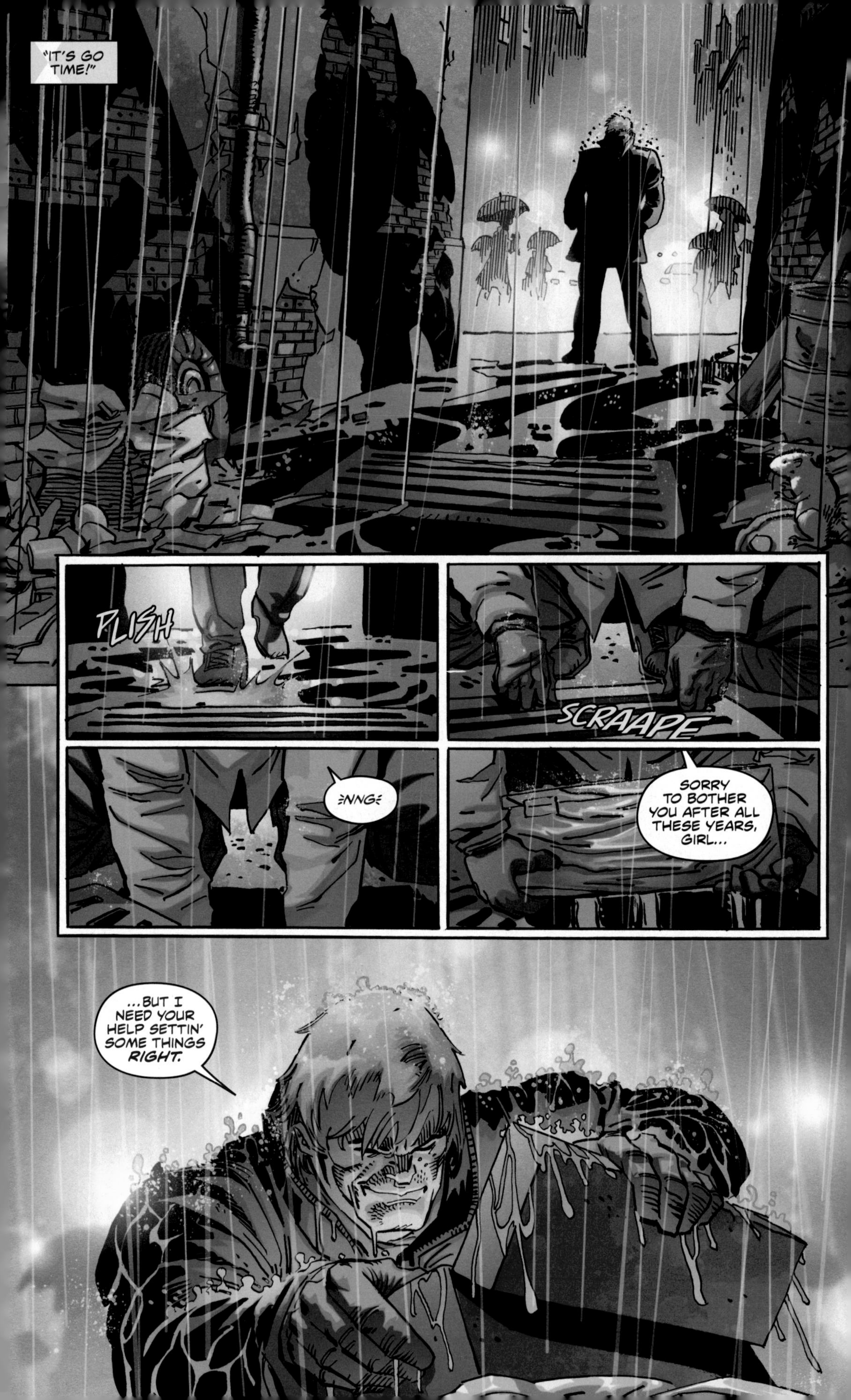
"IT'S GO TIME!"
PLISH
SCRAAPE
NNG
SORRY TO BOTHER YOU AFTER ALL THESE YEARS, GIRL...
...BUT I NEED YOUR HELP SETTIN' SOME THINGS RIGHT.

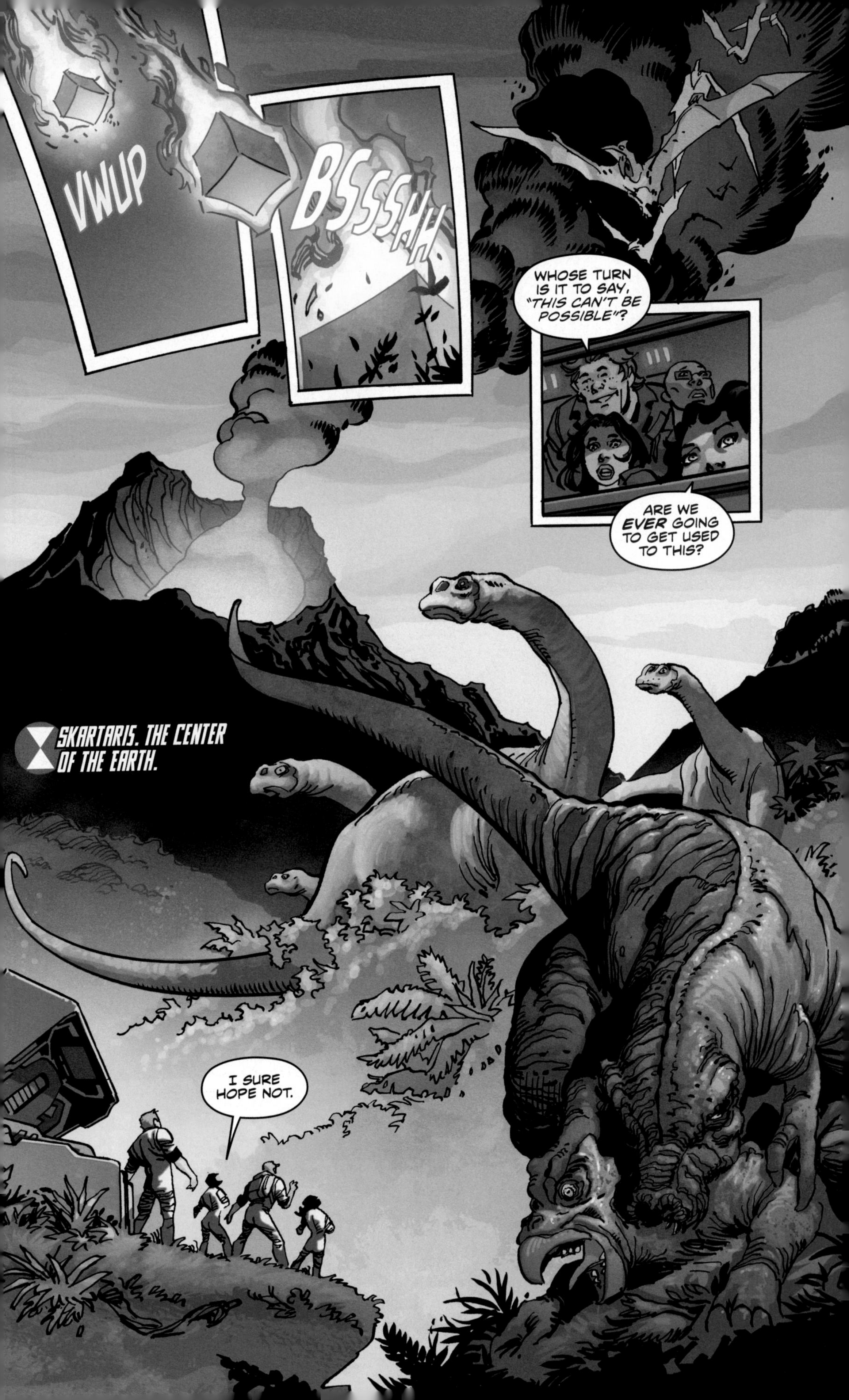
VWUP
BSSSHH
WHOSE TURN IS IT TO SAY, "THIS CAN'T BE POSSIBLE"?
ARE WE EVER GOING TO GET USED TO THIS?
SKARTARIS. THE CENTER OF THE EARTH.
I SURE HOPE NOT.

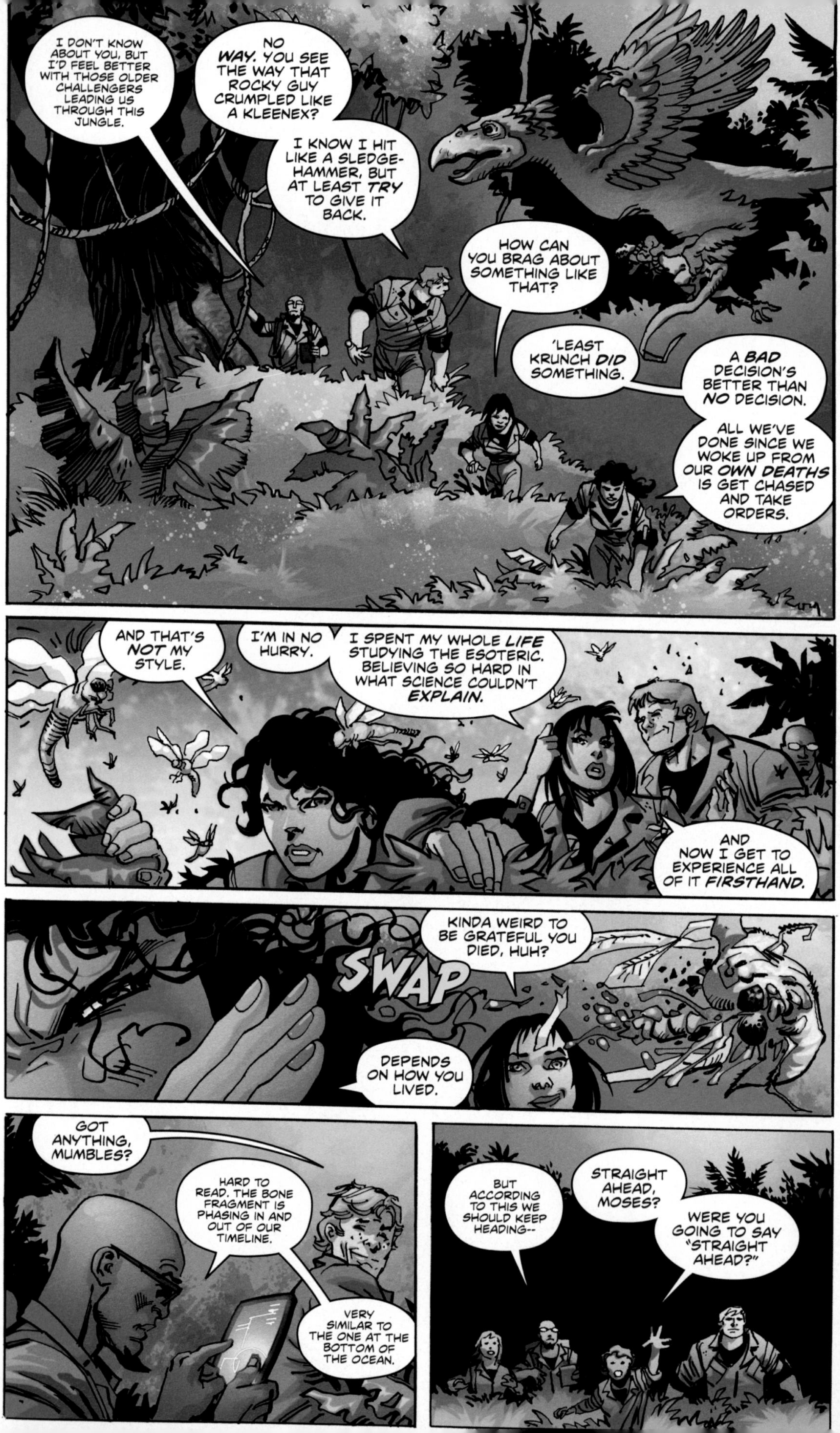
I DON'T KNOW ABOUT YOU, BUT I'D FEEL BETTER WITH THOSE OLDER CHALLENGERS LEADING US THROUGH THIS JUNGLE.
NO WAY. YOU SEE THE WAY THAT ROCKY GUY CRUMPLED LIKE A KLEENEX?
I KNOW I HIT LIKE A SLEDGE-HAMMER, BUT AT LEAST TRY TO GIVE IT BACK.
HOW CAN YOU BRAG ABOUT SOMETHING LIKE THAT?
'LEAST KRUNCH DID SOMETHING.
A BAD DECISION'S BETTER THAN NO DECISION.
ALL WE'VE DONE SINCE WE WOKE UP FROM OUR OWN DEATHS IS GET CHASED AND TAKE ORDERS.
AND THAT'S NOT MY STYLE.
I'M IN NO HURRY.
I SPENT MY WHOLE LIFE STUDYING THE ESOTERIC. BELIEVING SO HARD IN WHAT SCIENCE COULDN'T EXPLAIN.
AND NOW I GET TO EXPERIENCE ALL OF IT FIRSTHAND.
SWAP
KINDA WEIRD TO BE GRATEFUL YOU DIED, HUH?
DEPENDS ON HOW YOU LIVED.
GOT ANYTHING, MUMBLES?
HARD TO READ. THE BONE FRAGMENT IS PHASING IN AND OUT OF OUR TIMELINE.
VERY SIMILAR TO THE ONE AT THE BOTTOM OF THE OCEAN.
BUT ACCORDING TO THIS WE SHOULD KEEP HEADING--
STRAIGHT AHEAD, MOSES?
WERE YOU GOING TO SAY "STRAIGHT AHEAD?"

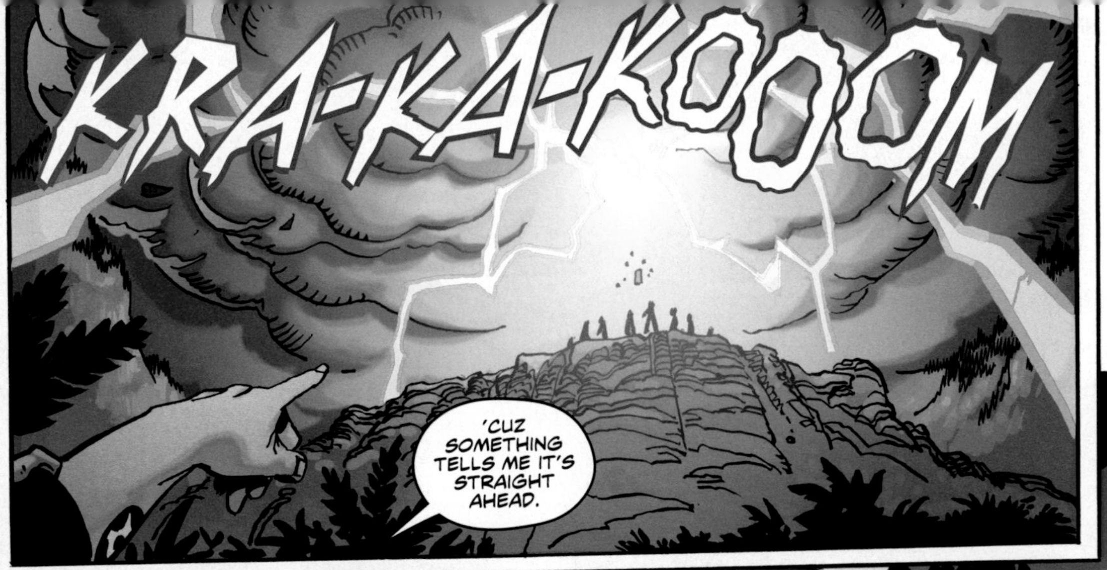
KRA-KA-KOOOM
'CUZ SOMETHING TELLS ME IT'S STRAIGHT AHEAD.

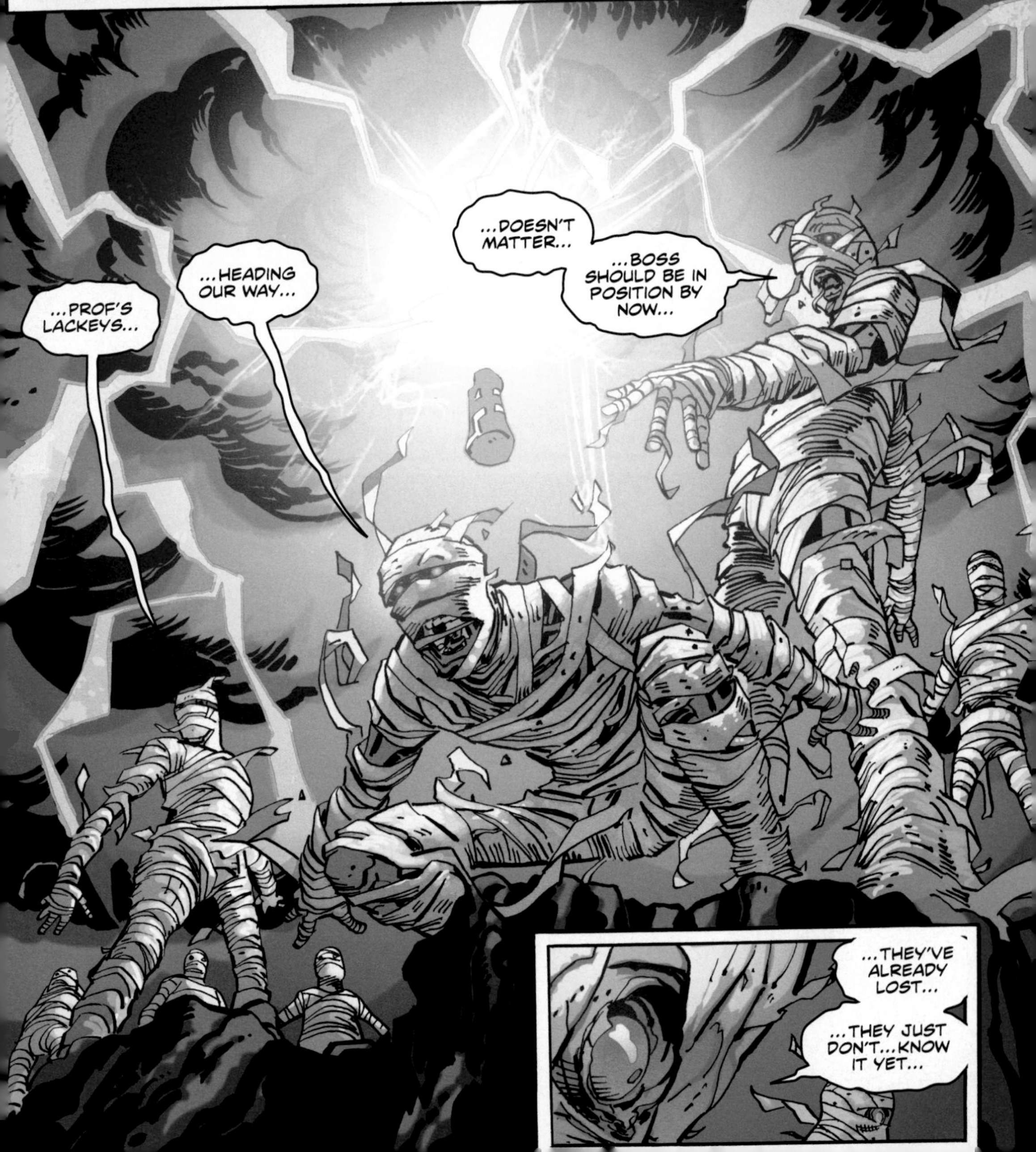
...PROF'S LACKEYS...
...HEADING OUR WAY...
...DOESN'T MATTER...
...BOSS SHOULD BE IN POSITION BY NOW...
...THEY'VE ALREADY LOST...
...THEY JUST DON'T...KNOW IT YET...

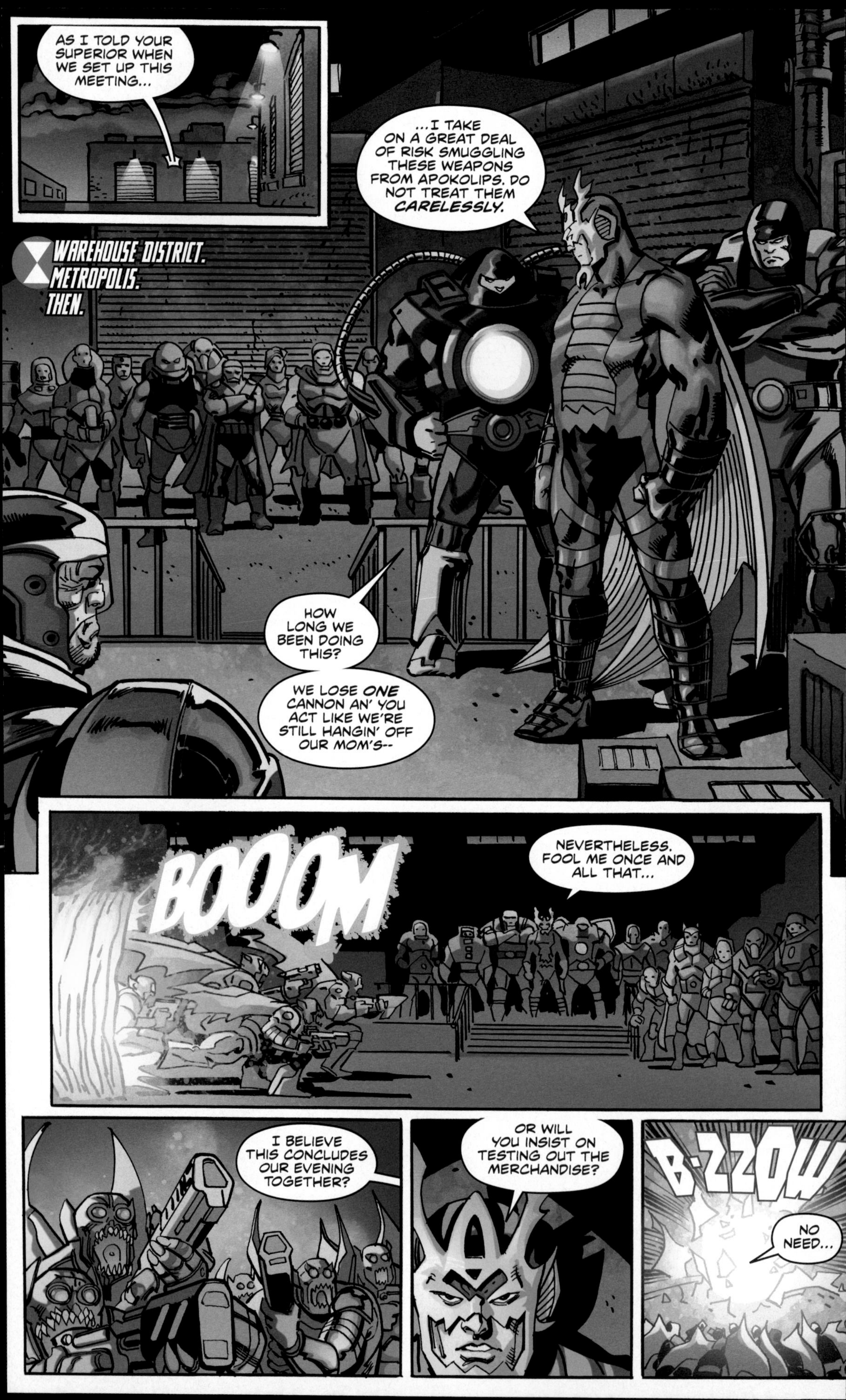

AS I TOLD YOUR SUPERIOR WHEN WE SET UP THIS MEETING...
...I TAKE ON A GREAT DEAL OF RISK SMUGGLING THESE WEAPONS FROM APOKOLIPS. DO NOT TREAT THEM CARELESSLY.
WAREHOUSE DISTRICT. METROPOLIS. THEN.
HOW LONG WE BEEN DOING THIS?
WE LOSE ONE CANNON AN' YOU ACT LIKE WE'RE STILL HANGIN' OFF OUR MOM'S--
BOOOM
NEVERTHELESS. FOOL ME ONCE AND ALL THAT...
I BELIEVE THIS CONCLUDES OUR EVENING TOGETHER?
OR WILL YOU INSIST ON TESTING OUT THE MERCHANDISE?
B-ZZOW
NO NEED...

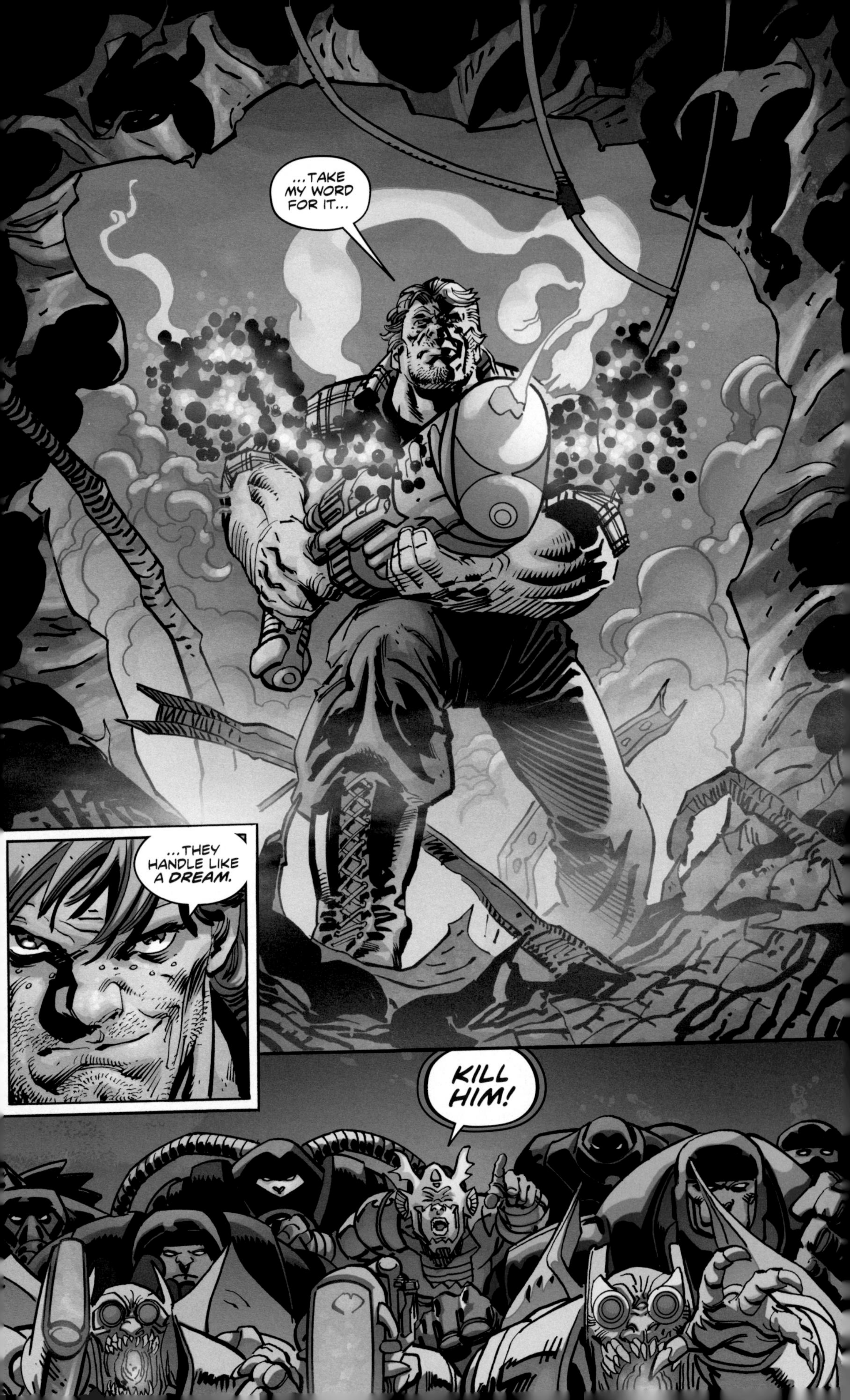
...TAKE MY WORD FOR IT...
...THEY HANDLE LIKE A *DREAM.*
KILL HIM!

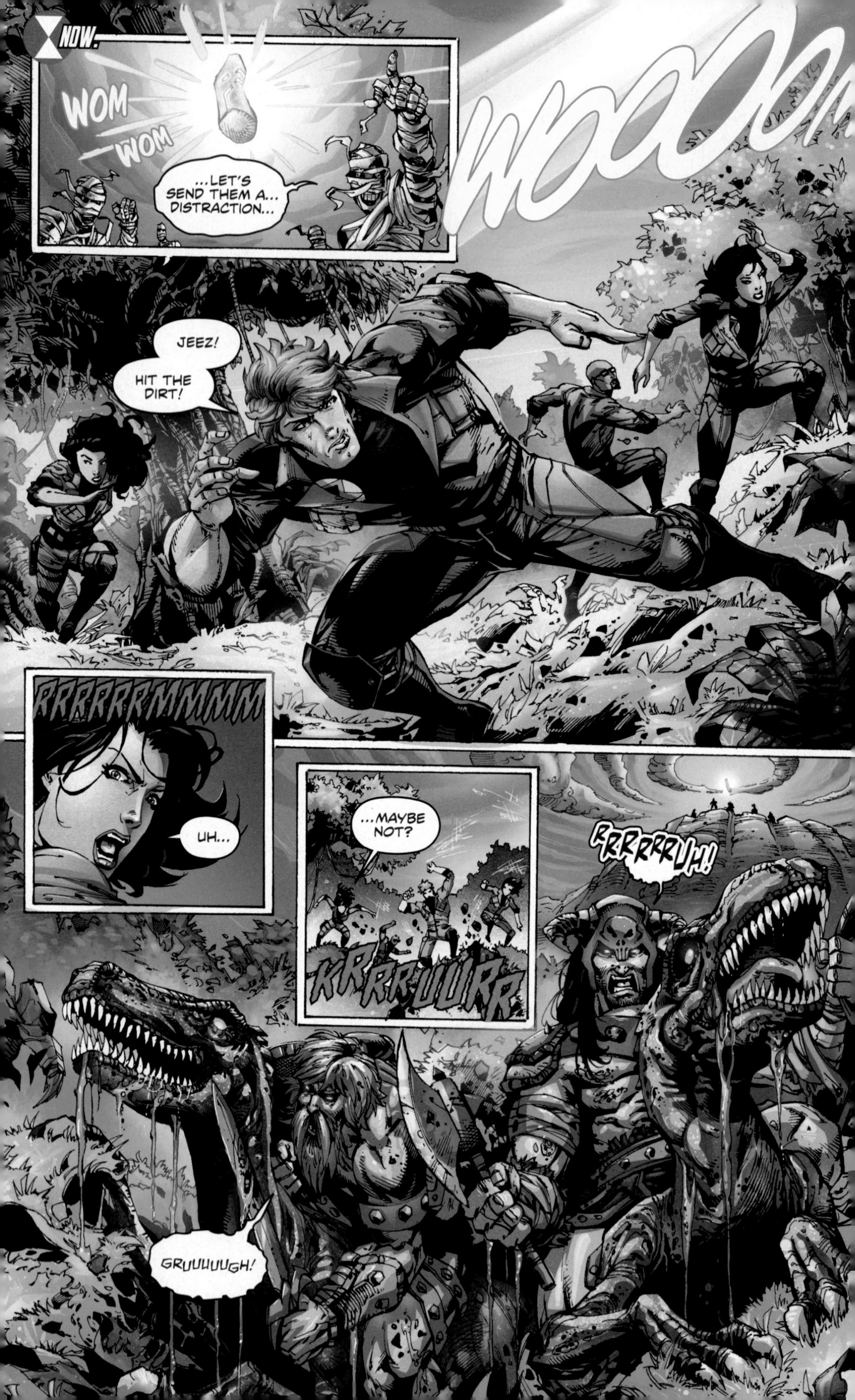
NOW.
WOM
WOM
...LET'S SEND THEM A... DISTRACTION...
JEEZ!
HIT THE DIRT!
RRRRRRMMMMM
UH...
...MAYBE NOT?
KRRRUURR
RRRRRRUH!
GRUUUUUGH!

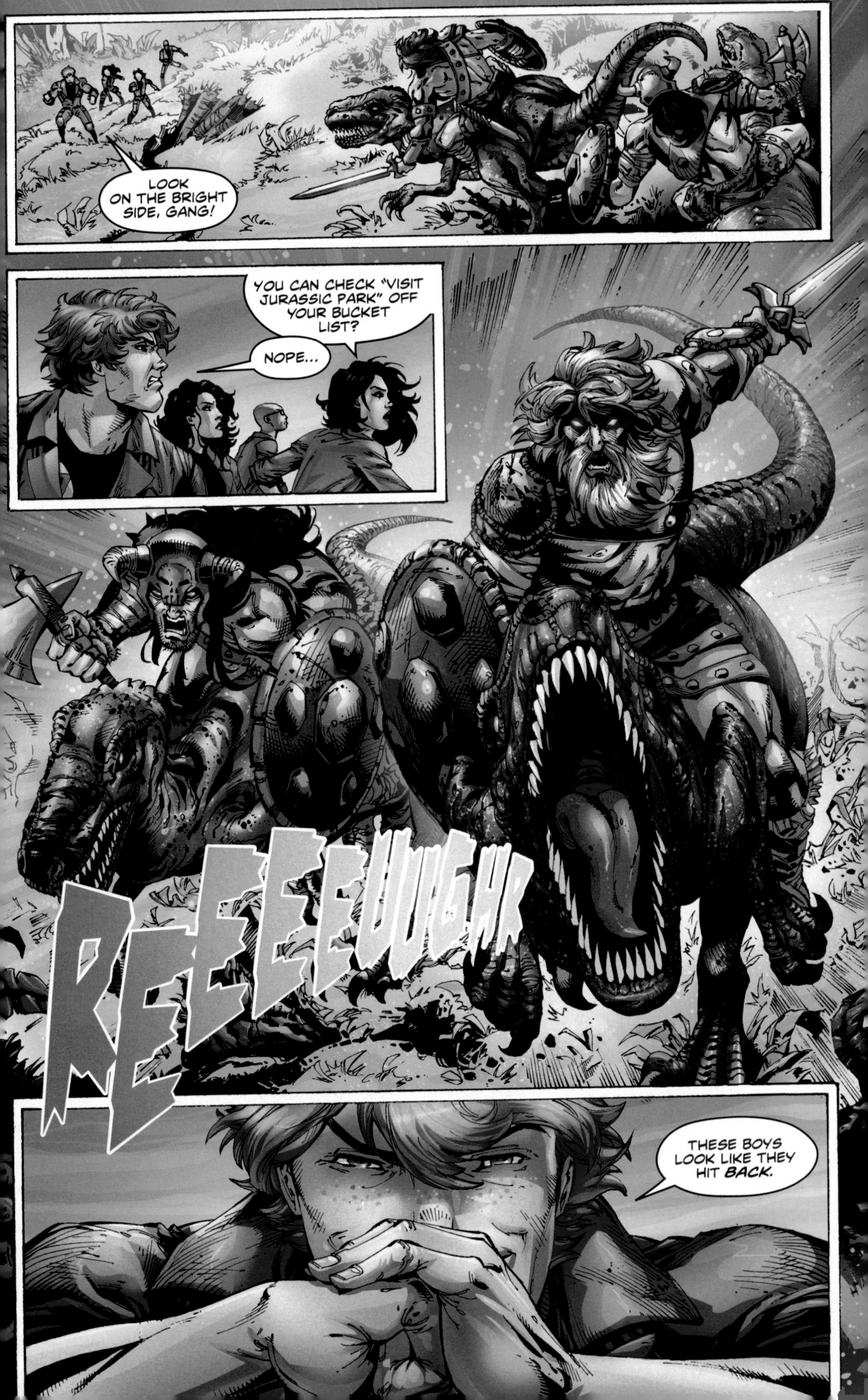
LOOK ON THE BRIGHT SIDE, GANG!
YOU CAN CHECK "VISIT JURASSIC PARK" OFF YOUR BUCKET LIST?
NOPE...
REEEEUUGHR
THESE BOYS LOOK LIKE THEY HIT BACK.

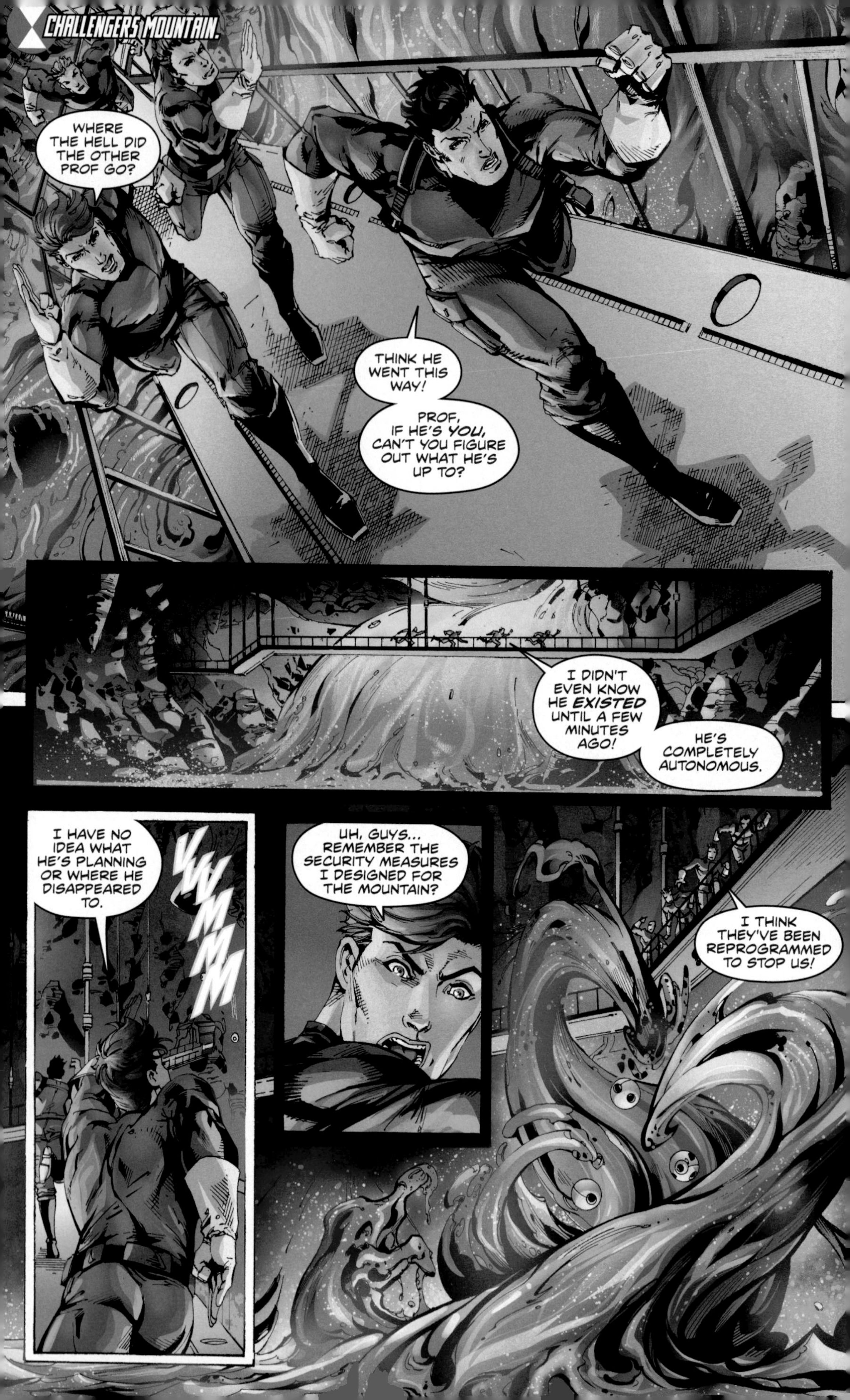
CHALLENGERS MOUNTAIN.
WHERE THE HELL DID THE OTHER PROF GO?
THINK HE WENT THIS WAY!
PROF, IF HE'S YOU, CAN'T YOU FIGURE OUT WHAT HE'S UP TO?
I DIDN'T EVEN KNOW HE EXISTED UNTIL A FEW MINUTES AGO!
HE'S COMPLETELY AUTONOMOUS.
I HAVE NO IDEA WHAT HE'S PLANNING OR WHERE HE DISAPPEARED TO.
VVMMM
UH, GUYS... REMEMBER THE SECURITY MEASURES I DESIGNED FOR THE MOUNTAIN?
I THINK THEY'VE BEEN REPROGRAMMED TO STOP US!

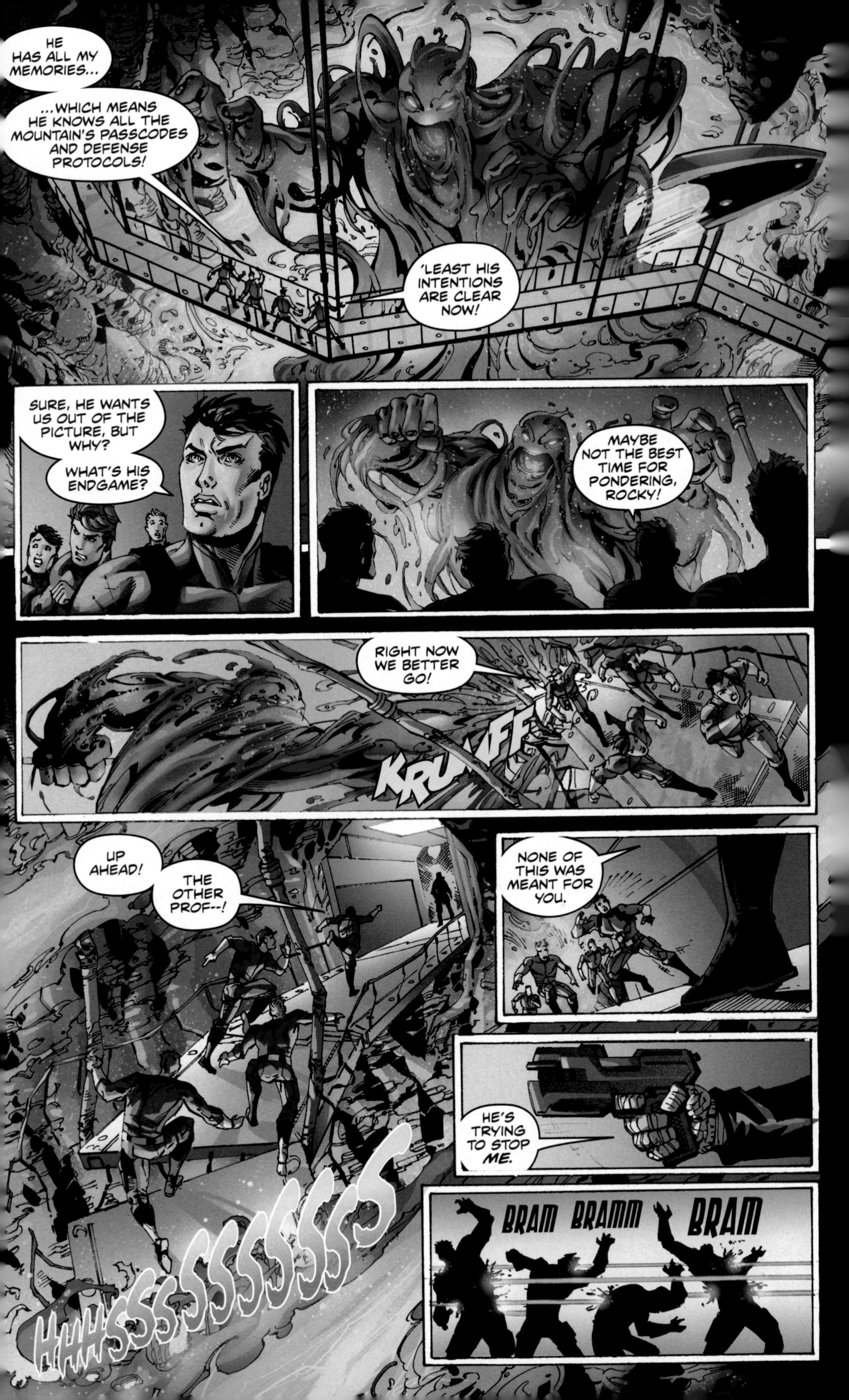
HE HAS ALL MY MEMORIES...
...WHICH MEANS HE KNOWS ALL THE MOUNTAIN'S PASSCODES AND DEFENSE PROTOCOLS!
'LEAST HIS INTENTIONS ARE CLEAR NOW!
SURE, HE WANTS US OUT OF THE PICTURE, BUT WHY?
WHAT'S HIS ENDGAME?
MAYBE NOT THE BEST TIME FOR PONDERING, ROCKY!
RIGHT NOW WE BETTER GO!
UP AHEAD!
THE OTHER PROF--!
HHHSSSSSSSSSSS
NONE OF THIS WAS MEANT FOR YOU.
HE'S TRYING TO STOP ME.
BRAM BRAMM BRAM

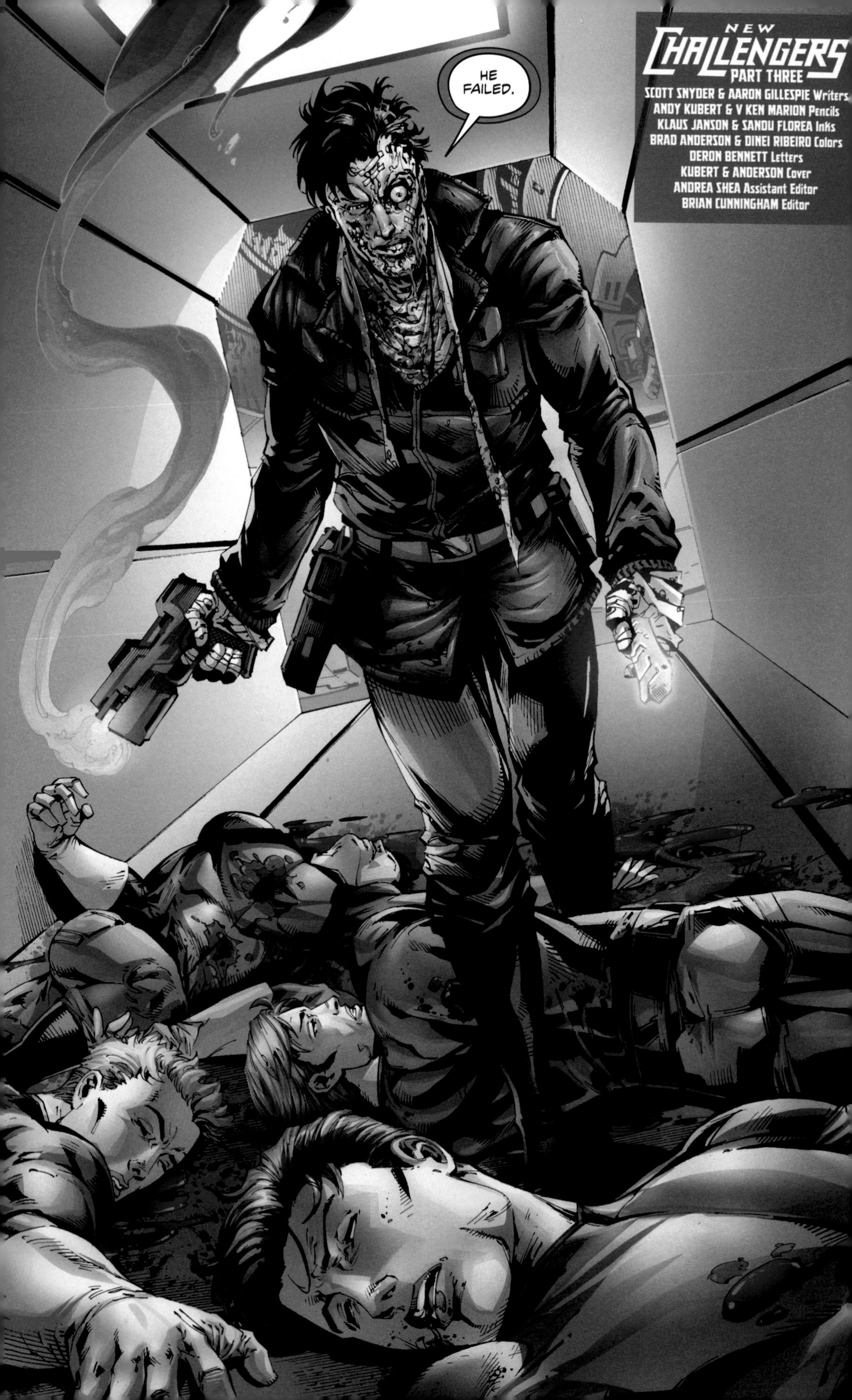
HE FAILED.
NEW CHALLENGERS PART THREE
SCOTT SNYDER & AARON GILLESPIE Writers
ANDY KUBERT & V KEN MARION Pencils
KLAUS JANSON & SANDU FLOREA Inks
BRAD ANDERSON & DINEI RIBEIRO Colors
DERON BENNETT Letters
KUBERT & ANDERSON Cover
ANDREA SHEA Assistant Editor
BRIAN CUNNINGHAM Editor

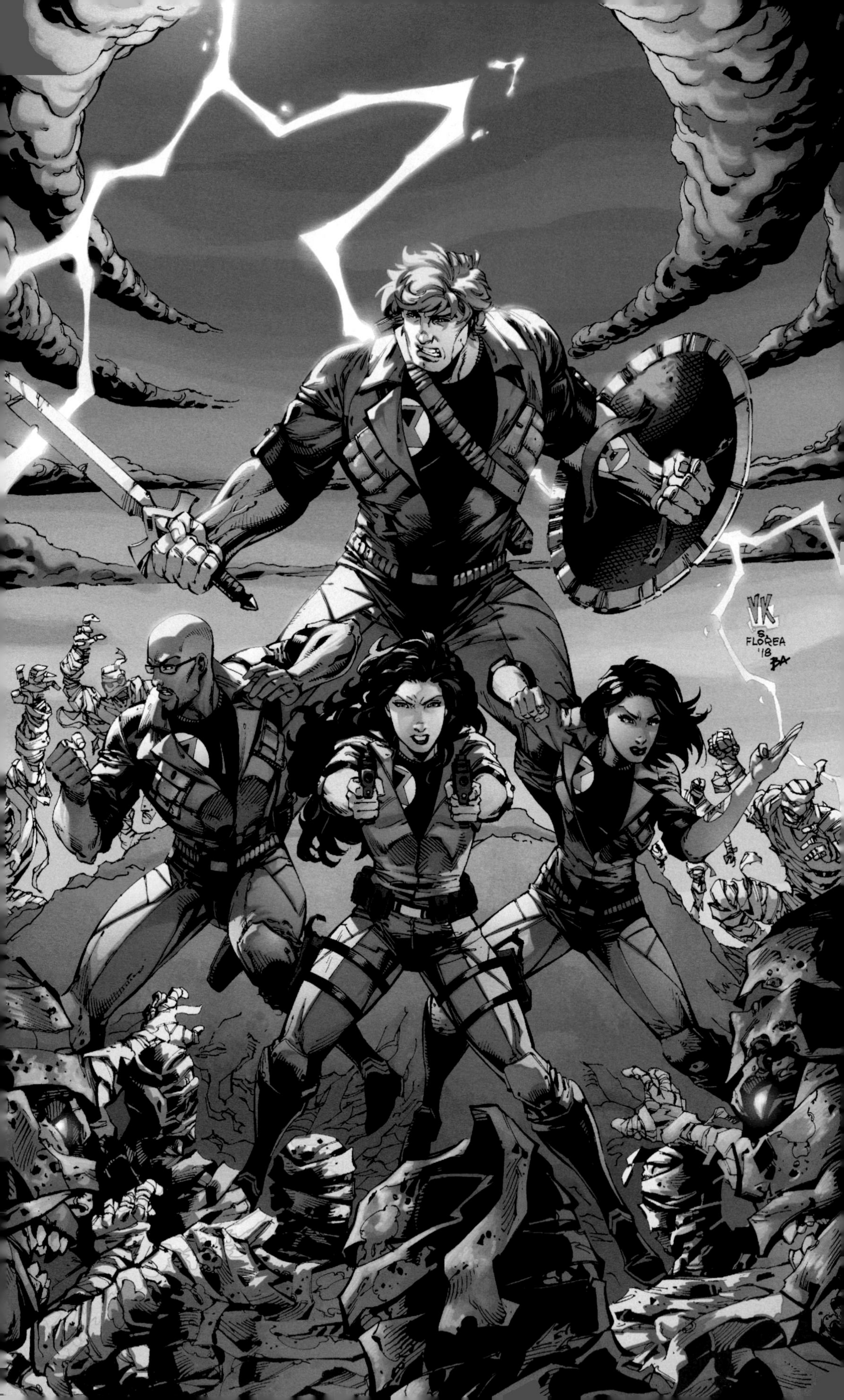
VK
S. FLOREA
'18
BA

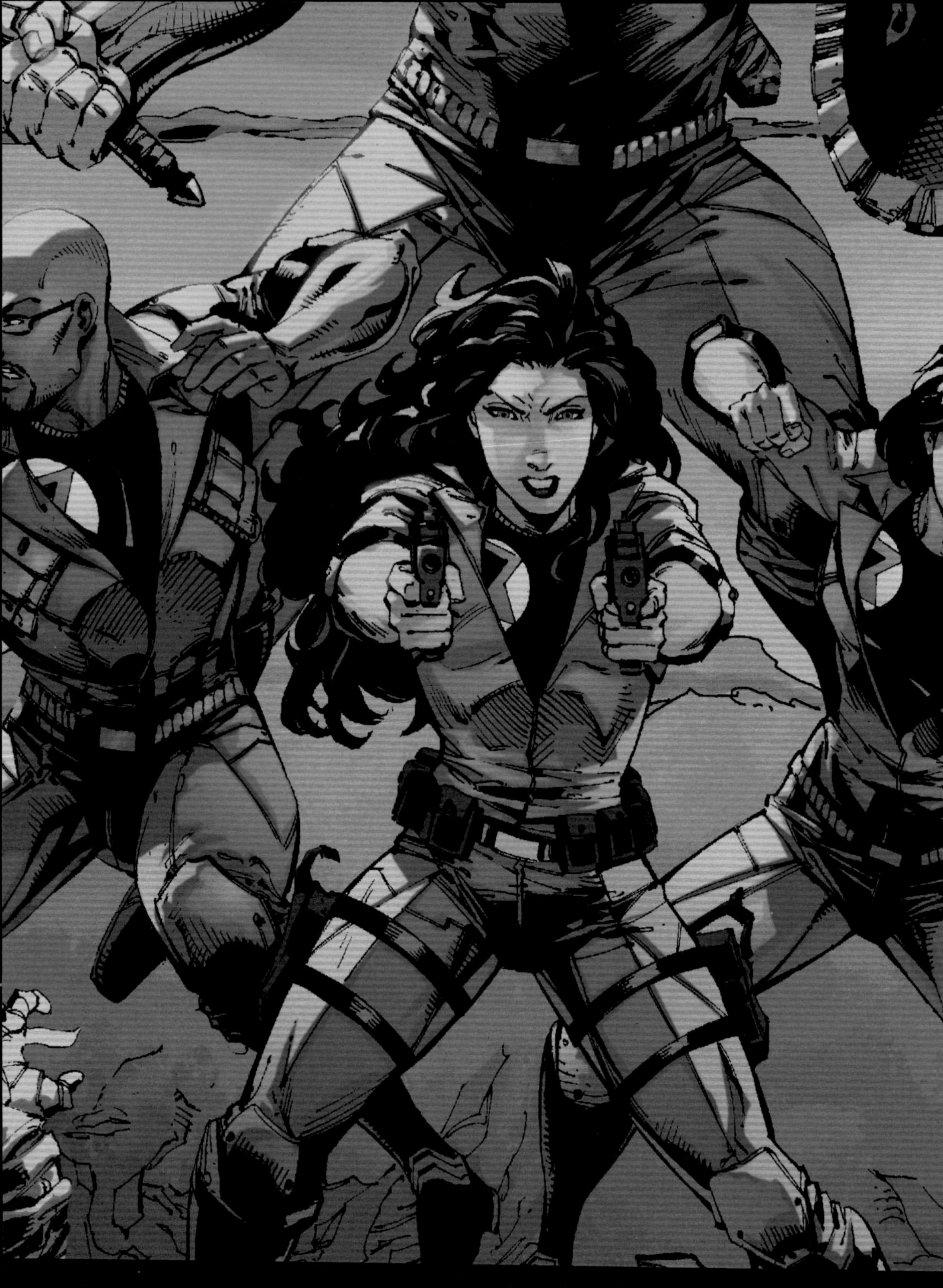

NEW CHALLENGERS
#4

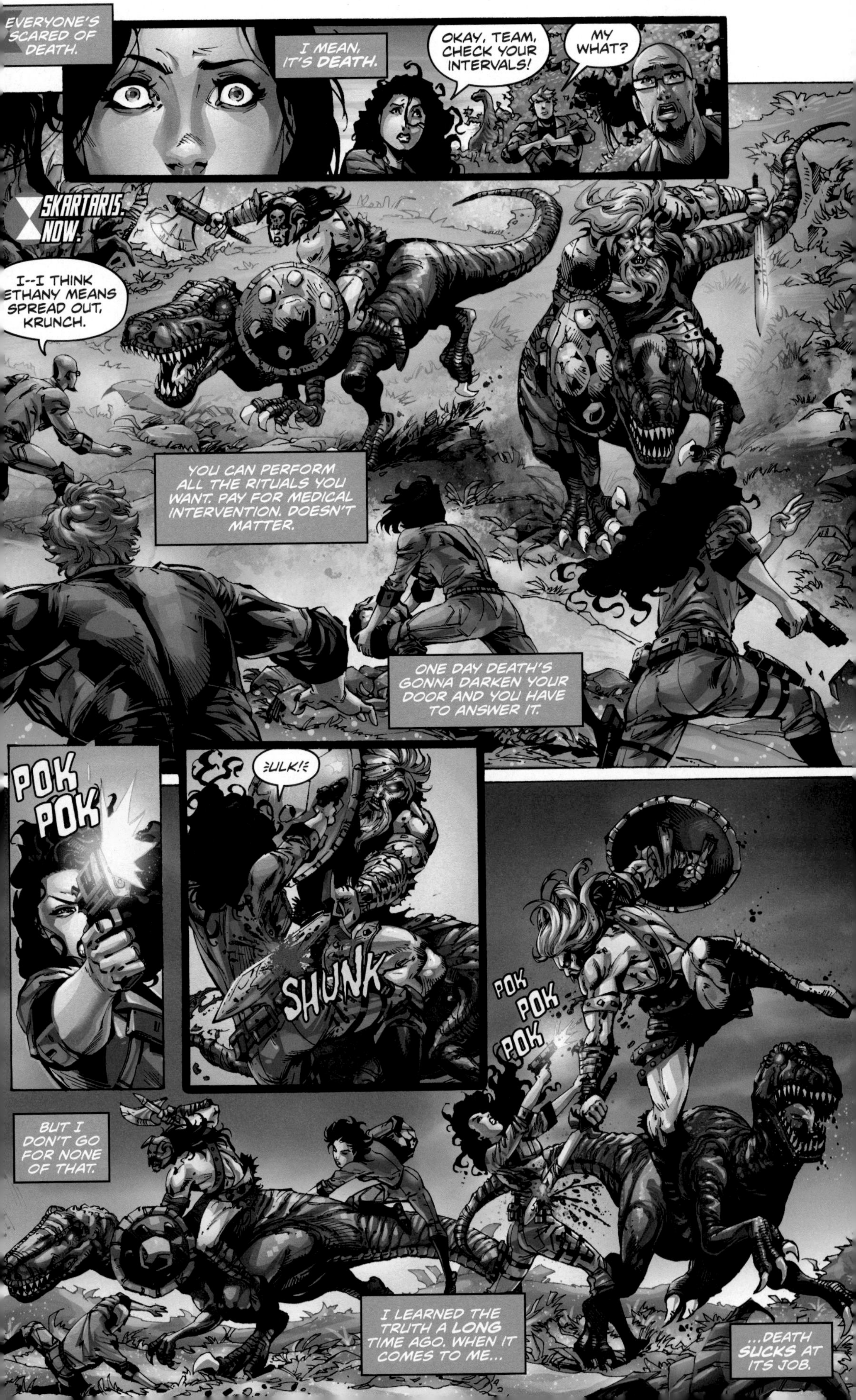

EVERYONE'S SCARED OF DEATH.
I MEAN, IT'S DEATH.
OKAY, TEAM, CHECK YOUR INTERVALS!
MY WHAT?
SKARTARIS. NOW.
I--I THINK ETHANY MEANS SPREAD OUT, KRUNCH.
YOU CAN PERFORM ALL THE RITUALS YOU WANT. PAY FOR MEDICAL INTERVENTION. DOESN'T MATTER.
ONE DAY DEATH'S GONNA DARKEN YOUR DOOR AND YOU HAVE TO ANSWER IT.
POK POK
ULK!
SHUNK
POK POK POK
BUT I DON'T GO FOR NONE OF THAT.
I LEARNED THE TRUTH A LONG TIME AGO. WHEN IT COMES TO ME...
...DEATH SUCKS AT ITS JOB.

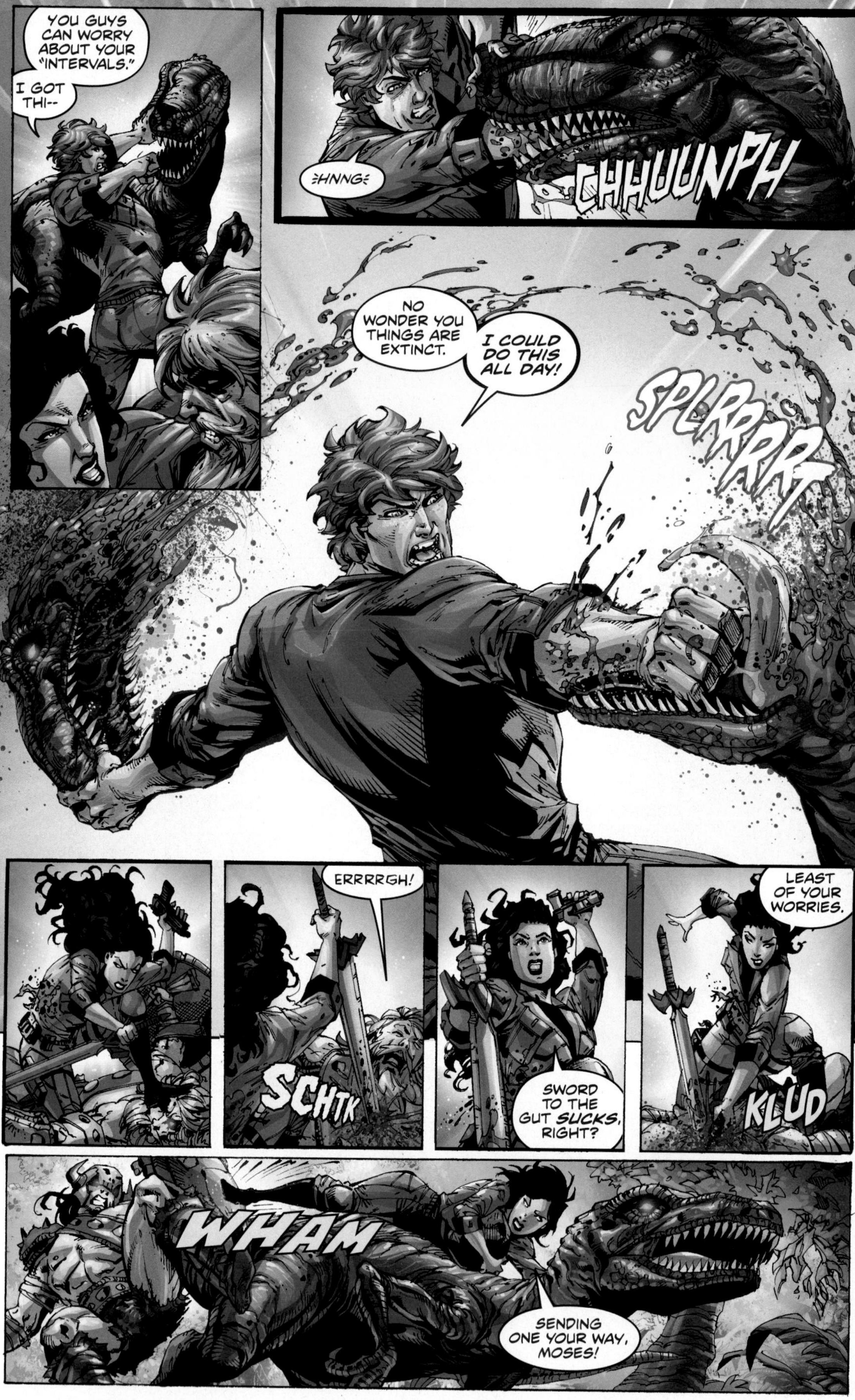
YOU GUYS CAN WORRY ABOUT YOUR "INTERVALS."
I GOT THI--
HNNG
CHHUUNPH
NO WONDER YOU THINGS ARE EXTINCT.
I COULD DO THIS ALL DAY!
SPLRRRRR
ERRRRGH!
SCHTK
SWORD TO THE GUT SUCKS, RIGHT?
LEAST OF YOUR WORRIES.
KLUD
WHAM
SENDING ONE YOUR WAY, MOSES!

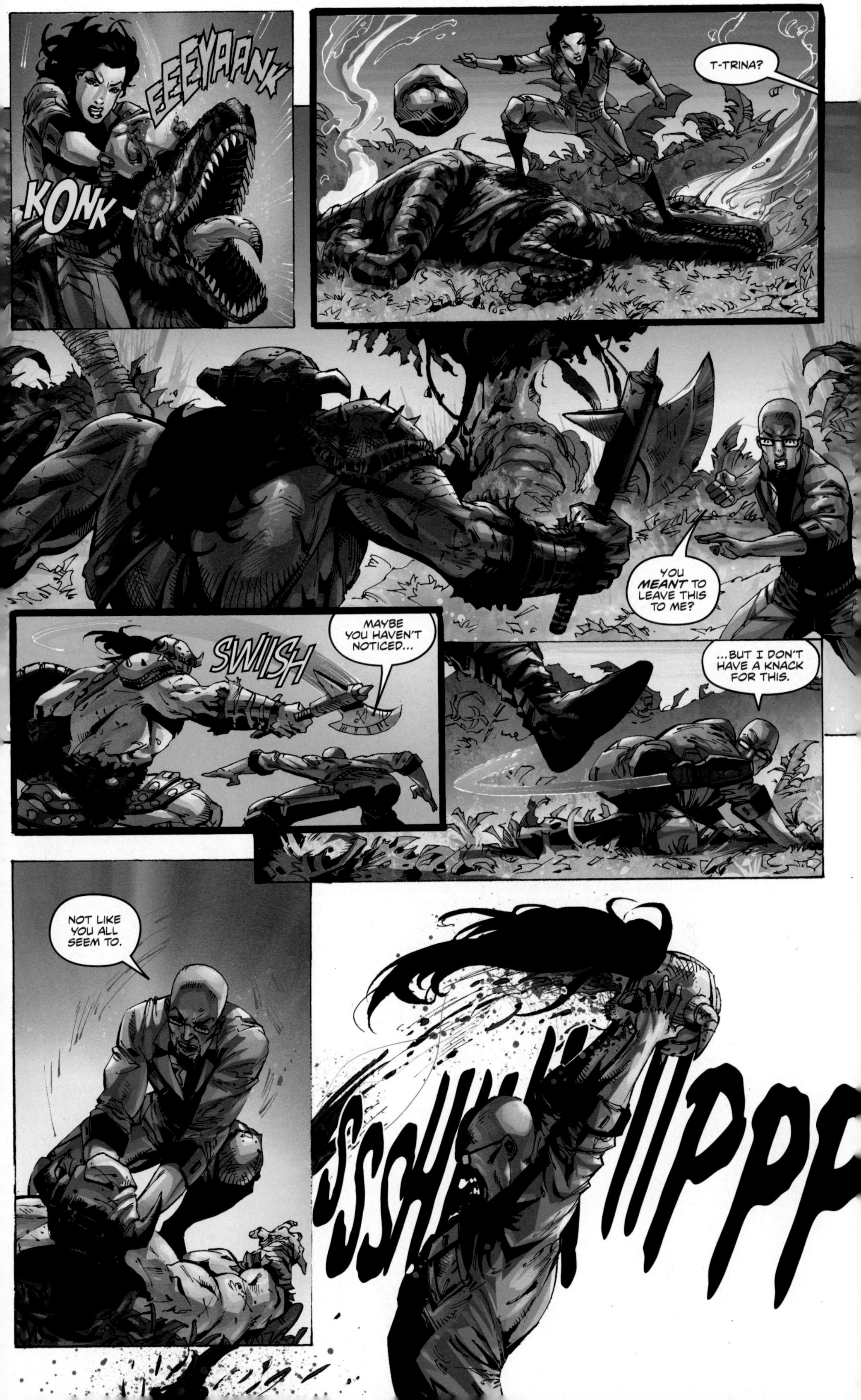
EEEYAANK
KONK
T-TRINA?
YOU MEANT TO LEAVE THIS TO ME?
SWISH
MAYBE YOU HAVEN'T NOTICED...
...BUT I DON'T HAVE A KNACK FOR THIS.
NOT LIKE YOU ALL SEEM TO.

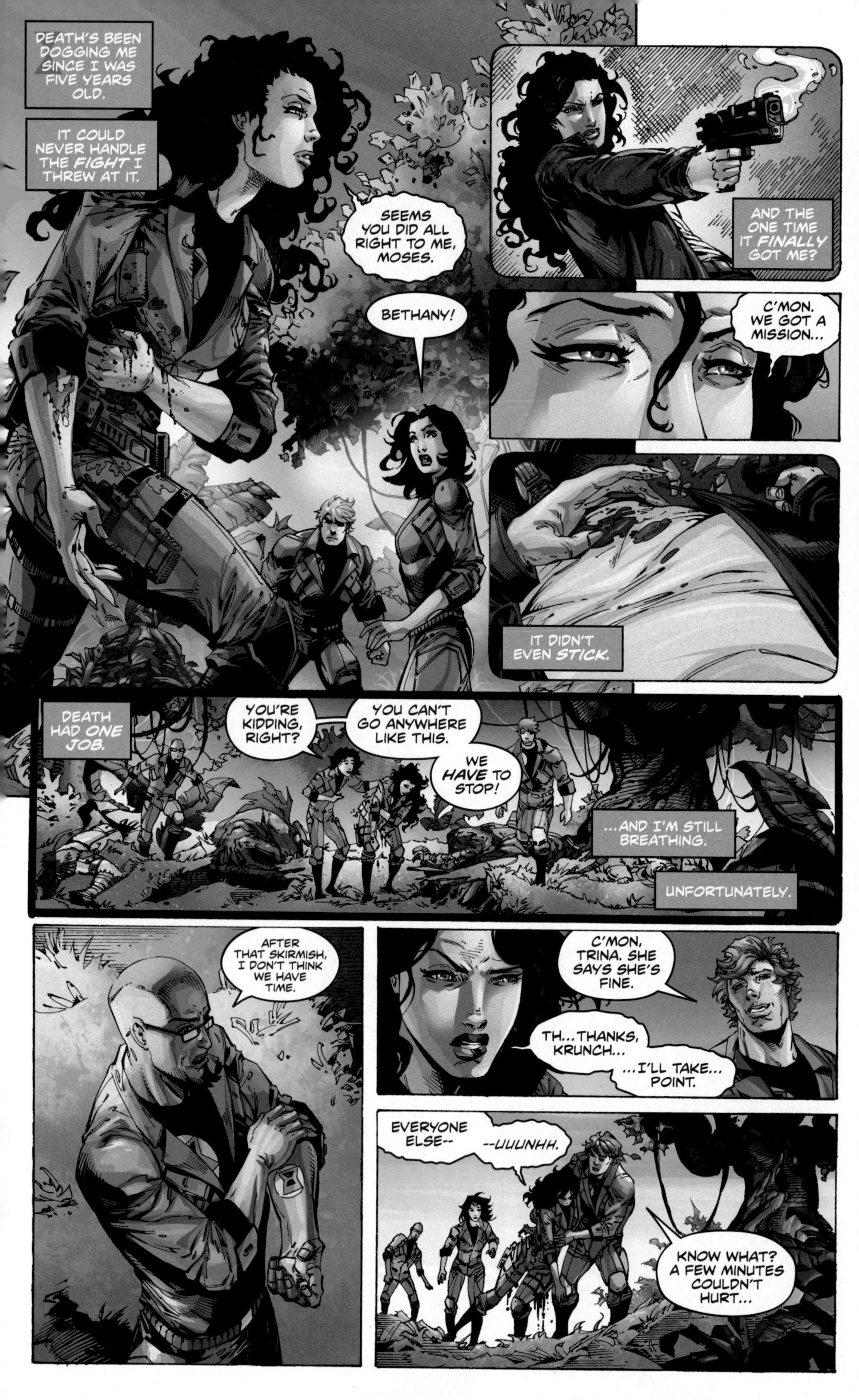
DEATH'S BEEN DOGGING ME SINCE I WAS FIVE YEARS OLD.
IT COULD NEVER HANDLE THE *FIGHT* I THREW AT IT.
SEEMS YOU DID ALL RIGHT TO ME, MOSES.
BETHANY!
AND THE ONE TIME IT *FINALLY* GOT ME?
C'MON. WE GOT A MISSION...
IT DIDN'T EVEN *STICK.*
DEATH HAD *ONE JOB.*
YOU'RE KIDDING, RIGHT?
YOU CAN'T GO ANYWHERE LIKE THIS.
WE *HAVE* TO STOP!
...AND I'M STILL BREATHING.
UNFORTUNATELY.
AFTER THAT SKIRMISH, I DON'T THINK WE HAVE TIME.
C'MON, TRINA. SHE SAYS SHE'S FINE.
TH...THANKS, KRUNCH...
...I'LL TAKE... POINT.
EVERYONE ELSE--
--UUUNHH.
KNOW WHAT? A FEW MINUTES COULDN'T HURT...

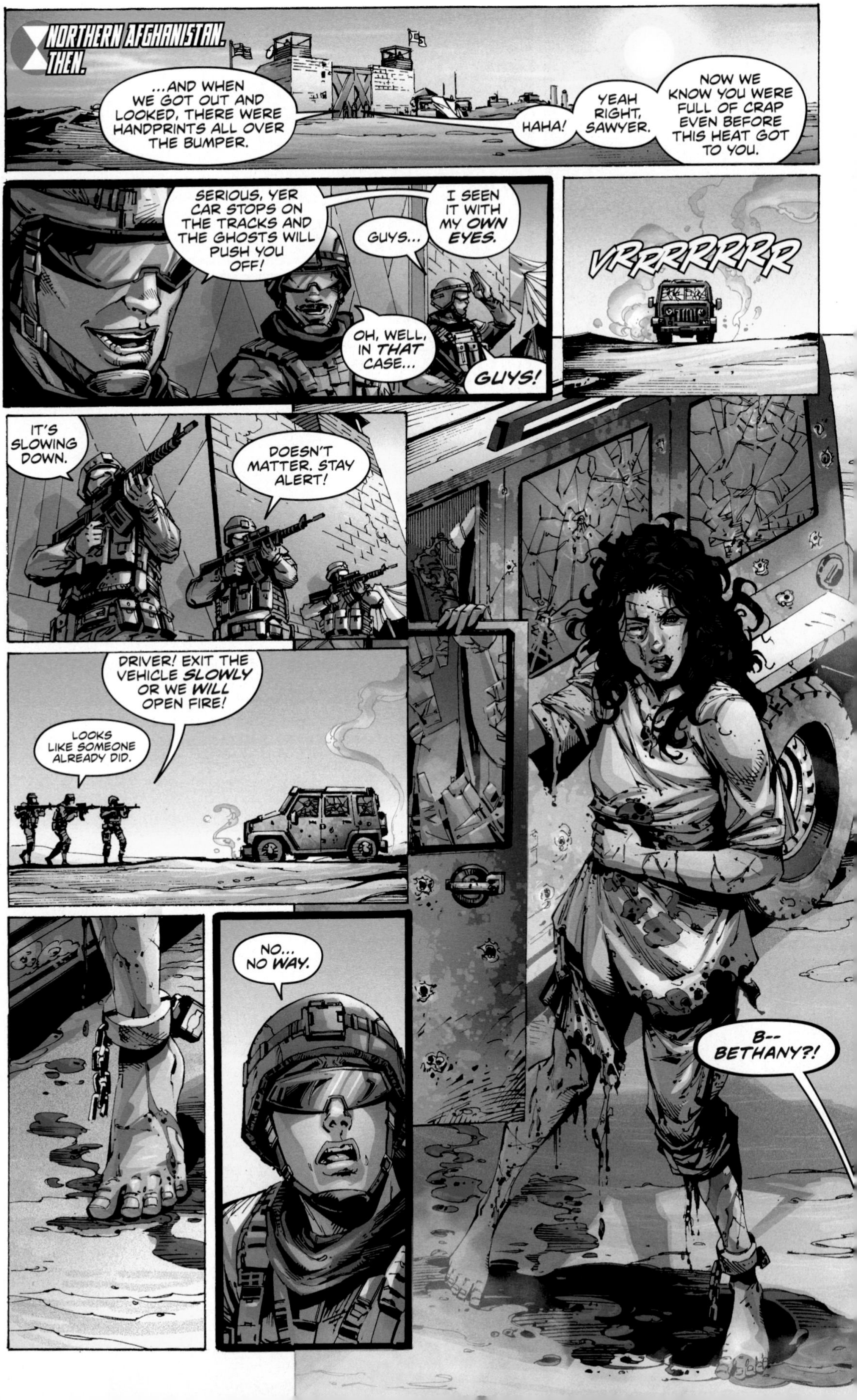
NORTHERN AFGHANISTAN. THEN.
...AND WHEN WE GOT OUT AND LOOKED, THERE WERE HANDPRINTS ALL OVER THE BUMPER.
HAHA!
YEAH RIGHT, SAWYER.
NOW WE KNOW YOU WERE FULL OF CRAP EVEN BEFORE THIS HEAT GOT TO YOU.
SERIOUS, YER CAR STOPS ON THE TRACKS AND THE GHOSTS WILL PUSH YOU OFF!
GUYS...
I SEEN IT WITH MY OWN EYES.
OH, WELL, IN THAT CASE...
GUYS!
VRRRRRRR
IT'S SLOWING DOWN.
DOESN'T MATTER. STAY ALERT!
DRIVER! EXIT THE VEHICLE SLOWLY OR WE WILL OPEN FIRE!
LOOKS LIKE SOMEONE ALREADY DID.
NO... NO WAY.
B-- BETHANY?!

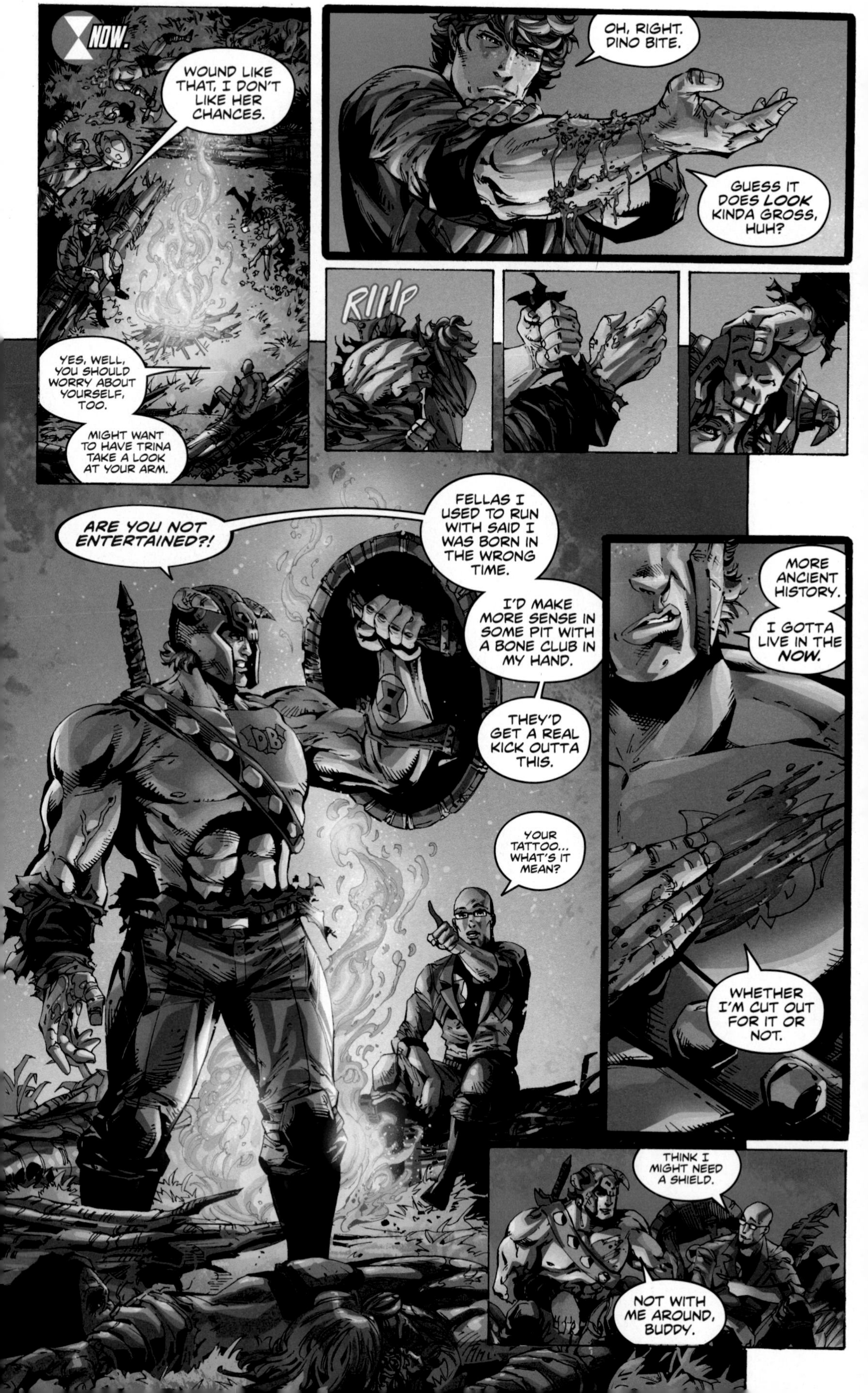

NOW.
WOUND LIKE THAT, I DON'T LIKE HER CHANCES.
YES, WELL, YOU SHOULD WORRY ABOUT YOURSELF, TOO.
MIGHT WANT TO HAVE TRINA TAKE A LOOK AT YOUR ARM.
OH, RIGHT. DINO BITE.
GUESS IT DOES LOOK KINDA GROSS, HUH?
RIIIP
ARE YOU NOT ENTERTAINED?!
FELLAS I USED TO RUN WITH SAID I WAS BORN IN THE WRONG TIME.
I'D MAKE MORE SENSE IN SOME PIT WITH A BONE CLUB IN MY HAND.
THEY'D GET A REAL KICK OUTTA THIS.
YOUR TATTOO... WHAT'S IT MEAN?
MORE ANCIENT HISTORY.
I GOTTA LIVE IN THE NOW.
WHETHER I'M CUT OUT FOR IT OR NOT.
THINK I MIGHT NEED A SHIELD.
NOT WITH ME AROUND, BUDDY.

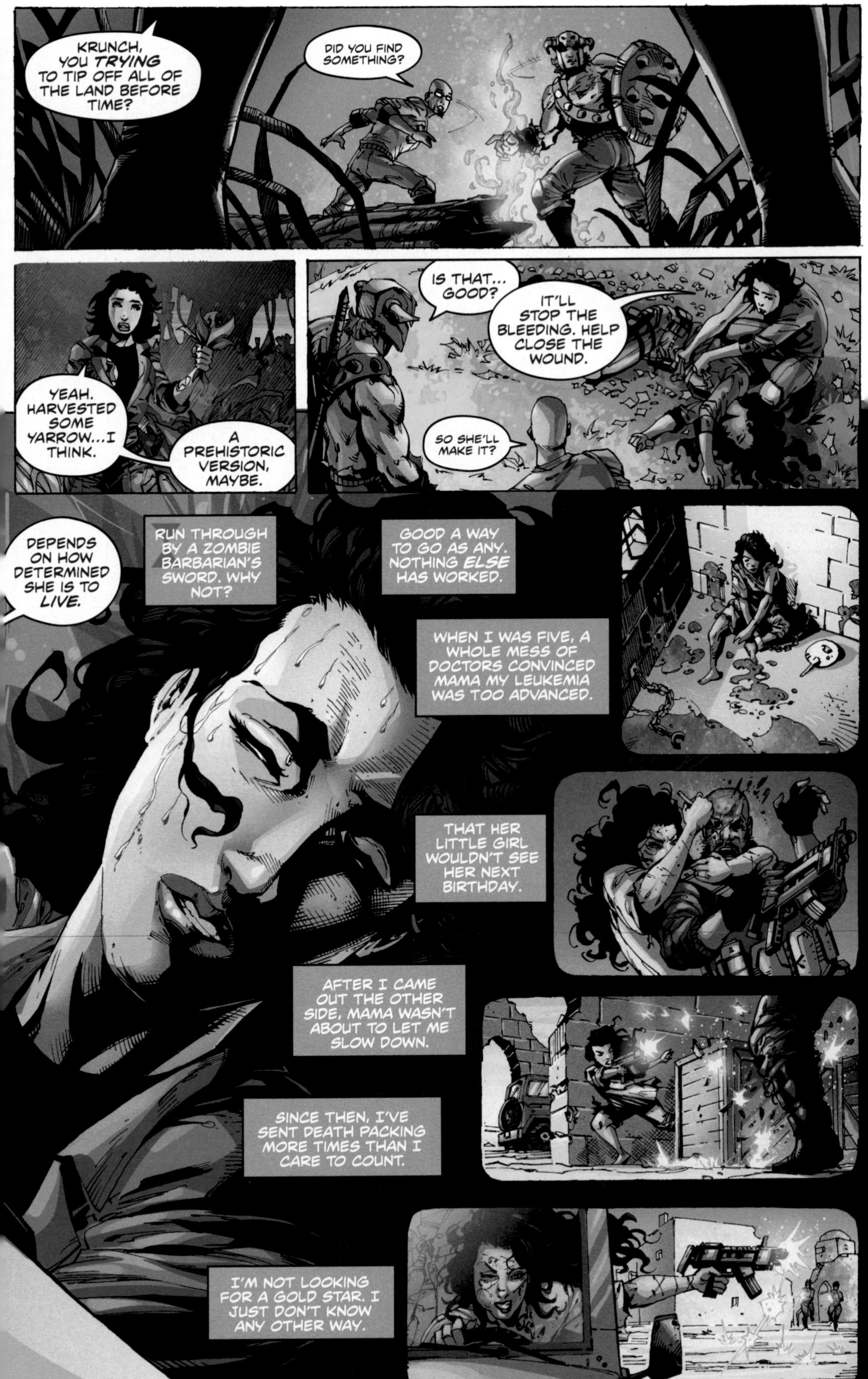
KRUNCH, YOU TRYING TO TIP OFF ALL OF THE LAND BEFORE TIME?
DID YOU FIND SOMETHING?
YEAH. HARVESTED SOME YARROW...I THINK.
A PREHISTORIC VERSION, MAYBE.
IS THAT... GOOD?
IT'LL STOP THE BLEEDING. HELP CLOSE THE WOUND.
SO SHE'LL MAKE IT?
DEPENDS ON HOW DETERMINED SHE IS TO LIVE.
RUN THROUGH BY A ZOMBIE BARBARIAN'S SWORD. WHY NOT?
GOOD A WAY TO GO AS ANY. NOTHING ELSE HAS WORKED.
WHEN I WAS FIVE, A WHOLE MESS OF DOCTORS CONVINCED MAMA MY LEUKEMIA WAS TOO ADVANCED.
THAT HER LITTLE GIRL WOULDN'T SEE HER NEXT BIRTHDAY.
AFTER I CAME OUT THE OTHER SIDE, MAMA WASN'T ABOUT TO LET ME SLOW DOWN.
SINCE THEN, I'VE SENT DEATH PACKING MORE TIMES THAN I CARE TO COUNT.
I'M NOT LOOKING FOR A GOLD STAR. I JUST DON'T KNOW ANY OTHER WAY.

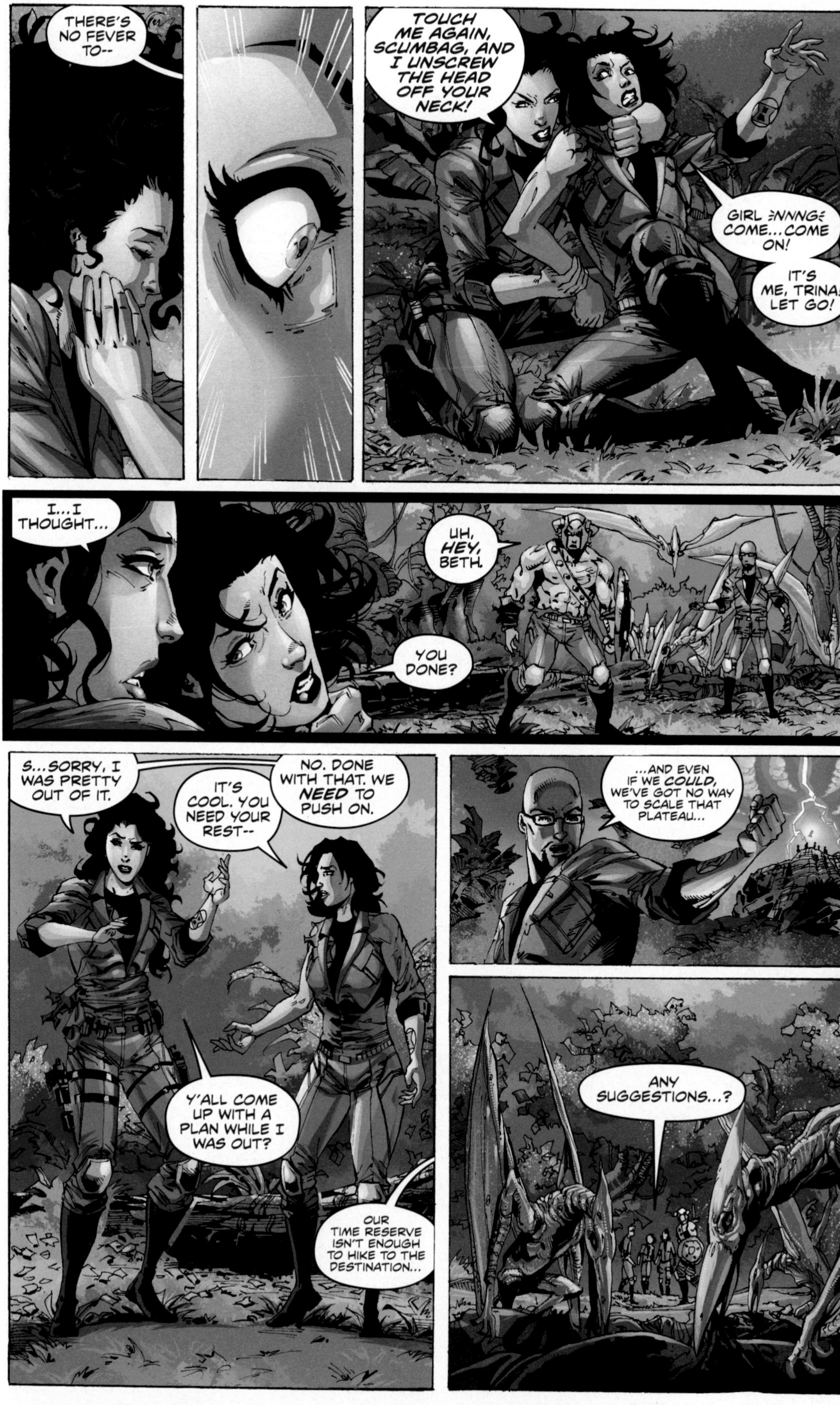
THERE'S NO FEVER TO--
TOUCH ME AGAIN, SCUMBAG, AND I UNSCREW THE HEAD OFF YOUR NECK!
GIRL =NNNG= COME...COME ON!
IT'S ME, TRINA! LET GO!
I...I THOUGHT...
UH, HEY, BETH.
YOU DONE?
S...SORRY, I WAS PRETTY OUT OF IT.
IT'S COOL. YOU NEED YOUR REST--
NO. DONE WITH THAT. WE NEED TO PUSH ON.
Y'ALL COME UP WITH A PLAN WHILE I WAS OUT?
OUR TIME RESERVE ISN'T ENOUGH TO HIKE TO THE DESTINATION...
...AND EVEN IF WE COULD, WE'VE GOT NO WAY TO SCALE THAT PLATEAU...
ANY SUGGESTIONS...?

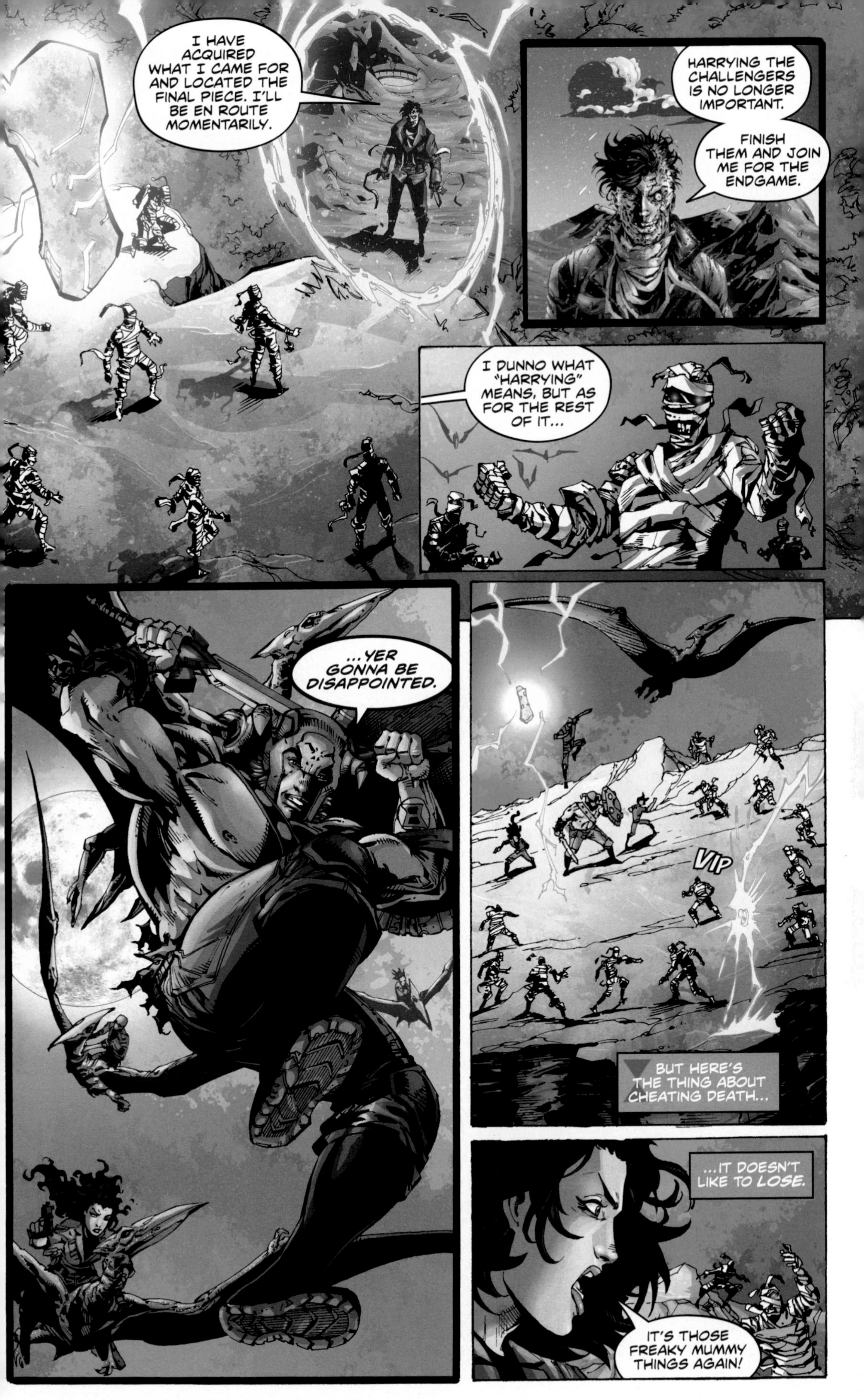
I HAVE ACQUIRED WHAT I CAME FOR AND LOCATED THE FINAL PIECE. I'LL BE EN ROUTE MOMENTARILY.
HARRYING THE CHALLENGERS IS NO LONGER IMPORTANT.
FINISH THEM AND JOIN ME FOR THE ENDGAME.
I DUNNO WHAT "HARRYING" MEANS, BUT AS FOR THE REST OF IT...
...YER GONNA BE DISAPPOINTED.
VIP
BUT HERE'S THE THING ABOUT CHEATING DEATH...
...IT DOESN'T LIKE TO *LOSE*.
IT'S THOSE FREAKY MUMMY THINGS AGAIN!

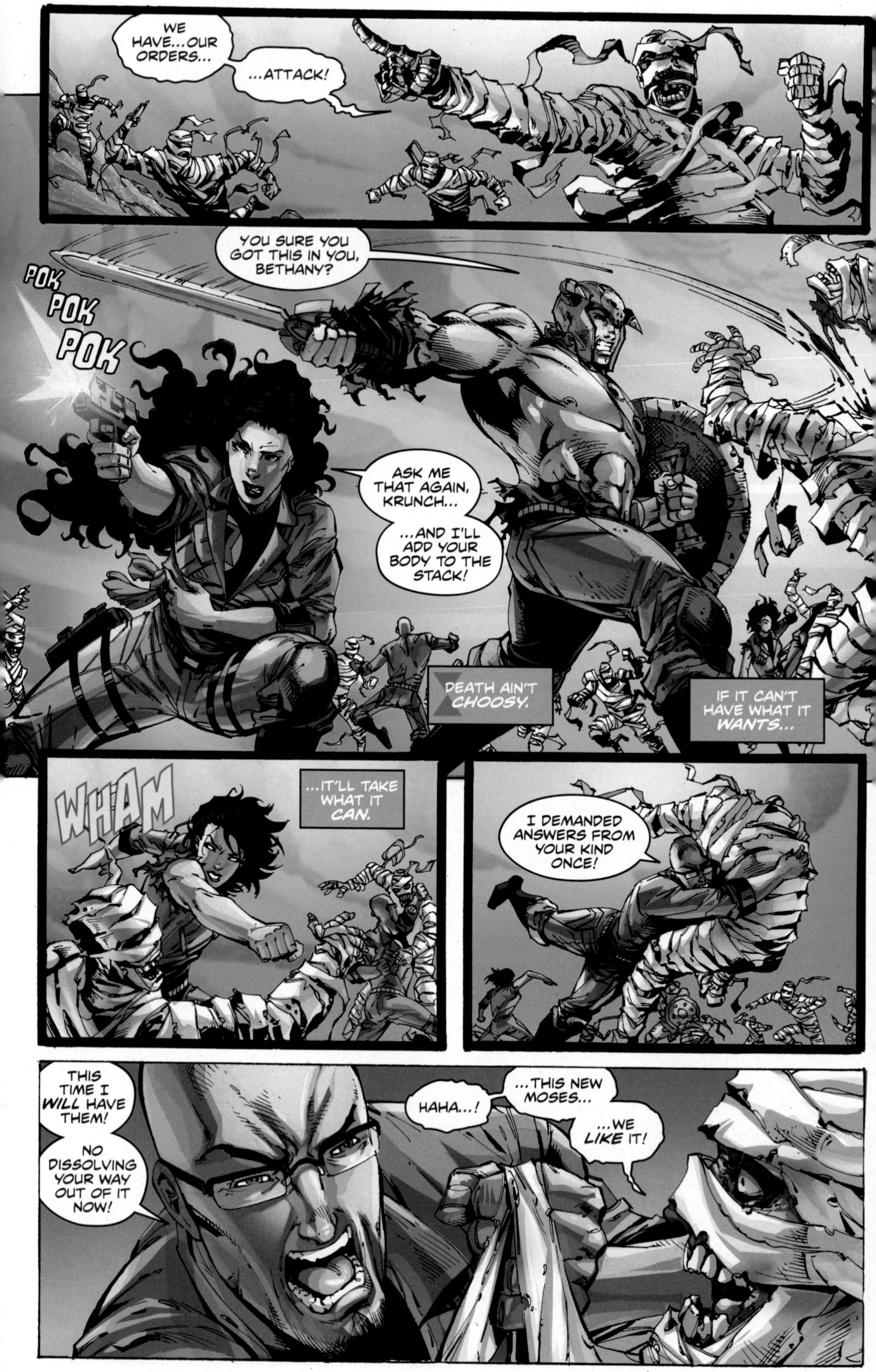
WE HAVE...OUR ORDERS...
...ATTACK!
YOU SURE YOU GOT THIS IN YOU, BETHANY?
POK
POK
POK
ASK ME THAT AGAIN, KRUNCH...
...AND I'LL ADD YOUR BODY TO THE STACK!
DEATH AIN'T CHOOSY.
IF IT CAN'T HAVE WHAT IT WANTS...
WHAM
...IT'LL TAKE WHAT IT CAN.
I DEMANDED ANSWERS FROM YOUR KIND ONCE!
THIS TIME I WILL HAVE THEM!
NO DISSOLVING YOUR WAY OUT OF IT NOW!
HAHA...!
...THIS NEW MOSES...
...WE LIKE IT!

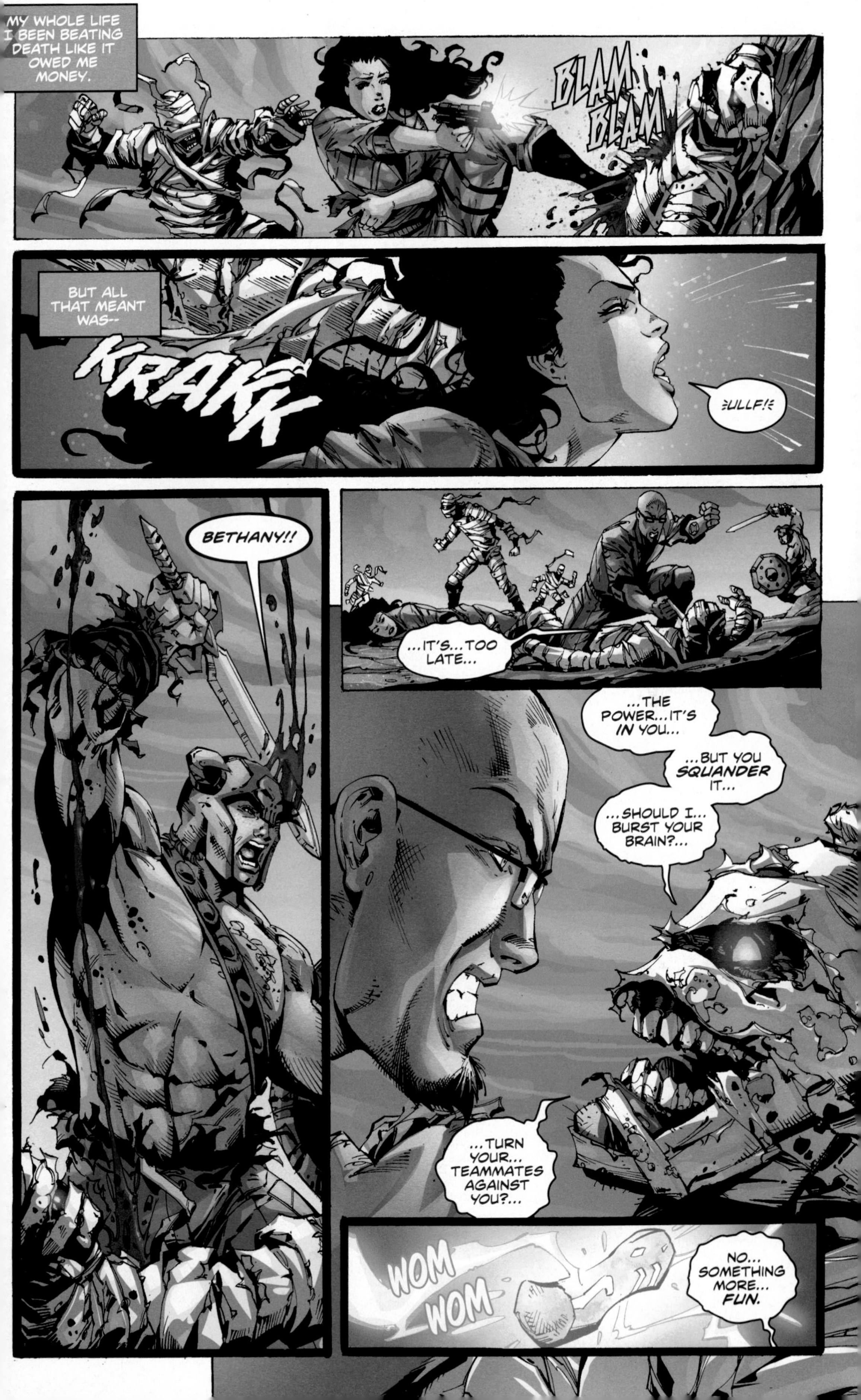
MY WHOLE LIFE I BEEN BEATING DEATH LIKE IT OWED ME MONEY.
BLAM BLAM
BUT ALL THAT MEANT WAS--
KRAKK
ULLF!
BETHANY!!
...IT'S...TOO LATE...
...THE POWER...IT'S IN YOU...
...BUT YOU SQUANDER IT...
...SHOULD I... BURST YOUR BRAIN?...
...TURN YOUR... TEAMMATES AGAINST YOU?...
WOM WOM
NO... SOMETHING MORE... FUN.

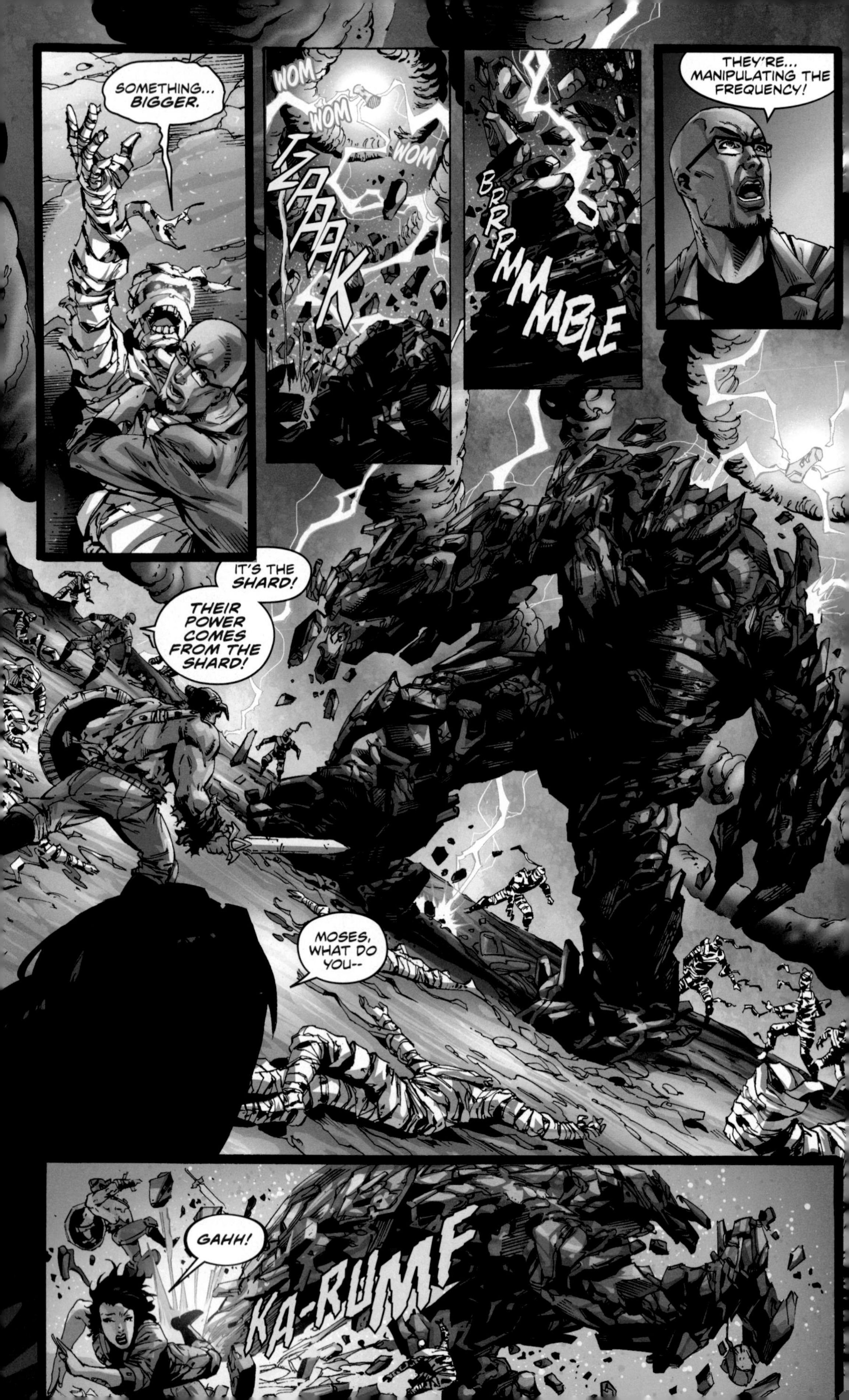
SOMETHING... BIGGER.
WOM
WOM
WOM
TZAAAK
BRRRMMMBLE
THEY'RE... MANIPULATING THE FREQUENCY!
IT'S THE SHARD!
THEIR POWER COMES FROM THE SHARD!
MOSES, WHAT DO YOU--
GAHH!
KA-RUMF

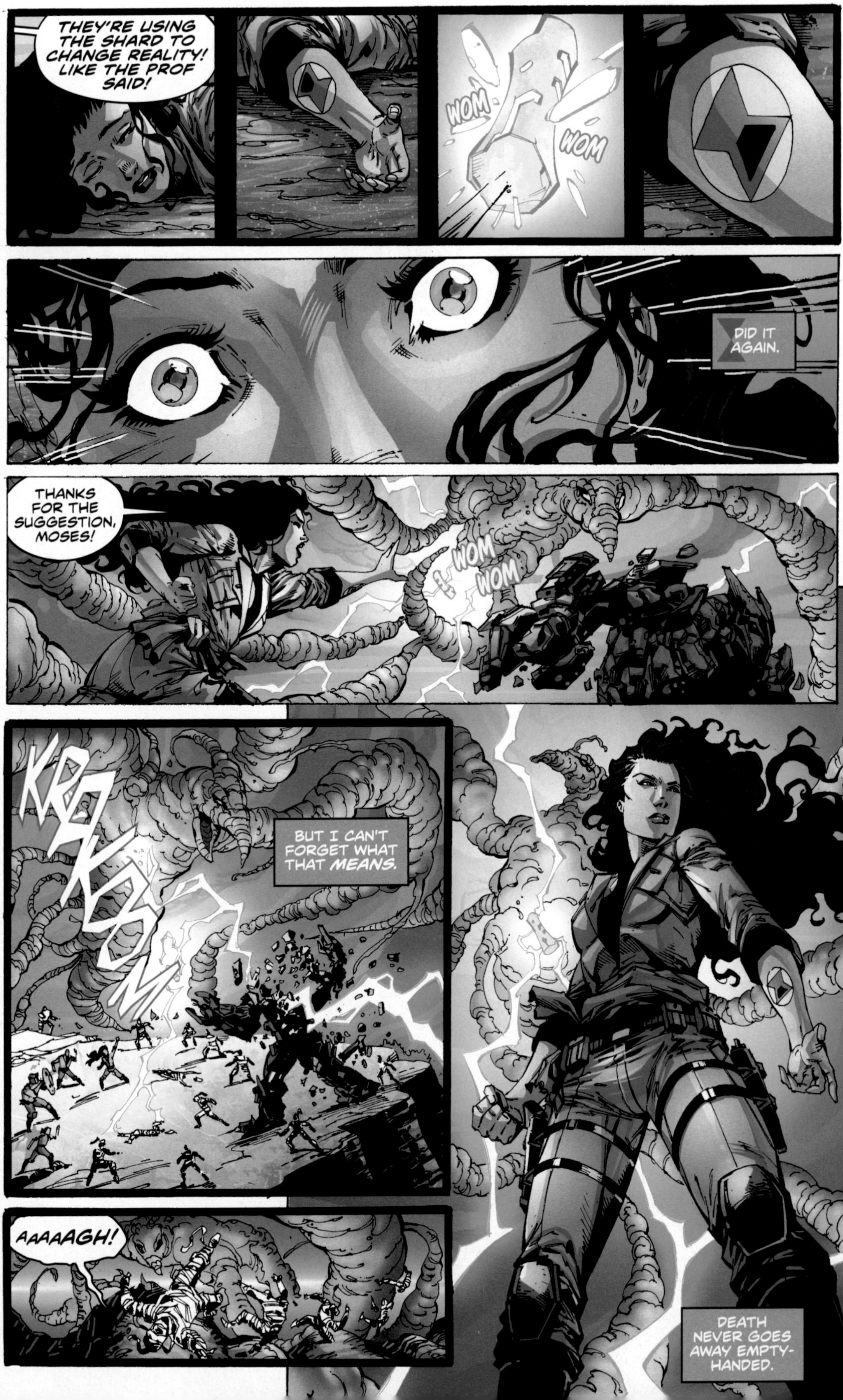
THEY'RE USING THE SHARD TO CHANGE REALITY! LIKE THE PROF SAID!
WOM
WOM
DID IT AGAIN.
THANKS FOR THE SUGGESTION, MOSES!
WOM
WOM
KRAKOOM
BUT I CAN'T FORGET WHAT THAT *MEANS.*
AAAAAGH!
DEATH NEVER GOES AWAY EMPTY-HANDED.

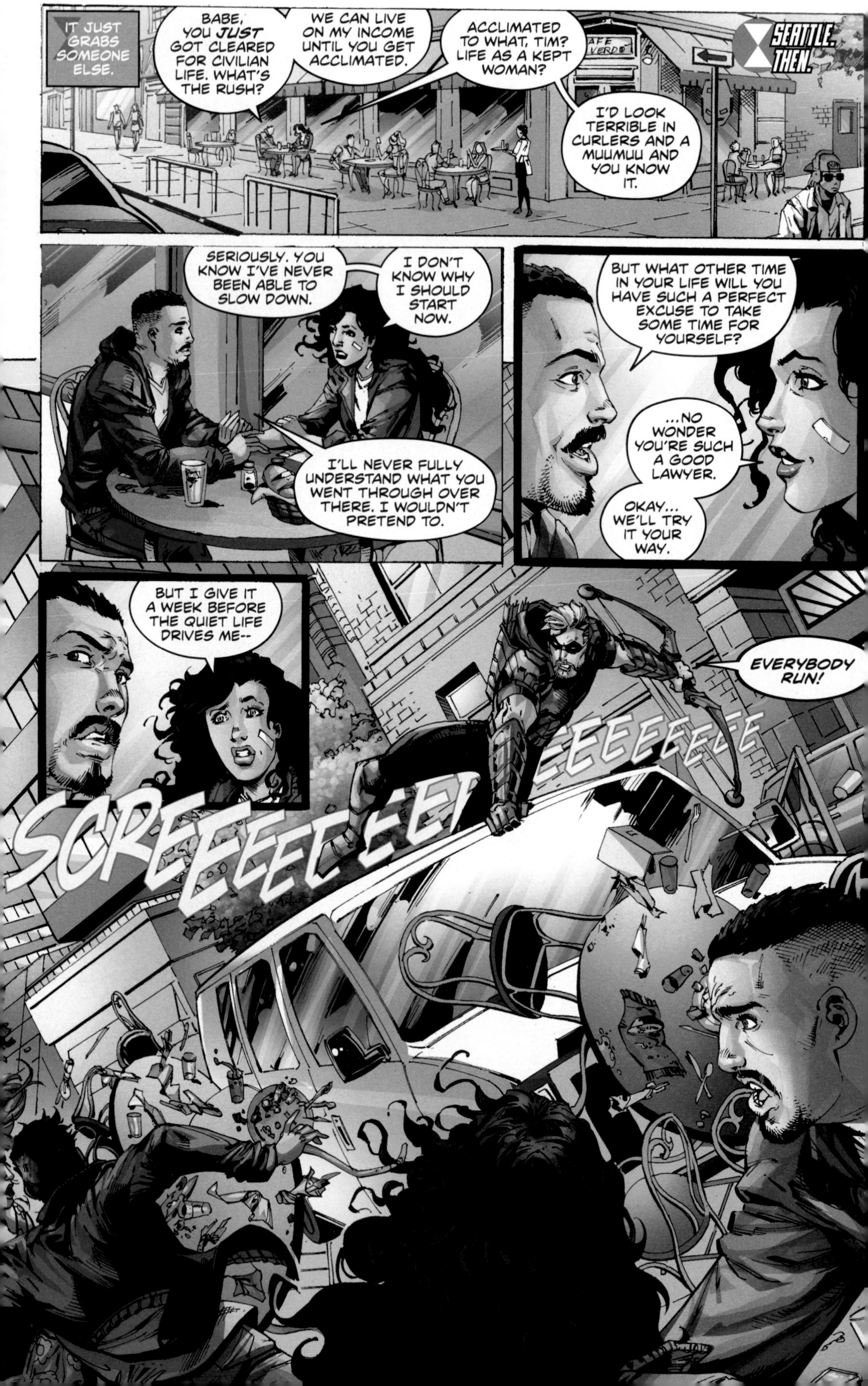
SEATTLE. THEN.
IT JUST GRABS SOMEONE ELSE.
BABE, YOU JUST GOT CLEARED FOR CIVILIAN LIFE. WHAT'S THE RUSH?
WE CAN LIVE ON MY INCOME UNTIL YOU GET ACCLIMATED.
ACCLIMATED TO WHAT, TIM? LIFE AS A KEPT WOMAN?
I'D LOOK TERRIBLE IN CURLERS AND A MUUMUU AND YOU KNOW IT.
SERIOUSLY. YOU KNOW I'VE NEVER BEEN ABLE TO SLOW DOWN.
I DON'T KNOW WHY I SHOULD START NOW.
I'LL NEVER FULLY UNDERSTAND WHAT YOU WENT THROUGH OVER THERE. I WOULDN'T PRETEND TO.
BUT WHAT OTHER TIME IN YOUR LIFE WILL YOU HAVE SUCH A PERFECT EXCUSE TO TAKE SOME TIME FOR YOURSELF?
...NO WONDER YOU'RE SUCH A GOOD LAWYER.
OKAY... WE'LL TRY IT YOUR WAY.
BUT I GIVE IT A WEEK BEFORE THE QUIET LIFE DRIVES ME--
EVERYBODY RUN!
SCREEEEEEEEEEEEEEEE

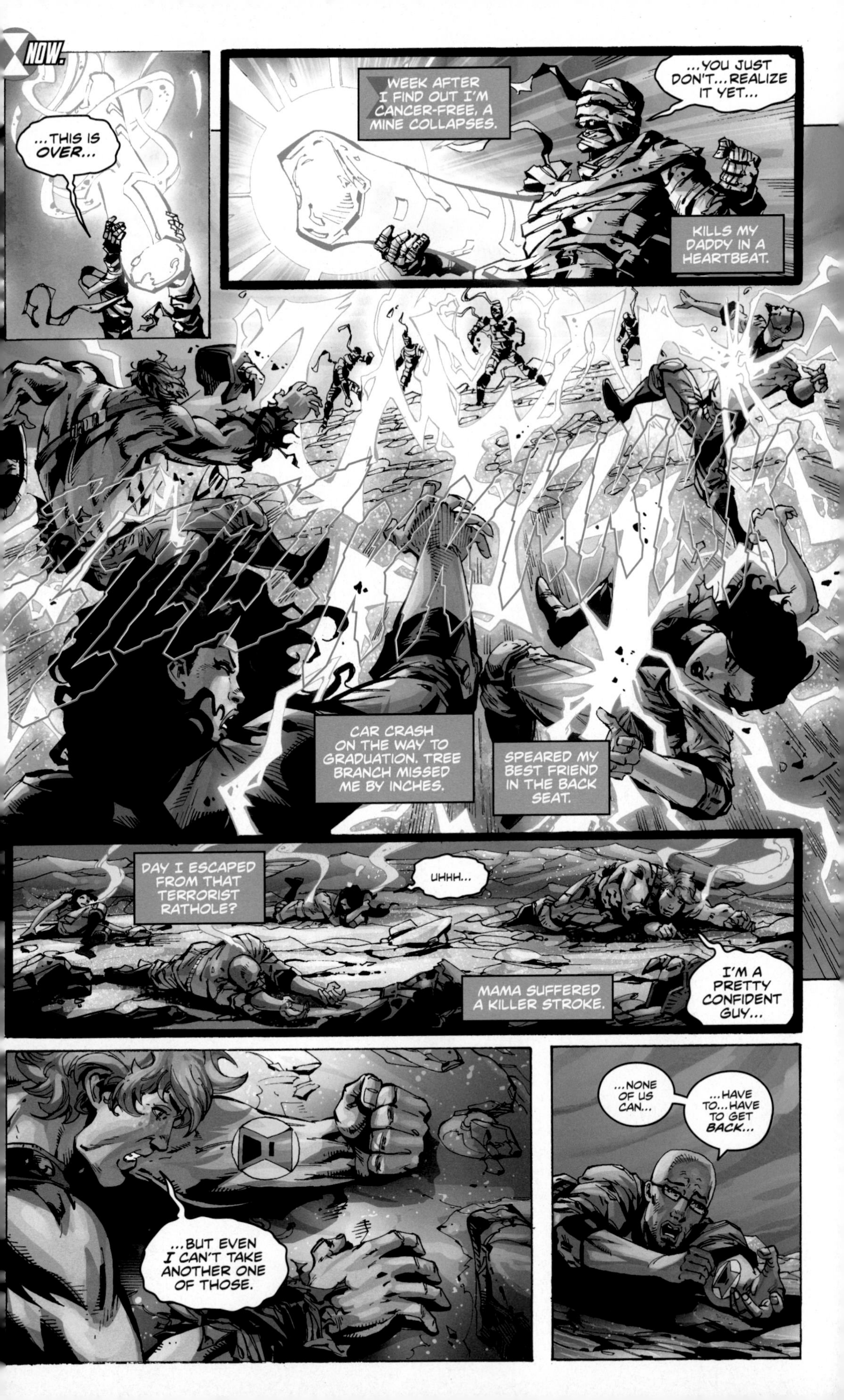
NOW.
...THIS IS OVER...
WEEK AFTER I FIND OUT I'M CANCER-FREE, A MINE COLLAPSES.
...YOU JUST DON'T...REALIZE IT YET...
KILLS MY DADDY IN A HEARTBEAT.
CAR CRASH ON THE WAY TO GRADUATION. TREE BRANCH MISSED ME BY INCHES.
SPEARED MY BEST FRIEND IN THE BACK SEAT.
DAY I ESCAPED FROM THAT TERRORIST RATHOLE?
UHHH...
MAMA SUFFERED A KILLER STROKE.
I'M A PRETTY CONFIDENT GUY...
...BUT EVEN I CAN'T TAKE ANOTHER ONE OF THOSE.
...NONE OF US CAN...
...HAVE TO...HAVE TO GET BACK...

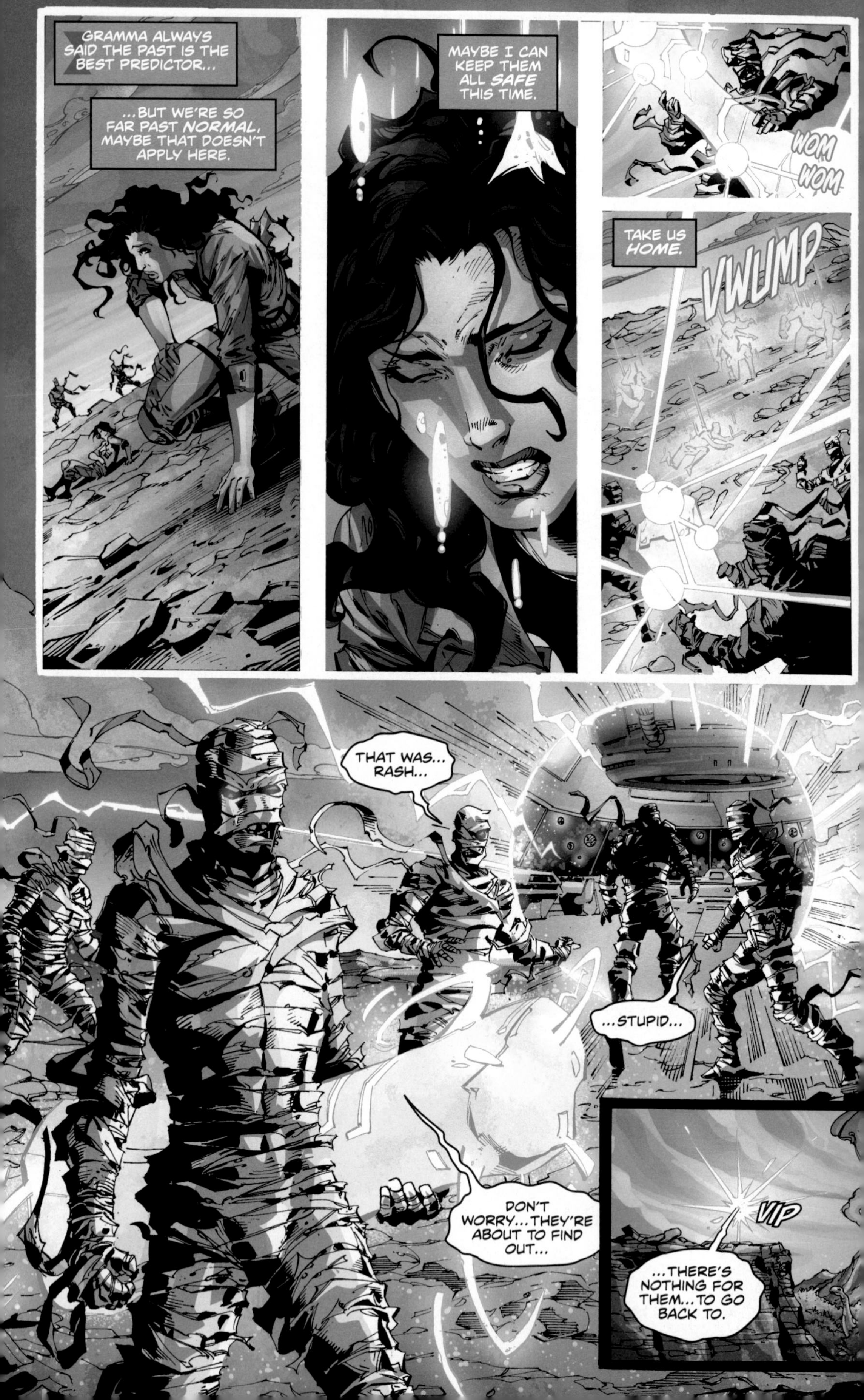
GRAMMA ALWAYS SAID THE PAST IS THE BEST PREDICTOR...
...BUT WE'RE SO FAR PAST NORMAL, MAYBE THAT DOESN'T APPLY HERE.
MAYBE I CAN KEEP THEM ALL SAFE THIS TIME.
WOM WOM
TAKE US HOME.
VWUMP
THAT WAS... RASH...
...STUPID...
DON'T WORRY...THEY'RE ABOUT TO FIND OUT...
VIP
...THERE'S NOTHING FOR THEM...TO GO BACK TO.

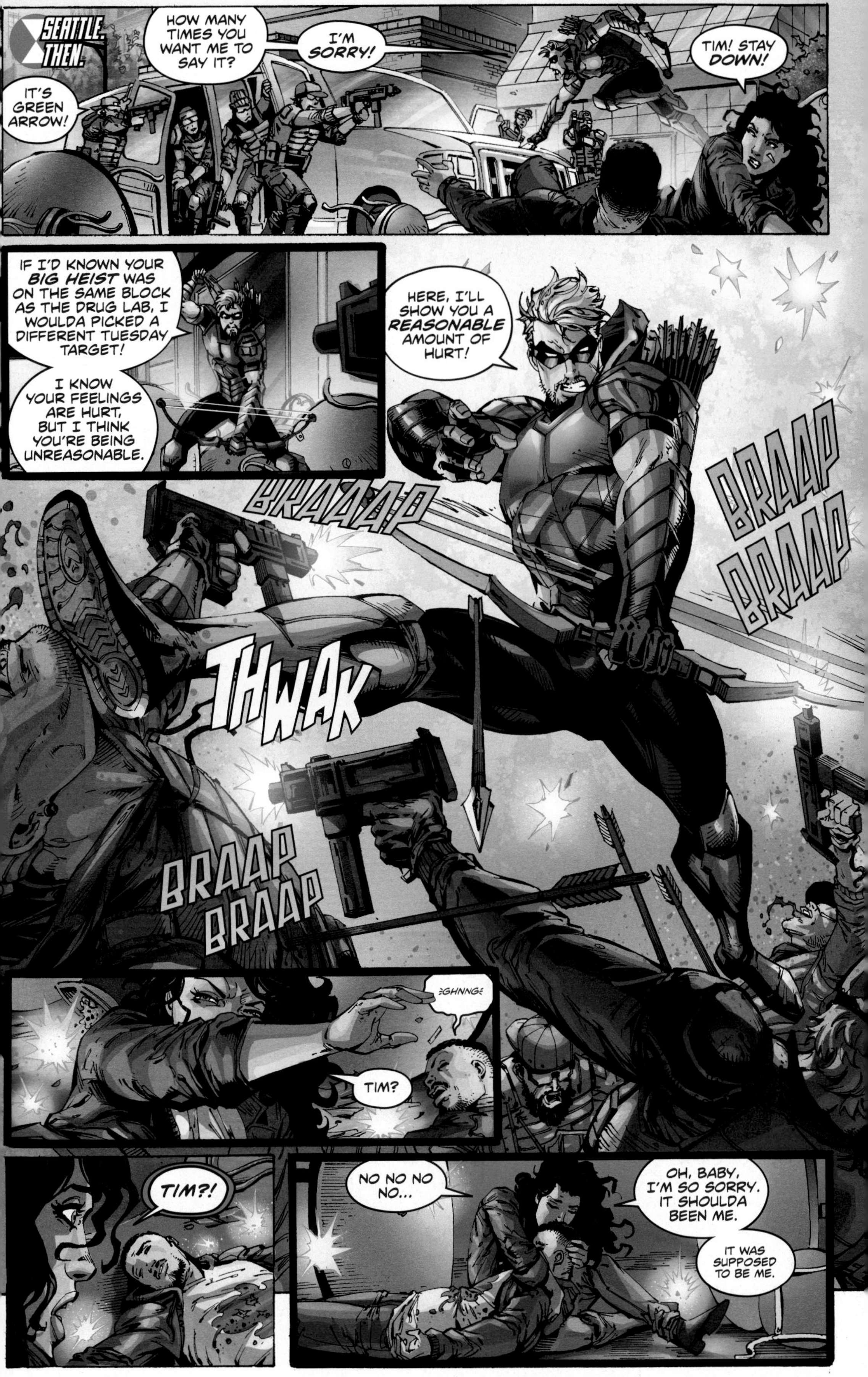
SEATTLE. THEN.
HOW MANY TIMES YOU WANT ME TO SAY IT?
I'M SORRY!
IT'S GREEN ARROW!
TIM! STAY DOWN!
IF I'D KNOWN YOUR BIG HEIST WAS ON THE SAME BLOCK AS THE DRUG LAB, I WOULDA PICKED A DIFFERENT TUESDAY TARGET!
I KNOW YOUR FEELINGS ARE HURT, BUT I THINK YOU'RE BEING UNREASONABLE.
HERE, I'LL SHOW YOU A REASONABLE AMOUNT OF HURT!
BRAAAP
BRAAP BRAAP
THWAK
BRAAP BRAAP
GHNNG
TIM?
TIM?!
NO NO NO NO...
OH, BABY, I'M SO SORRY. IT SHOULDA BEEN ME.
IT WAS SUPPOSED TO BE ME.

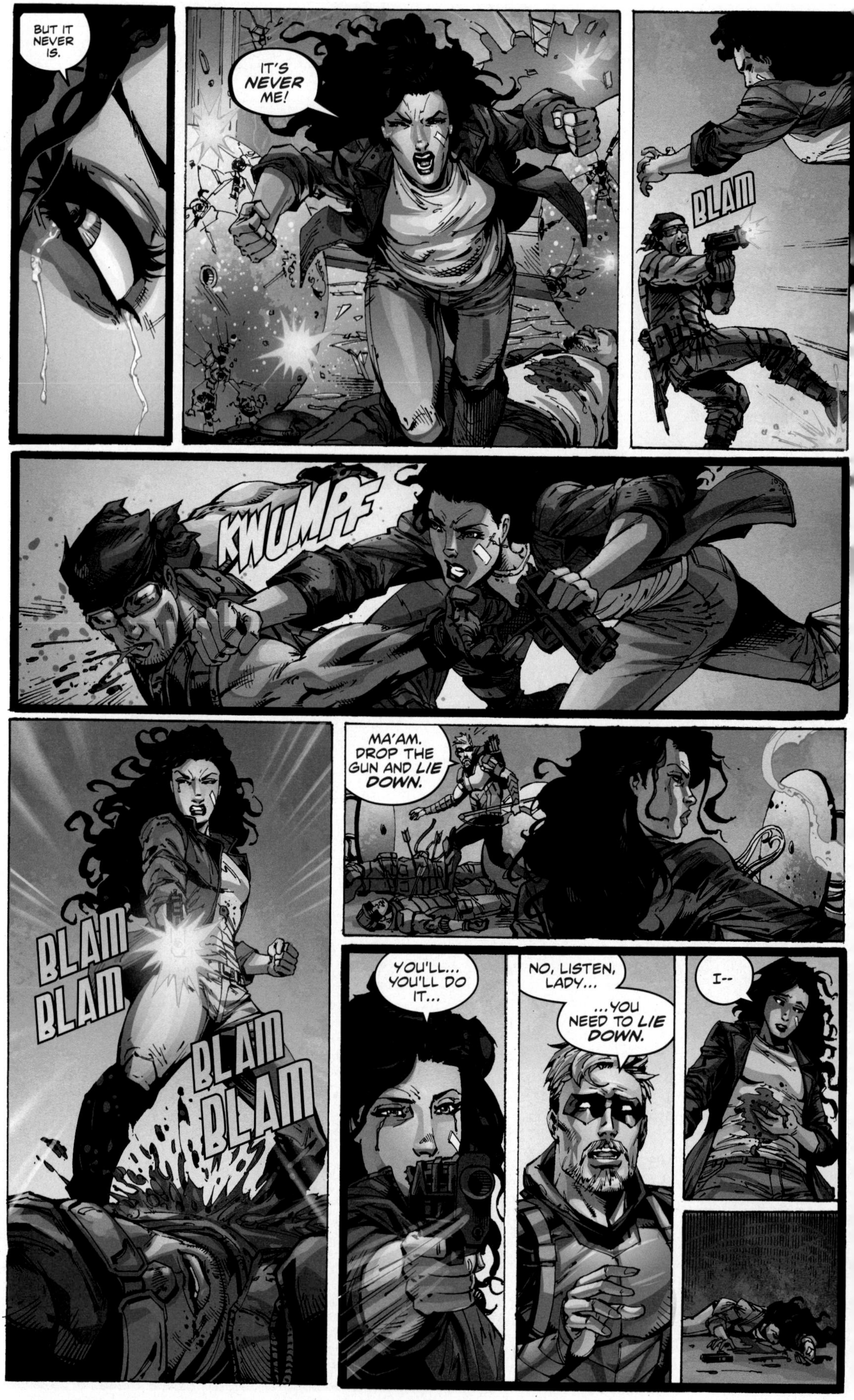

BUT IT NEVER IS.
IT'S NEVER ME!
BLAM
KWUMPF
BLAM BLAM
BLAM BLAM
MA'AM. DROP THE GUN AND LIE DOWN.
YOU'LL... YOU'LL DO IT...
NO, LISTEN, LADY...
...YOU NEED TO LIE DOWN.
I--

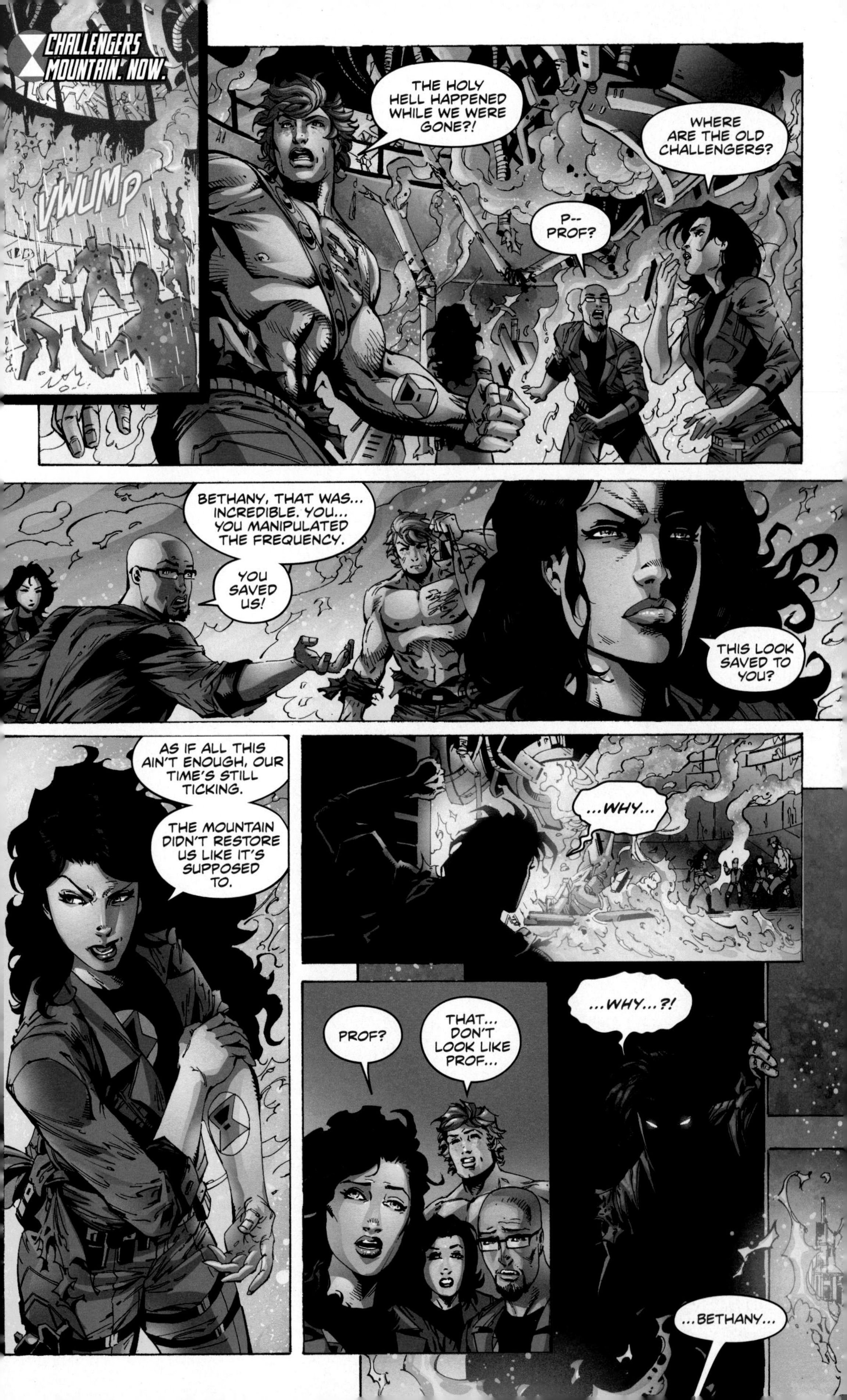
CHALLENGERS MOUNTAIN: NOW.
VWUMP
THE HOLY HELL HAPPENED WHILE WE WERE GONE?!
WHERE ARE THE OLD CHALLENGERS?
P-- PROF?
BETHANY, THAT WAS... INCREDIBLE. YOU... YOU MANIPULATED THE FREQUENCY.
YOU SAVED US!
THIS LOOK SAVED TO YOU?
AS IF ALL THIS AIN'T ENOUGH, OUR TIME'S STILL TICKING.
THE MOUNTAIN DIDN'T RESTORE US LIKE IT'S SUPPOSED TO.
...WHY...
PROF?
THAT... DON'T LOOK LIKE PROF...
...WHY...?!
...BETHANY...

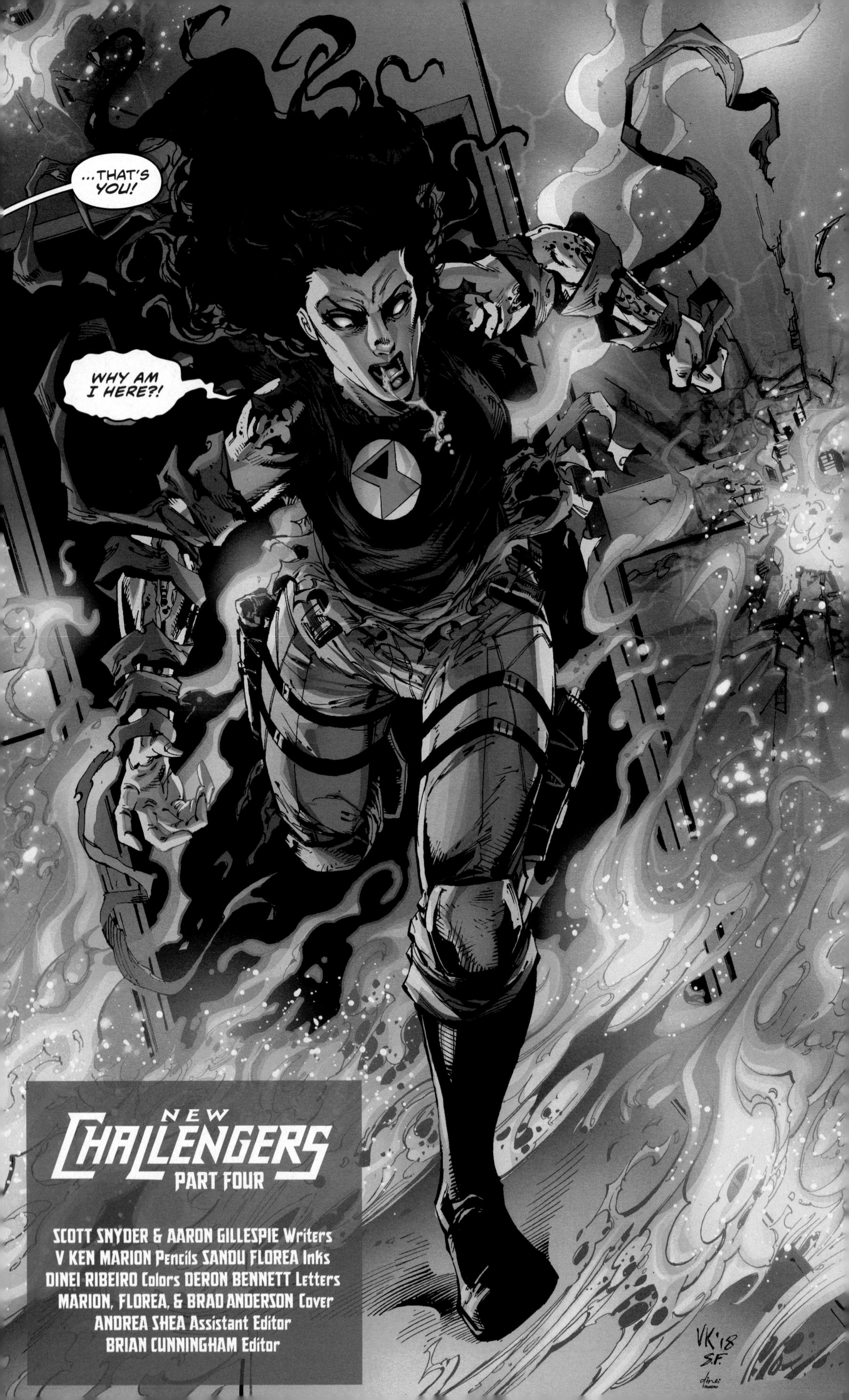
...THAT'S YOU!
WHY AM I HERE?!
NEW CHALLENGERS
PART FOUR
SCOTT SNYDER & AARON GILLESPIE Writers
V KEN MARION Pencils SANDU FLOREA Inks
DINEI RIBEIRO Colors DERON BENNETT Letters
MARION, FLOREA, & BRAD ANDERSON Cover
ANDREA SHEA Assistant Editor
BRIAN CUNNINGHAM Editor
VK'18
S.F.

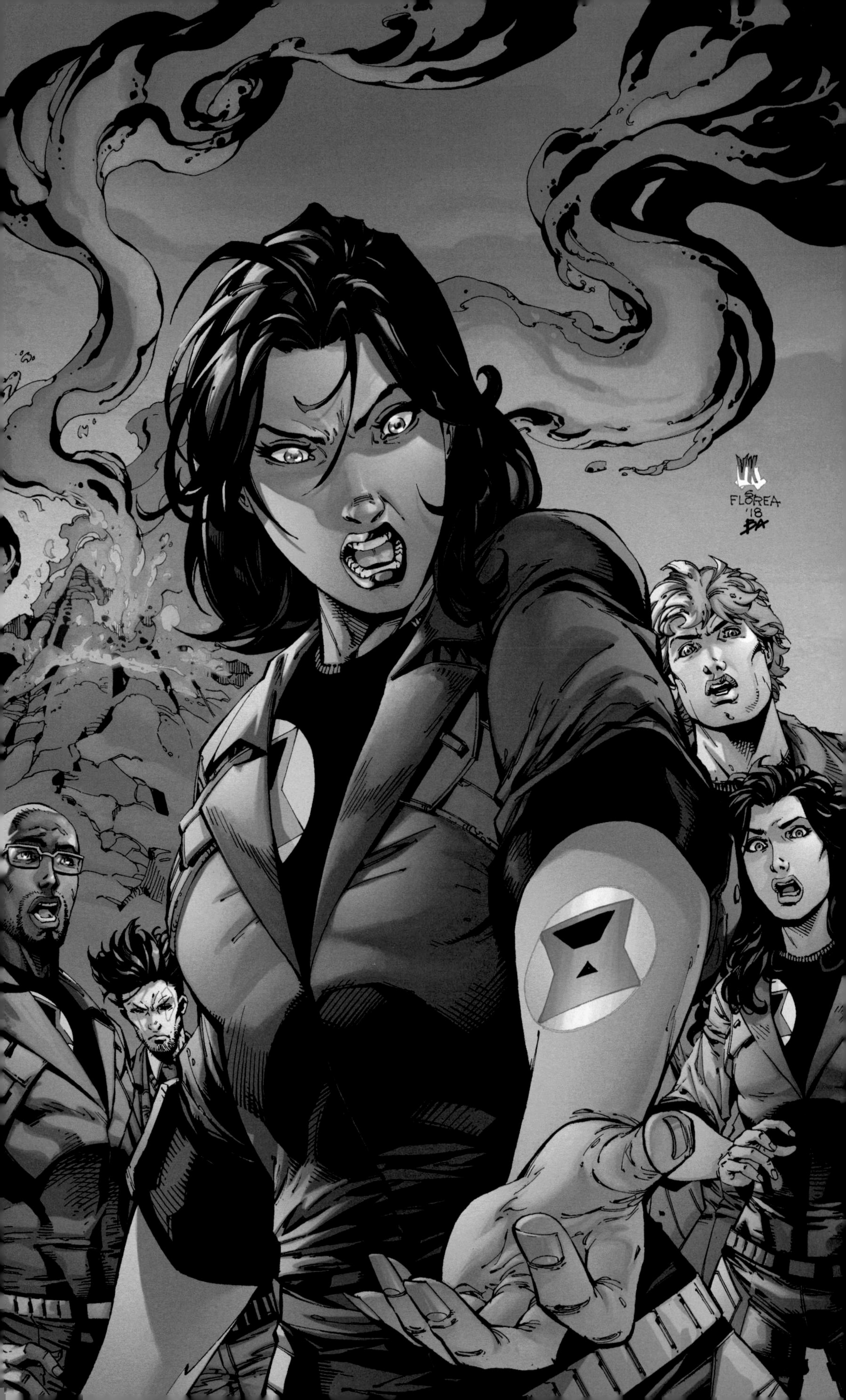
FLOREA
'18

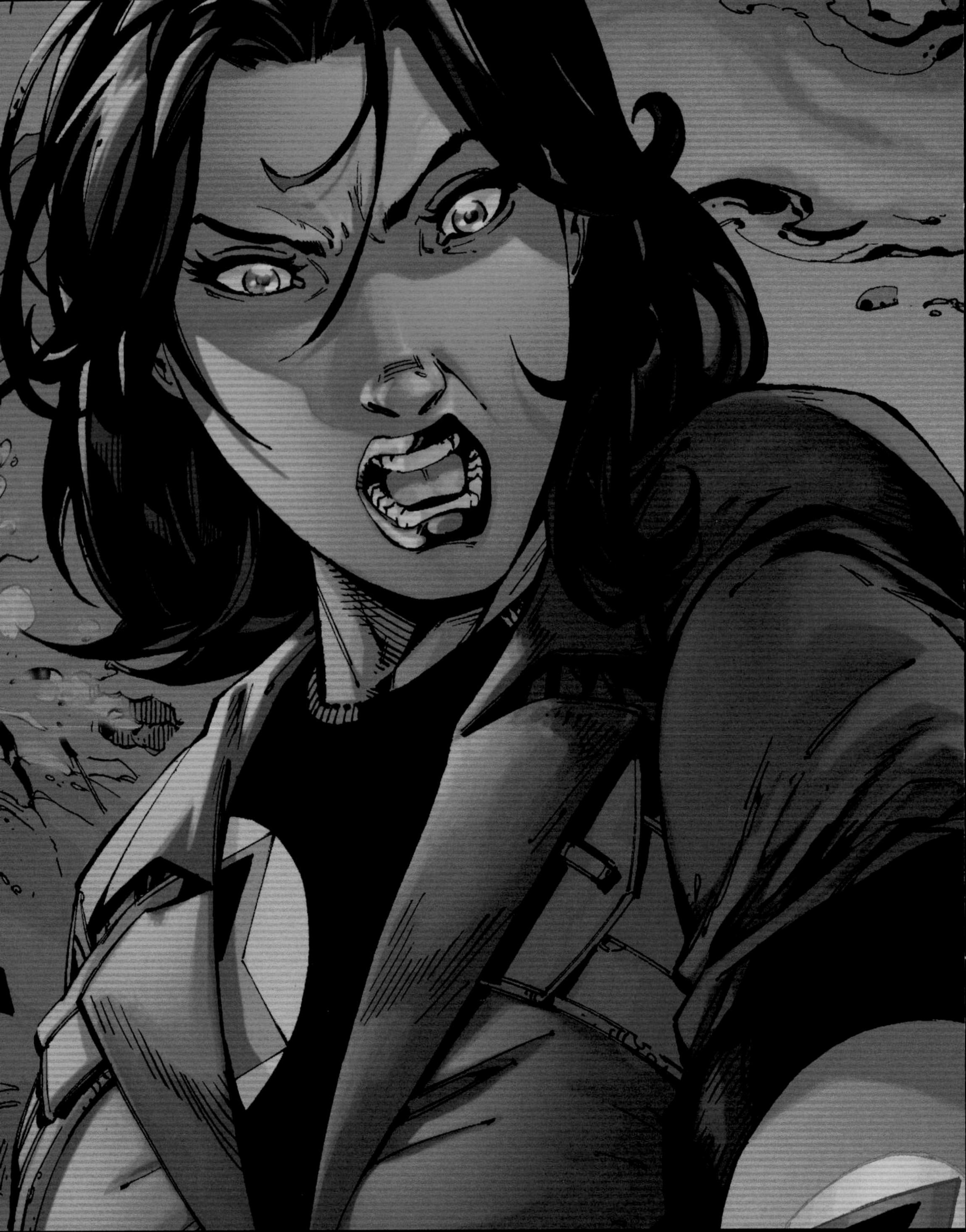

NEW CHALLENGERS
#5

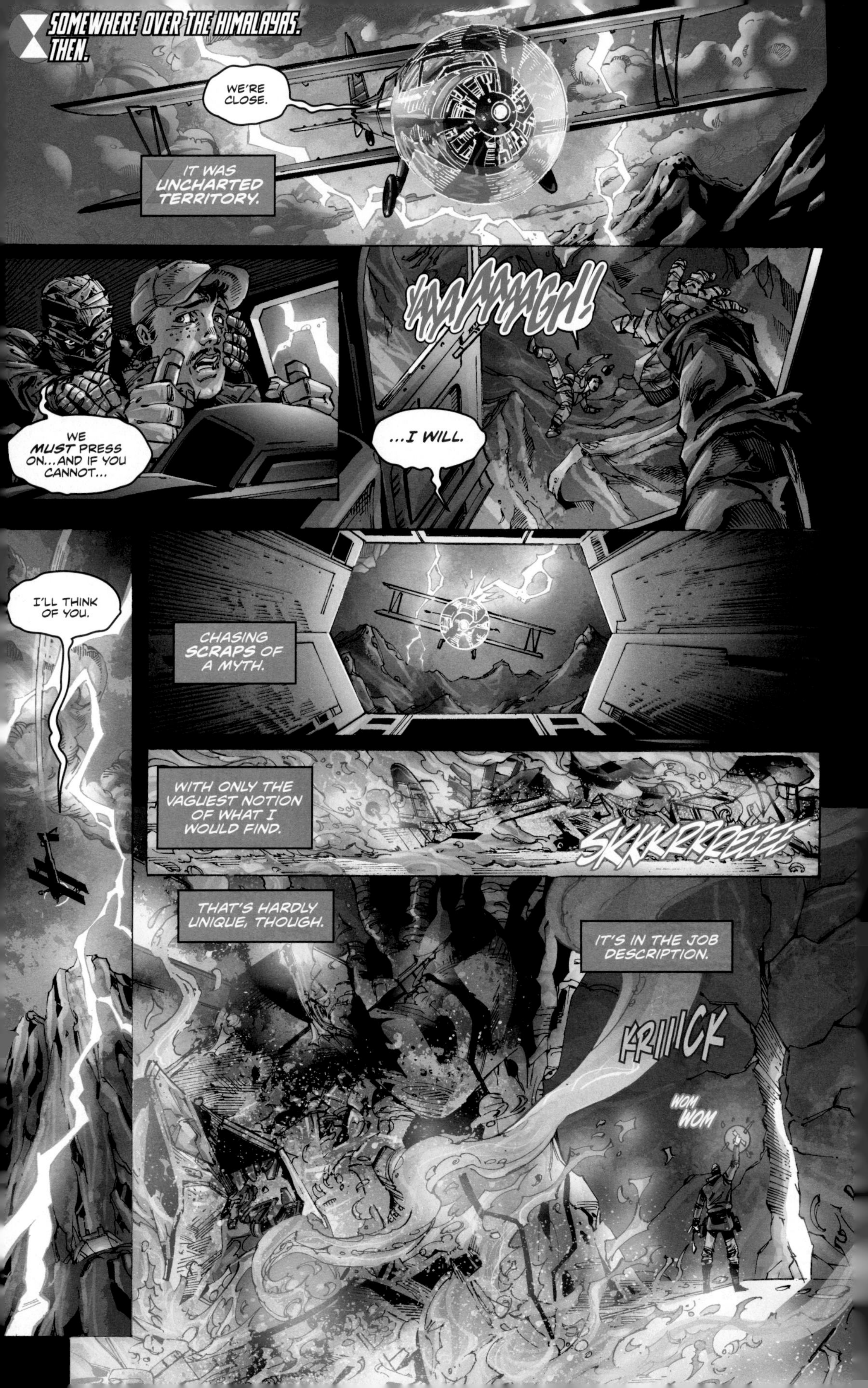
SOMEWHERE OVER THE HIMALAYAS. THEN.
WE'RE CLOSE.
IT WAS UNCHARTED TERRITORY.
WE MUST PRESS ON...AND IF YOU CANNOT...
YAAAAAAAGH!
...I WILL.
I'LL THINK OF YOU.
CHASING SCRAPS OF A MYTH.
WITH ONLY THE VAGUEST NOTION OF WHAT I WOULD FIND.
SKKKRRREEEE
THAT'S HARDLY UNIQUE, THOUGH.
IT'S IN THE JOB DESCRIPTION.
KRIIICK
WOM WOM

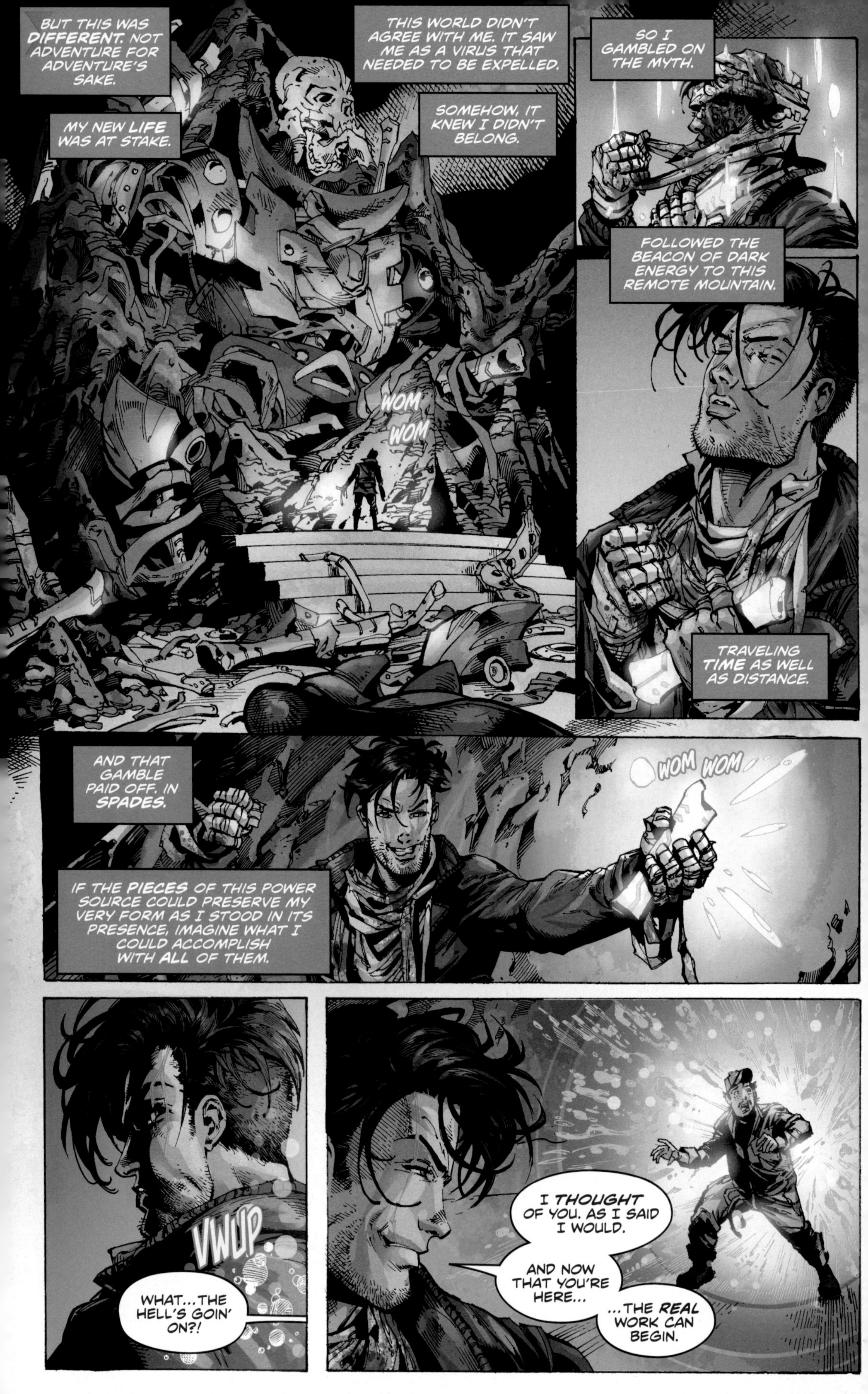
BUT THIS WAS DIFFERENT. NOT ADVENTURE FOR ADVENTURE'S SAKE.
MY NEW LIFE WAS AT STAKE.
THIS WORLD DIDN'T AGREE WITH ME. IT SAW ME AS A VIRUS THAT NEEDED TO BE EXPELLED.
SOMEHOW, IT KNEW I DIDN'T BELONG.
WOM
WOM
SO I GAMBLED ON THE MYTH.
FOLLOWED THE BEACON OF DARK ENERGY TO THIS REMOTE MOUNTAIN.
TRAVELING TIME AS WELL AS DISTANCE.
AND THAT GAMBLE PAID OFF. IN SPADES.
WOM WOM
IF THE PIECES OF THIS POWER SOURCE COULD PRESERVE MY VERY FORM AS I STOOD IN ITS PRESENCE, IMAGINE WHAT I COULD ACCOMPLISH WITH ALL OF THEM.
VWUP
WHAT...THE HELL'S GOIN' ON?!
I THOUGHT OF YOU. AS I SAID I WOULD.
AND NOW THAT YOU'RE HERE...
...THE REAL WORK CAN BEGIN.

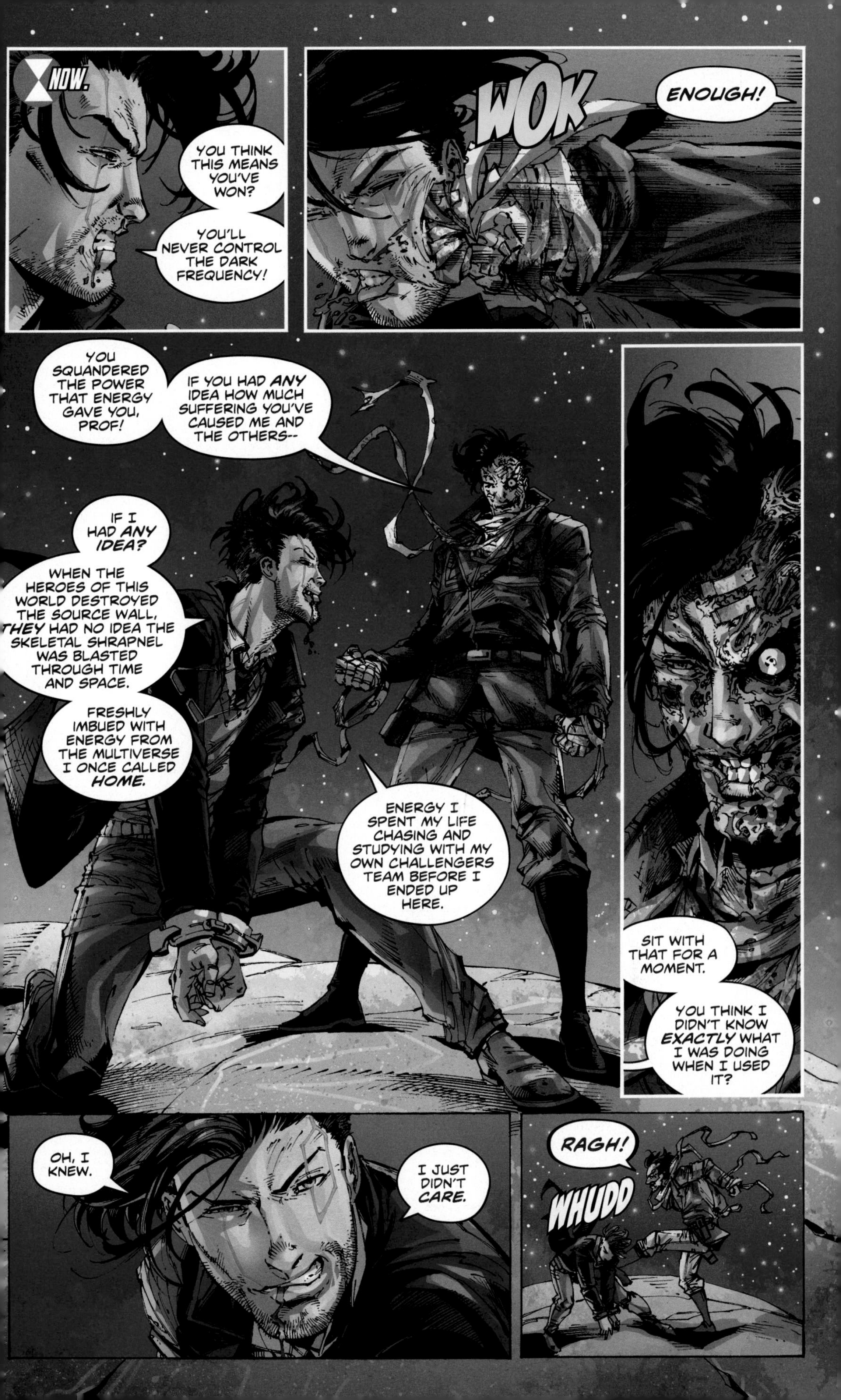
NOW.
YOU THINK THIS MEANS YOU'VE WON?
YOU'LL NEVER CONTROL THE DARK FREQUENCY!
WOK
ENOUGH!
YOU SQUANDERED THE POWER THAT ENERGY GAVE YOU, PROF!
IF YOU HAD ANY IDEA HOW MUCH SUFFERING YOU'VE CAUSED ME AND THE OTHERS--
IF I HAD ANY IDEA?
WHEN THE HEROES OF THIS WORLD DESTROYED THE SOURCE WALL, THEY HAD NO IDEA THE SKELETAL SHRAPNEL WAS BLASTED THROUGH TIME AND SPACE.
FRESHLY IMBUED WITH ENERGY FROM THE MULTIVERSE I ONCE CALLED HOME.
ENERGY I SPENT MY LIFE CHASING AND STUDYING WITH MY OWN CHALLENGERS TEAM BEFORE I ENDED UP HERE.
SIT WITH THAT FOR A MOMENT.
YOU THINK I DIDN'T KNOW EXACTLY WHAT I WAS DOING WHEN I USED IT?
OH, I KNEW.
I JUST DIDN'T CARE.
RAGH!
WHUDD

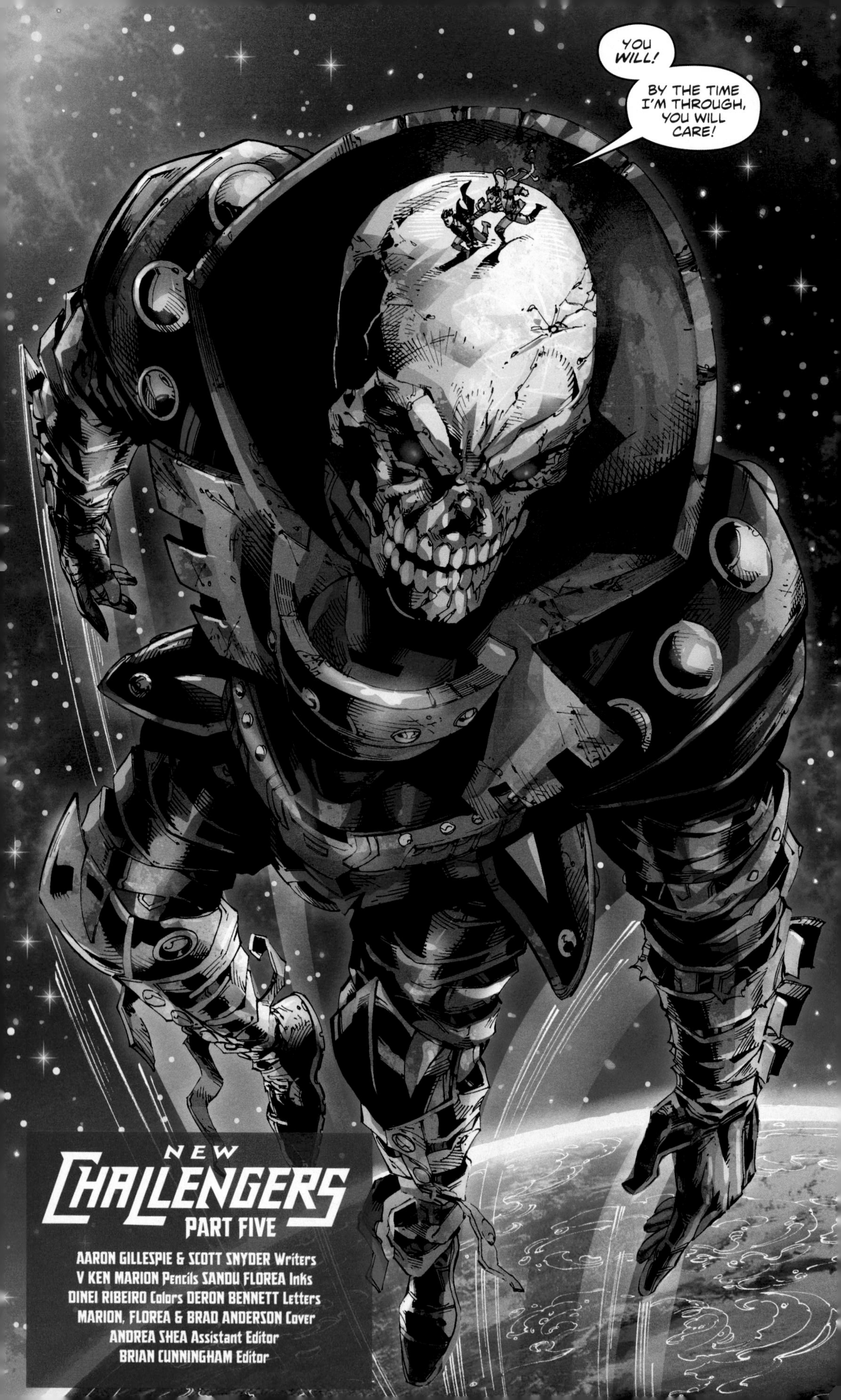
YOU WILL!
BY THE TIME I'M THROUGH, YOU WILL CARE!
NEW CHALLENGERS
PART FIVE
AARON GILLESPIE & SCOTT SNYDER Writers
V KEN MARION Pencils SANDU FLOREA Inks
DINEI RIBEIRO Colors DERON BENNETT Letters
MARION, FLOREA & BRAD ANDERSON Cover
ANDREA SHEA Assistant Editor
BRIAN CUNNINGHAM Editor

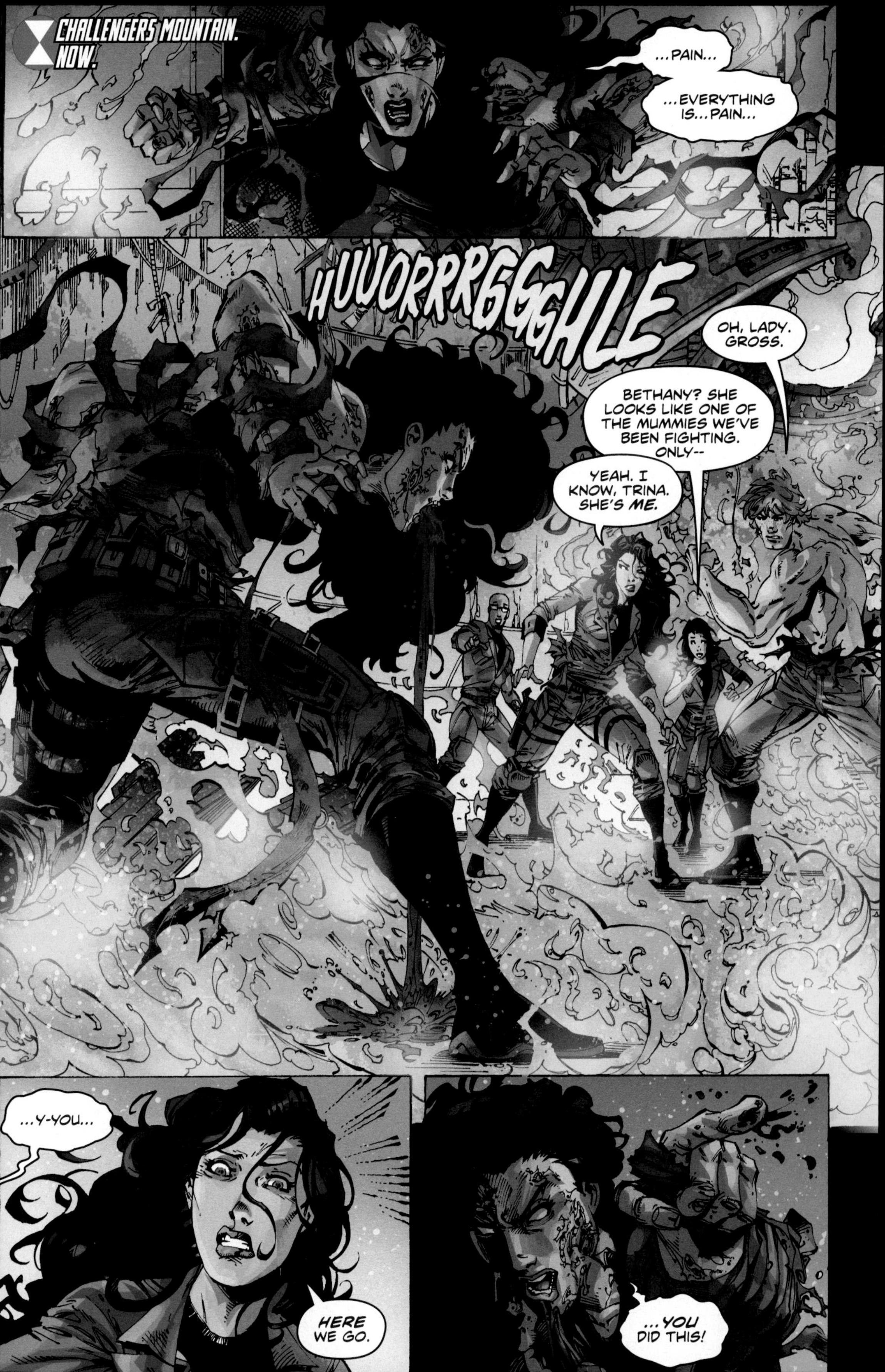
CHALLENGERS MOUNTAIN. NOW.
...PAIN...
...EVERYTHING IS...PAIN...
HUUORRRGGGHLE
OH, LADY. GROSS.
BETHANY? SHE LOOKS LIKE ONE OF THE MUMMIES WE'VE BEEN FIGHTING. ONLY--
YEAH. I KNOW, TRINA. SHE'S ME.
...Y-YOU...
HERE WE GO.
...YOU DID THIS!

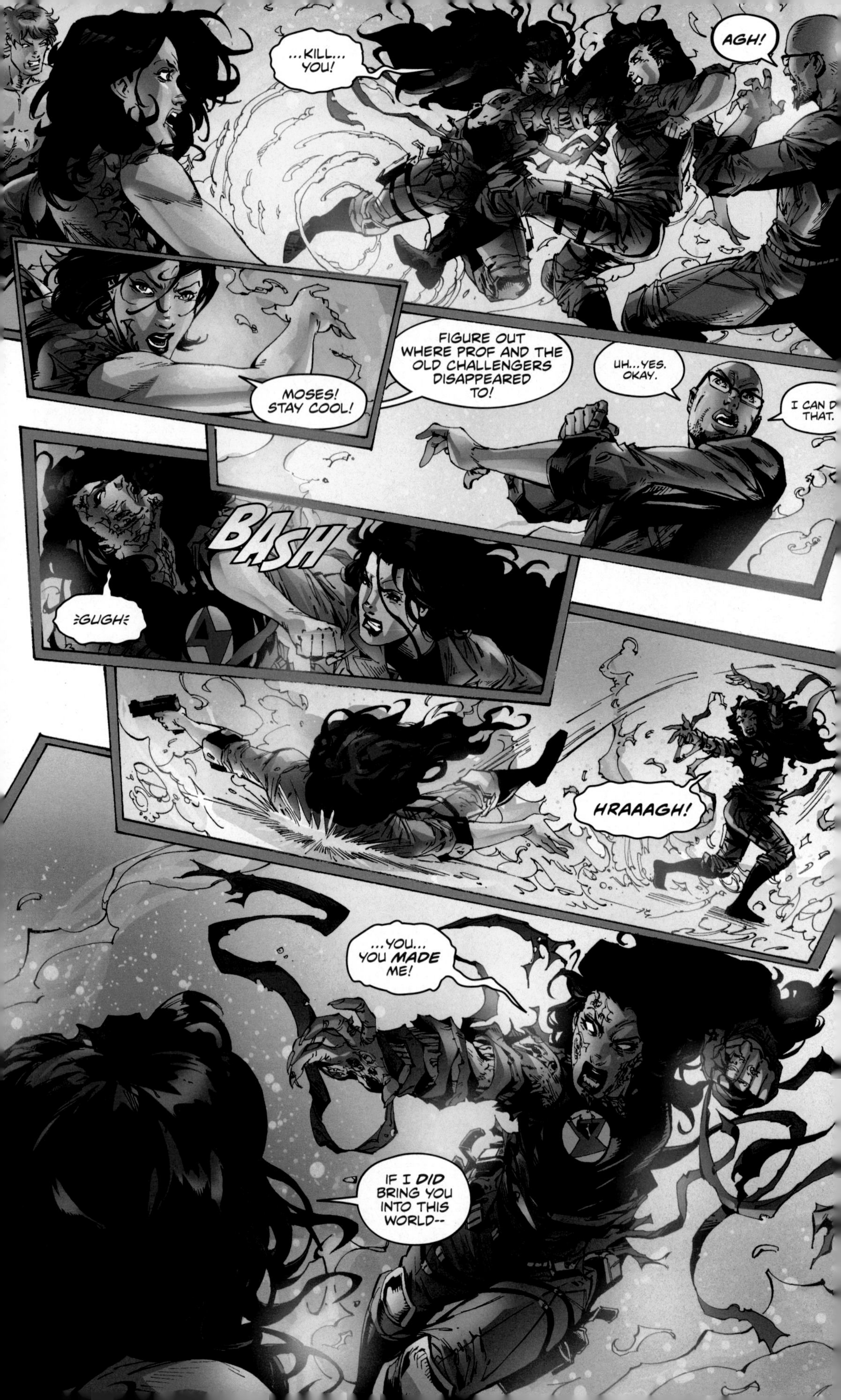

...KILL... YOU!
AGH!
MOSES! STAY COOL!
FIGURE OUT WHERE PROF AND THE OLD CHALLENGERS DISAPPEARED TO!
UH...YES. OKAY.
I CAN D THAT.
BASH
GUGH
HRAAAGH!
...YOU... YOU MADE ME!
IF I DID BRING YOU INTO THIS WORLD--

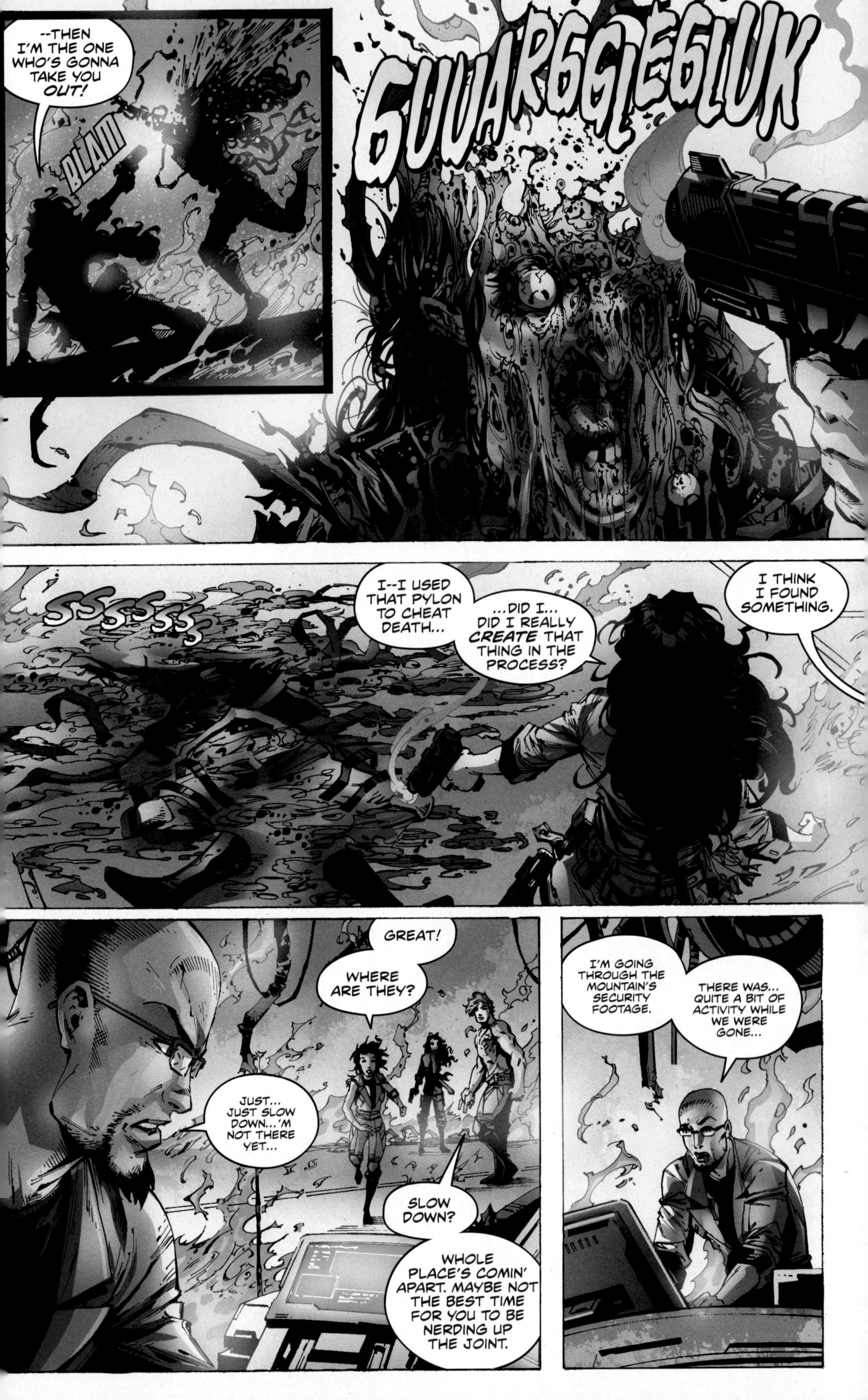
--THEN I'M THE ONE WHO'S GONNA TAKE YOU *OUT!*
BLAM
GUUARGGLEGLUK
SSSSSS
I--I USED THAT PYLON TO CHEAT DEATH...
...DID I... DID I REALLY *CREATE* THAT THING IN THE PROCESS?
I THINK I FOUND SOMETHING.
GREAT!
WHERE ARE THEY?
JUST... JUST SLOW DOWN...'M NOT THERE YET...
SLOW DOWN?
WHOLE PLACE'S COMIN' APART. MAYBE NOT THE BEST TIME FOR YOU TO BE NERDING UP THE JOINT.
I'M GOING THROUGH THE MOUNTAIN'S SECURITY FOOTAGE.
THERE WAS... QUITE A BIT OF ACTIVITY WHILE WE WERE GONE...

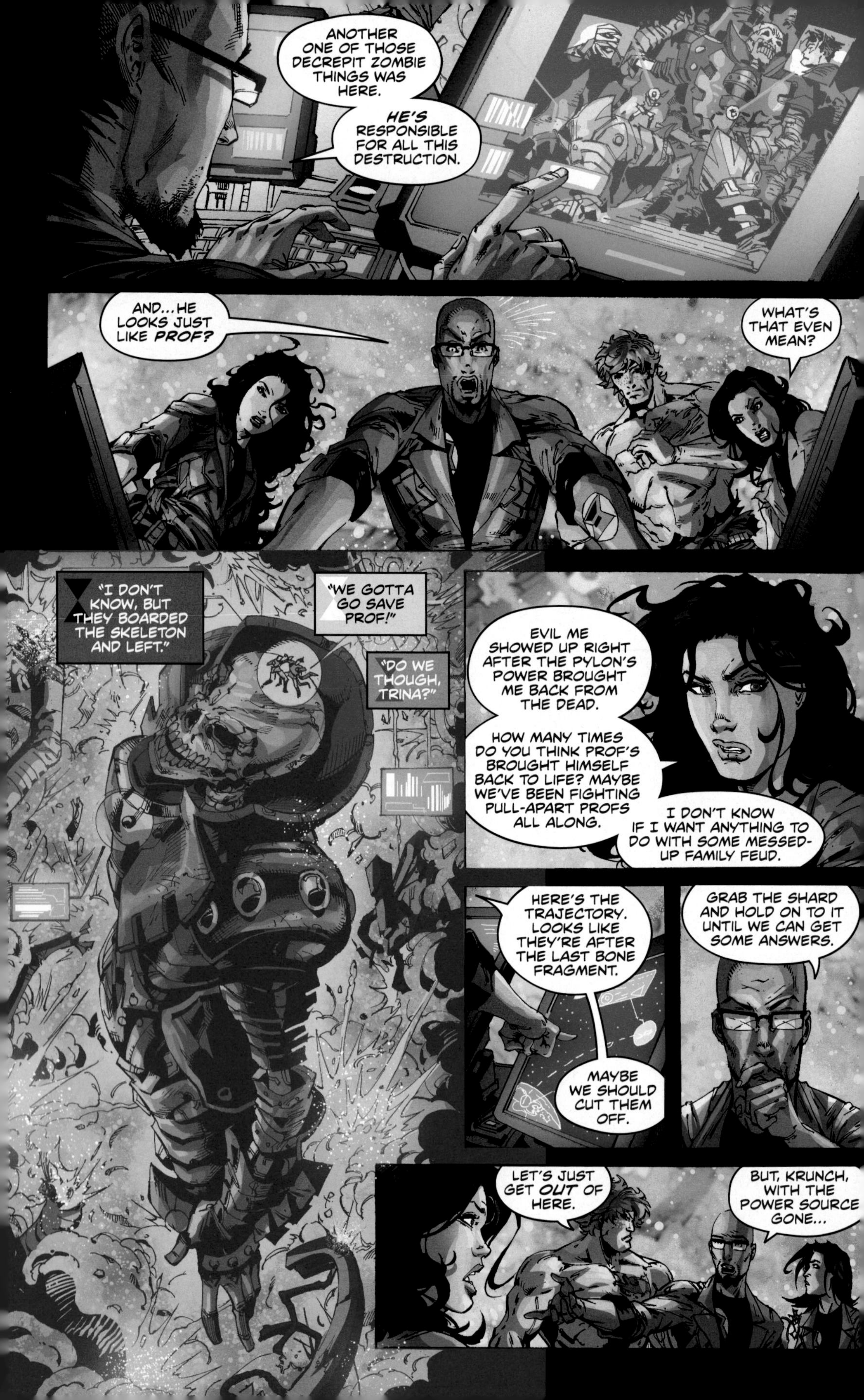
ANOTHER ONE OF THOSE DECREPIT ZOMBIE THINGS WAS HERE.
HE'S RESPONSIBLE FOR ALL THIS DESTRUCTION.
AND...HE LOOKS JUST LIKE PROF?
WHAT'S THAT EVEN MEAN?
"I DON'T KNOW, BUT THEY BOARDED THE SKELETON AND LEFT."
"WE GOTTA GO SAVE PROF!"
"DO WE THOUGH, TRINA?"
EVIL ME SHOWED UP RIGHT AFTER THE PYLON'S POWER BROUGHT ME BACK FROM THE DEAD.
HOW MANY TIMES DO YOU THINK PROF'S BROUGHT HIMSELF BACK TO LIFE? MAYBE WE'VE BEEN FIGHTING PULL-APART PROFS ALL ALONG.
I DON'T KNOW IF I WANT ANYTHING TO DO WITH SOME MESSED-UP FAMILY FEUD.
HERE'S THE TRAJECTORY. LOOKS LIKE THEY'RE AFTER THE LAST BONE FRAGMENT.
MAYBE WE SHOULD CUT THEM OFF.
GRAB THE SHARD AND HOLD ON TO IT UNTIL WE CAN GET SOME ANSWERS.
LET'S JUST GET OUT OF HERE.
BUT, KRUNCH, WITH THE POWER SOURCE GONE...

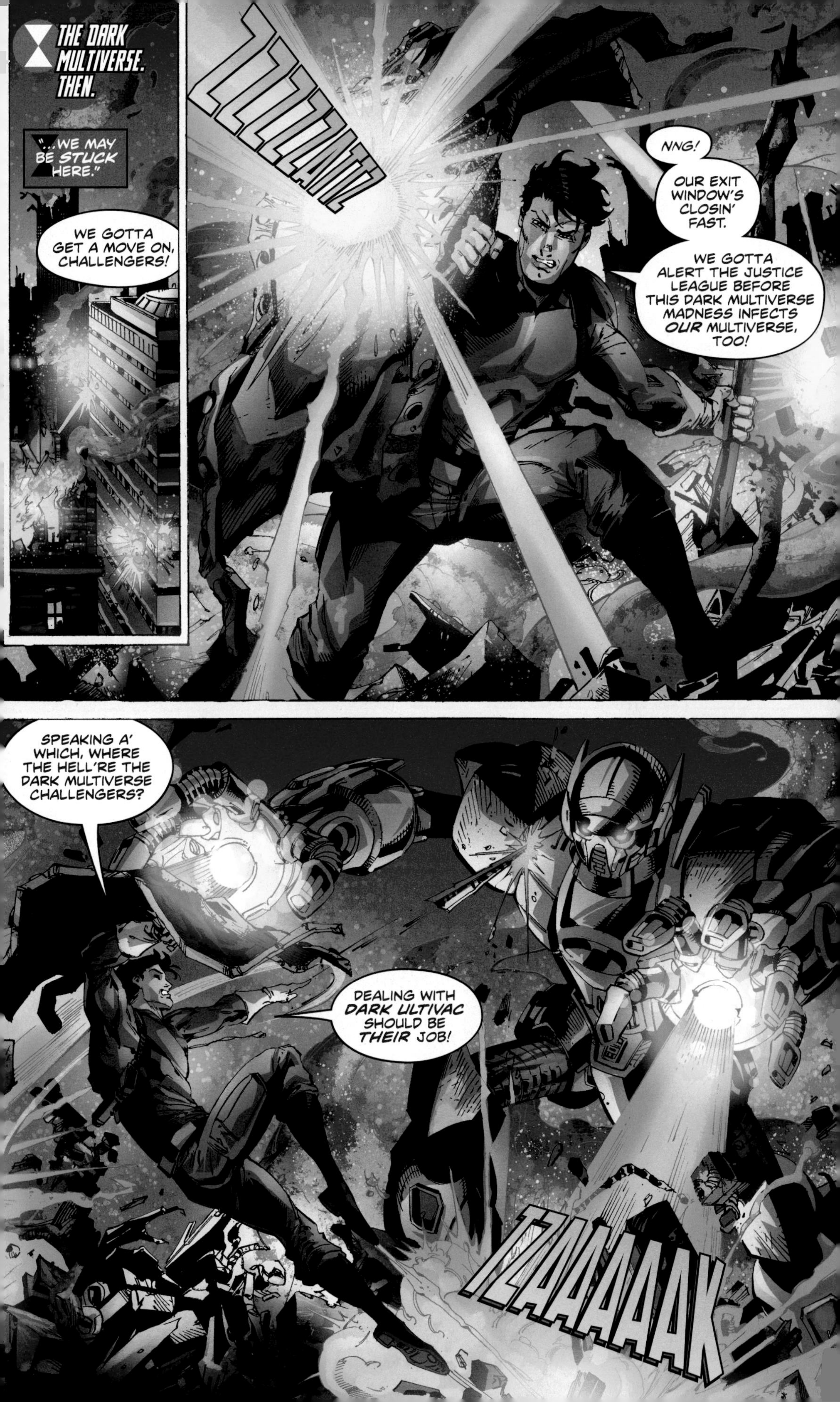

THE DARK MULTIVERSE. THEN.
"...WE MAY BE STUCK HERE."
ZZZZZZAAAAAT
WE GOTTA GET A MOVE ON, CHALLENGERS!
NNG!
OUR EXIT WINDOW'S CLOSIN' FAST.
WE GOTTA ALERT THE JUSTICE LEAGUE BEFORE THIS DARK MULTIVERSE MADNESS INFECTS OUR MULTIVERSE, TOO!
SPEAKING A' WHICH, WHERE THE HELL'RE THE DARK MULTIVERSE CHALLENGERS?
DEALING WITH DARK ULTIVAC SHOULD BE THEIR JOB!
TZAAAAAK

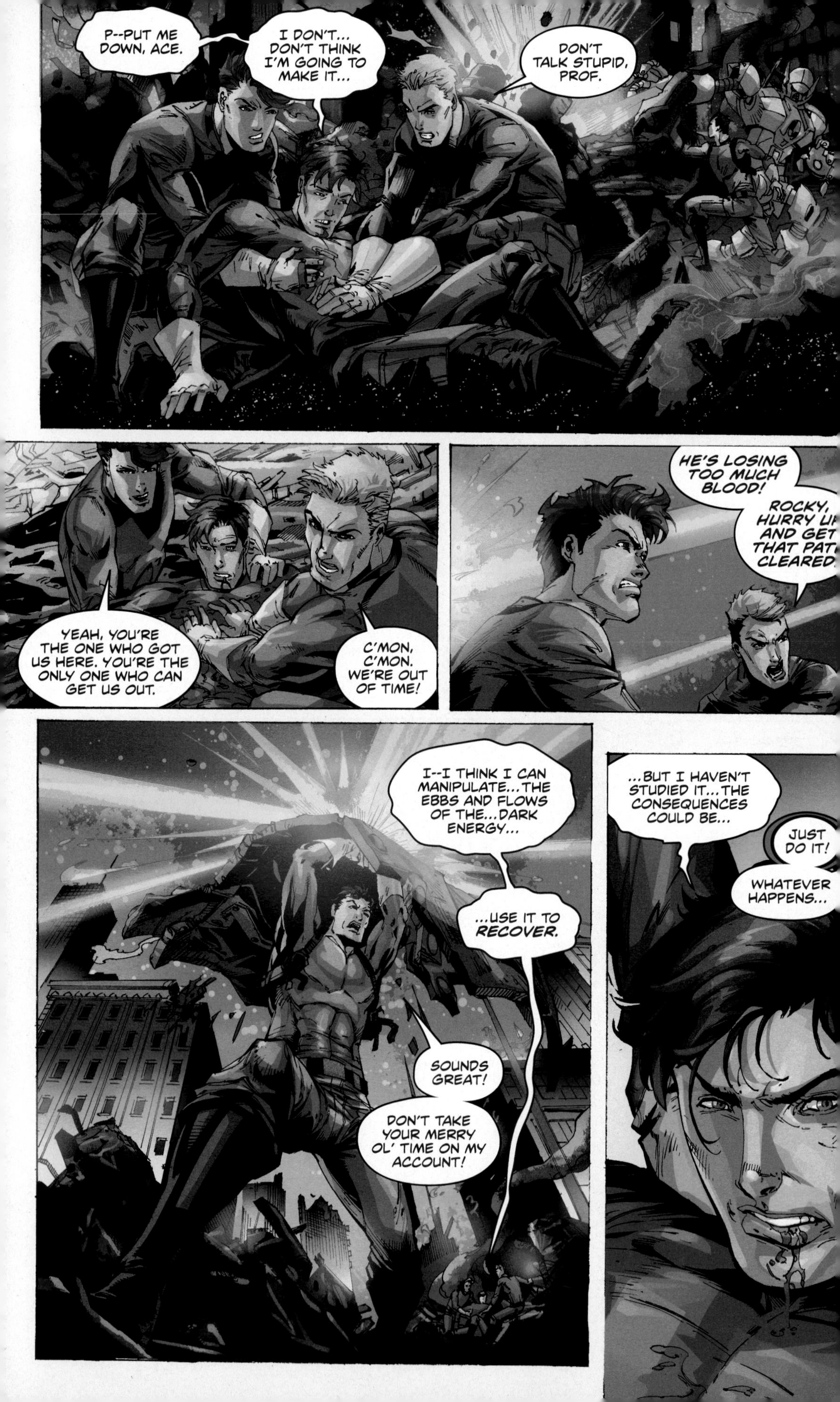
P--PUT ME DOWN, ACE.
I DON'T... DON'T THINK I'M GOING TO MAKE IT...
DON'T TALK STUPID, PROF.
YEAH, YOU'RE THE ONE WHO GOT US HERE. YOU'RE THE ONLY ONE WHO CAN GET US OUT.
C'MON, C'MON. WE'RE OUT OF TIME!
HE'S LOSING TOO MUCH BLOOD!
ROCKY, HURRY U AND GET THAT PAT CLEARED
I--I THINK I CAN MANIPULATE...THE EBBS AND FLOWS OF THE...DARK ENERGY...
...USE IT TO RECOVER.
SOUNDS GREAT!
DON'T TAKE YOUR MERRY OL' TIME ON MY ACCOUNT!
...BUT I HAVEN'T STUDIED IT...THE CONSEQUENCES COULD BE...
JUST DO IT!
WHATEVER HAPPENS...

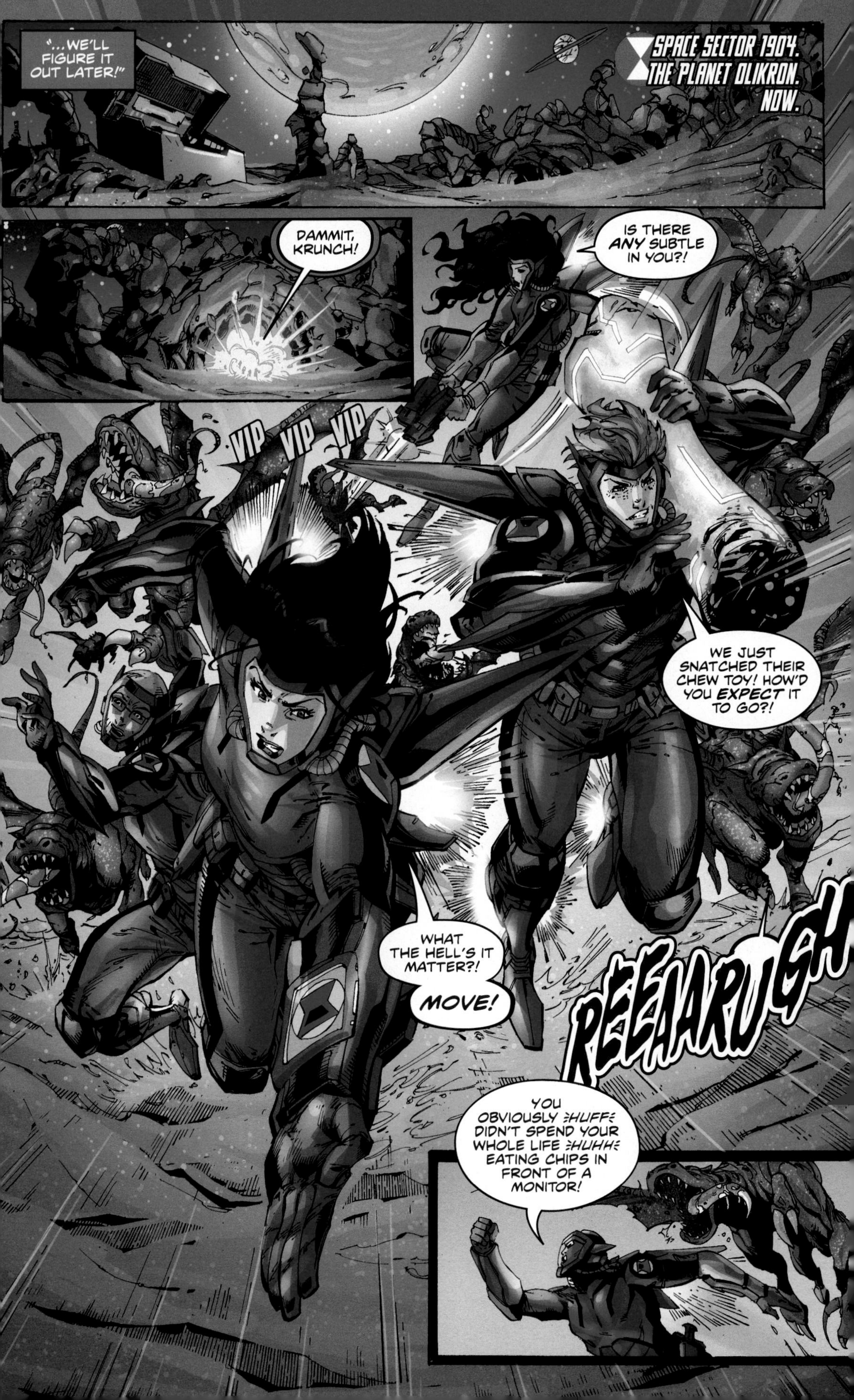
"...WE'LL FIGURE IT OUT LATER!"
SPACE SECTOR 1904. THE PLANET OLIKRON. NOW.
DAMMIT, KRUNCH!
IS THERE ANY SUBTLE IN YOU?!
VIP VIP VIP
WE JUST SNATCHED THEIR CHEW TOY! HOW'D YOU EXPECT IT TO GO?!
WHAT THE HELL'S IT MATTER?! MOVE!
REEAARUGH
YOU OBVIOUSLY HUFF DIDN'T SPEND YOUR WHOLE LIFE HUHH EATING CHIPS IN FRONT OF A MONITOR!

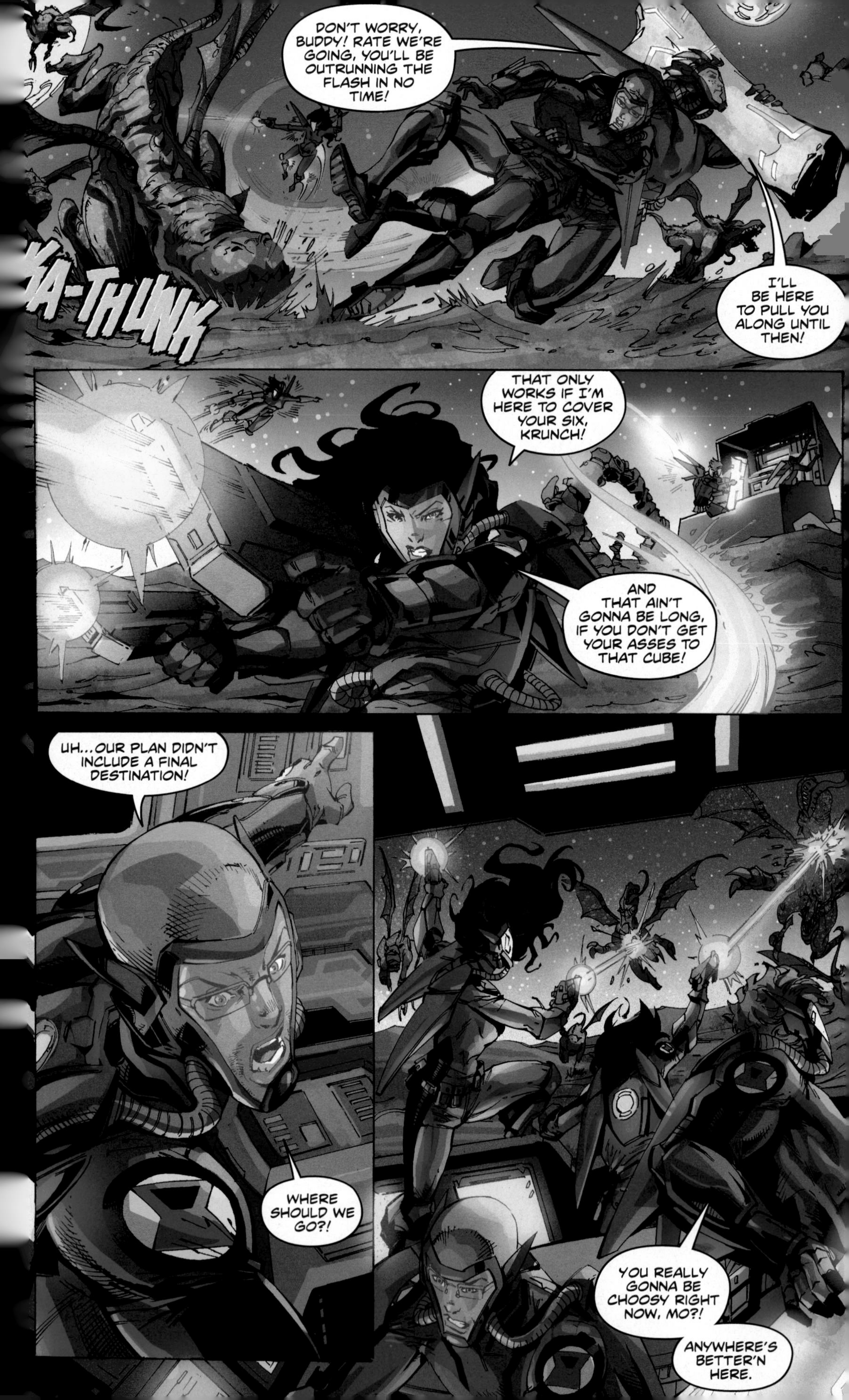
DON'T WORRY, BUDDY! RATE WE'RE GOING, YOU'LL BE OUTRUNNING THE FLASH IN NO TIME!
I'LL BE HERE TO PULL YOU ALONG UNTIL THEN!
KA-THUNK
THAT ONLY WORKS IF I'M HERE TO COVER YOUR SIX, KRUNCH!
AND THAT AIN'T GONNA BE LONG, IF YOU DON'T GET YOUR ASSES TO THAT CUBE!
UH...OUR PLAN DIDN'T INCLUDE A FINAL DESTINATION!
WHERE SHOULD WE GO?!
YOU REALLY GONNA BE CHOOSY RIGHT NOW, MO?!
ANYWHERE'S BETTER'N HERE.

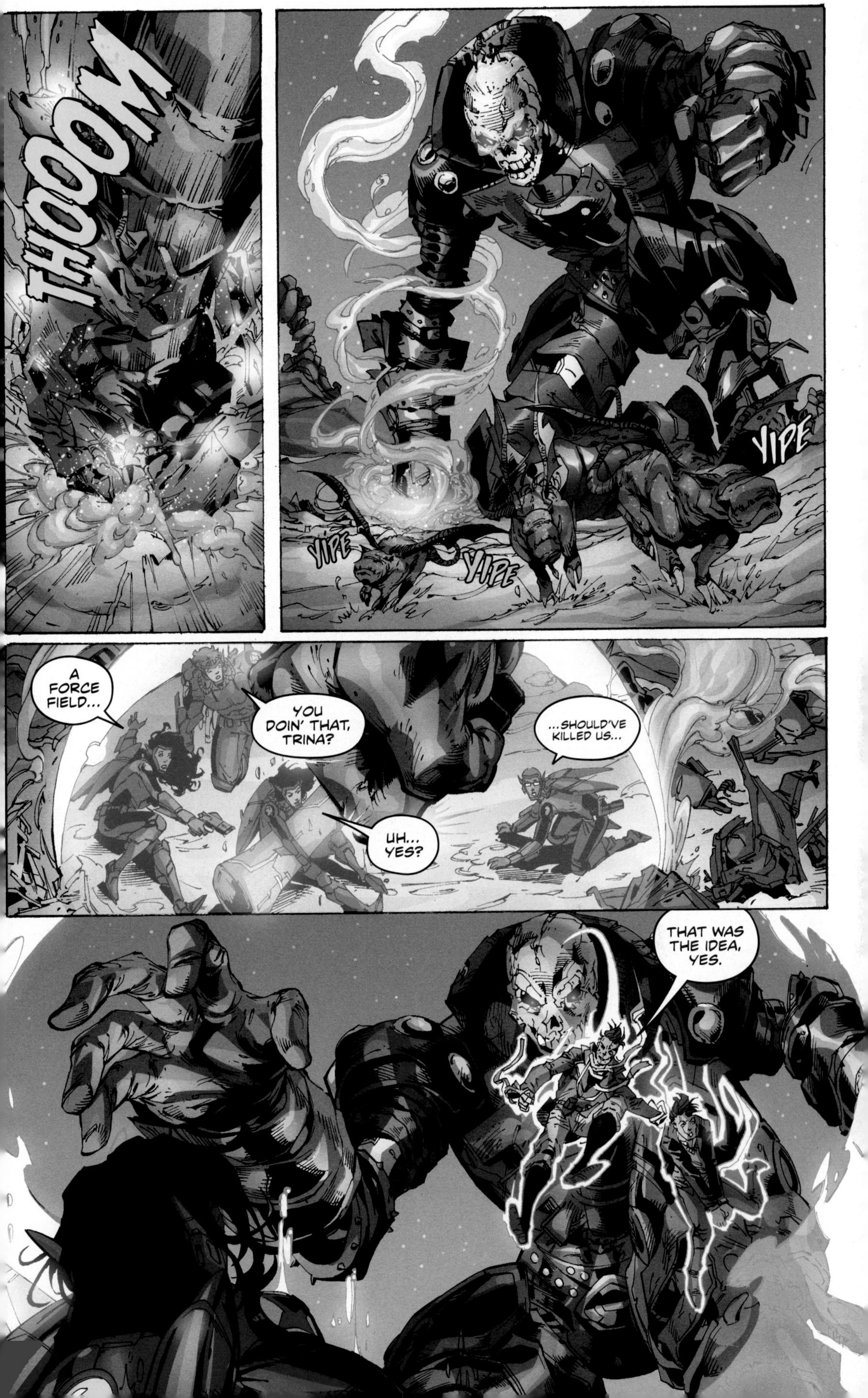
THOOOM
YIPE
YIPE
YIPE
A FORCE FIELD...
YOU DOIN' THAT, TRINA?
UH... YES?
...SHOULD'VE KILLED US...
THAT WAS THE IDEA, YES.

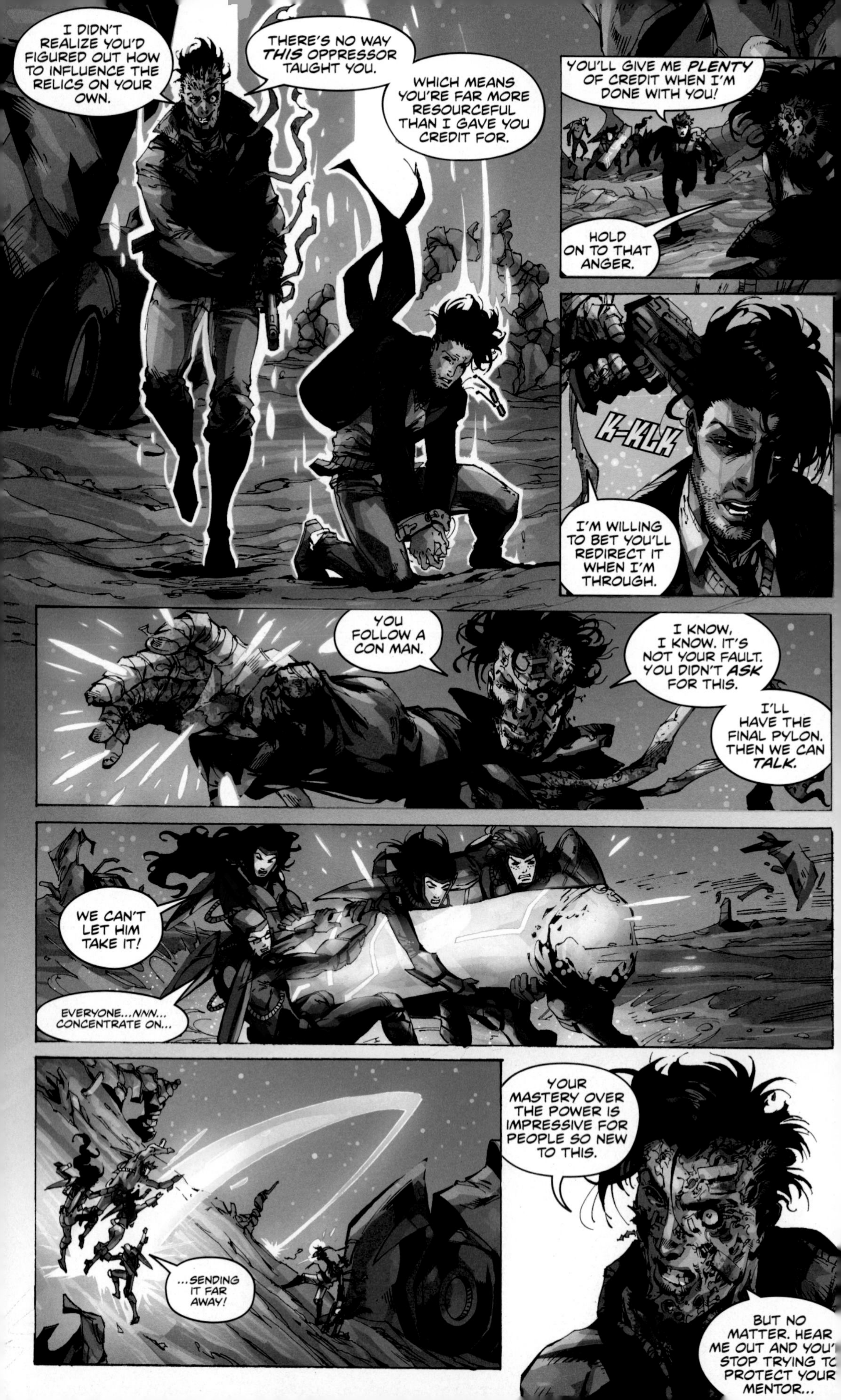
I DIDN'T REALIZE YOU'D FIGURED OUT HOW TO INFLUENCE THE RELICS ON YOUR OWN.
THERE'S NO WAY *THIS* OPPRESSOR TAUGHT YOU.
WHICH MEANS YOU'RE FAR MORE RESOURCEFUL THAN I GAVE YOU CREDIT FOR.
YOU'LL GIVE ME *PLENTY* OF CREDIT WHEN I'M DONE WITH YOU!
HOLD ON TO THAT ANGER.
K-KLK
I'M WILLING TO BET YOU'LL REDIRECT IT WHEN I'M THROUGH.
YOU FOLLOW A CON MAN.
I KNOW, I KNOW. IT'S NOT YOUR FAULT. YOU DIDN'T *ASK* FOR THIS.
I'LL HAVE THE FINAL PYLON. THEN WE CAN *TALK.*
WE CAN'T LET HIM TAKE IT!
EVERYONE...NNN... CONCENTRATE ON...
...SENDING IT FAR AWAY!
YOUR MASTERY OVER THE POWER IS IMPRESSIVE FOR PEOPLE SO NEW TO THIS.
BUT NO MATTER. HEAR ME OUT AND YOU' STOP TRYING TO PROTECT YOUR MENTOR...

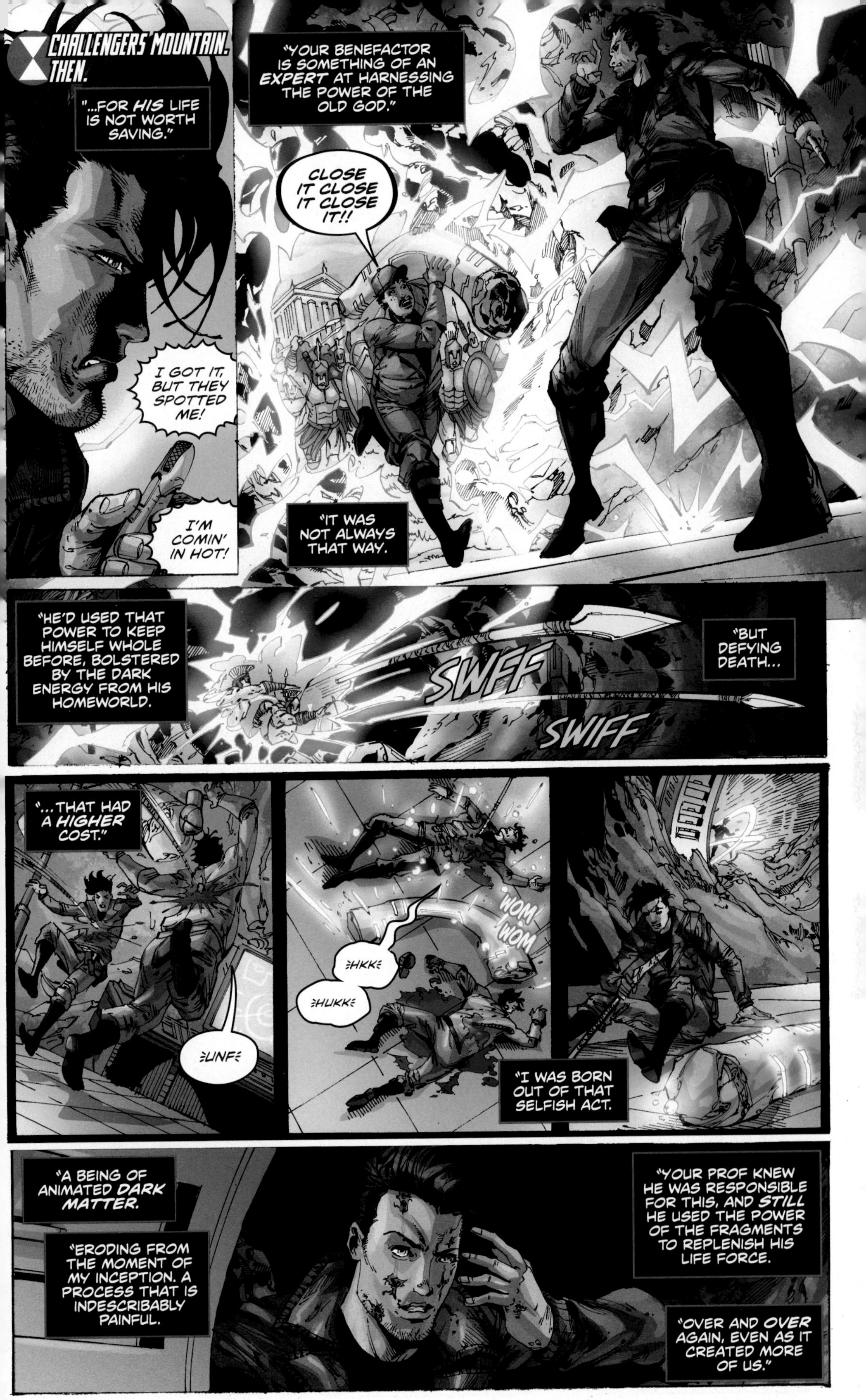

CHALLENGERS MOUNTAIN. THEN.
"...FOR HIS LIFE IS NOT WORTH SAVING."
I GOT IT, BUT THEY SPOTTED ME!
I'M COMIN' IN HOT!
"YOUR BENEFACTOR IS SOMETHING OF AN EXPERT AT HARNESSING THE POWER OF THE OLD GOD."
CLOSE IT CLOSE IT CLOSE IT!!
"IT WAS NOT ALWAYS THAT WAY.
"HE'D USED THAT POWER TO KEEP HIMSELF WHOLE BEFORE, BOLSTERED BY THE DARK ENERGY FROM HIS HOMEWORLD.
SWFF
SWIFF
"BUT DEFYING DEATH...
"...THAT HAD A HIGHER COST."
UNF
WOM WOM
HKK
HUKK
"I WAS BORN OUT OF THAT SELFISH ACT.
"A BEING OF ANIMATED DARK MATTER.
"ERODING FROM THE MOMENT OF MY INCEPTION. A PROCESS THAT IS INDESCRIBABLY PAINFUL.
"YOUR PROF KNEW HE WAS RESPONSIBLE FOR THIS, AND STILL HE USED THE POWER OF THE FRAGMENTS TO REPLENISH HIS LIFE FORCE.
"OVER AND OVER AGAIN, EVEN AS IT CREATED MORE OF US."

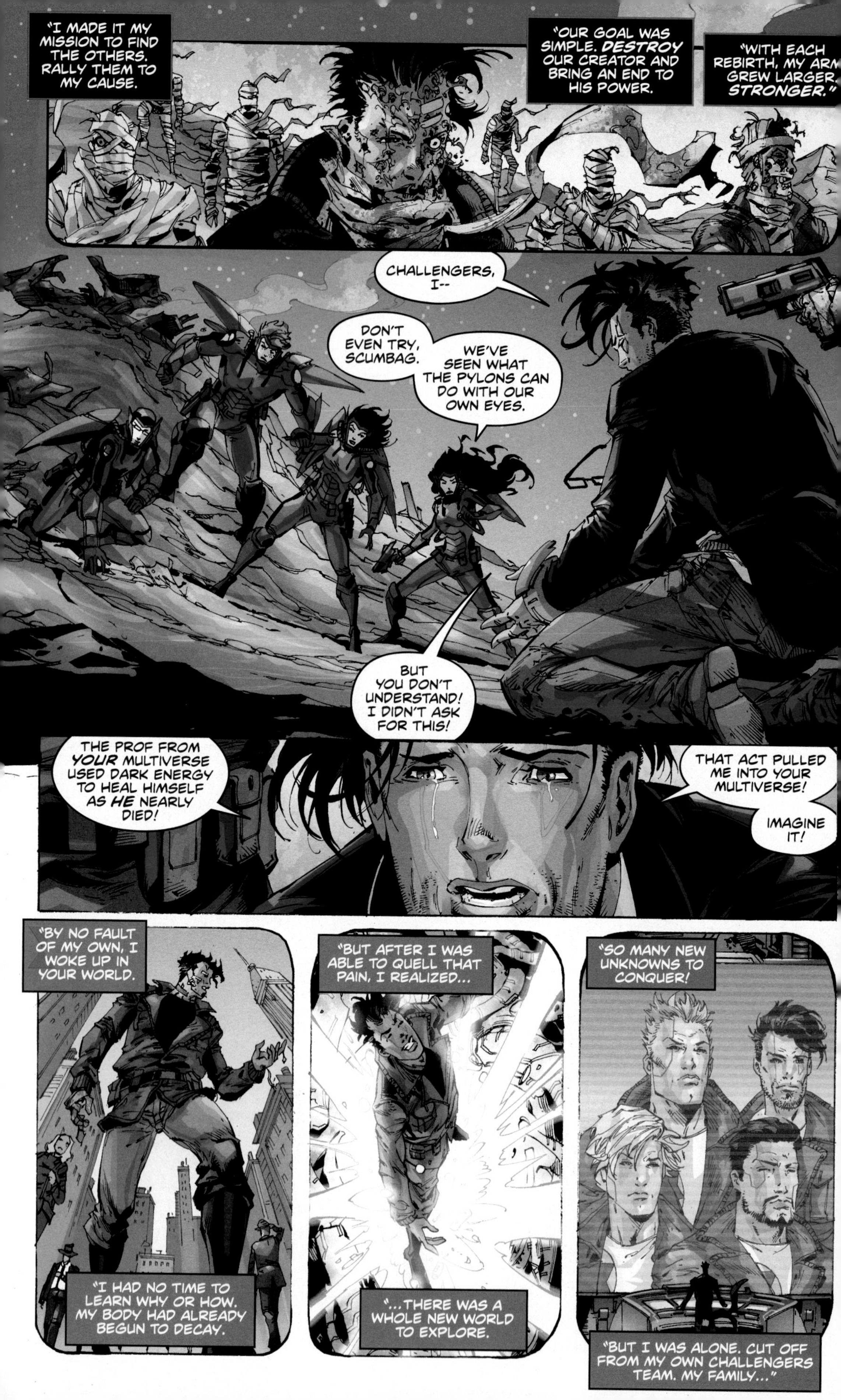
"I MADE IT MY MISSION TO FIND THE OTHERS. RALLY THEM TO MY CAUSE.
"OUR GOAL WAS SIMPLE. *DESTROY* OUR CREATOR AND BRING AN END TO HIS POWER.
"WITH EACH REBIRTH, MY ARM GREW LARGER. *STRONGER.*"
CHALLENGERS, I--
DON'T EVEN TRY, SCUMBAG.
WE'VE SEEN WHAT THE PYLONS CAN DO WITH OUR OWN EYES.
BUT YOU DON'T UNDERSTAND! I DIDN'T ASK FOR THIS!
THE PROF FROM *YOUR* MULTIVERSE USED DARK ENERGY TO HEAL HIMSELF AS *HE* NEARLY DIED!
THAT ACT PULLED ME INTO YOUR MULTIVERSE!
IMAGINE IT!
"BY NO FAULT OF MY OWN, I WOKE UP IN YOUR WORLD.
"I HAD NO TIME TO LEARN WHY OR HOW. MY BODY HAD ALREADY BEGUN TO DECAY.
"BUT AFTER I WAS ABLE TO QUELL THAT PAIN, I REALIZED...
"...THERE WAS A WHOLE NEW WORLD TO EXPLORE.
"SO MANY NEW UNKNOWNS TO CONQUER!
"BUT I WAS ALONE. CUT OFF FROM MY OWN CHALLENGERS TEAM. MY FAMILY..."

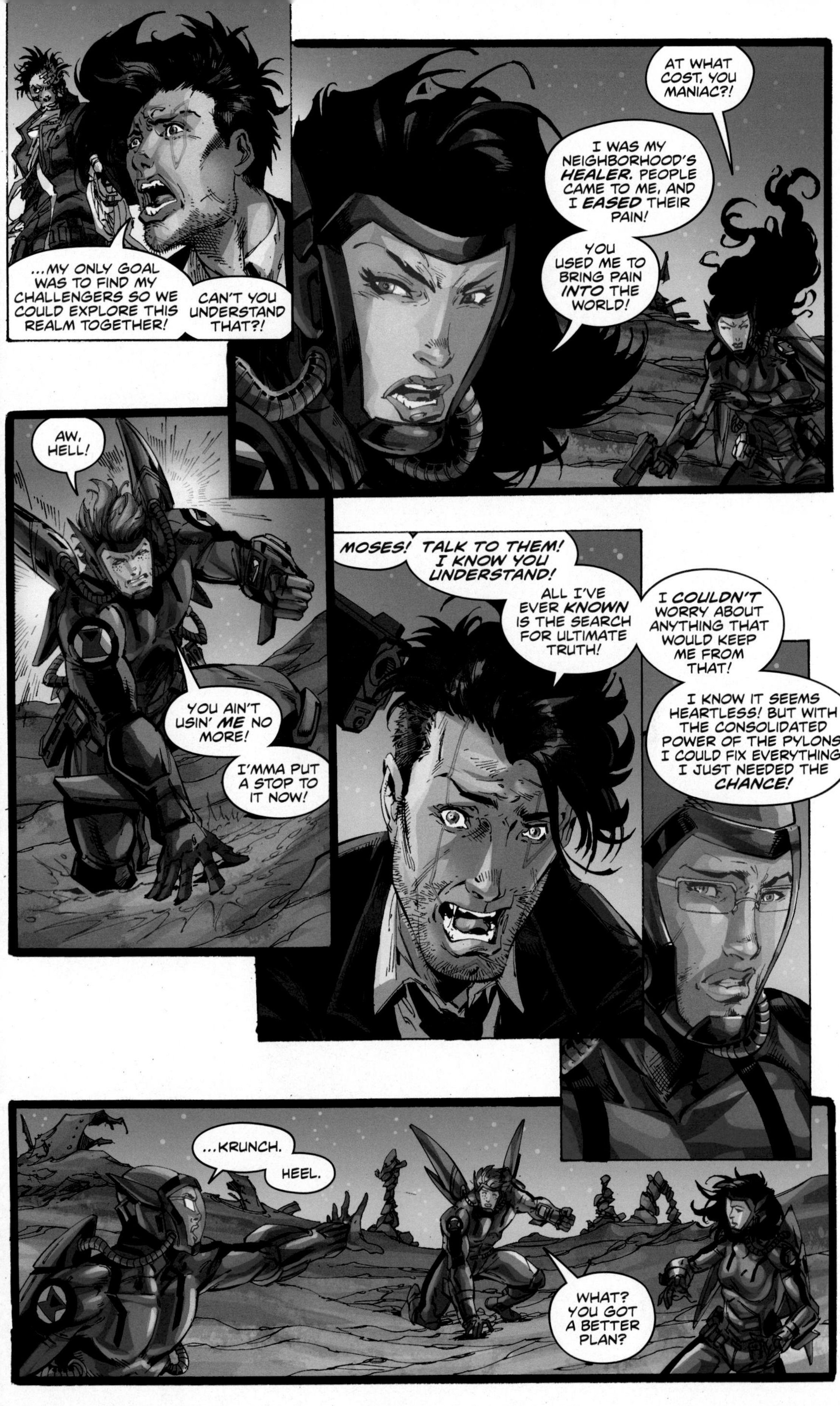
...MY ONLY GOAL WAS TO FIND MY CHALLENGERS SO WE COULD EXPLORE THIS REALM TOGETHER!
CAN'T YOU UNDERSTAND THAT?!
AT WHAT COST, YOU MANIAC?!
I WAS MY NEIGHBORHOOD'S HEALER. PEOPLE CAME TO ME, AND I EASED THEIR PAIN!
YOU USED ME TO BRING PAIN INTO THE WORLD!
AW, HELL!
YOU AIN'T USIN' ME NO MORE!
I'MMA PUT A STOP TO IT NOW!
MOSES!
TALK TO THEM! I KNOW YOU UNDERSTAND!
ALL I'VE EVER KNOWN IS THE SEARCH FOR ULTIMATE TRUTH!
I COULDN'T WORRY ABOUT ANYTHING THAT WOULD KEEP ME FROM THAT!
I KNOW IT SEEMS HEARTLESS! BUT WITH THE CONSOLIDATED POWER OF THE PYLONS, I COULD FIX EVERYTHING! I JUST NEEDED THE CHANCE!
...KRUNCH.
HEEL.
WHAT? YOU GOT A BETTER PLAN?

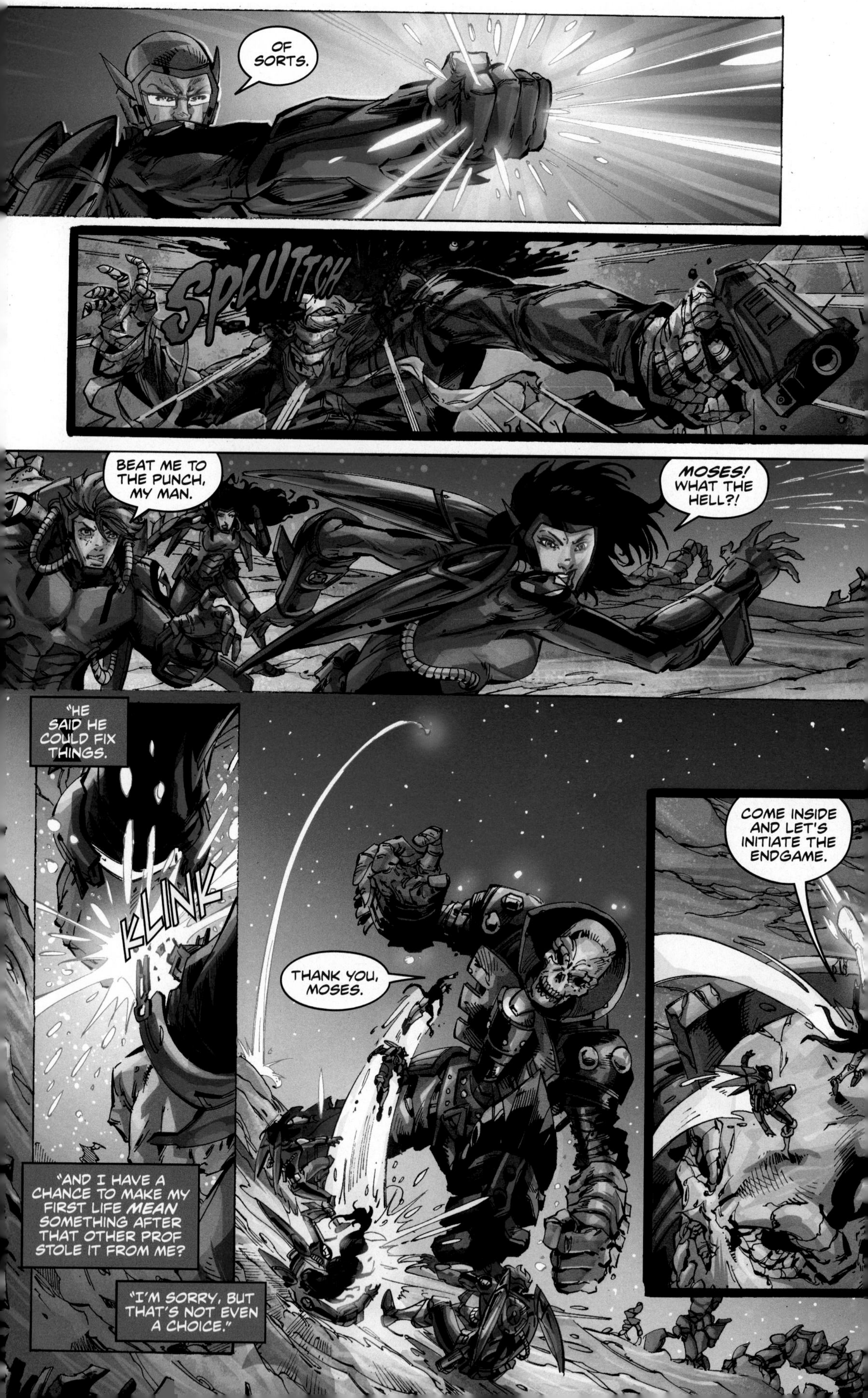

OF SORTS.
SPLUTTCH
BEAT ME TO THE PUNCH, MY MAN.
MOSES! WHAT THE HELL?!
"HE SAID HE COULD FIX THINGS.
KLINK
"AND I HAVE A CHANCE TO MAKE MY FIRST LIFE *MEAN* SOMETHING AFTER THAT OTHER PROF STOLE IT FROM ME?
"I'M SORRY, BUT THAT'S NOT EVEN A CHOICE."
THANK YOU, MOSES.
COME INSIDE AND LET'S INITIATE THE ENDGAME.

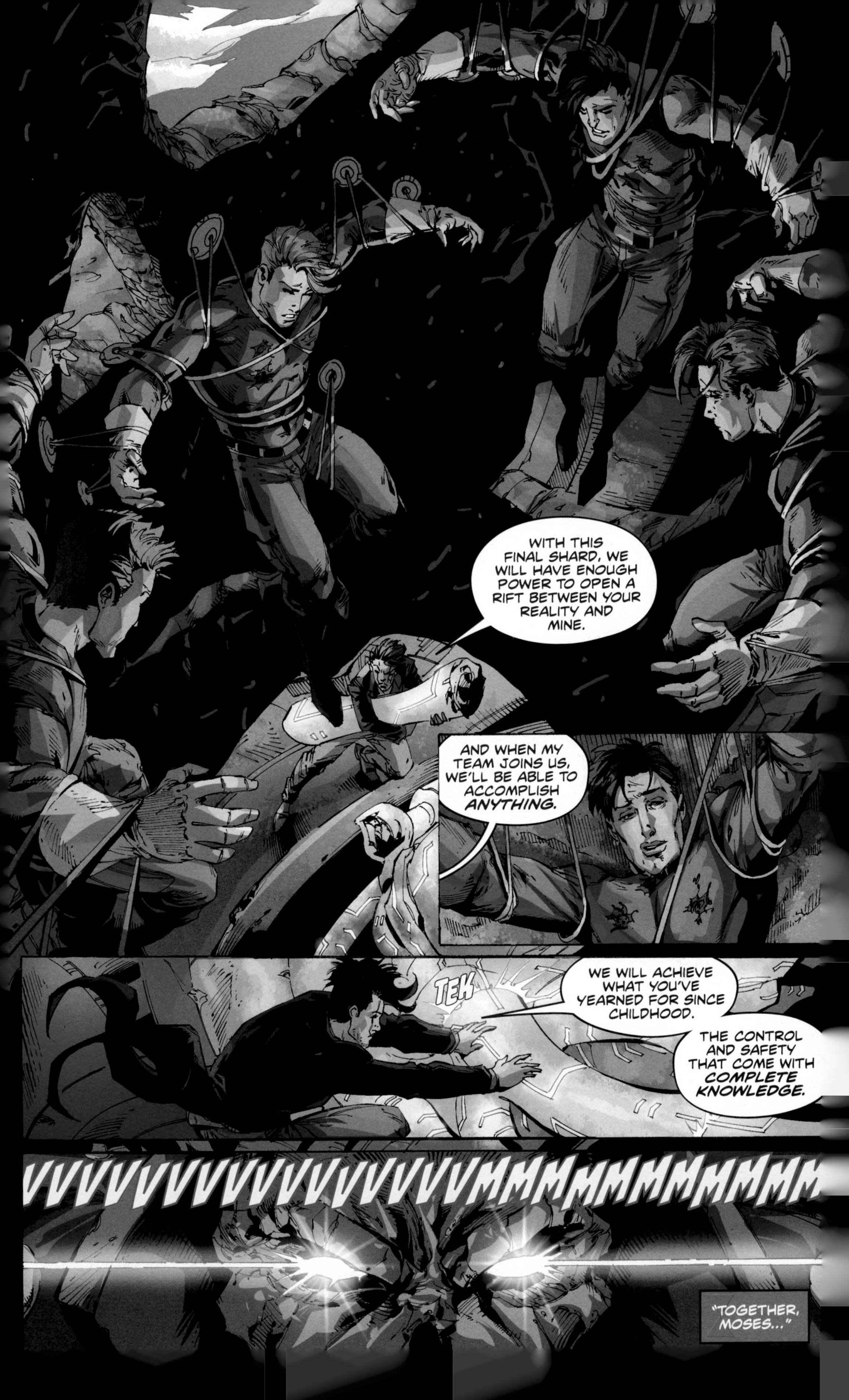
WITH THIS FINAL SHARD, WE WILL HAVE ENOUGH POWER TO OPEN A RIFT BETWEEN YOUR REALITY AND MINE.
AND WHEN MY TEAM JOINS US, WE'LL BE ABLE TO ACCOMPLISH ANYTHING.
TEK
WE WILL ACHIEVE WHAT YOU'VE YEARNED FOR SINCE CHILDHOOD.
THE CONTROL AND SAFETY THAT COME WITH COMPLETE KNOWLEDGE.
VVVVVVVVVVVVVVVVVVVVVMMMMMMMMMMMMMM
"TOGETHER, MOSES..."

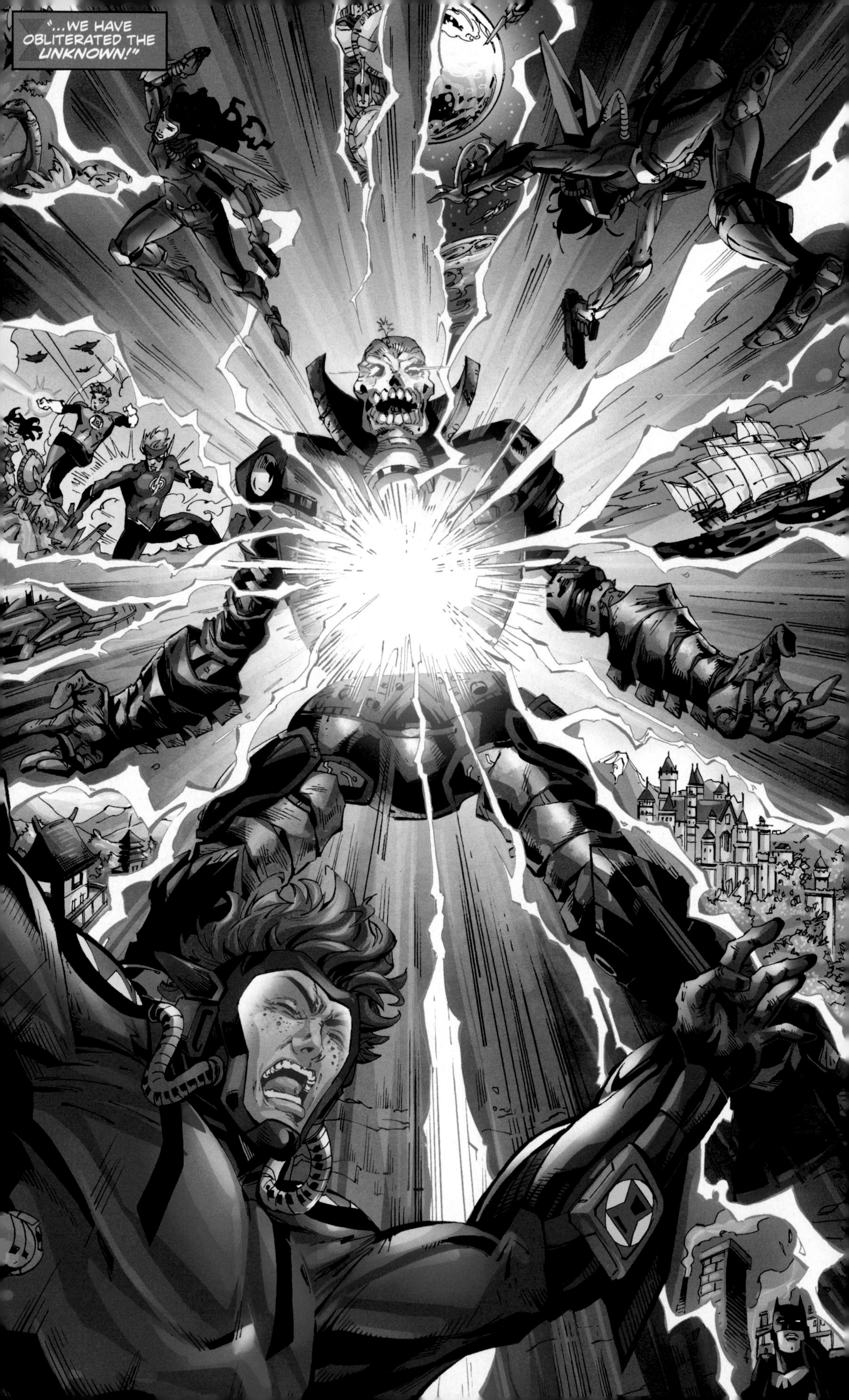
"...WE HAVE OBLITERATED THE UNKNOWN!"

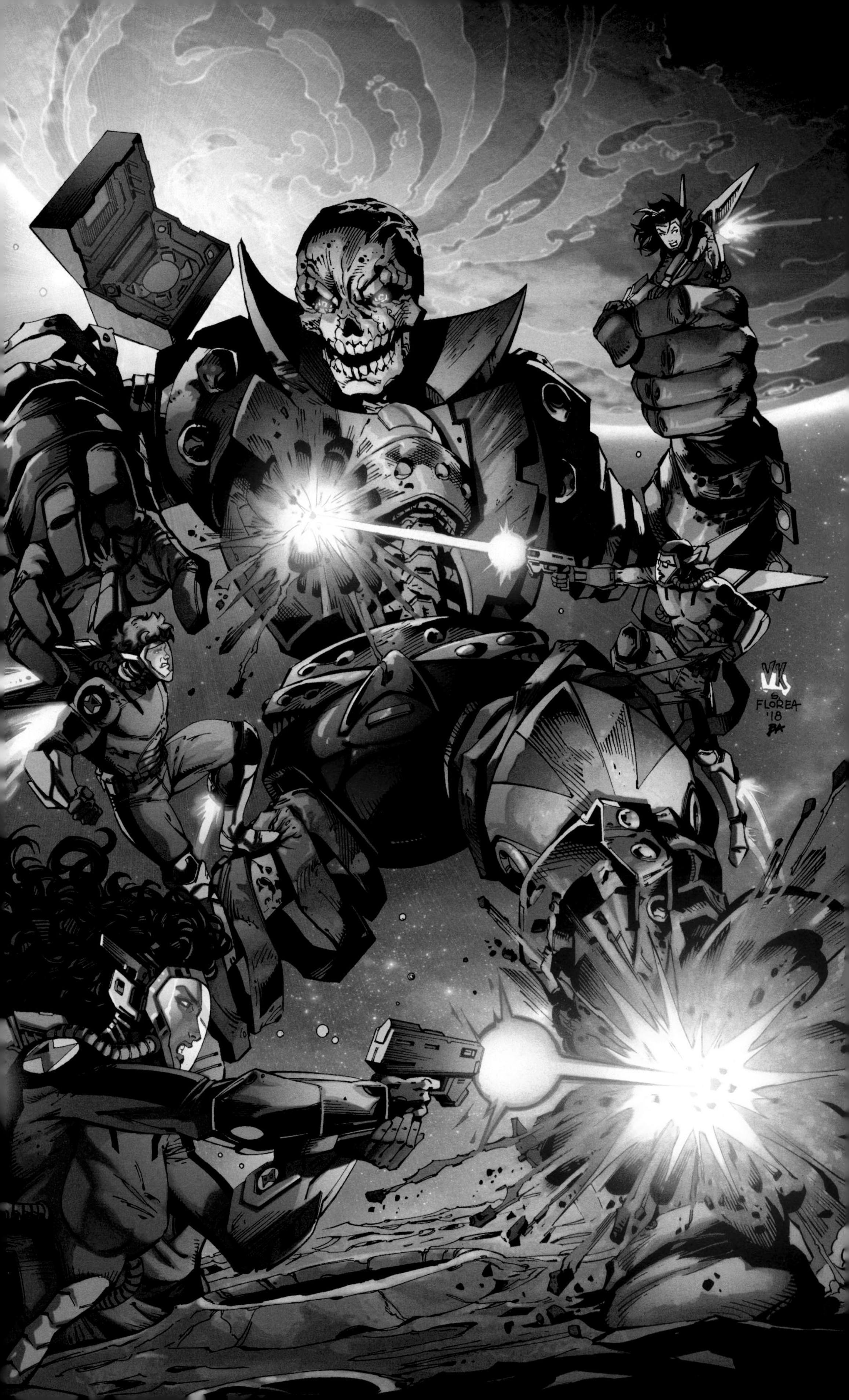
S. FLOREA
'18

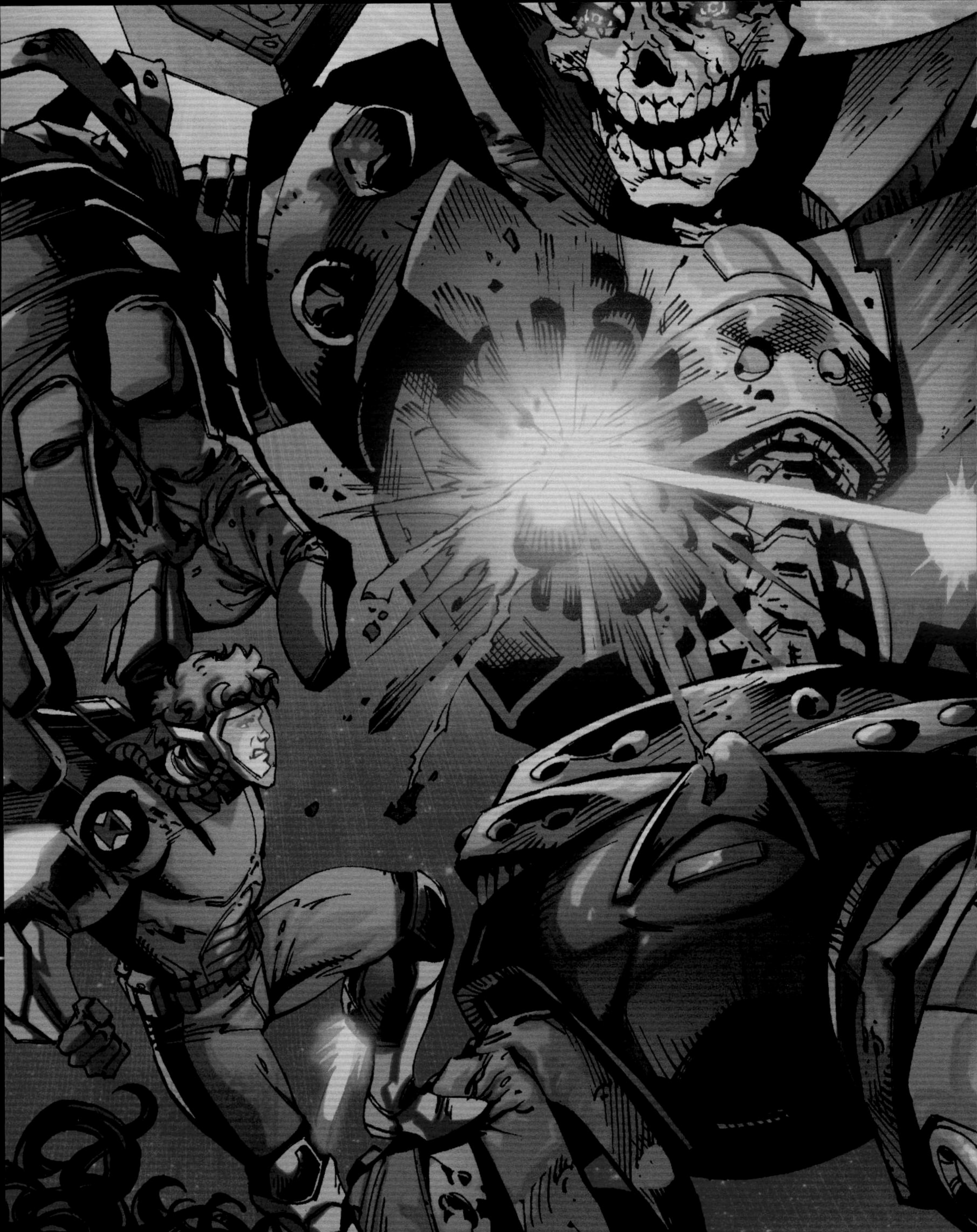

NEW CHALLENGERS
#6

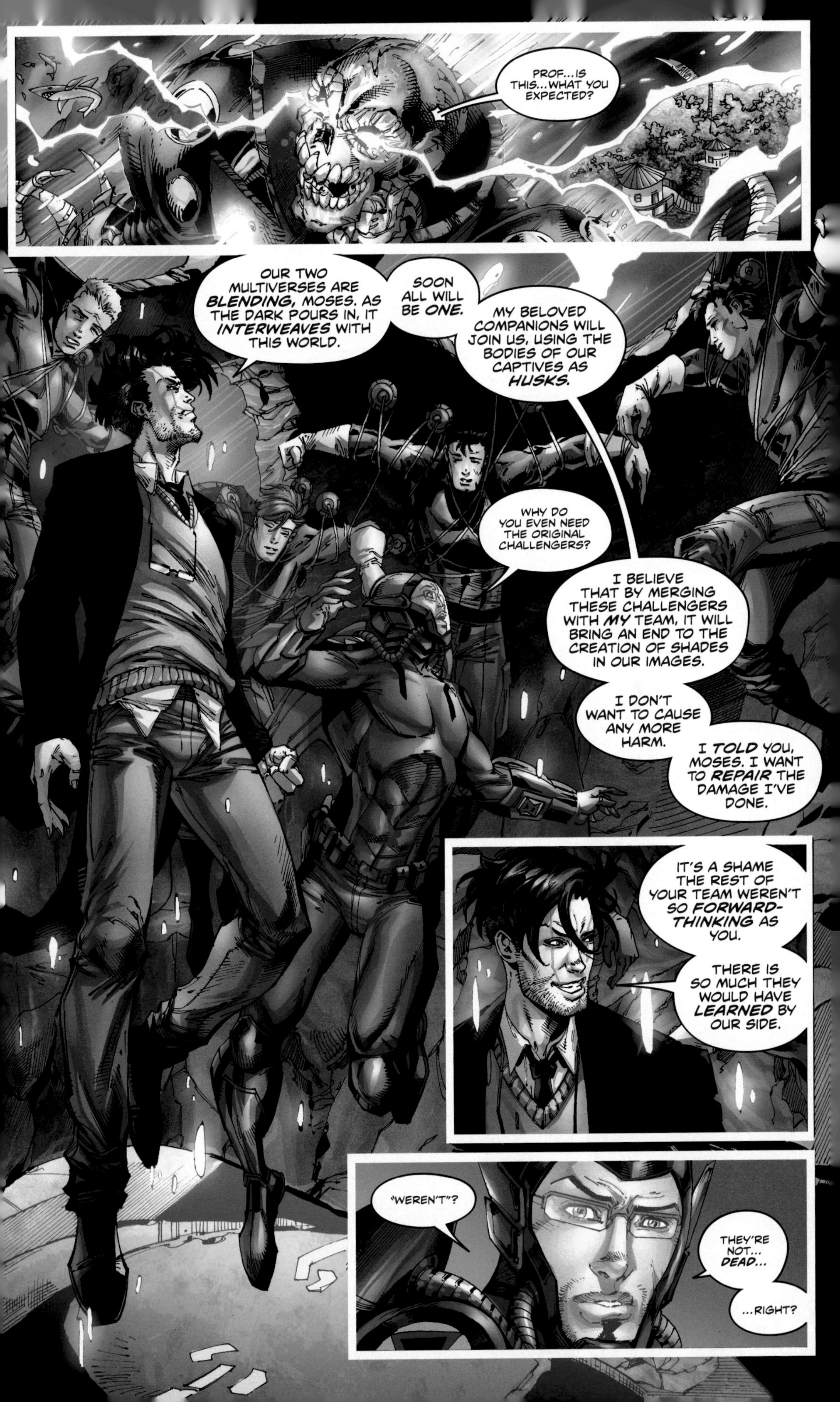

PROF...IS THIS...WHAT YOU EXPECTED?
OUR TWO MULTIVERSES ARE BLENDING, MOSES. AS THE DARK POURS IN, IT INTERWEAVES WITH THIS WORLD.
SOON ALL WILL BE ONE.
MY BELOVED COMPANIONS WILL JOIN US, USING THE BODIES OF OUR CAPTIVES AS HUSKS.
WHY DO YOU EVEN NEED THE ORIGINAL CHALLENGERS?
I BELIEVE THAT BY MERGING THESE CHALLENGERS WITH MY TEAM, IT WILL BRING AN END TO THE CREATION OF SHADES IN OUR IMAGES.
I DON'T WANT TO CAUSE ANY MORE HARM.
I TOLD YOU, MOSES. I WANT TO REPAIR THE DAMAGE I'VE DONE.
IT'S A SHAME THE REST OF YOUR TEAM WEREN'T SO FORWARD-THINKING AS YOU.
THERE IS SO MUCH THEY WOULD HAVE LEARNED BY OUR SIDE.
"WEREN'T"?
THEY'RE NOT... DEAD...
...RIGHT?

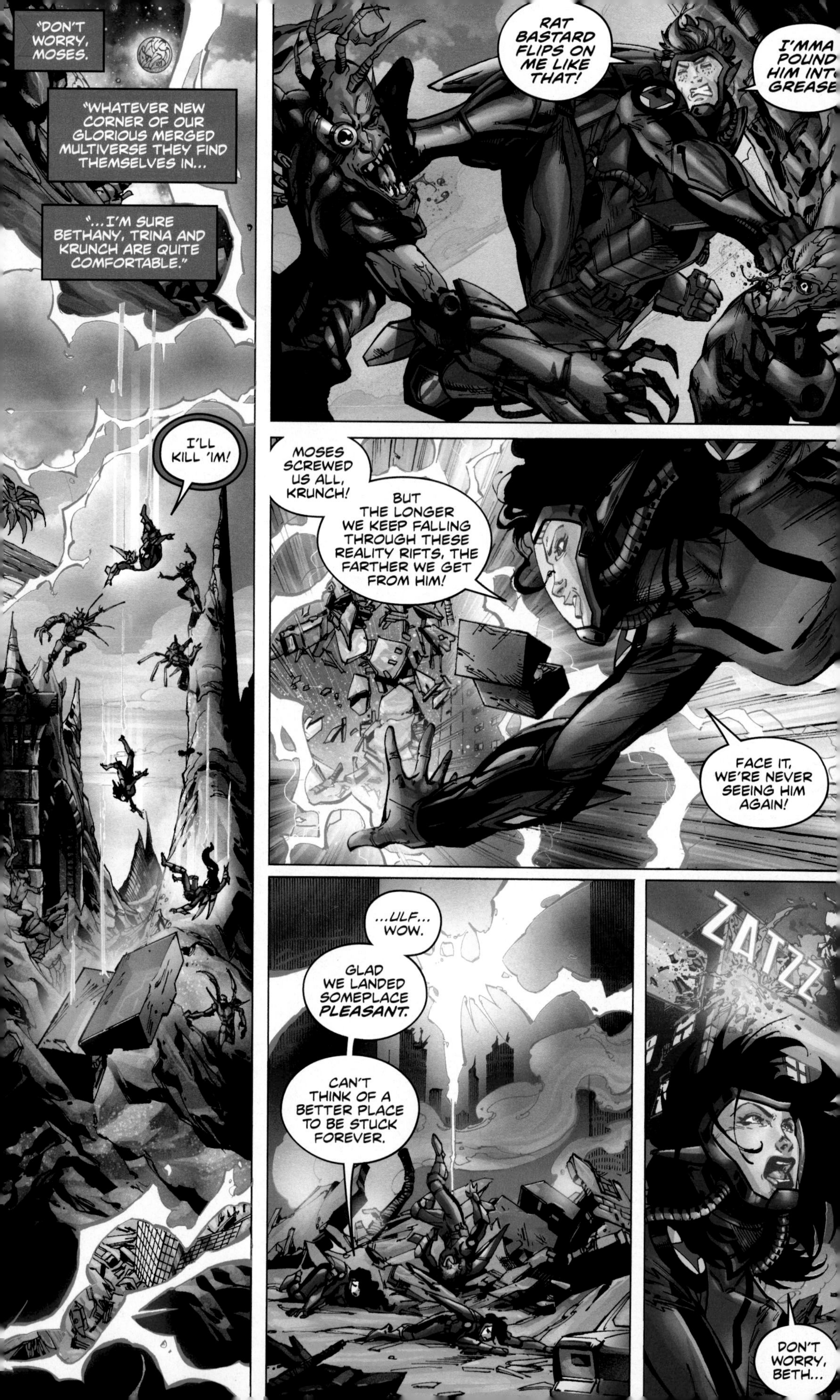
"DON'T WORRY, MOSES.
"WHATEVER NEW CORNER OF OUR GLORIOUS MERGED MULTIVERSE THEY FIND THEMSELVES IN...
"...I'M SURE BETHANY, TRINA AND KRUNCH ARE QUITE COMFORTABLE."
I'LL KILL 'IM!
RAT BASTARD FLIPS ON ME LIKE THAT!
I'MMA POUND HIM INTO GREASE
MOSES SCREWED US ALL, KRUNCH!
BUT THE LONGER WE KEEP FALLING THROUGH THESE REALITY RIFTS, THE FARTHER WE GET FROM HIM!
FACE IT, WE'RE NEVER SEEING HIM AGAIN!
...ULF... WOW.
GLAD WE LANDED SOMEPLACE PLEASANT.
CAN'T THINK OF A BETTER PLACE TO BE STUCK FOREVER.
ZATZZ
DON'T WORRY, BETH...

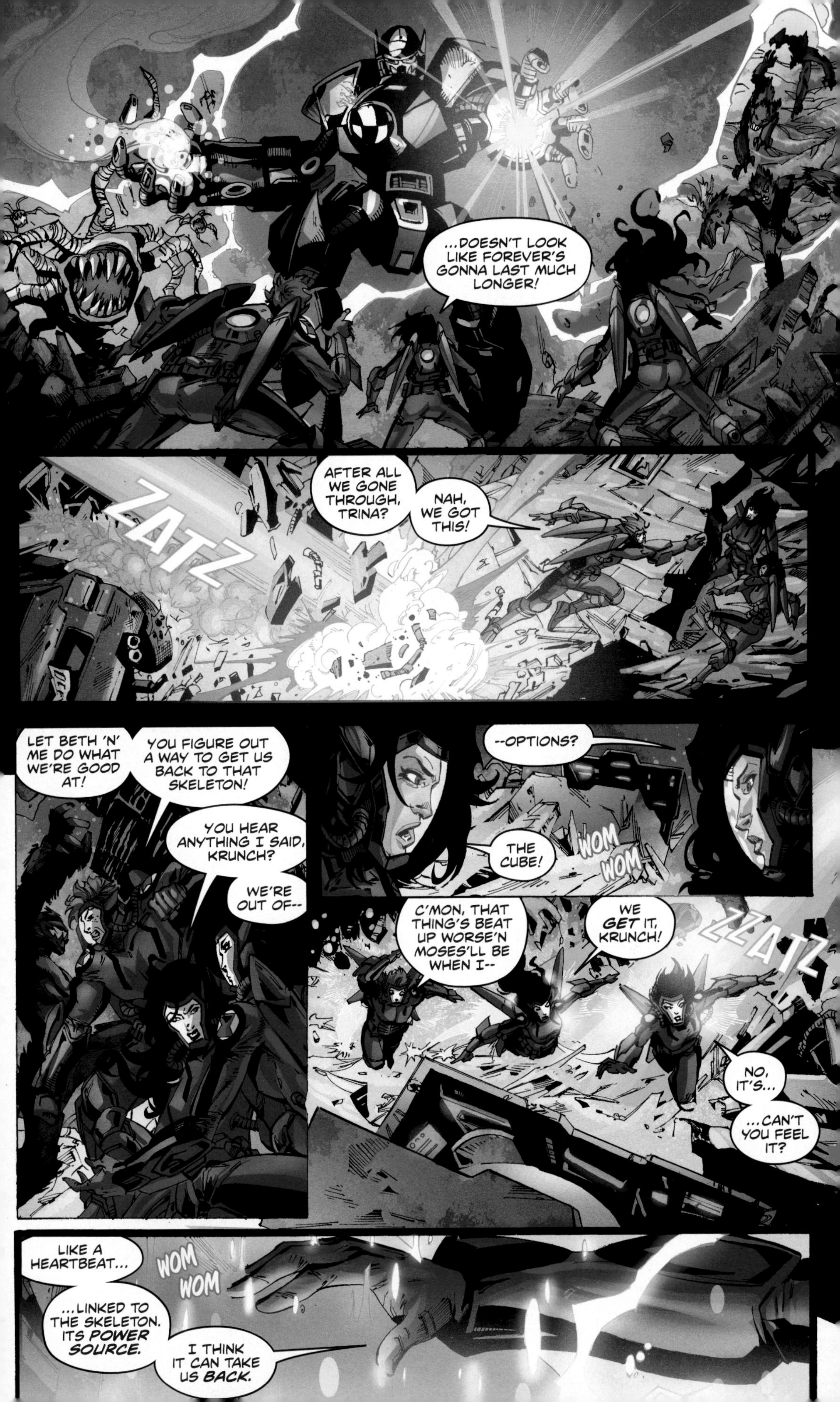
...DOESN'T LOOK LIKE FOREVER'S GONNA LAST MUCH LONGER!
ZATZ
AFTER ALL WE GONE THROUGH, TRINA?
NAH, WE GOT THIS!
LET BETH 'N' ME DO WHAT WE'RE GOOD AT!
YOU FIGURE OUT A WAY TO GET US BACK TO THAT SKELETON!
YOU HEAR ANYTHING I SAID, KRUNCH?
WE'RE OUT OF--
--OPTIONS?
THE CUBE!
WOM WOM
C'MON, THAT THING'S BEAT UP WORSE'N MOSES'LL BE WHEN I--
WE GET IT, KRUNCH!
ZZATZ
NO, IT'S...
...CAN'T YOU FEEL IT?
LIKE A HEARTBEAT...
WOM WOM
...LINKED TO THE SKELETON. ITS POWER SOURCE.
I THINK IT CAN TAKE US BACK.

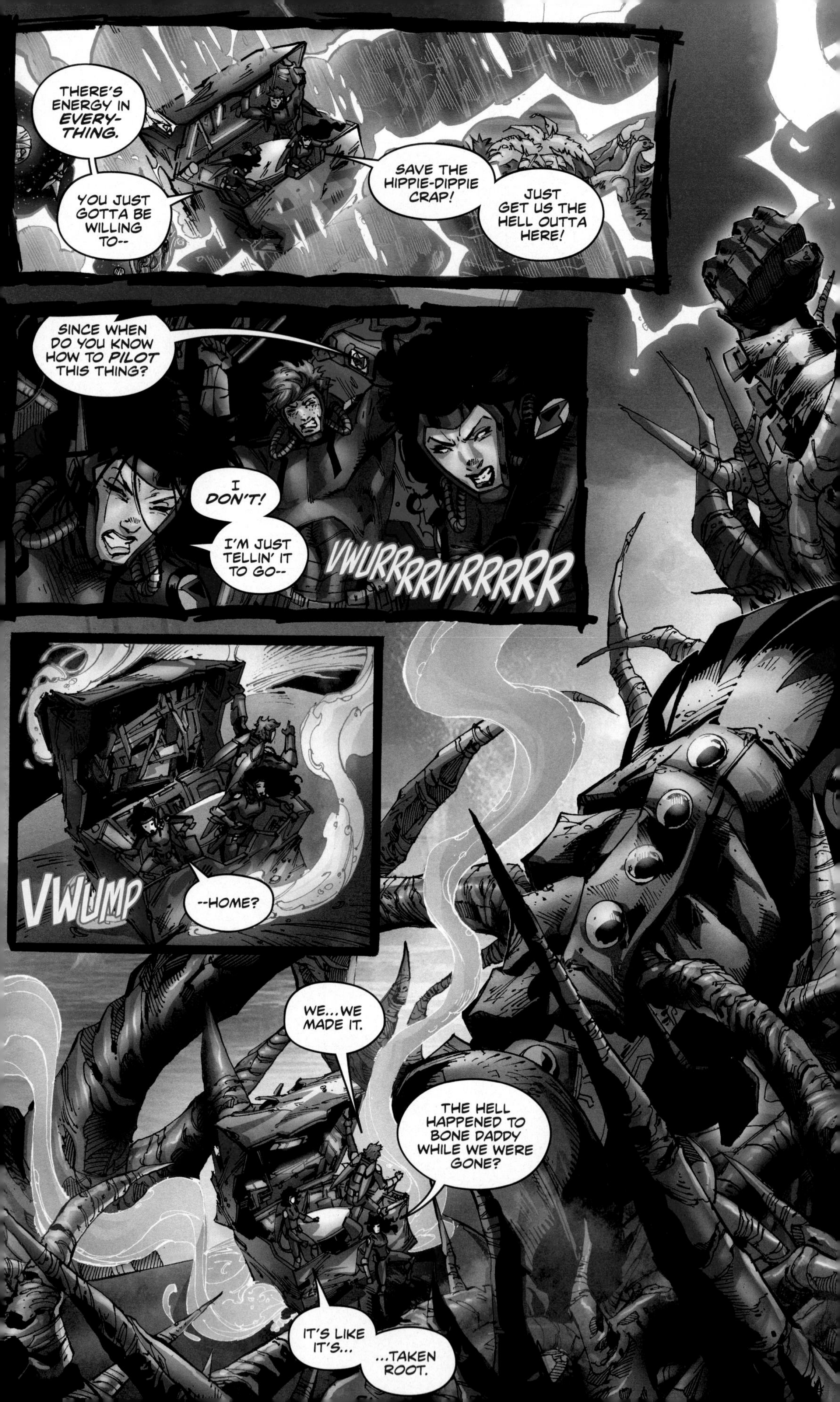
THERE'S ENERGY IN EVERYTHING.
YOU JUST GOTTA BE WILLING TO--
SAVE THE HIPPIE-DIPPIE CRAP!
JUST GET US THE HELL OUTTA HERE!
SINCE WHEN DO YOU KNOW HOW TO PILOT THIS THING?
I DON'T!
I'M JUST TELLIN' IT TO GO--
VWURRRRRVRRRRR
VWUMP
--HOME?
WE...WE MADE IT.
THE HELL HAPPENED TO BONE DADDY WHILE WE WERE GONE?
IT'S LIKE IT'S...
...TAKEN ROOT.

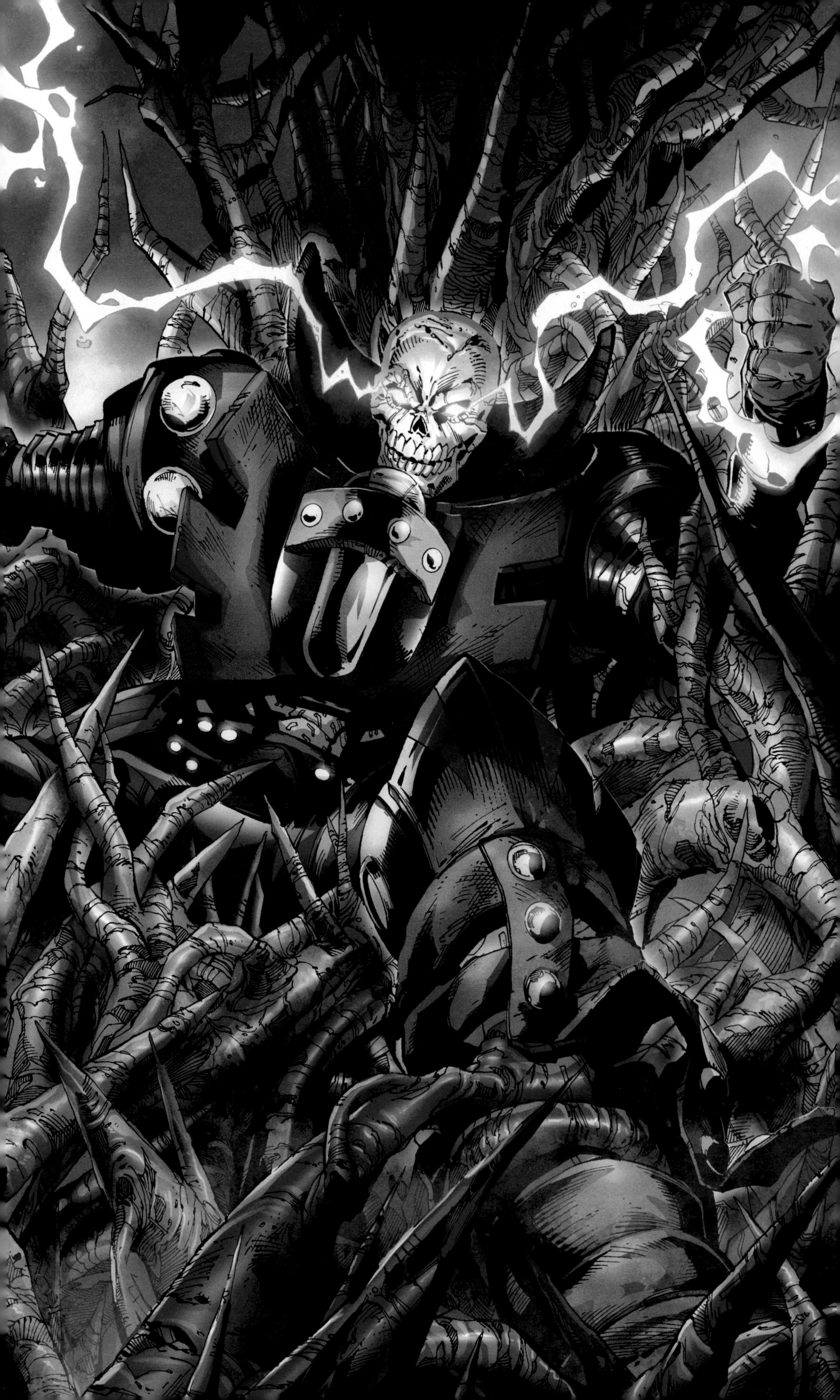

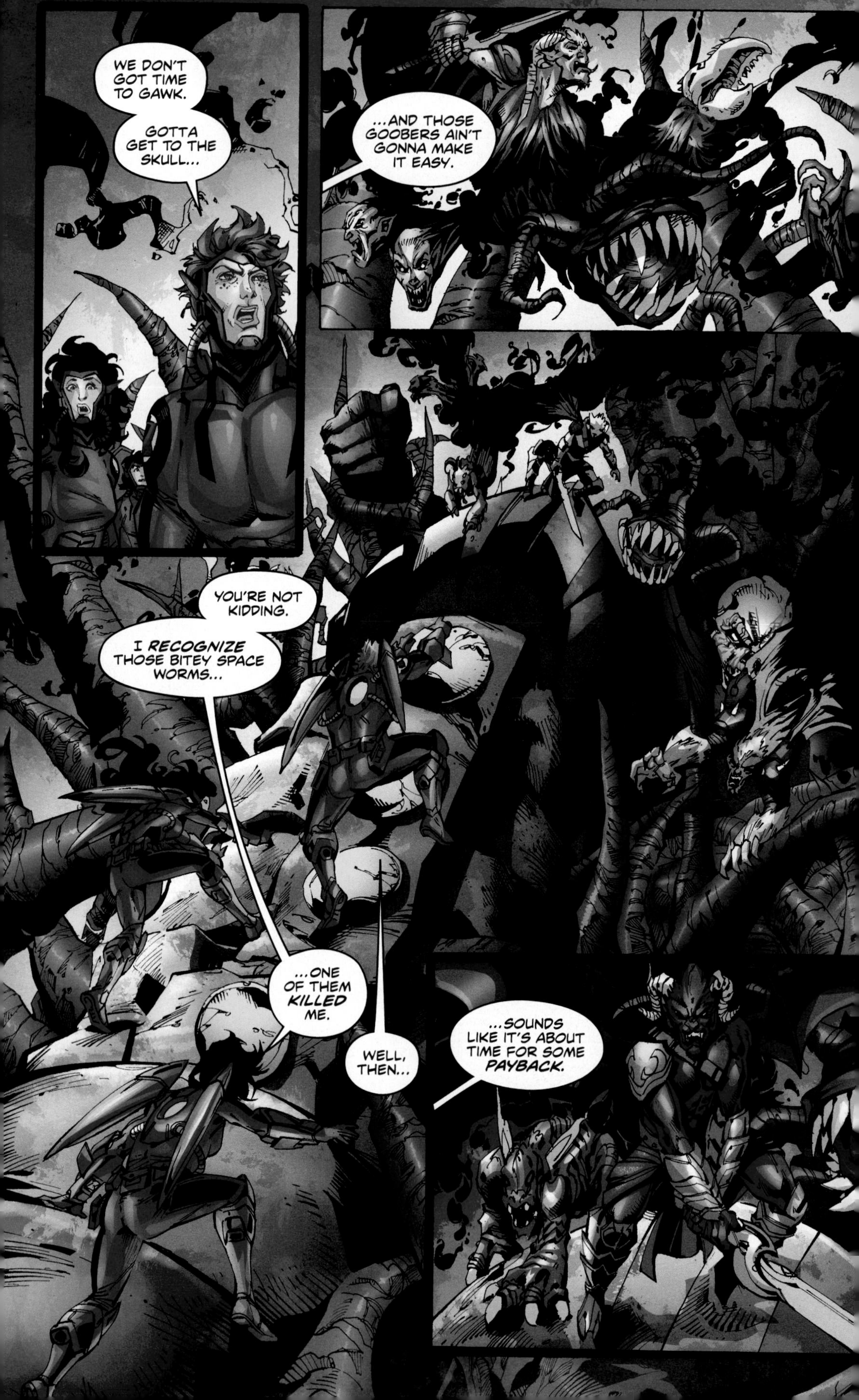
WE DON'T GOT TIME TO GAWK.
GOTTA GET TO THE SKULL...
...AND THOSE GOOBERS AIN'T GONNA MAKE IT EASY.
YOU'RE NOT KIDDING.
I *RECOGNIZE* THOSE BITEY SPACE WORMS...
...ONE OF THEM *KILLED* ME.
WELL, THEN...
...SOUNDS LIKE IT'S ABOUT TIME FOR SOME *PAYBACK*.

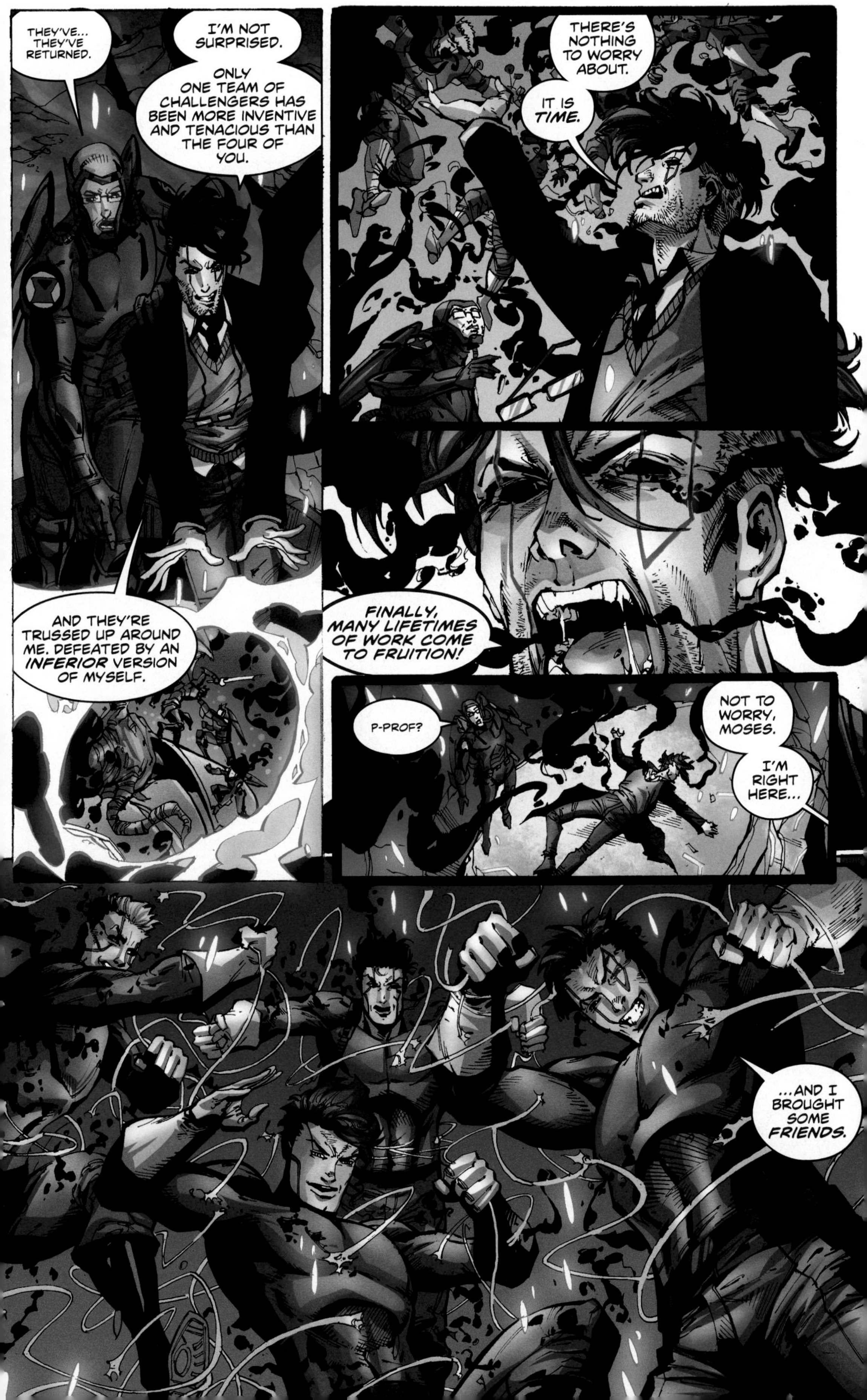
THEY'VE... THEY'VE RETURNED.
I'M NOT SURPRISED.
ONLY ONE TEAM OF CHALLENGERS HAS BEEN MORE INVENTIVE AND TENACIOUS THAN THE FOUR OF YOU.
AND THEY'RE TRUSSED UP AROUND ME. DEFEATED BY AN *INFERIOR* VERSION OF MYSELF.
THERE'S NOTHING TO WORRY ABOUT.
IT IS *TIME.*
FINALLY, MANY LIFETIMES OF WORK COME TO FRUITION!
P-PROF?
NOT TO WORRY, MOSES.
I'M RIGHT HERE...
...AND I BROUGHT SOME *FRIENDS.*

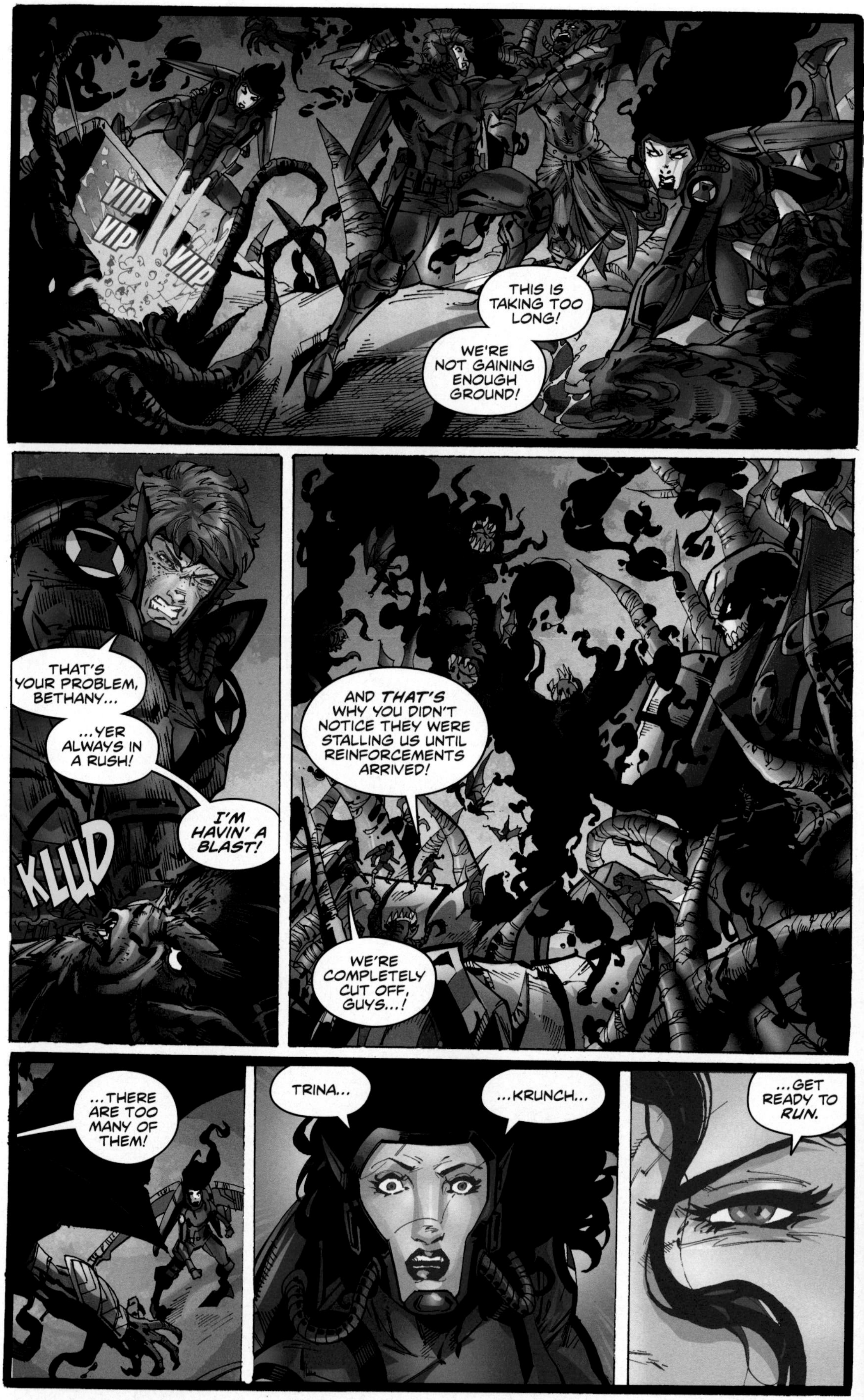
VIIP
VIP
VIIP
THIS IS TAKING TOO LONG!
WE'RE NOT GAINING ENOUGH GROUND!
THAT'S YOUR PROBLEM, BETHANY...
...YER ALWAYS IN A RUSH!
I'M HAVIN' A BLAST!
KLUD
AND THAT'S WHY YOU DIDN'T NOTICE THEY WERE STALLING US UNTIL REINFORCEMENTS ARRIVED!
WE'RE COMPLETELY CUT OFF, GUYS...!
...THERE ARE TOO MANY OF THEM!
TRINA...
...KRUNCH...
...GET READY TO RUN.

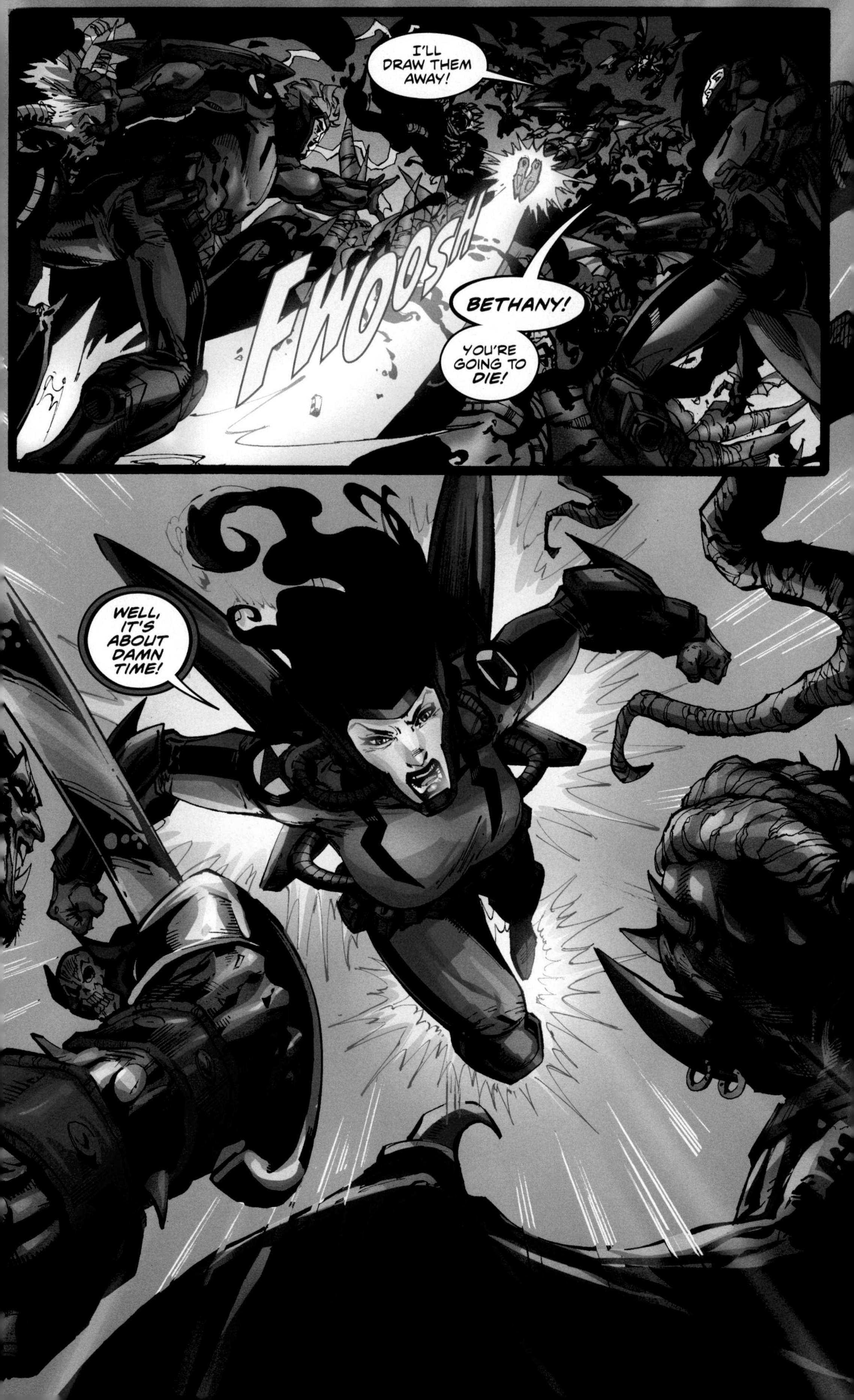
I'LL DRAW THEM AWAY!
FWOOSH
BETHANY!
YOU'RE GOING TO DIE!
WELL, IT'S ABOUT DAMN TIME!

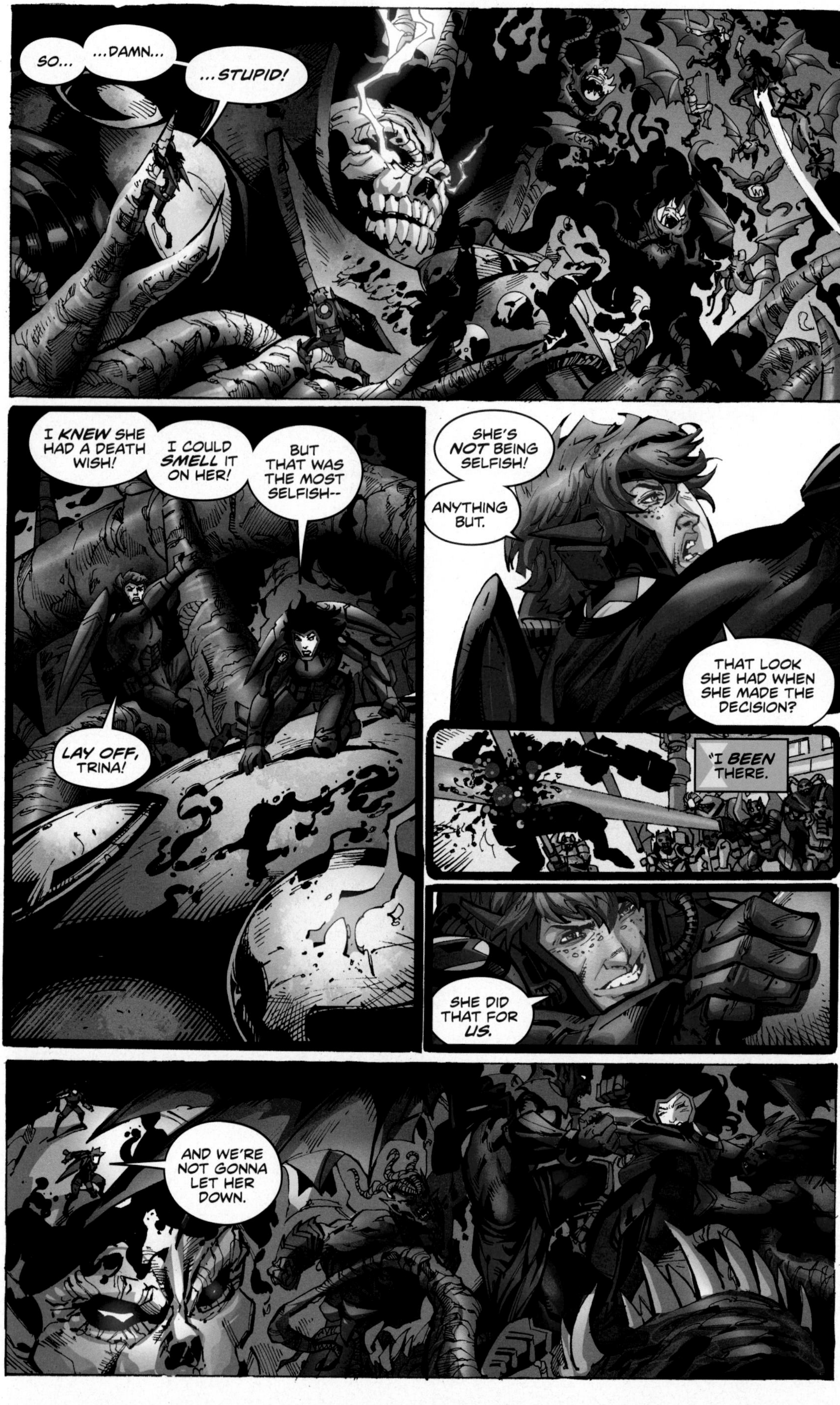

SO...
...DAMN...
...STUPID!
I KNEW SHE HAD A DEATH WISH!
I COULD SMELL IT ON HER!
BUT THAT WAS THE MOST SELFISH--
LAY OFF, TRINA!
SHE'S NOT BEING SELFISH!
ANYTHING BUT.
THAT LOOK SHE HAD WHEN SHE MADE THE DECISION?
"I BEEN THERE.
SHE DID THAT FOR US.
AND WE'RE NOT GONNA LET HER DOWN.

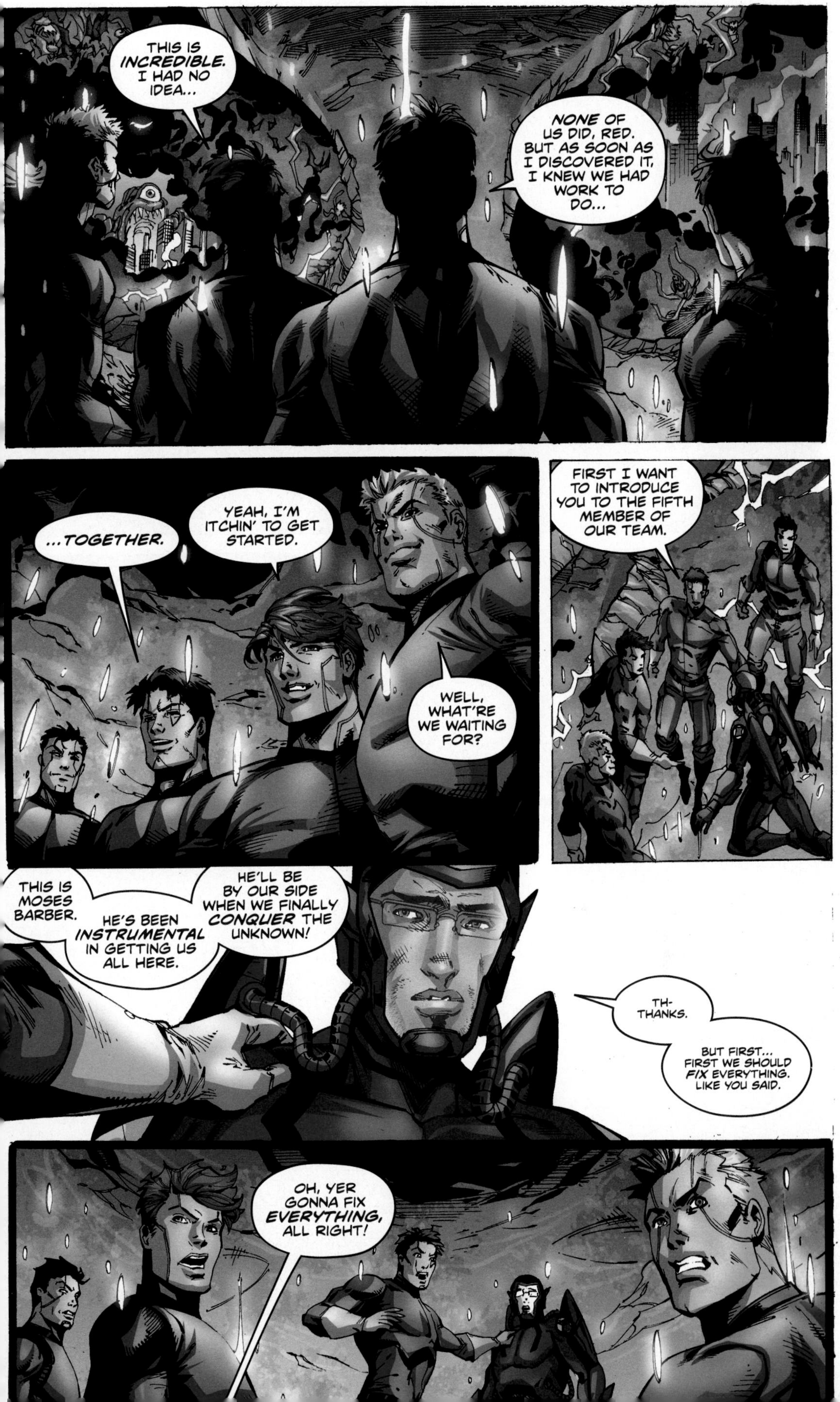
THIS IS INCREDIBLE. I HAD NO IDEA...
NONE OF US DID, RED. BUT AS SOON AS I DISCOVERED IT, I KNEW WE HAD WORK TO DO...
...TOGETHER.
YEAH, I'M ITCHIN' TO GET STARTED.
WELL, WHAT'RE WE WAITING FOR?
FIRST I WANT TO INTRODUCE YOU TO THE FIFTH MEMBER OF OUR TEAM.
THIS IS MOSES BARBER.
HE'S BEEN INSTRUMENTAL IN GETTING US ALL HERE.
HE'LL BE BY OUR SIDE WHEN WE FINALLY CONQUER THE UNKNOWN!
TH- THANKS.
BUT FIRST... FIRST WE SHOULD FIX EVERYTHING. LIKE YOU SAID.
OH, YER GONNA FIX EVERYTHING, ALL RIGHT!

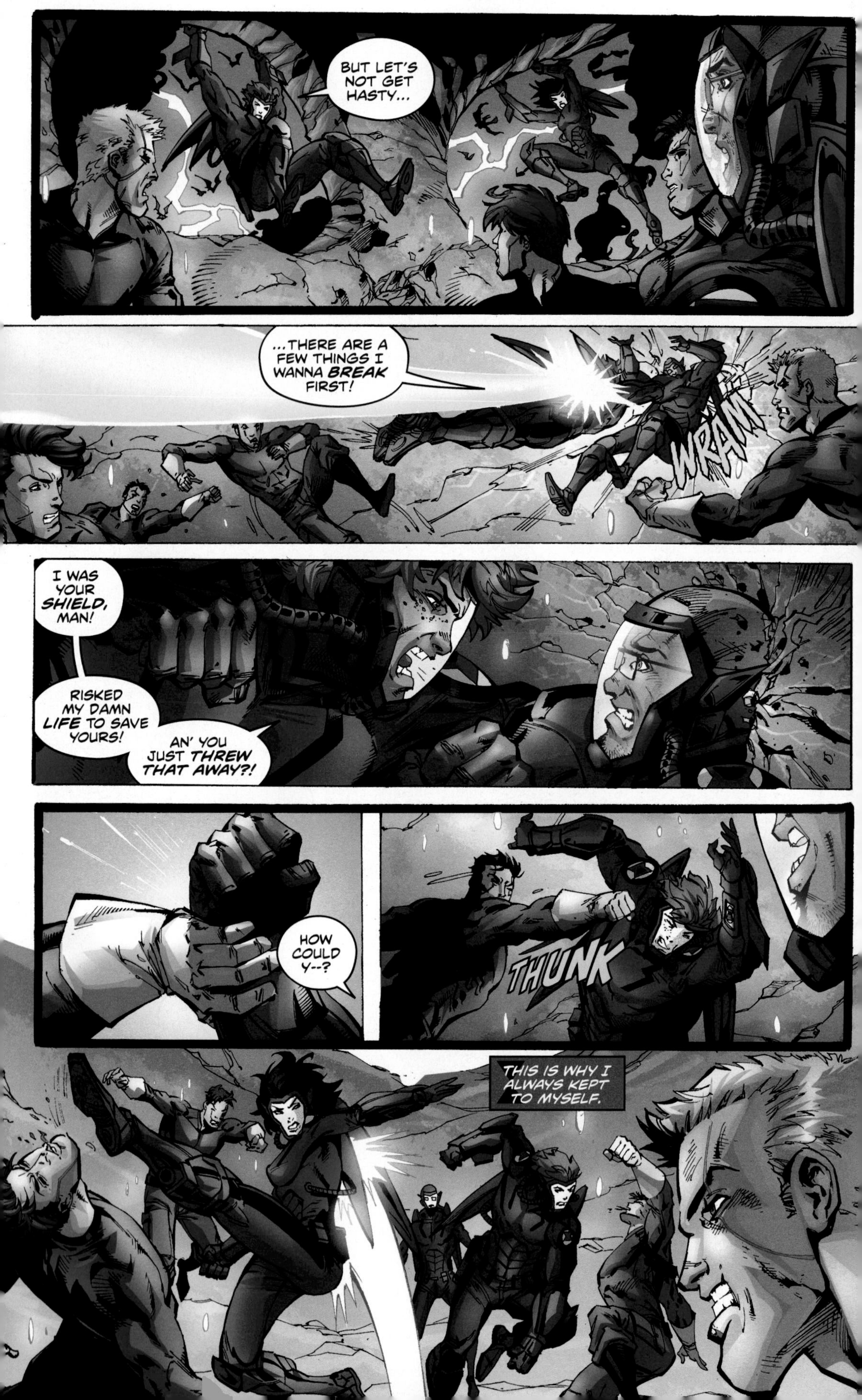
BUT LET'S NOT GET HASTY...
...THERE ARE A FEW THINGS I WANNA *BREAK* FIRST!
WRAM
I WAS YOUR *SHIELD,* MAN!
RISKED MY DAMN *LIFE* TO SAVE YOURS!
AN' YOU JUST *THREW THAT AWAY?!*
HOW COULD Y--?
THUNK
THIS IS WHY I ALWAYS KEPT TO MYSELF.

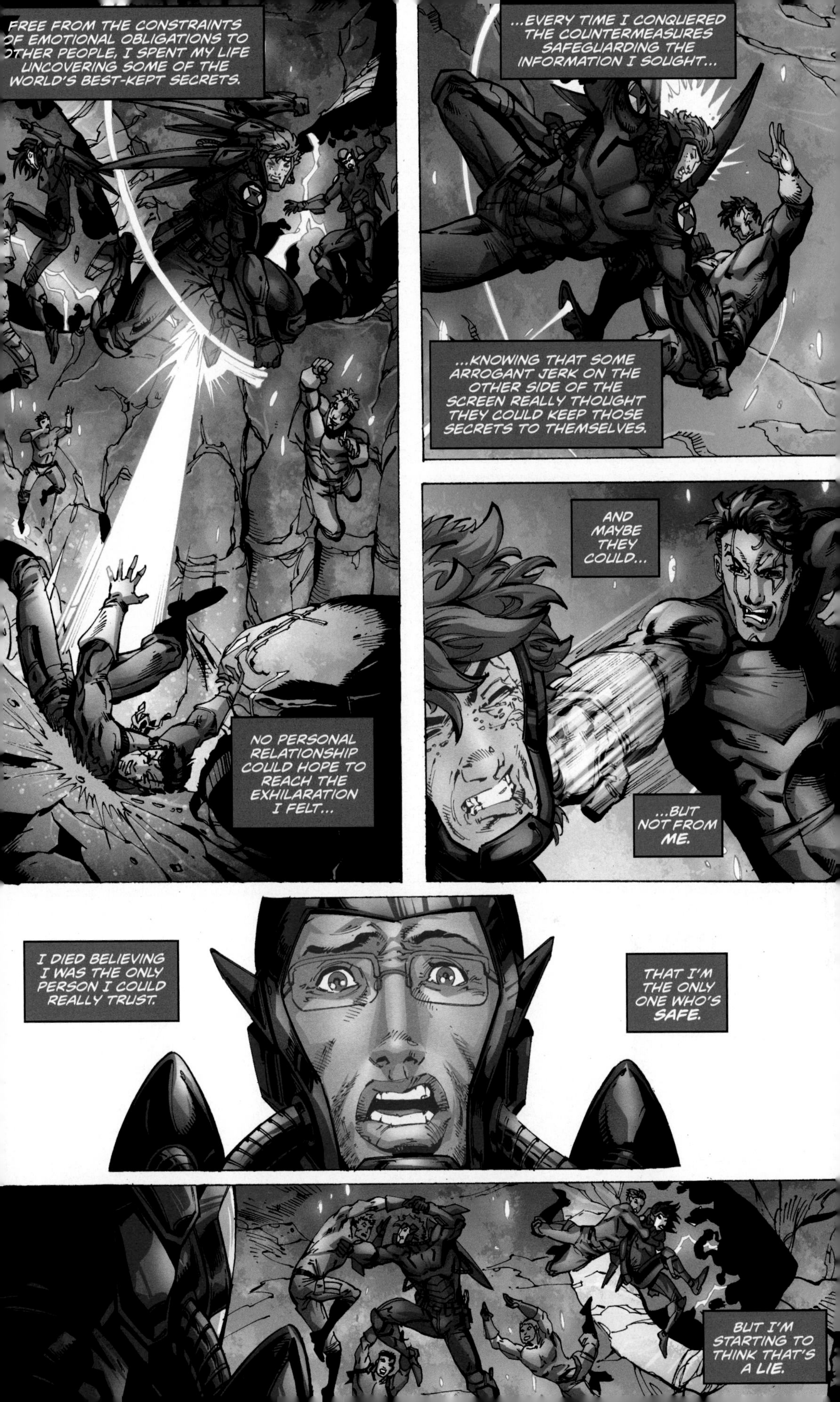
FREE FROM THE CONSTRAINTS OF EMOTIONAL OBLIGATIONS TO OTHER PEOPLE, I SPENT MY LIFE UNCOVERING SOME OF THE WORLD'S BEST-KEPT SECRETS.
NO PERSONAL RELATIONSHIP COULD HOPE TO REACH THE EXHILARATION I FELT...
...EVERY TIME I CONQUERED THE COUNTERMEASURES SAFEGUARDING THE INFORMATION I SOUGHT...
...KNOWING THAT SOME ARROGANT JERK ON THE OTHER SIDE OF THE SCREEN REALLY THOUGHT THEY COULD KEEP THOSE SECRETS TO THEMSELVES.
AND MAYBE THEY COULD...
...BUT NOT FROM ME.
I DIED BELIEVING I WAS THE ONLY PERSON I COULD REALLY TRUST.
THAT I'M THE ONLY ONE WHO'S SAFE.
BUT I'M STARTING TO THINK THAT'S A LIE.

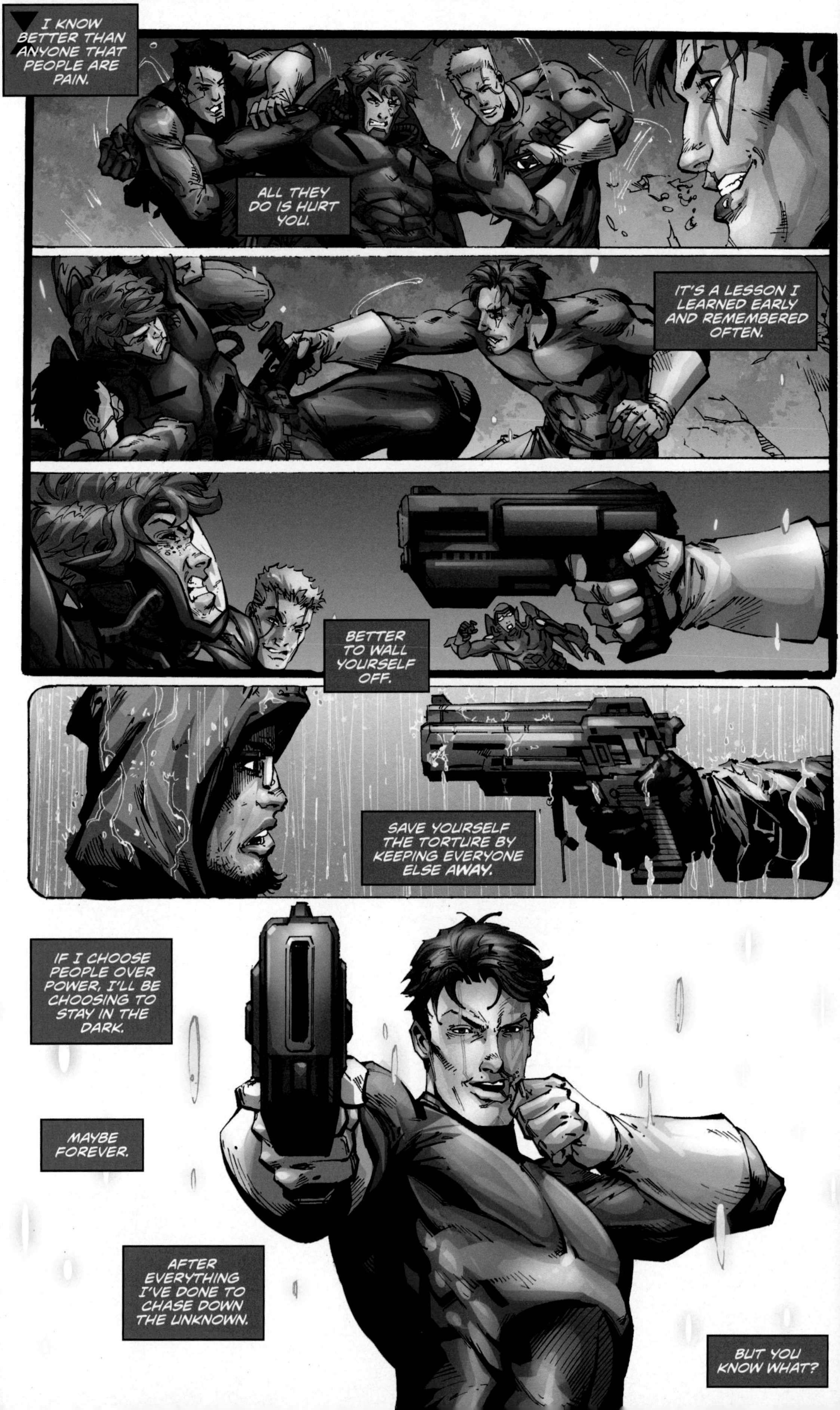
I KNOW BETTER THAN ANYONE THAT PEOPLE ARE PAIN.
ALL THEY DO IS HURT YOU.
IT'S A LESSON I LEARNED EARLY AND REMEMBERED OFTEN.
BETTER TO WALL YOURSELF OFF.
SAVE YOURSELF THE TORTURE BY KEEPING EVERYONE ELSE AWAY.
IF I CHOOSE PEOPLE OVER POWER, I'LL BE CHOOSING TO STAY IN THE DARK.
MAYBE FOREVER.
AFTER EVERYTHING I'VE DONE TO CHASE DOWN THE UNKNOWN.
BUT YOU KNOW WHAT?

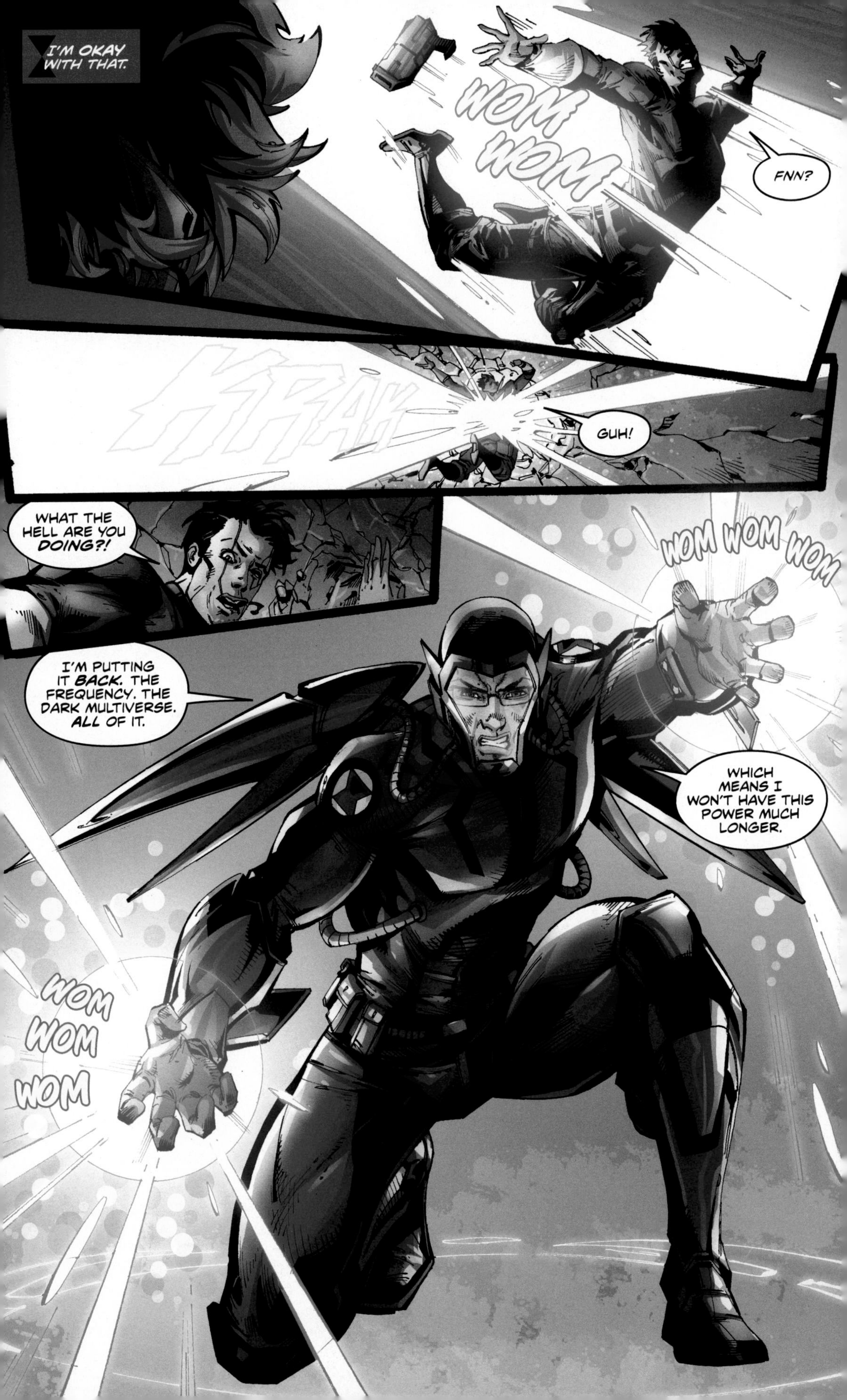
I'M OKAY WITH THAT.
WOM WOM
FNN?
KRAK
GUH!
WHAT THE HELL ARE YOU DOING?!
WOM WOM WOM
I'M PUTTING IT BACK. THE FREQUENCY. THE DARK MULTIVERSE. ALL OF IT.
WHICH MEANS I WON'T HAVE THIS POWER MUCH LONGER.
WOM WOM WOM

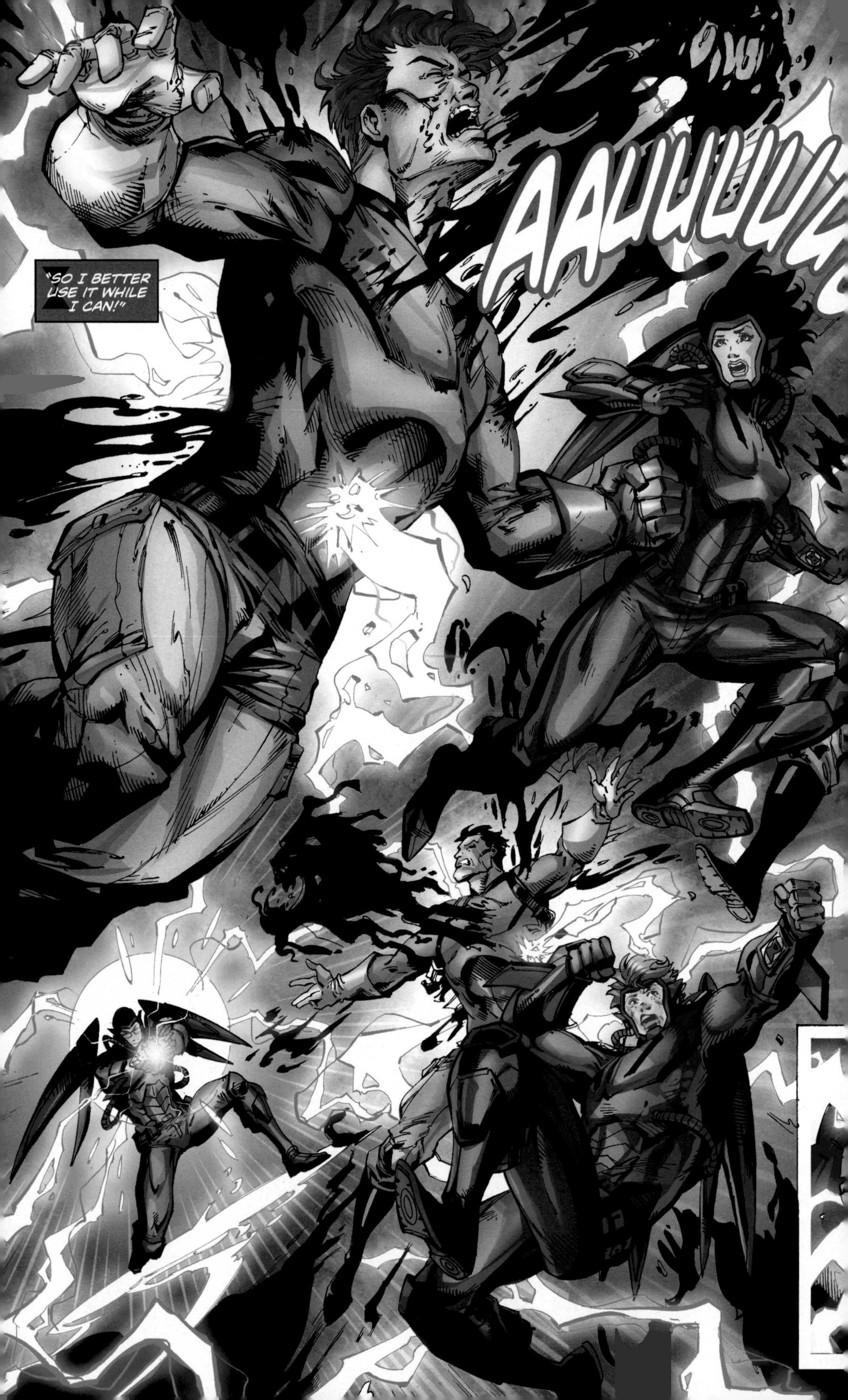
"SO I BETTER USE IT WHILE I CAN!"
AAUUUUU

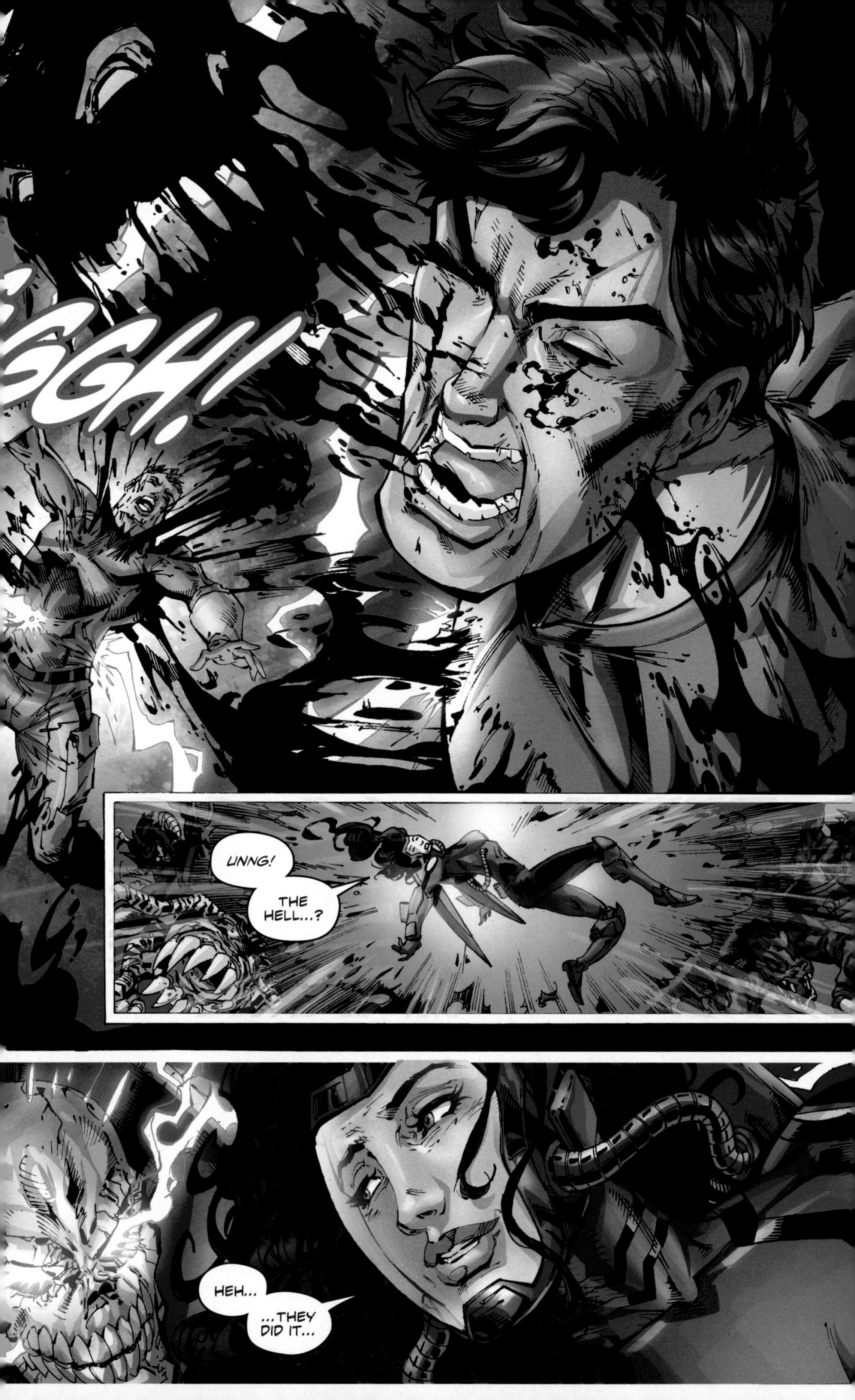
UNNG!
THE HELL...?
HEH...
...THEY DID IT...

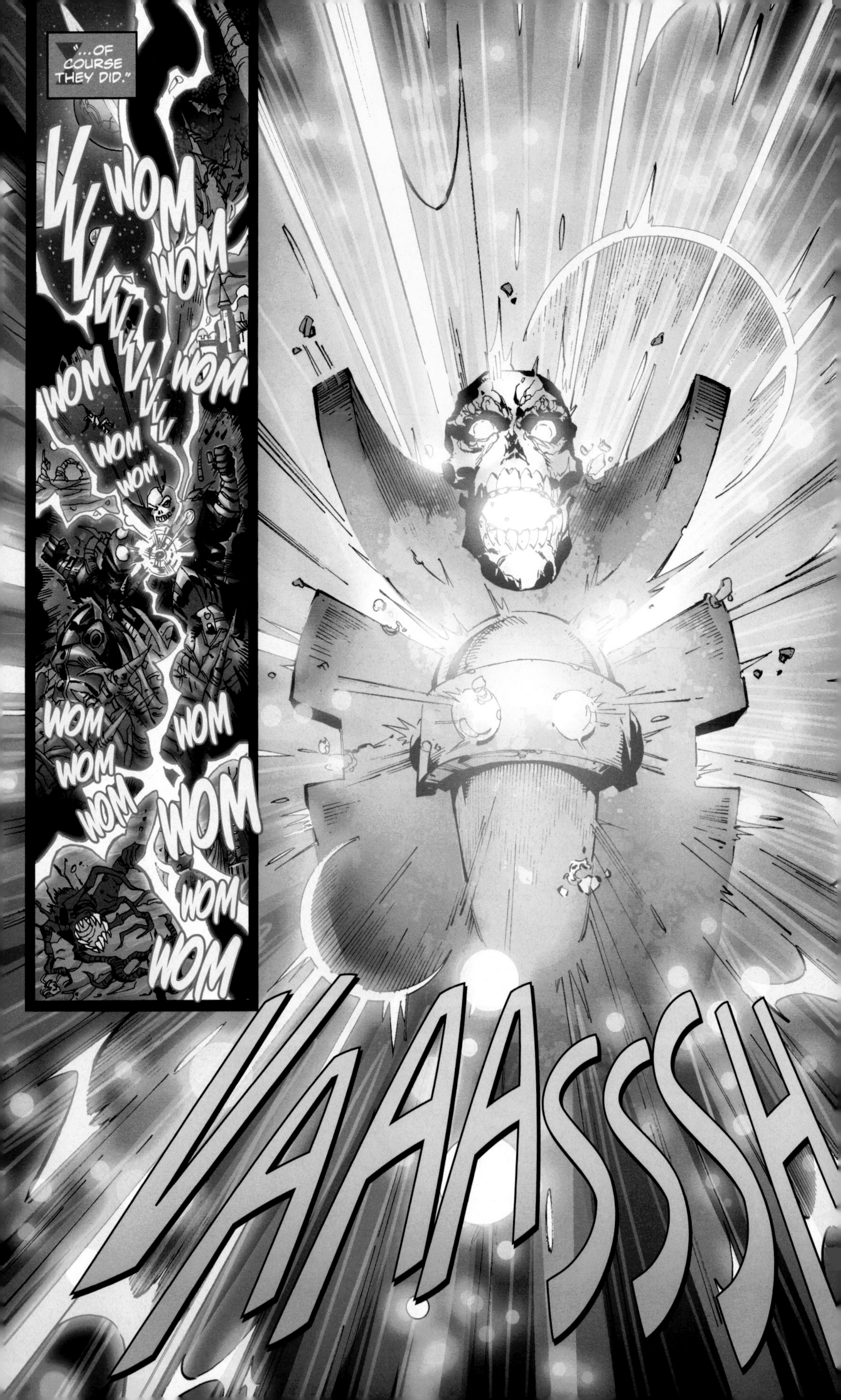
"...OF COURSE THEY DID."
VVVVVVVVVVVV
WOM WOM WOM WOM WOM WOM WOM
WOM WOM WOM WOM WOM WOM WOM WOM
VAAASSSH

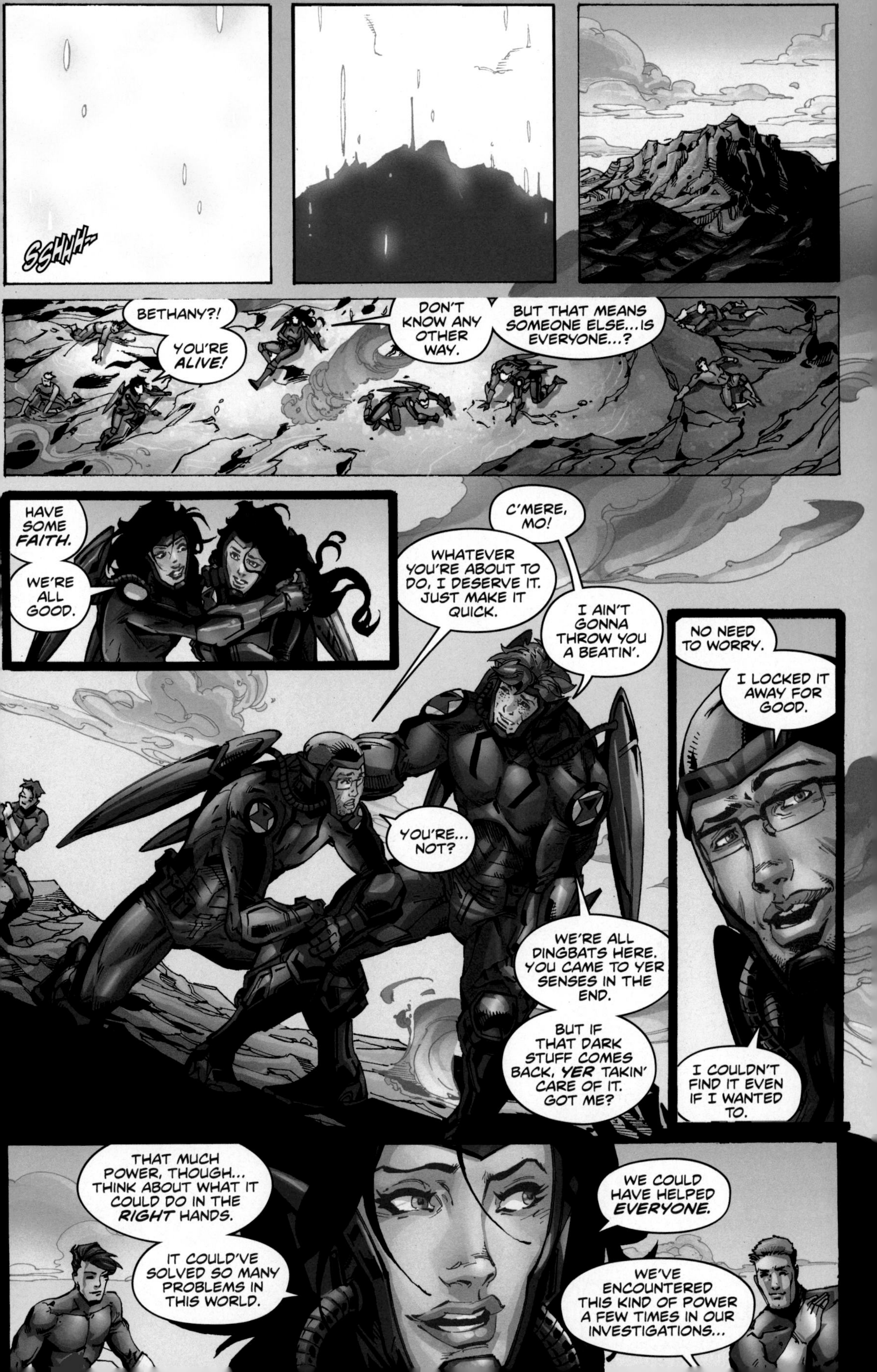
SSHHH--
BETHANY?!
YOU'RE ALIVE!
DON'T KNOW ANY OTHER WAY.
BUT THAT MEANS SOMEONE ELSE... IS EVERYONE...?
HAVE SOME FAITH.
WE'RE ALL GOOD.
C'MERE, MO!
WHATEVER YOU'RE ABOUT TO DO, I DESERVE IT. JUST MAKE IT QUICK.
I AIN'T GONNA THROW YOU A BEATIN'.
YOU'RE... NOT?
WE'RE ALL DINGBATS HERE. YOU CAME TO YER SENSES IN THE END.
BUT IF THAT DARK STUFF COMES BACK, YER TAKIN' CARE OF IT. GOT ME?
NO NEED TO WORRY.
I LOCKED IT AWAY FOR GOOD.
I COULDN'T FIND IT EVEN IF I WANTED TO.
THAT MUCH POWER, THOUGH... THINK ABOUT WHAT IT COULD DO IN THE RIGHT HANDS.
IT COULD'VE SOLVED SO MANY PROBLEMS IN THIS WORLD.
WE COULD HAVE HELPED EVERYONE.
WE'VE ENCOUNTERED THIS KIND OF POWER A FEW TIMES IN OUR INVESTIGATIONS...

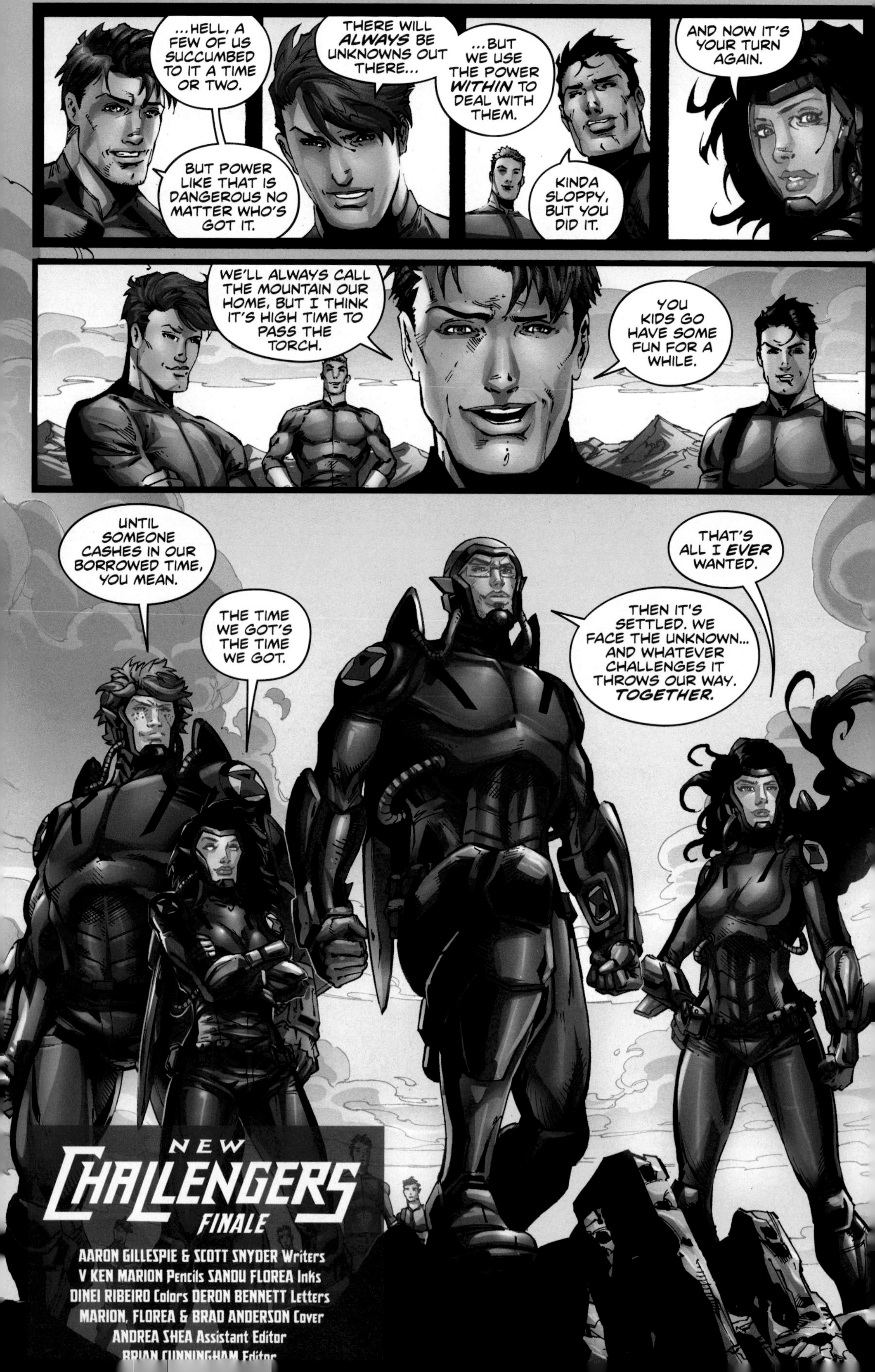
...HELL, A FEW OF US SUCCUMBED TO IT A TIME OR TWO.
BUT POWER LIKE THAT IS DANGEROUS NO MATTER WHO'S GOT IT.
THERE WILL ALWAYS BE UNKNOWNS OUT THERE...
...BUT WE USE THE POWER WITHIN TO DEAL WITH THEM.
KINDA SLOPPY, BUT YOU DID IT.
AND NOW IT'S YOUR TURN AGAIN.
WE'LL ALWAYS CALL THE MOUNTAIN OUR HOME, BUT I THINK IT'S HIGH TIME TO PASS THE TORCH.
YOU KIDS GO HAVE SOME FUN FOR A WHILE.
UNTIL SOMEONE CASHES IN OUR BORROWED TIME, YOU MEAN.
THE TIME WE GOT'S THE TIME WE GOT.
THEN IT'S SETTLED. WE FACE THE UNKNOWN... AND WHATEVER CHALLENGES IT THROWS OUR WAY. TOGETHER.
THAT'S ALL I EVER WANTED.
NEW CHALLENGERS
FINALE
AARON GILLESPIE & SCOTT SNYDER Writers
V KEN MARION Pencils SANDU FLOREA Inks
DINEI RIBEIRO Colors DERON BENNETT Letters
MARION, FLOREA & BRAD ANDERSON Cover
ANDREA SHEA Assistant Editor
BRIAN CUNNINGHAM Editor

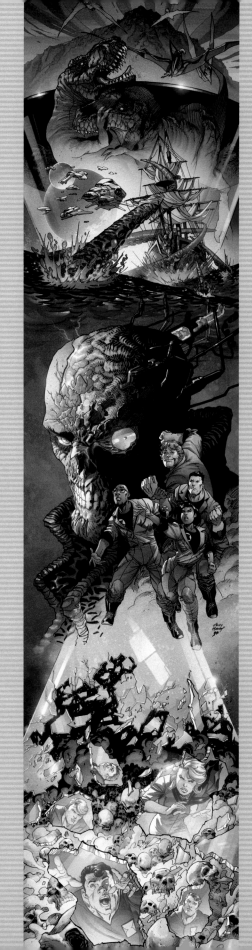

NEW CHALLENGERS #1 FOLD-OUT COVER

artwork by ANDY KUBERT with BRAD ANDERSON

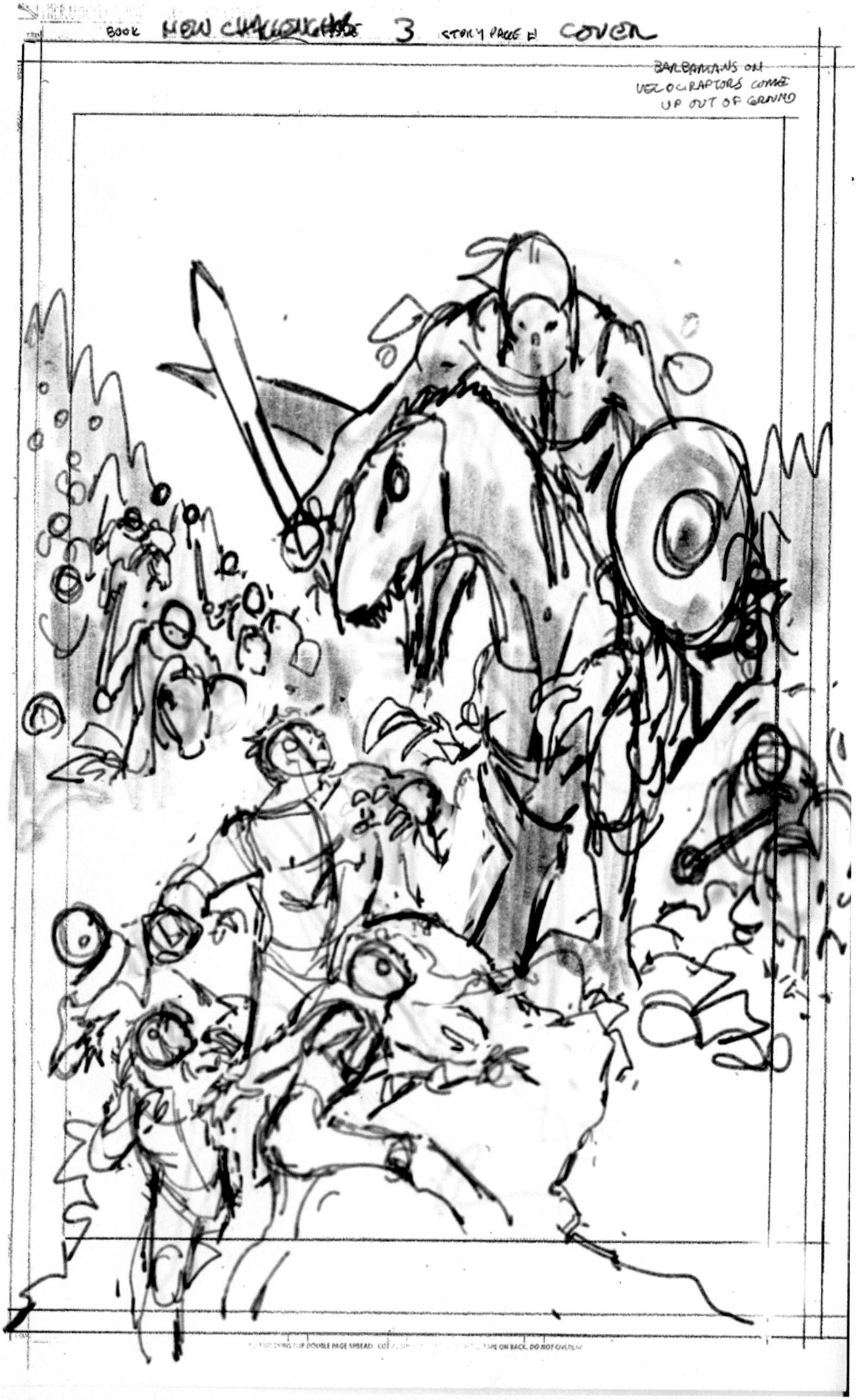
BOOK NEW CHALLENGERS 3 STORY PAGE # COVER
BARBARIANS ON VELOCIRAPTORS COME UP OUT OF GROUND
DOUBLE PAGE SPREAD
TAPE ON BACK. DO NOT OVERLAP

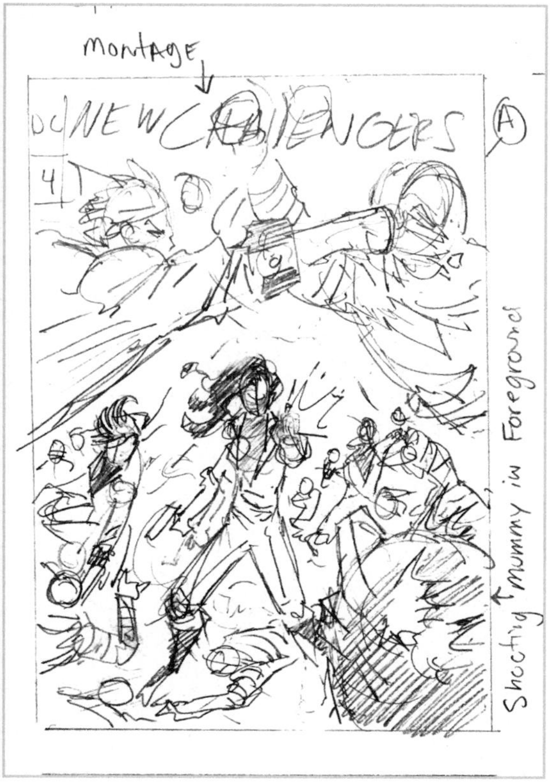
montage
DC
4
NEW CHALLENGERS
A
Shooting mummy in Foreground

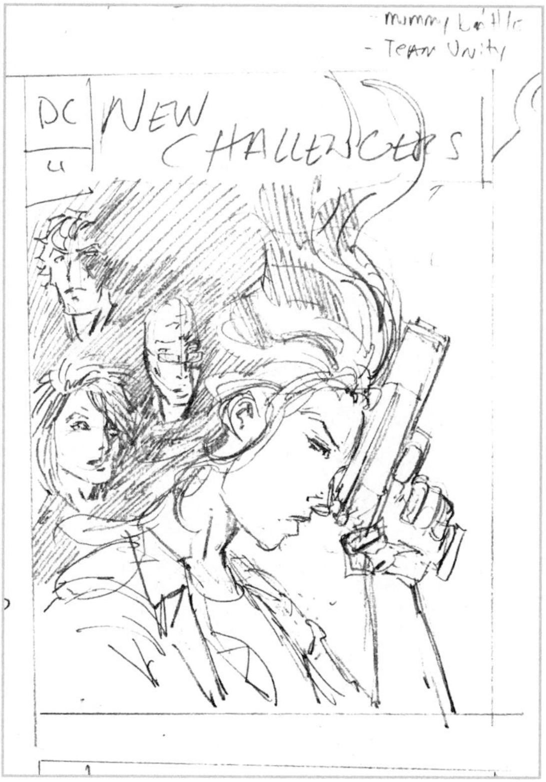
- mummy battle
- Team Unity
DC
4
NEW CHALLENGERS

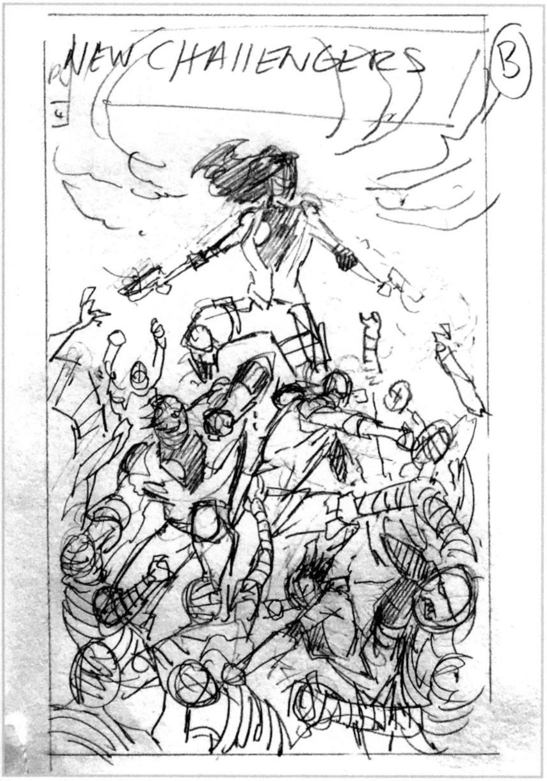
NEW CHALLENGERS
B

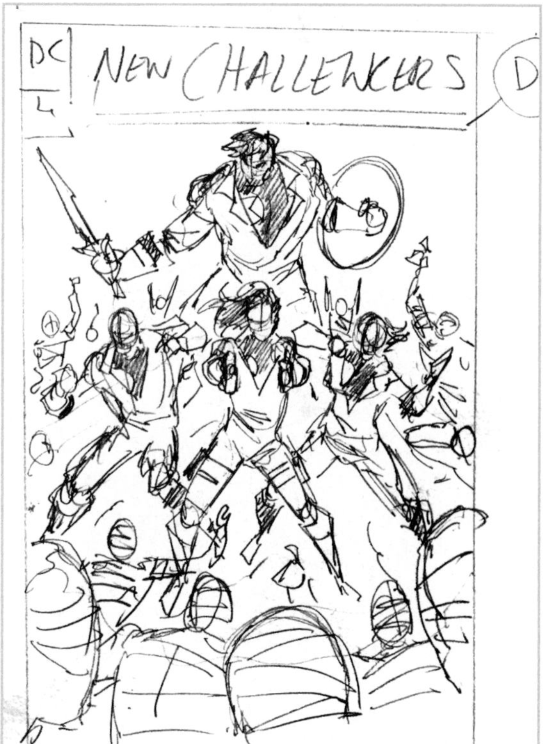
DC
4
NEW CHALLENGERS
D

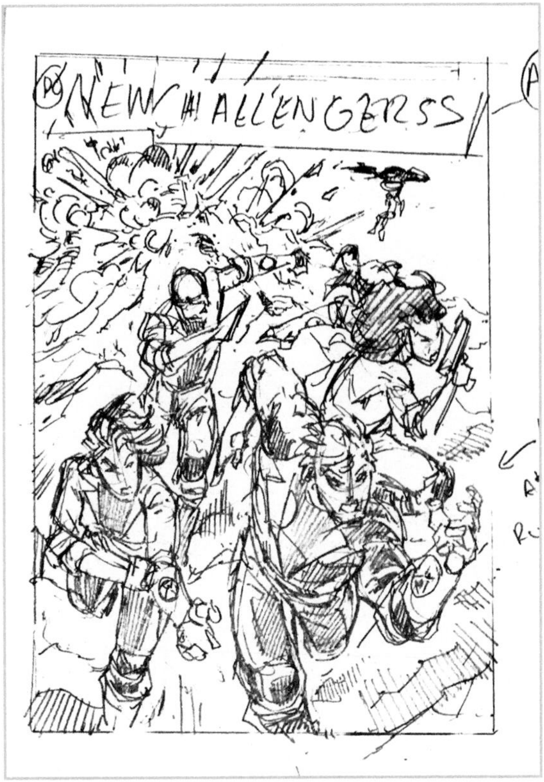
DC
NEW CHALLENGERS
A

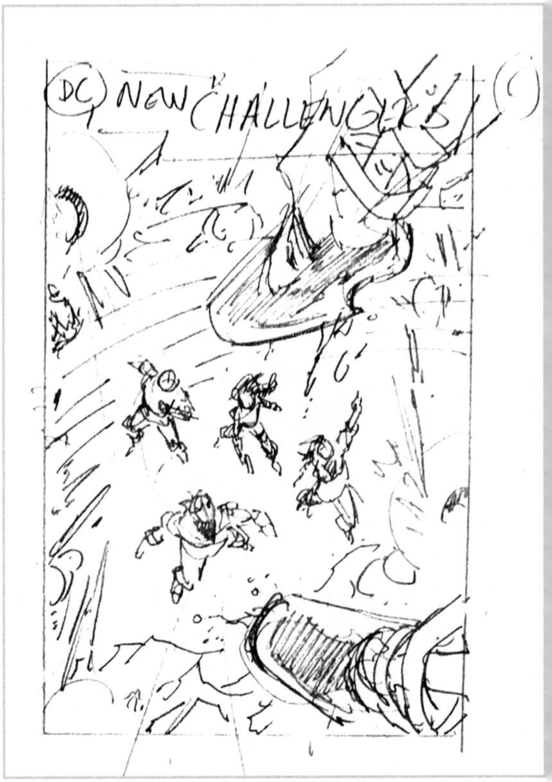
DC
NEW CHALLENGERS
C

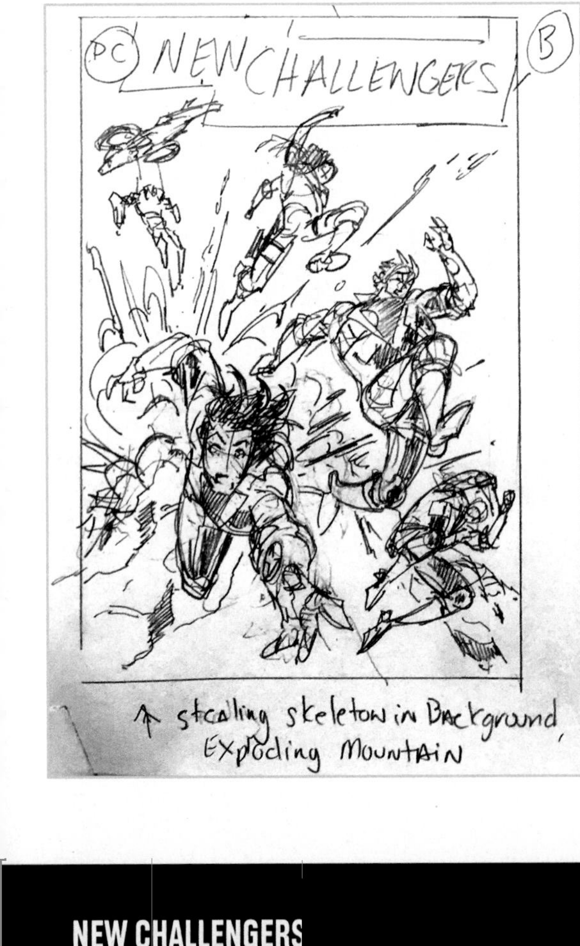
DC
NEW CHALLENGERS
B
stealing skeleton in Background
Exploding Mountain

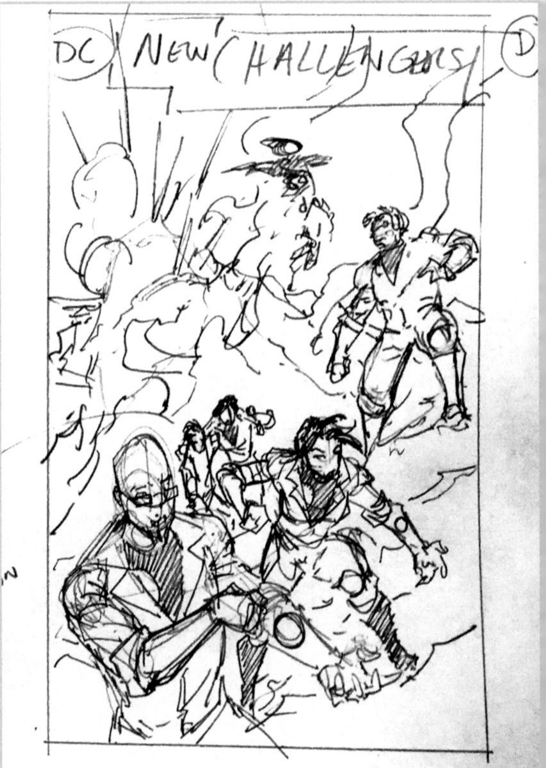
DC
NEW CHALLENGERS
D

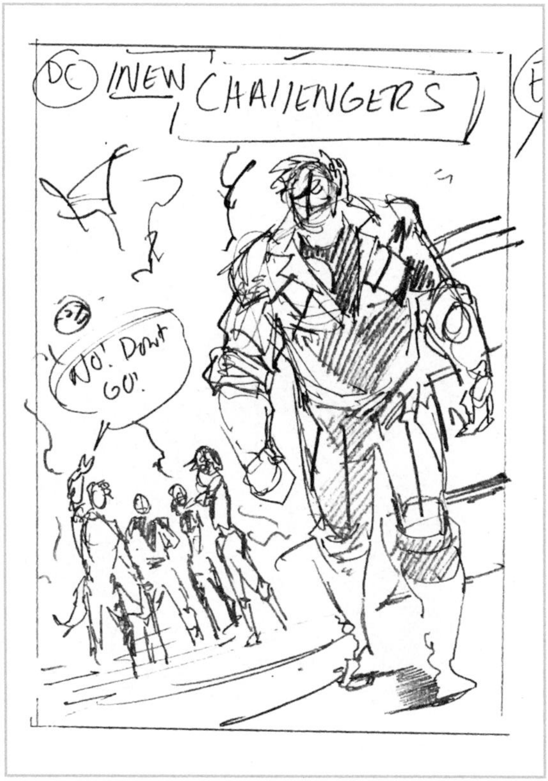
DC
NEW CHALLENGERS
NO! DON'T GO!

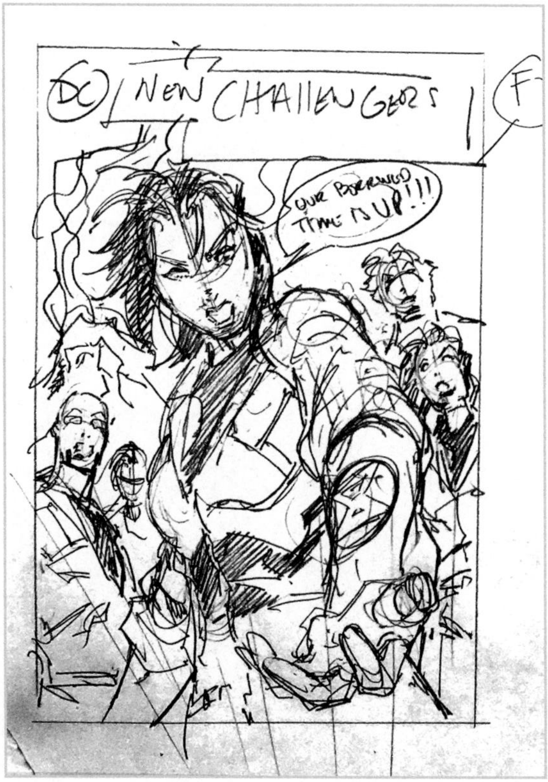
DC
NEW CHALLENGERS
F
OUR BORROWED TIME IS UP!!!

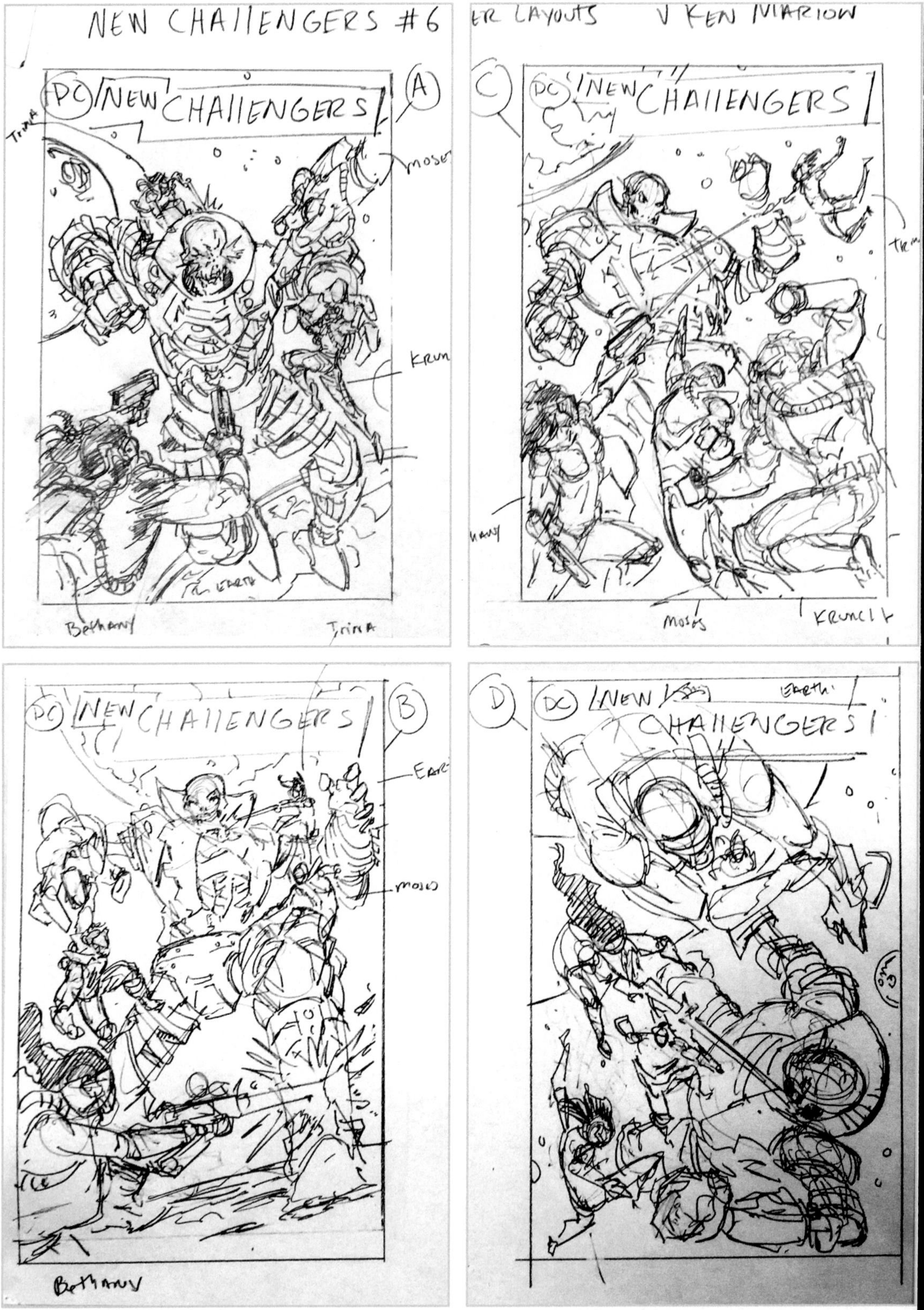
NEW CHALLENGERS #6
ER LAYOUTS
V KEN MARION
A
DC NEW CHALLENGERS
TRINA
MOSES
KRUN
BETHANY
TRINA
C
DC NEW CHALLENGERS
KRUNCH
MOSES
B
DC NEW CHALLENGERS
MOSES
BETHANY
D
DC NEW CHALLENGERS

NEW CHALLENGERS #6 COVER SKETCHES BY V KEN MARION

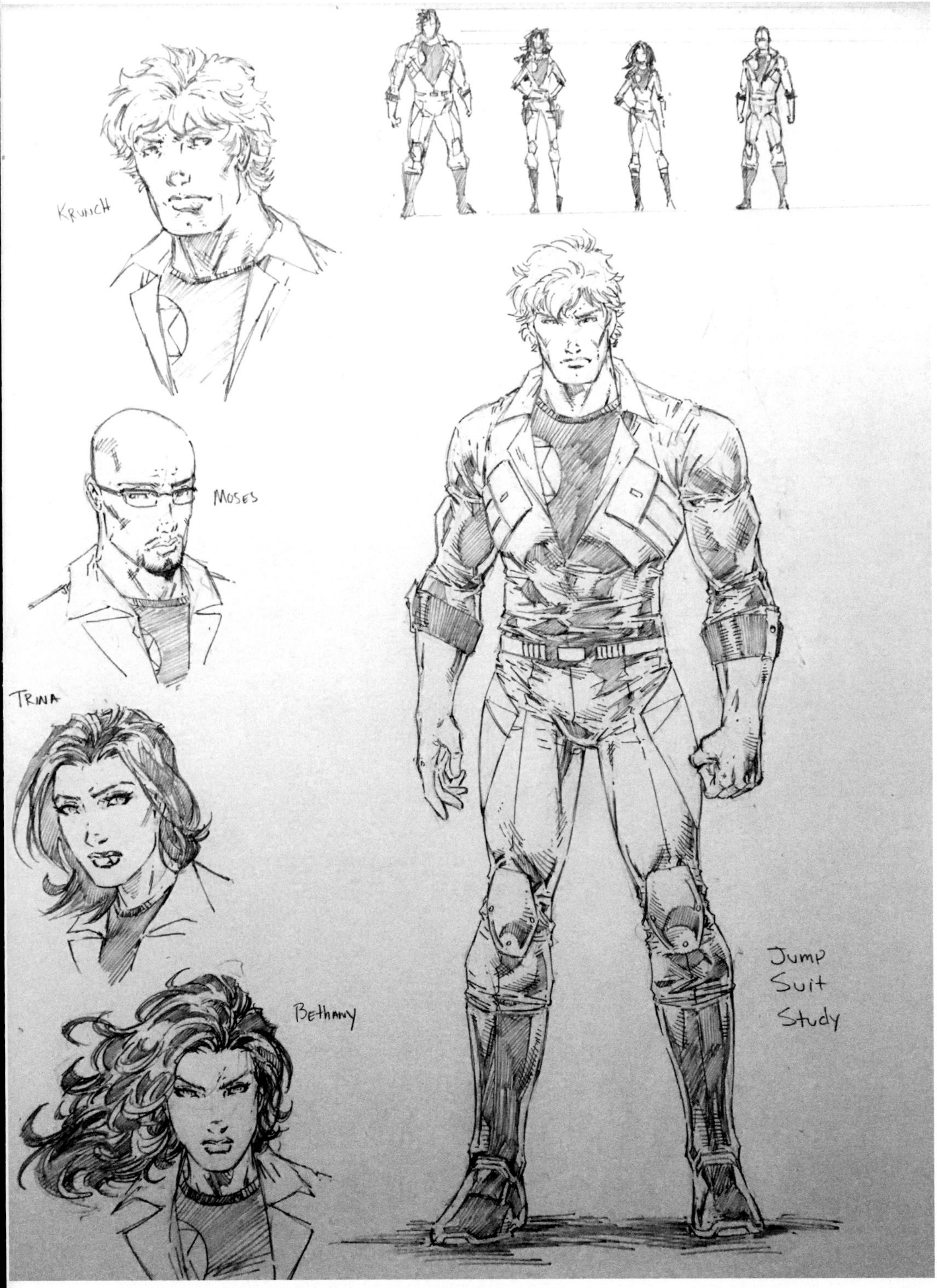
KRUNCH
MOSES
TRINA
Bethany
Jump
Suit
Study

NEW CHALLENGERS CHARACTER STUDIES BY V KEN MARION

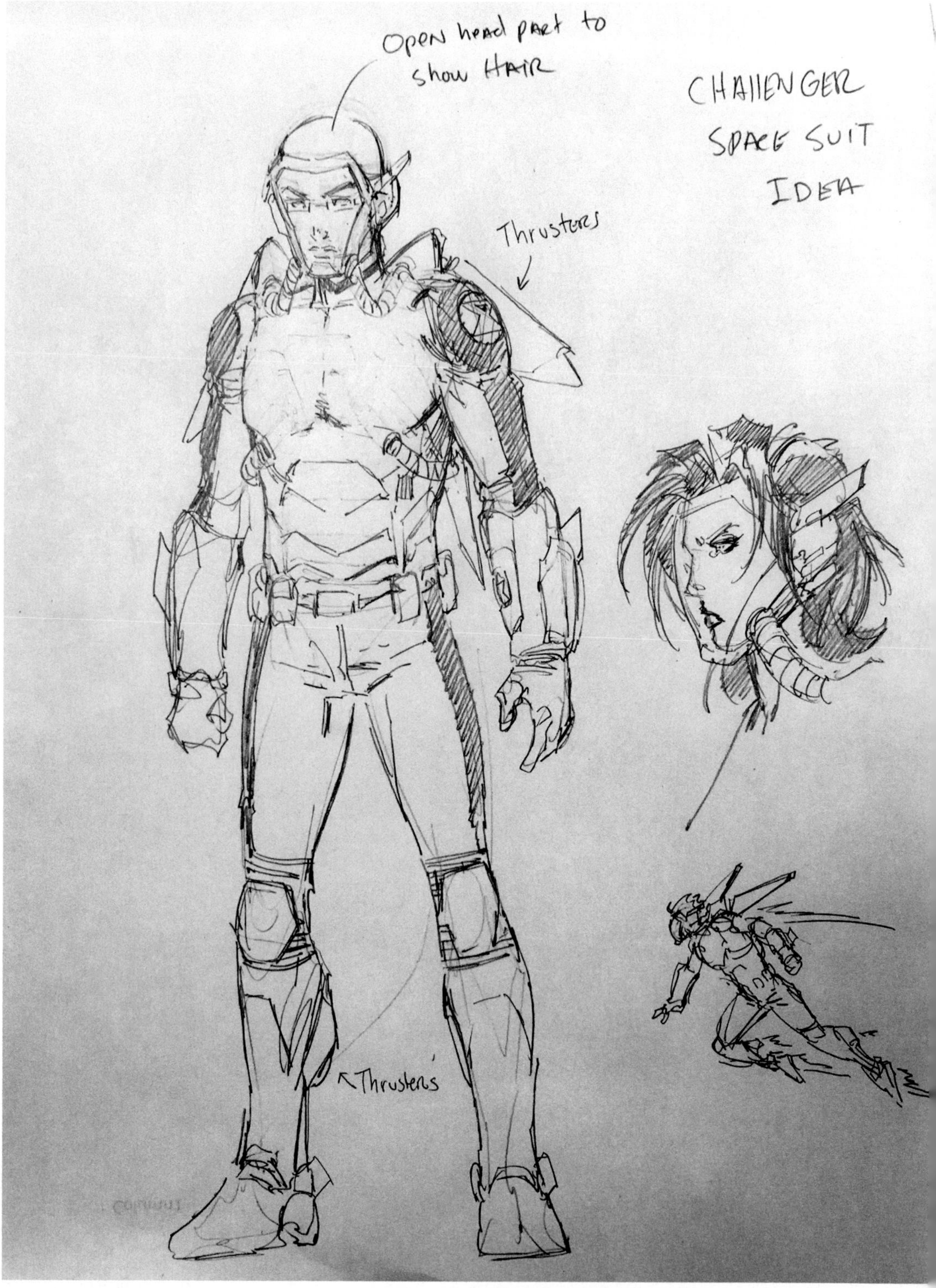
Open head part to show HAIR
CHALLENGER SPACE SUIT IDEA
Thrusters
Thrusters